ADVANCES IN MEDICAL PSYCHOTHERAPY AND PSYCHODIAGNOSIS

VOLUME 11: 2002–2003

*American Board of
Medical Psychotherapists
and Psychodiagnosticians*

KENDALL/HUNT PUBLISHING COMPANY
4050 Westmark Drive   Dubuque, Iowa 52002

Information for Contributors

This series gives preference to articles that report empirical or conceptual work in which behavioral or psychological methods of treatment are related to areas that are "medical" in the broad sense. Articles will also be accepted that deal with the wider areas of disease prevention, health, and wellness, insofar as they relate to psychology and psychotherapy. The volume's purpose is to provide a forum for dissemination of scientific findings as well as practical information and conceptual integration of existing knowledge in the broad areas of overlap between health and disease on the one hand, and psychology and the psychotherapies on the other. Selected book reviews in this area will also be considered. Manuscripts may be six to thirty pages long. They must be double-spaced on one side of the page and submitted in triplicate (one original and two photocopies) to Dr. William Tsushima, Editor, *Advances,* c/o ABMPP Central Office, Park Plaza Medical Bldg., 345 24th Avenue North, Nashville, TN 37203, e-mail: americanbd@aol.com, fax: 615-327-9235. An abstract of 100 to 300 words should accompany the text, and all figures and artwork must be camera-ready. Whenever possible, a diskette is desirable. Manuscripts should be written in accordance with the current edition of the style manual of the American Psychological Association. The editorial review process ordinarily takes about three months. Further information about the submission of manuscripts can be obtained from Dr. Tsushima's office. Authors of accepted manuscripts will be asked to submit a copy of their article on diskette (further information will be provided at the appropriate time). Membership inquiries should be sent to American Board of Medical Psychotherapists and Psychodiagnosticians, Park Plaza Medical Building, 345 24th Avenue North, Suite 201, Nashville, TN 37203-1520 (Telephone # 615-327-2984, Fax # 615-327-9235).

Advances in Medical Psychotherapy and Psychodiagnosis

Volume 11   2002–2003

Advances in Medical Psychotherapy and Psychodiagnosis
2002–2003, Volume 11, pp. 1–8

Comparison of MMPI-2 Scores of White and Japanese American Medical Patients

William T. Tsushima
Straub Clinic & Hospital
Honolulu, Hawaii

Vincent G. Tsushima
Fukunago, Matayoshi, Hershey and Ching

Abstract

This study compared the Minnesota Multiphasic Personality Inventory-2 (MMPI-2) scores of 196 medical patients classified by race (White or Japanese Americans). Multiple regression analyses failed to show significant race differences with the MMPI-2 scales. Item analyses evaluating the two racial groups on the 370 MMPI-2 items found only 1 item that significantly differentiated the White and Japanese American patients. A second study compared the two racial groups of medical patients with a sample of 32 normal subjects on the 13 MMPI-2 scales. Univariate analyses of variance revealed significant differences between both racial groups of medical patients and the normals on nearly all of the MMPI-2 scales. Limitations of this study were discussed and more research on the MMPI-2 with ethnic minority groups is strongly encouraged.

The normative sample of the Minnesota Multiphasic Personality Inventory-2 (MMPI-2; Butcher, Dahlstrom, Graham, Tellegen & Kaemmer, 1989) is considerably larger and more representative of the general U.S. population than that of the original MMPI, which was comprised of 724 Caucasian visitors at the University of Minnesota Hospitals. The MMPI-2 normative sample consisted of 1,138 men and 1,462 women from diverse geographic regions of the country, with representatives of minority groups: African Americans (12.1%), Hispanics (2.8%), Native Americans (2.9%), and Asian Americans (0.7%). Although the MMPI-2 normative sample is substantially more ethnically diverse than the original MMPI standardization sample, Okazaki and Sue (2000) print out that Asian Americans, who comprised 3% of the U.S. population in 1990, were inadequately represented in the MMPI-2 standardization sample, raising questions of test bias and possible sociocultural effects upon Asian American MMPI-2 scores.

This study was conducted under the auspices of the Pacific Health Research Institute with a grant from the George F. Straub Trust, Hawaii Community Foundation.

Correspondence concerning this article should be addressed to William T. Tsushima, Ph.D., Department of Psychiatry and Psychology, Straub Clinic and Hospital, 888 South King Street, Honolulu, Hawaii, 96813.

Research on the use of the original MMPI with Asian Americans has been notably sparse. In their comprehensive survey of MMPI patterns of American minorities, Dahlstrom, Lachar and Dahlstrom (1986) found only 6 articles pertaining to Asian Americans. The authors cited a large-scale unpublished tabulation of MMPI records accumulated by the Roche Psychiatric Service Institute in 1978, including T-score means and standard deviations for a subgroup of 282 Asian Americans seen in the mental health settings, with insignificant differences between Asians and Caucasians for any of the basic scales. Because of the limited data available on Asian Americans, Greene (1987) cautioned use of this test with such individuals.

MMPI-2 research with ethnic minority samples has also been meager. In one of the few published articles, Timbrook and Graham (1994) compared the MMPI-2 scores of 140 African Americans and 1,468 White subjects who were part of the MMPI restandardization sample. When subjects were matched by age, education and income, the African American men scored significantly higher on Scale 8 than the White men, while African American women scored statistically higher on Scales 4, 5 and 9 than the White women. However, all of the mean differences were less than 5 T-score points, representing small-to-medium effect sizes (Cohen, 1997).

Canul and Cross (1994) studied the MMPI-2 results of 51 Mexican-American college students and found that the L and K scale scores, but not the MF scale, were influenced by racial identity attitudes and levels of acculturation. However, none of the MMPI-2 clinical scales were included in the Canul and Cross article. Data of 25 Chinese foreign college students (Stevens, Kwan & Graybill, 1993) and of 11 minority male police officer candidates (Kornfeld, 1995) have also been reported, but the small number of subjects in these studies preclude reliable conclusions. In a study involving a relatively large number of ethnic minority subjects (Sue, Keefe, Enomoto, Durvasula & Chao, 1996), 133 Asian American college students, including 35 Chinese, 15 Filipino, 13 Japanese, 34 Korean, 23 Vietnamese, and 13 "other Asians," were compared with 91 White students on the MMPI-2. Significant group differences emerged on Scales 1, 2, 4, 6, 7, 8, and 0, with Asian American students showing greater elevations on the MMPI-2 clinical scales than the White students. The research also revealed that the less acculturated Asian American students differed more from the White students than the more acculturated Asian American students. Finally, in a meta-analytic review of 31 years of MMPI/MMPI-2 research comparing European Americans, African Americans and Latino Americans, the authors concluded that MMPI/MMPI-2 differences between these groups were trivial (Nagayama Hall, Bansal & Lopez, 1999).

The research literature, thus, reveals limited information about the MMPI-2 scores of ethnic minority group members. Presumably the MMPI-2 is often administered to ethnic minority group subjects; thus, it is important to provide comparisons of MMPI-2 scores between White and other minority subjects. The present investigation was designed to evaluate the MMPI-2 responses of White and Japanese American outpatient medical patients who presented physical symptoms that were suspected to be affected by psychological factors. Based on previous research on the original MMPI (Dahlstrom, Lachar & Dahlstrom, 1986) and our earlier study comparing the MMPI scores of White and Japanese American medical and neurological patients in which no racial/ethnic differences were found (Tsushima & Onorato, 1982), it was hypothesized that there are insignificant differences between the White and Japanese American medical patients on the MMPI-2 scales.

Study 1: Comparison of White and Japanese Americans

Method

Subjects

The MMPI-2 records were obtained from White and Japanese American medical outpatients at the Psychiatry and Psychology Department of a private medical center in Honolulu, Hawaii over a four-year period. In Hawaii, Whites and Japanese Americans are about equally represented, and together they comprise about 50% of the state's total population. All subjects were born in the United States. The racial or ethnic group identification was indicated through self-report by each patient when initially registering at the medical center. None of the subjects were from mixed racial parentage.

The study involved 196 patients who were referred by their physicians for an MMPI-2 after presenting various health problems, such as fatigue, pain, or insomnia, which were suspected to be related to psychological influences. The patients had no previous psychiatric history.

Subjects included 130 Whites (64 males, 66 females) and 66 Japanese (29 males, 37 females) Americans.

The mean age of the patients was 44.38 years (SD = 13.74), and the mean education was 14.37 years (SD = 2.68). Univariate analyses of variance (ANOVA) revealed no significant differences in terms of age, $F(1,183) = 0.878$, $p = .35$, and education $F(1,183) = 0.019$, $p = .89$, between the White and Japanese American patients.

The K-corrected T-scores for the three validity scales and 10 basic scales were obtained from the first 370 items of the MMPI-2. Based on the recommendations of Butcher, Graham, and Ben-Porath (1995), subjects were excluded from the study if any of the following criteria were met: more than 100 unanswered items, Scales L and K greater than T-80, and greater than a Scale F raw score of 30. A total of 4 subjects were excluded using these criteria, including two Whites and two Japanese Americans.

Results

The means and standard deviations (SD) of the 13 MMPI-2 scale scores of the 130 White and 66 Japanese American patients are presented in Table 1. Multiple regression analyses were performed to determine the amount of variance in each scale accounted for by race. Race did not account for a significant amount of variance in any of the 13 MMPI-2 scales, i.e., no F score achieved a level of significance at the $p < .01$ level. It should be noted, however, that the power of this analysis, given the sample size, was only .50.

Although no significant race factor was detected in the multiple regression analyses, item analyses were conducted to identify specific items or behaviors that differentiated the two racial groups. The 370 MMPI-2 items were analyzed, comparing the two racial groups while setting a Bonferroni adjustment level at .00013 to control for familywise error. A significant Mann-Whitney U was obtained for only one item that substantially differentiated the White and Japanese American patients.

Study 2: Comparison of Medical Patients and Normals

A second study was conducted to compare the MMPI-2 scores of White and Japanese American medical patients to the scores of a sample of normal subjects. Significant differences between patients and normal subjects would support the contention that the MMPI-2 is equally valid for use with White and Japanese American medical patients.

Method

Subjects

The MMPI-2 records were obtained from 32 non-medical subjects, or Normals, with no suspected medical or psychological conditions, who were being evaluated as part of a screening process for

Table 1
MMPI-2 Means and Standard Deviations of White and Japanese American Medical Patients and Normals

Scale	White		Japanese		Normals	
	M	SD	M	SD	M	SD
L	52.24	8.83	54.32	11.12	58.16	12.22
F	55.85	12.80	57.29	16.51	40.91	4.90
K	50.18	11.64	50.30	10.38	59.94	8.13
Hs	66.12	13.71	66.27	11.64	49.97	8.01
D	64.42	13.94	67.24	14.85	46.28	5.55
Hy	66.53	14.93	64.61	13.16	51.41	8.99
Pd	57.25	12.87	54.12	11.12	51.38	9.04
MF	49.00	9.24	51.23	10.98	45.50	10.17
Pa	58.97	14.51	57.32	15.41	48.94	8.61
Pt	61.98	13.91	63.20	13.55	47.94	7.44
Sc	60.22	14.00	61.24	14.71	48.41	7.76
Ma	51.29	9.46	50.63	12.67	48.00	6.41
Si	51.16	11.67	54.91	10.68	43.59	6.73

employment. Eleven were applying for a pilot position for a major airlines, 10 were applying for a security guard position, and 11 were applying for the ministry. All of the Normals were males. The subjects included 24 Whites, 2 Japanese Americans, 3 Chinese Americans, 1 Korean American, 1 Pacific Islander American, and 1 African American.

The average age of the Normals was 42.00 years (SD = 13.27) and their average years of education was 15.42 (SD = 3.02). One-way ANOVAs revealed no significant differences between the White medical patients, the Japanese American medical patients, and the Normals in terms of age, $F (2,216) = 0.69$, $p = .504$, and education, $F (2,223) = 1.99$, $p = .138$.

To assess the validity of the MMPI-2 with White and Japanese medical patients, scores of the 13 MMPI-2 scales were compared with those of the Normal subjects.

Results

The means and SDs of the 13 MMPI-2 scale scores of the Normal Ss are found in Table 1. One-way ANOVAs were performed on the 13 MMPI-2 scales, comparing the two racial groups of medical patients and the group of Normal Ss. Significant differences were found on all of the scales except

Scale 9, F (2,225) = 1.35, p = .262. A significant difference of $p <$ .0001 was found on seven scales (F, K, 1, 3, 7, 8 and 10). Other significant findings $p <$ .05 were on Scales 2 ($p <$ .001), 6 ($p <$ .002), L ($p <$ .011), 4 ($p <$ .025), and 5 ($p <$ .028).

Post hoc t-tests revealed significant differences between the Normals and both racial groups of medical patients on nearly all of the MMPI-2 scales. Whites and Normals differed on all of the scales except Scale 5 (p = .907). The Japanese and Normals differed on all of the scales except Scales L (p = .560), 4 (p = .154) and 5 (p = .717).

Discussion

Although the revised MMPI-2 has been in use since 1989, very few empirical studies concerning the test performance of ethnic minority groups have been conducted, and practically none for Asian American samples. Thus, the present investigation, which found that the amount of variance accounted for by race was inconsequential for all 13 MMPI-2 scales, provides relatively unique data of this widely used test instrument with a sample of Japanese American patients.

The results of the present study are similar to our earlier research with the original MMPI comparing White and Japanese American medical and neurological patients (Tsushima & Onorato, 1982), and consistent with the meta-analytic review that found no noteworthy differences in MMPI/MMPI-2 scores of European Americans, African Americans and Latino Americans (Nagayama Hall, Bansal & Lopez, 1999). The present findings are at odds with Sue and his associates (1996) who found substantial differences on the MMPI-2 between Asian Americans and White college students. It should be noted that the Sue study dealt with a "normal" population with no control over the influences of psychopathology among the groups investigated. As Pritchard and Rosenblatt (1980) pointed out in their review article, MMPI differences in unequated samples may be due to actual differences in psychopathology that the test is accurately measuring. Sue *et al.* (1996) stated that the MMPI-2 differences observed in their research "may simply reflect that Asian Americans as a minority group experience greater difficulties in their daily lives and as a result have more elevated profiles than do Whites (p. 216)." The present study controlled for psychopathology by including only psychophysiological disorders, which probably accounts for the conflicting results. As noted in our previous investigation (Tsushima & Onorato, 1982), if psychopathology classifications are held constant, sociocultural differences reported with the MMPI-2 diminish and seem nonsignificant.

A distinct aspect of this research was the analysis of individual items, comparing the White and Japanese Americans across the 370 MMPI-2 items. No study ever examined White and Asian American responses on the items of the original MMPI (Dahlstrom, Lachar & Dahlstrom, 1986). Individual item analyses could identify specific responses that differ between the two racial groups; however, only one MMPI-2 item was found to vary significantly between the Whites and Japanese Americans, a finding that can be attributed to chance. Thus, the item analyses, along with the multiple regression analyses, imply that the MMPI-2 evaluations of Japanese American Ss would not be noticeably affected by sociocultural influences.

In his critique of MMPI studies of ethnic differences, Greene (1987) stated that research in this area rarely considers an assessment of empirical correlates of the scales. While it is interesting to compare the scores of two racial or ethnic groups, Greene asserted that it is even more important to determine if the pattern of responses is manifested in any external manner. The present study found that the White and Japanese American medical patients differed significantly from a group of Normals on nearly all of the MMPI-2 scales and especially on Scales 1, 2 and 3, which are well known to be elevated among those suspected of psychophysiological problems (Gass, 1992; Keller & Butcher, 1991). Thus, the present findings lend support to the notion that the MMPI-2 is a valid measure when employed with Japanese American medical patients with possible somatization issues.

Because of important methodological limitations of this study, much caution is urged in interpreting these results. The relatively small number of Japanese American subjects increased the probability of a Type II error and these results may be difficult to replicate. The terms "White" and "Japanese

American" were imprecise groupings based on an assumption that those identified as belonging in one group share common psychological or sociocultural characteristics. No effort was made to measure acculturation and ethnic identification and the degree to which individuals adhere to American cultural practices or to traditional ethnic attitudes. Studies of ethnicity and race yield more conclusive evidence when cultural and psychological variables are clearly conceptualized and measured (Betancourt & Lopez, 1993; Greene, 1987; Okazaki & Sue, 1995).

Inadequate sampling and small sample size are frequent problems in many investigations of ethnic groups (Okazaki & Sue, 1995). Japanese Americans are scattered throughout the U.S., although somewhat more concentrated on the West Coast and in Hawaii. The present research, which covered a 4-year period, included only 66 Japanese Americans, most of whom were born and raised in Hawaii; how well they represent the various Japanese Americans on the continental U.S. is uncertain. Greene (1987) recommended that at least 130 Ss are needed in an ethnic group to examine differences on the MMPI. To achieve a desired minimum power level of .80, Butcher, Graham and Ben-Porath (1995) proposed that 326 participants are required in MMPI-2 research. Thus, although this is the largest number of Asian Americans involved in a published study of the MMPI-2, the size of the current sample limits confidence in the generalizability of the findings.

Only Japanese Americans were involved in this research. Thus, we do not know how other minority groups including other Asian Americans would compare with Whites on the MMPI-2. Furthermore, because only medical patients referred for psychological testing were investigated, how different clinical samples, such as psychiatric inpatients and outpatients, would respond on this test is not known.

Although the similarities between Whites and Japanese Americans offer some promise, Dana (1988) warned that the MMPI is a culturally influenced test instrument "with limitations that increase as cultures become more dissimilar from Anglo-American middle-class behavior and attitudes." The revised MMPI-2 appears psychometrically similar to its predecessor and requires continued investigation with ethnic minority populations to assess the possibilities of test bias.

References

Betancourt, H., & Lopez, S.R. (1993). The study of culture, ethnicity, and race in American psychology. *American Psychologist, 48,* 629–637.

Butcher, J.N., Dahlstrom, W.G., Graham, J.R., Tellegen, A., & Kaemmer, B. (1989). *Minnesota Multiphasic Personality Inventory-2 (MMPI-2): Manual for administration and scoring.* Minneapolis: University of Minnesota Press.

Butcher, J.N., Graham, J.R., & Ben-Porath, Y.S. (1995). Methodological problems and issues in MMPI, MMPI-2, and MMPI-A research. *Psychological Assessment, 7,* 320–329.

Canul, G.D., & Cross, H.J. (1994). The influence of acculturation and racial identity attitudes on Mexican-Americans' MMPI-2 performance. *Journal of Clinical Psychology, 50,* 736–745.

Cohen, J. (1997). *Statistical power analysis for the behavioral sciences* (Rev. ed.). San Diego, CA: Academic Press.

Dahlstrom, W.G., Lachar, D., & Dahlstrom, L.E. (1986). *MMPI patterns of American minorities.* Minneapolis, MN: University of Minnesota Press.

Dana, R.H. (1988). Culturally diverse groups and MMPI interpretation. *Professional Psychology: Research and Practice, 5,* 490–495.

Gass, C.S. (1992). MMPI-2 interpretation of patients with cerebrovascular disease: A correction factor. *Archives of Clinical Neuropsychology, 7,* 17–27.

Greene, R.L. (1987). Ethnicity and MMPI performance: A review. *Journal of Consulting and Clinical Psychology, 55,* 497–512.

Keller, L.S., & Butcher, J.N. (1991). *Assessment of chronic pain with the MMPI-2.* Minneapolis: University of Minnesota Press.

Kornfeld, A.P. (1995). Police officer candidate MMPI-2 performances: Gender, ethnic, and normative factors. *Journal of Clinical Psychology, 51,* 536–540.

Nagayama Hall, G.C., Bansal, A., & Lopez, I.R. (1999). Ethnicity and psychopathology: A meta-analytic review of 31 years of comparative MMPI/MMPI-2 research. *Psychological Assessment, 11,* 186–197.

Okazaki, S., & Sue, S. (1995). Methodological issues in assessment research with ethnic minorities. *Psychological Assessment, 7,* 367–375.

Okazaki, S., & Sue, S. (2000). Implications of test revisions for assessment with Asian Americans. *Psychological Assessment, 12,* 272–280.

Pritchard, D.A., & Rosenblatt, A. (1980). Racial bias in the MMPI: A methodological review. *Journal of Consulting and Clinical Psychology, 48,* 263–267.

Stevens, M.J., Kwan, K.L., & Graybill, D. Comparison of MMPI-2 scores of foreign Chinese and Caucasian-American students (1993). *Journal of Clinical Psychology, 49,* 23–27.

Sue, S., Keefe, K., Enomoto, K., Durvasula, R.S., & Chao, R. (1996). Asian American and White College Students' performance on the MMPI-2. In J.N. Butcher (Ed.), *International Adaptions of the MMPI-2: Research and Clinical Applications* (pp. 206–218). Minneapolis: University of Minnesota Press.

Timbrook, R.E., & Graham, J.R. (1994). Ethnic differences on the MMPI-2? *Psychological Assessment, 6,* 212–217.

Tsushima, W.T., & Onorato, V.A. (1982). Comparison of MMPI scores of White and Japanese-American medical patients. *Journal of Consulting and Clinical Psychology, 50,* 150–151.

Advances in Medical Psychotherapy and Psychodiagnosis
2002–2003, Volume 11, pp. 9–18

A Psycholegal Perspective: The Lack of Neuropsychological Examination Following Significant Brain Trauma Can Be Costly

Lewis M. Etcoff and Karen E. Sims
Neuropsychology and Psychotherapy Associates, Las Vegas, Nevada

Scott M. Abbott
Kamer, Zucker, & Abbott Attorneys At Law, Las Vegas, Nevada

Michelle G. Carro
Neuropsychology and Psychotherapy Associates, Las Vegas, Nevada

Abstract

After any significant head trauma or brain-related disorder, adequate neuropsychological follow-up should be the standard of care in helping a person to recover (e.g., to provide an understanding of their strengths and weaknesses and what can be expected during recovery). Unfortunately, as the following case highlights, the absence of this step can be costly in both monetary and emotional terms. The following case is a unique one of a woman who suffered arteriovenous malformations in the right cerebral hemisphere, which resulted in a massive intracranial bleed, requiring neurosurgical intervention. Her neurosurgery was successful, but when she eventually returned to work in the same management position she previously held, her co-workers and supervisors recognized that she was not the same manager. Unfortunately, and as a direct result of the location of her brain lesions, she had no awareness of her job-related difficulties. She eventually brought suit against her employer, claiming discrimination. Had she been referred by her neurosurgeon for neuropsychological evaluation prior to having returned to work, this lawsuit would not likely have occurred; but as a result of the neurosurgeon's assumption that his patient recovered fully in all respects, what turned out to be considerable cognitive and perceptual disabilities were not discovered in a timely enough fashion, resulting in a most unusual lawsuit.

Introduction

Significant alterations in brain function, whether the result of structural, metabolic or electrochemical abnormalities, can disturb human abilities to feel, sense, perceive, think, concentrate, remember, plan and behave. Any of these abilities, alone or in combination, when disturbed can impair a person's ability to return to work following a significant brain lesion (Guilmette & Kastner, 1996; Lezak, 1995).

Although a person's basic abilities may appear to recover fully following successful neurosurgery, more subtle changes in functioning may not be immediately apparent to the patient, her loved ones, friends or colleagues (Prigatano, G.P. & Schacter, D.L. 1991). It may only be over months or longer when the brain-injured person returns to work that she or her colleagues perceive her job performance to have significantly declined.

If the brain-injured patient's treating physician realizes that a variety of subtle yet significant changes in functioning can occur following a brain event, the physician may refer the patient for comprehensive neuropsychological evaluation following the initial rehabilitative period, with a major goal of the evaluation to determine whether there are neuropsychological impairments; and if there are, to determine how and to what extent they might obstruct this person's successful return to work (McMahon & Shaw, 1996).

In the following case, referral to a neuropsychologist was never made by the patient's physician, which reinforced the patient's incorrect belief that she was no different in ability following ruptured aneurysms and subsequent neurosurgery. Thus, she returned to work to the same management position she previously held, beginning at first part-time and eventually returning full time. Her colleagues, supervisors, and customers soon recognized that she wasn't the same person she had been previously. To her great chagrin, her supervisors and colleagues pointed out to her the serious job-related mistakes she was making. Complicating matters, because there was a massive intraventricular hemorrhage in her right cerebral hemisphere, she suffered anosagnosia, a common phenomenon associated with right hemisphere insult (Giacino & Cicerone, 1998). In other words, she was unaware of the changes that had taken place in her cognitive functions. As a result of having no insight into her behavioral and cognitive deficits, she believed that the criticisms made of her were both incorrect and unjust. Her company demoted her in order to try to help her regain her job skills, but she perceived that this demotion was unwarranted, and so concluded that her superiors were discriminating against her based on a misperception that she was disabled. This led to her voluntarily leaving her position and soon after retaining a personal injury attorney who filed a discrimination lawsuit against her company under the Americans with Disabilities Act (ADA) (EEOC, 1991, 1992; Sachs & Redd, 1994).

One of the earliest assessments which a plaintiff or defense attorney needs to make in a discrimination lawsuit is of the plaintiff. This is an especially important determination in those cases where the plaintiff alleges that he or she sustained an injury, either physical or psychological. When a plaintiff alleges that injury was suffered because of the opposing party's either intentional or negligent conduct, it is the plaintiff whom jurors most want to hear from in order to learn such things as the manifestations of the injury and its level of severity. Ordinarily in these cases, plaintiffs have the benefit of assistance from doctors who have treated them. These doctors can then offer corroborative testimony to the plaintiff by describing the plaintiff's symptoms, level of functioning, treatment, and overall prognosis. Because jurors are rarely experienced in the fields of medicine and psychology, a plaintiff's testimony, coupled with that of a doctor, can be very powerful influences before a jury.

At the same time, injury claims asserted by plaintiffs are usually heavily subjective. While doctors who have provided treatment can offer guidance to a jury on more objective factors, the practical reality is that the plaintiff is often the only one who can comprehensively testify about the injury and its effects (or in this case, lack of injury and absence of effects). Sometimes, plaintiffs, in their zeal to litigate claims, exaggerate or even fabricate their injuries. Even more problematic are those cases where a plaintiff honestly believes that she has been injured, despite the fact that the surrounding circumstances do not support that theory. On the other hand, as in this case, plaintiffs can also minimize the serious changes that have taken place as a result of their injuries (Williams, 1997).

Unlike physical injuries such as broken bones, which can be objectively established through the means of an x-ray, psychological injuries alleged in civil litigation are more difficult to prove. Cases involving claims of intentional employment discrimination with accompanying psychological injuries are often of this nature. A plaintiff in a job discrimination lawsuit may claim that she suffered anxiety and depression as a result of harassing conduct of colleagues or supervisors, for example, on the job. She may even offer medical and psychological testimony regarding her treatment for such conditions. The plaintiff's attorney must establish whether the facts of the case are consistent with the damages the plaintiff alleges have taken place. The defense attorney, on the other hand, must determine how to counterbalance the impact of that evidence. One of the resources available to both attorneys in this scenario is a neuropsychological evaluation of the plaintiff. These types of evaluations, when performed ethically, are designed to provide a more objective barometer of the plaintiff's psychological state by being performed by an outside examiner who has no prior familiarity with the plaintiff (Giuliano, Barth, Hawk & Ryan, 1997).

At the same time, however, attorneys must exercise prudence in determining whether a particular plaintiff should be evaluated. Evaluations of this sort are often quite expensive, in that they involve substantial time spent by the clinician reviewing records, interviewing and testing the plaintiff, and formulating conclusions based upon the information gathered. Even more significant is the potential that neuropsychological evaluations can "backfire" on the requesting party. For example, a clinician asked by a defense attorney to perform an evaluation of a plaintiff may determine that the plaintiff has sustained a substantial psychological injury, and may further conclude that such injury was likely precipitated by the conduct alleged. In this case, the defendant will have expended substantial monies and will have obtained nothing more than yet another adverse witness whom the plaintiff will gladly want to utilize to strengthen his or her allegations. Conversely, a clinician retained by plaintiff's counsel may conclude there was no significant injury as alleged. Therefore, attorneys must be judicious in their use of these evaluations.

The following plaintiff was referred for an independent neuropsychological evaluation by the attorney representing the defendant, her employer. This case is particularly unusual because the plaintiff was alleging she was not impaired whereas the defendant believed she was impaired.

Method

Subject and Case History (All identifying information has been changed to protect the privacy of the individual.)

Ms. Meredith Malone was a 32-year-old college graduate, employed as a restaurant manager for a large restaurant chain. She had been hired at the restaurant four years earlier, first as a manager trainee, then as an assistant manager. She had been working as a restaurant manager for two years, with performance evaluations reflecting above-average performance in all measured areas. She was described in her performance evaluations as a very determined manager who set and achieved goals appropriately. In fact, she was being considered for another promotion when she developed an acute headache, nausea, vomiting and lethargy at work, causing her to literally collapse. She was taken by co-workers to a nearby hospital where an angiography and cerebral arteriogram were performed. The consulting neurosurgeon diagnosed Ms. Malone with a congenital massive intraventricular hemorrhage secondary to a congenital arteriovenous malformation (AVM) coming off the choroidal artery with two small aneurysms. She was given only a 10% chance of survival. A lengthy neurosurgery was performed to remove the aneurysms and insert a ventricular shunt into her right lateral ventricle, which removed some of the blood and relieved some of the pressure that had built up in her head. Following neurosurgery, Ms. Malone developed significant right temporal lobe edema and a small subdural hematoma. Once these medical conditions were dealt with, her physicians stated that they thought she made a remarkable recovery.

Ms. Malone's one-month hospitalization was relatively unremarkable but for the fact that she developed significant seizure activity and was prescribed Dilantin by the neurologist who was responsible for her care.

Approximately six weeks post neurosurgery, Ms. Malone followed up with her neurosurgeon, who noted that she was doing extremely well and was without neurological deficits or visual field problems, although she did report feeling a bit unsteady. A CT Scan of the head showed marked improvement three months post neurosurgery. The neurologist also noted continued improvement. Ms. Malone was still taking Dilantin 300 mg b.i.d. for seizure activity and Tylenol No. 3 for headaches as needed. Her gait and cerebellar functioning were normal, and she had resumed driving. Four months post surgery, Ms. Malone was seizure-free but was experiencing some intermittent dizziness. Several months later, however, Ms. Malone experienced at least one more grand mal seizure and began experiencing episodes of déjà vu and mouth drooling.

During the recovery period, there was no mention made to any of Ms. Malone's doctors that she was experiencing any cognitive difficulties or personality changes despite the fact that these would be common sequelae after a massive intraventricular hemorrhage. Ms. Malone's neurosurgeon perceived that she did not have brain damage, although his visits with her lasted, at most, 15 minutes. As a result, Ms. Malone was never referred for a formal neuropsychological evaluation despite the nature of her injuries and symptoms the type of which can result from right hemisphere dysfunction or insults (Joseph, 1990).

Six months following Ms. Malone's neurosurgery, she returned to her previous employment but on a part-time basis. Almost immediately upon her return to work, Ms. Malone was observed to have a variety of difficulties. Although Ms. Malone's immediate supervisor was pleased by her enthusiasm to get back to work, he quickly observed a marked change in her work performance. Prior to her neurosurgery, Ms. Malone had been a manager who required very little supervision and learned new things with dispatch. After she returned, however, she did not seem to be the same person. Her supervisor noticed that she now required intense supervision to ensure that job-related tasks were performed satisfactorily. It was noted she was "not up to speed" and needed to relearn skills she had previously mastered. She was socially inappropriate with co-workers and alienated co-workers and customers alike. Her leadership skills became unsatisfactory. She was described as confrontational and insensitive as well as insubordinate. Her language became inappropriate. She began calling in sick frequently, leaving early from work, and demonstrating memory difficulties, such as remembering where documents were stored. She also had trouble remembering restaurant policies and conversations with co-workers. On one occasion, she forgot the PIN number and set off the restaurant's alarm system. On another occasion, she left the safe wide open with money inside. She also had difficulty with certain bookkeeping responsibilities and made frequent arithmetic errors. Ms. Malone's supervisor attempted to work with her to improve her performance; however, when she was confronted with her mistakes, she became angry and defensive. Notably, she had previously gotten along well with her supervisor. Her supervisor perceived that Ms. Malone was refusing to take responsibility for her mistakes and lapses in judgment. Inasmuch as Ms. Malone's performance failed to measurably improve, her employer decided to transfer her to another location and downgrade her managerial responsibilities. This change in work assignment also involved a loss of pay. Ms. Malone was upset by this decision and viewed it as some type of punitive action. By contrast, her employer suggested the demotion was an attempt to help her regain lost skills with the benefit of additional supervisory support.

Ms. Malone worked in her new position as assistant manager for a total of six months before resigning her employment. In those six months, she claimed that her new supervisor harassed her constantly, pressuring her to seek another job because she could not perform to his satisfaction. Like his predecessor, this new supervisor also had to address work-related deficiencies. Because Ms. Malone did not like the supervisor, she became very defensive when he criticized her performance. She claimed that this particular supervisor harassed her to the point where she felt she needed to leave her job. She then resigned and filed a lawsuit against her employer under the Americans with Disabilities Act (ADA), with specific charges of Breach of Contract, Intentional and/or Negligent Infliction of Emotional Distress and Retaliation.

Legal Considerations

In her lawsuit, Ms. Malone alleged that her employer had discriminated against her on the basis of disability under the ADA in the form of demoting her and then forcing her to resign. In a typical ADA case, the plaintiff alleges that he or she was subjected to discriminatory treatment because he or she is disabled in some physical or psychological way. In Ms. Malone's case, however, she took the opposite position. She contended that she was not disabled at all, and that her medical condition and accompanying neurosurgery had no effect on her ability to properly perform her job duties. Instead, she claimed that her employer, acting through its supervisors, falsely perceived her as disabled and discriminated against her based on that assumption by demoting her.

As a general matter, a defense attorney's usage of a neuropsychological evaluation in civil litigation is geared toward attacking the plaintiff's case theory. For example, this type of evaluation may reveal that, notwithstanding the plaintiff's allegations, no discernible psychological injury exists. It also may show that the plaintiff is exaggerating the manifestations of the alleged injury. In those situations where the evaluation does reveal some degree of injury, it can also be tremendously helpful in exploring and uncovering other potential sources of the injury, separate and distinct from what the plaintiff claims as the precipitating factor. These are all types of issues which a defense attorney wants to put before a judge and jury.

Early on in this case, the employer needed to determine how it was going to address Ms. Malone's allegations. Both Ms. Malone and her treating physicians were inclined to testify that she suffered no noticeable deficits in her mental functioning following her neurosurgery. The employer, however, had the testimony of her two supervisors who, although not trained in the intricacies of medicine and psychology, would be able to attest to their observations of her job performance and the types of problems that were occurring. Although the supervisors' testimony would be helpful, a professional opinion as to Ms. Malone's post-surgical level of functioning would be needed to rebut the testimony of Ms. Malone and her doctors.

The employer thus made the decision to have Ms. Malone submit to a neuropsychological evaluation. As previously stated, there was a risk to perform this evaluation in that if it were determined that Ms. Malone indeed did not suffer any impairment, that determination would prove very useful to Ms. Malone's case presentation. This calculated risk was nevertheless necessary because the lack of any objective support for the employer's position that Ms. Malone was actually impaired would be glaring in front of a jury.

Procedure

Prior to the subject being evaluated, a thorough review of relevant records was performed, including medical records prior to, related to, and following Ms. Malone's neurosurgery. Ms. Malone's educational records were also reviewed in order to determine a base rate of prior academic functioning. Additionally, occupational records from the restaurant were reviewed, including performance evaluations, notices of achievement and reprimands from before the neurosurgery and after Ms. Malone's return to work (Sbordonne and Saul, 2000). Prior to the scheduled neuropsychological examination, Ms. Malone was sent a letter outlining what she could expect from the evaluation and describing informed consent. Furthermore, informed consent was provided orally prior to the commencement of the evaluation. Ms. Malone understood the purpose of the evaluation, the role of the neuropsychologist in litigation, and consented to proceed.

The neuropsychologist conducted a lengthy interview of Ms. Malone, accompanied by her husband, in which her subjective complaints were gathered over a several-hour period. Additionally, in order to evaluate Ms. Malone's cognitive behavioral functioning, a complete neuropsychological test battery was performed. Testing was accomplished by the neuropsychologist and a Master's level psychometrist. The standard administration and scoring procedures were followed for each test. The following tests were performed over a two-day period: Wechsler Adult Intelligence Scale—III (WAIS-III) (Wechsler, 1997); Wechsler Memory Scale—III (WMS-III) (Wechsler, 1997); Lateral Dominance Examination; Halstead-Reitan Neuropsychological Test Battery (Reitan and Wilson, 1993); Hooper Visual Organization Test (Hooper, 1958; Western Psychological Services, 1983); Rey Complex Figure Test (Meyers and Meyers, 1995); Wide Range Achievement Test—3 (WRAT-3) (Wilkinson, 1993); Gross Motor Examination; Stroop Color-Word Test (Golden, 1978); Minnesota Multiphasic Personality Inventory—2 (MMPI-2) (Hathaway and McKinley, 1989); and Millon Clinical Multiaxial Inventory—III (MCMI-III) (Millon, Davis & Millon, 1997).

Results

Test Behavior

Ms. Malone presented without abnormalities of gait, speech, attention, or mood. Remarkable were several occasions that she behaved inappropriately, making sarcastic remarks and mimicking the neuropsychologist's nonverbal gestures. Equally notable was Ms. Malone's complete lack of insight that her behaviors were inappropriate. During tests she found difficult, Ms. Malone became easily frustrated and called the tests "stupid." Her emotions of anger and frustration were manifested in raw form with insufficient self-control. Nevertheless, motivation was adequate, and there were no behavioral signs or test results consistent with malingering or willful symptom exaggeration (Etcoff and Kampfer, 1996).

Neuropsychological Test Results

Tests of gross motor skills were unremarkable but for a mild construction dyspraxia and slightly better dexterity with the right versus left hand. Differences between the hands were subtle, however.

Consistent with a right hemisphere temporal lobe bleed, two left eye upper quadrant suppressions and two left ear auditory suppressions were noted. Furthermore, left-sided tactile perception was impaired in comparison to right-sided tactile perception, which was normal.

Compared to estimated premorbid levels of functioning, there was a mild diminution in working memory on the WAIS-III and WMS-III Working Memory Indices. Divided attention was also diminished, as evidenced on the Trails B and the Stroop Color-Word component.

Using a regression formula to estimate premorbid intelligence (Barona, 1984), Ms. Malone's Verbal IQ would likely have been approximately 114 (83rd percentile). On current testing, her WAIS-III Verbal IQ was 88 (21st percentile), suggesting there was an approximate two standard deviation loss of verbal skills subsequent to Ms. Malone's neurologic event and surgery.

Additionally, there were significant losses in academic skills, as measured on the WRAT-3 in Reading (5th percentile, fifth grade), Spelling (18th percentile, seventh grade), and Computational Arithmetic (16th percentile, seventh grade).

A premorbid estimate of Ms. Malone's perceptual organizational abilities (Barona, 1984) indicates her Performance IQ would likely have been approximately 111 (77th percentile). On current testing, her WAIS-III Performance IQ was 91 (27th percentile). Although this score is within the average range, it does suggest a decline from previous estimated levels of functioning. Furthermore, on tests measuring more complex visual problem solving, Ms. Malone scored very poorly. For example, on the WAIS-III Block Design Subtest, her performance fell at the 9th percentile; and on the Booklet Category Test, she made 113 out of 208 errors for a T-Score equivalent of 13, a score falling in the severe range of impairment (Heaton, Grant & Matthews, 1991).

On several tests and measures of reasoning, hypothesis testing, and problem solving, Ms. Malone performed quite poorly. For example, the Tactual Performance Test (TPT) had to be discontinued after the first of three trials because Ms. Malone couldn't deduce any method that would accomplish the task. Rather, she persisted with a trial-and-error approach until she finally refused to continue several minutes into the task. Had she finished the task, at the rate she was performing, she would have performed in the severely impaired range. Additionally, her responses on the WAIS-III Comprehension Subtest were concrete and simplistic, suggesting significant deficits in verbal reasoning. Finally, her WAIS-III Full Scale IQ was measured at an 89 (23rd percentile), an approximate 24-point drop from her estimated premorbid Full Scale IQ of 113 (81st percentile).

Verbal and visual memory skills were grossly deteriorated both on the WMS-III and Rey Complex Figure Test (RCFT). Her ability to encode information visually was measured at the 3rd percentile on the WMS-III Visual Immediate Index and beneath the 1st percentile on the RCFT. Ms. Malone's ability to encode auditory-verbal information fell at the 1st percentile on the WMS-III Auditory Immediate Index. Delayed recollection was measured at the 2nd percentile on the WMS-III General Memory Index and beneath the 1st percentile on the RCFT. Even with visual and auditory-verbal cues, Ms. Malone's delayed recognition of information, both visual and verbal, was extremely impaired.

During her evaluation, Ms. Malone did not appear depressed or overly anxious. She didn't appear to be experiencing significant emotional discomfort. Consistent with her clinical presentation, objective personality test results indicated that she did not perceive herself as experiencing emotional turmoil to any significant degree.

Discussion

The position of restaurant manager required the job incumbent to be adaptable to changes in technology, customer needs, schedules and procedures. The position also required the ability to be team oriented and cooperative. Ms. Malone's supervisors and co-workers perceived that she was no longer the same capable restaurant manager upon returning to work; that she kept forgetting company policies and procedures (even after they were retaught) as well as co-worker and customer conversations she had heard less than an hour before. Their perceptions were consistent with her WMS-III General Memory Index Score of 70 (2nd percentile). Additionally, the contention that Ms. Malone could not relearn managerial tasks and procedures despite whether they were presented auditorily or visually was consistent with the WMS-III Immediate Memory Index Score of 61 (< 1st percentile).

Ms. Malone's co-workers' perceptions that she was making poor decisions that required immediate problem solving, common sense and judgment was evident in her performances on the Category Test, Tactual Performance Test, and WAIS-III Full Scale IQ of 89 (23rd percentile).

Ms. Malone's fifth grade reading skills could very well have interfered with her ability to read and understand company or other manual publications as well as all other forms of written communication. Her compromised spelling skills (7th grade) would have interfered with her ability to write a variety of communications, including performance evaluations, letters and memos to customers, coworkers, management and company officials. Her compromised arithmetic skills (7th grade) would likely have interfered with the job requirements having to do with bookkeeping and financial reporting. Her employer might have been able to accommodate these academic losses to some degree by providing her with computer software that could read written materials to her, a spell check, and a calculator; but to what extent would these accommodations have assured the company that Ms. Malone's work product would have been acceptable? How many arithmetic errors could the company be reasonably expected to tolerate? How much extra supervision could the company reasonably have been required to provide to assure Ms. Malone's work product accuracy?

One can argue that the most significant neuropsychological deficit suffered by Ms. Malone was her lack of self-awareness that she had so many recently acquired information processing impairments (Sherer, Bergloff, Levin, High, Oden & Nick, 1998). Without adequate self-awareness, Ms. Malone could not have been expected to gauge her effect on subordinates, colleagues, supervisors, or customers. Also, Ms. Malone's low frustration tolerance and tendency to become verbally disinhibited when she became frustrated could not have been long tolerated or accommodated in the workplace.

For all of the above-mentioned reasons, a preponderance of the neuropsychological evidence indicated that Ms. Malone would not have been able to function successfully or independently in her previous job as a restaurant manager.

It was recommended that Ms. Malone be given supportive feedback from the neuropsychologist whenever her attorney decided in consultation with her and her husband that such feedback would be advisable, given her legal case. It was also recommended that Ms. Malone be provided supportive psychotherapy in order to help her understand the profound effects of her brain injury on her daily cognitive functioning and social skills (Prigatano, 1991). Unfortunately for Ms. Malone, such neuropsychological support had not been provided before her return to work, as her evaluation results were classic sequelae to a right hemisphere injury (Joseph, 1990).

Furthermore, it was recommended that Ms. Malone consider allowing her husband to be given feedback from the neuropsychologist or her psychotherapist regarding her impairments and disabilities so that Mr. Malone might become a fully informed partner in helping to improve the quality of his wife's life. Finally, it was suggested and hoped that Ms. Malone would consent to providing her neurosurgeon with a copy of her neuropsychological evaluation in order to remind him of the importance of neuropsychological follow-up in cases where significant brain insult has occurred.

From a legal perspective, the neuropsychological evaluation proved useful on two levels. First, it provided objective, unchallenged evidence which demonstrated significant impairments suffered by Ms. Malone. From the attorney's perspective, had the case gone to trial, that evidence would have likely been persuasive to a jury, particularly the deficits Ms. Malone had in reading, spelling, and arithmetic.

Second, and perhaps more importantly, the neuropsychological evaluation provided a frank assessment to Ms. Malone of the extent of her limitations. As previously stated, none of her treating physicians believed that she was experiencing any cognitive difficulties, and therefore she had no reason to believe that her brain injury had resulted in any long-term neuropsychological deficits. With the evaluation, however, Ms. Malone was confronted, for the first time, with the fact that she was a different person, as her colleagues and supervisors at work had earlier observed. That recognition by Ms. Malone represented a turning point in the case. Where previously she and her attorney had been aggressive in their pursuit of her discrimination claims, they now had to re-evaluate the merits of her case. Ultimately, the case was settled for a nominal sum, representing a victory for both parties.

References

Equal Employment Opportunity Commission (1991). *The Americans with Disabilities Handbook.* Washington, D.C.: Author.

Equal Employment Opportunity Commission (1992). *A technical assistance manual on the employment provisions (Title 1) of the Americans with Disabilities Act.* Washington, D.C.: Author.

Etcoff, L.M., & Kampfer, K.M. (1996). Practical guidelines in the use of symptom validity and other psychological tests to measure malingering and symptom exaggeration in traumatic brain injury cases. *Neuropsychology Review,* 6, 171–201.

Ethical principles of psychologists and code of conduct. (1992, December). American Psychologist.

Giacino, J.T. & Cicerone, K.D. (1998). Varieties of deficit unawareness after brain injury. *Journal of Head Trauma Rehabilitation, 13*(5): 1–15.

Golden, C.J. (1978). *Stroop color and word test.* Chicago, Illinois: Stoelting Company.

Giuliano, A.J., Barth, J.T., Hawk, G.L. & Ryan, T.V. (1997). The forensic neuropsychologist: Precedent, roles, and problems. In A.E. Puente & C.R. Reynolds (Series Eds.) & R.J. McCaffrey, A.D. Williams, J.M. Fisher & L.C. Lang (Vol. Eds.), *The practice of forensic neuropsychology: Meeting challenges in the courtroom* (pp. 1–35). New York: Plenum Press.

Guilmette, T.J. & Kostner, M.P. (1996). The prediction of vocational functioning from neuropsychological data. In R.J. Sbordonne & C.J. Long (Eds.), *Ecological validity of neuropsychological testing.* Delray Beach, Florida: GR Press/St. Lucie Press.

Heaton, R.K., Grand, I. & Matthews, C.G. (1991). Comprehensive norms for an expanded Halstead-Reitan battery. Odessa, Fl. Psychological Assessment Resources, Inc.

Joseph, R.S. (1990). Neuropsychology, neuropsychiatry, and behavioral neurology. In A.E. Puente & C.R. Reynolds (Series Eds.), *Critical issues in neuropsychology.* New York: Plenum Press.

Lezak, M.D. (1995). *Neuropsychological assessment:* Third edition. New York: Oxford University Press.

McMahon, B.T. & Shaw, L.R. (1996). Neuropsychology and rehabilitation counseling: Bridging the gap. In R.J. Sbordonne & C.J. Long (Eds.), *Ecological validity of neuropsychological testing.* Delray Beach, Florida: GR Press/St. Lucie Press.

Meyers, J.E. & Meyers, K.R. (1995). Rey complex figure test and recognition trial: Professional manual. Fl., Psychological Assessment Resources, Inc.

Millon, T., Millon, C. & Davis, R. (1994). *Millon clinical multiaxial inventory-III.* Minneapolis, Minnesota: National Computer Systems, Inc.

Meyers, J.E. & Meyers, K.R. (1995). *Rey complex figure test and recognition trial professional manual.* Odessa, Florida: Psychological Assessment Resources, Inc.

Prigatano, G.P. & Schacter, D.L. (Eds.) (1991). *Awareness of deficit after brain injury: Clinical and theoretical issues.* New York: Oxford University Press.

Prigatano, G.P. (1991). Disordered mind, wounded soul: The emerging role of psychotherapy in rehabilitation after brain injury. *Journal of Head Trauma Rehabilitation, 6*(4): 1–10.

Reitan, R.M. & Wolfson, D. (1993). *The Halstead-Reitan neuropsychological test battery: Theory and clinical interpretation* (2nd Ed.). Tucson, Arizona: Neuropsychology Press.

Sachs, P.R. & Redd, C.A. (1994). The American's with Disabilities Act and individuals with neurological impairments. In S.M. Bruyere & J. O'Keefe (Vol. Eds.), *Implications of the Americans with Disabilities Act for psychology* (pp. 85–101). Washington, D.C.: American Psychological Association.

Sbordonne, R.J. and Saul, R.E. (2000). Neuropsychology for healthcare professionals and attorneys: 2nd Ed. Boca Raton, Fl. CRC Press.

Sherer, M., Bergloff, P., Levin E., High, W.M., Jr., Oden, K.E. & Nick, T.G. (1998). Impaired awareness and employment outcome after traumatic brain injury. *Journal of Head Trauma Rehabilitation, 13*(5): 52–61.

Specialty guidelines for forensic psychologists. (1991). *Law and Human Behavior,* 15, 655–665.

Wilkenson, G.S. (1993). *The wide range achievement test—third edition.* Wilmington, Delaware: Wide Range, Jastak Inc.

Williams, A.D. (1997). The forensic evaluation of adult traumatic brain injury. In A. E. Puente & C.R. Reynolds (Series Eds.) & R.J. McCaffrey, A.D. Williams, J.M. Fisher & L.C. Laing (Vol. Eds.), *The practice of forensic neuropsychology: Meeting challenges in the courtroom* (pp. 37–56). New York: Plenum Press.

Wechsler, D. (1997). *The Wechsler memory scale—third edition.* San Antonio, Texas: Psychological Corporation.

Wechsler, D. (1997). *The Wechsler adult intelligence scale—third edition.* San Antonio, Texas: Psychological Corporation.

Western Psychological Services (1983). *Hooper visual organization test.* Los Angeles, California: Author.

Advances in Medical Psychotherapy and Psychodiagnosis
2002–2003, Volume 11, pp. 19–34

Behavioral Healthcare and Education:
The Nature, Course and Application of
Risk Reduction Programming

Jerald Cilente, Ph.D.
Staten Island, NY

Abstract

Risk reduction programming is examined as a hybrid of health promotion and prevention programs. The major impetus comes from adapting current human services programming to the specific needs of individuals who seek help. The process of adapting these programs requires the professional counselor to develop a sensitivity of telonics for behavioral change, through a design-emergent synergy. This manual delineates telonics as a heuristic for developing risk reduction programming by considering the major health models that are applied to general health issues and specifically to substance abuse and related problems. Underlying cognitive structures are assumed to be the self regulating agent when an intention to improve one's health is established. Finally, an organismic-developmental-systems perspective encapsulates the theoretical and practical integration of telonics for education and treatment programming.

Introduction

Risk reduction is a generic concept for hybrid programs that arise from health promotion and prevention. The health and human services field has been progressively moving towards the task of being accountable for services rendered. Consequently, multivariate and eclectic treatment strategies evolve in order to give a client the best chance to manage his/her problem, for which help was sought. At times, the behavioral change technology may not be empirically validated and components of an individual's treatment plans may not be best, especially when the goal is to reduce the threats of harm or risk for the problem at hand. Therefore, programs in nonprofit agencies may need better guidelines for accountability to maintain their services. The task for the professional counselor in the field of health and human services would be to identify a need for such a program, and then, develop its parameters and behavioral change technology for successful outcome. Jaros and Baker (1998) called this process "telonics." Telonics undergirds the comprehensive view of technological innovation, from its conception to its modifications and usefulness in an area of treatment and education . The telonic process may also be applied in risk reduction because the changes in behavioral change technology should be thoughtfully constructed in light of eclectic treatment packages. It provides the theoretical framework for evaluating the quality of our actions where processes are created within a certain ethos that have definite goals. Furthermore, goals vary and change in structure when the need arises. Therefore, telonics guides the purposeful and qualitative process of behavioral change technology by the design-emergent synergy of eclecticism—a process that may be intuitively understood, but needs to be uncovered when a sense of timing is required for intervening in a client's progress and relapses.

Any new program in risk reduction should assume telonic qualities. Risk reduction technology should be considered within the context of health promotion, disease prevention and disease management. According to Taylor (1995) health promotion takes on an integrated stance because it attempts to change the attitudes and behaviors of individuals throughout their life span. Simultaneously, it helps practitioners identify people "at risk" so they can implement strategies to offset or monitor those risks. Theories about health promotion attempt to improve the quality of life proactively; disease prevention utilizes assumptions derived from a perceived threat to one's health; disease management models distinguish the guidelines that govern treatment and prevention. All use implicit assumptions about behavior change technology which should be anchored in experimentation and application—a test of utilizing the implicit assumptions of telonics. The development of behavioral change technology becomes an emergent synthesis when relevant, selected models and techniques are thoughtfully reconstructed to qualitatively fit the needs of a program and a specific population or disorder.

This paper provides a heuristic for the telonic process in risk reduction. It discusses the relevant models in our ethos that may be applied to minimize harm, and also to develop adequate behavioral interventions for such programs. It is not solely meant to give examples of risk reduction programs nor does it suggest a "correct" way to develop them. However, its intention is to start the telonic process. Where it goes from there will be entrusted to the counselor's knowledge, problem solving skills and the freedom to persuade and convince funding sources to perform the needed outcome research for such programs.

Risk Factors

What are risk factors?

According to Justice (1988):

> A risk factor is any characteristic, condition or behavior we have that increases our chances of getting sick . . . Risk factors—anything in our thinking, behavior, body or environment that increases the likelihood of illness—are opposed by "resistance resources" we possess . . . The balance between risk factors and resistance resources largely determines whether we get sick or stay healthy. (Justice, 1988, p. 30, 33)

Blair Justice implies that risk vulnerability trades off with resistance resources. Furthermore it is a biopsychosocial phenomenon. Therefore, when considering developing a risk reduction program, the disease or disorder should be considered within a context.

Bernard and Krupat (1994) see risk factors as a probability that certain signs or symptoms are associated with a disease of disorder. Therefore, conditions will occur in people where these symptoms are not addressed. They imply that life style and behavior are correlated with illness. Life style and behavioral risk factors do not cause a disease or a disorder; however they may contribute to increased vulnerability of its development. Taylor (1995) gives examples and discusses the benefits of risk reduction strategies towards health enhancing behaviors, such as exercise, accident prevention and weight control. She also delineates the benefits of risk reduction strategies for health compromising behaviors, such as substance abuse and smoking. All of these ideas and strategies are viewed from the biopsychosocial perspective.

Individuals suffering from psychiatric disorders have also benefited from risk reduction. Ever since Zubin and Spring (1977) developed the diathesis-stress model of schizophrenia, strategies emerged to help patients foster person-environment transactions within the limitations of their supports. Consequently, those suffering from depression, divorce, poor peer relationships and anxiety also capitalized on these programs (Curran and Monti, 1982).

An example of present day risk reduction has emerged within the problem of substance abuse. Catania et al. (1990) generated some programs to teach clients how to reduce the contraction and/or the spread of HIV/AIDS through an emergent behavioral technology. It raises a client's awareness about the effort one has to expend in order to change one's interpersonal processing with other drug related behaviors.

Risk factors for illness also correlate with peoples' life styles. These are the everyday behavioral patterns associated with the development of a chronic disease or a disorder. Sarafino (1994) believes that chronic diseases are the chief health problems in today's society and they draw money out of our health care dollars. Identifying risk factors, teaching people how to be aware of them, and providing them with their own idiosyncratic problem solving strategy to manage these disorders may have long term effects for health problems within a certain context. Consequently, this idea promotes large-scale prevention programs. However, regardless of the size of a program, the important point for the counselor is to learn how to target a problem and then to develop a program to minimize incrementally the damage that can be done to one's health and to others—this is the essence of risk reduction. It is not meant to guarantee one's safety. However, it is designed to work with problems at a low threshold while allowing the client to accept responsibility and practice change strategies outside the program.

Health Models to Consider in Risk Reduction

Risk reduction will eventually be built upon an eclectic model that attempts to explain and predict the perceived effort needed to change one's behavior, in order to foster enhanced person-environment transactions, within the person's environment of choice. This undoubtedly is a complex cognitive skill. A sense of well being associated with the quality of an individual's life represents a critical cognitive component in health models. Therefore, if one can adopt a personal, ecological strategy to appraise threats to wellness, then there is a potential to decrease the danger or harm of exacerbating a disease or a disorder.

The Biopsychosocial Model

The biopsychosocial model developed by Engel (1980) has been applied to theories and treatments pertaining to health and illness. It comes from the evolution of a changing perspective within a general systems theory that puts cognition in the center of perceived person-environment transactions that influences coping. At that time, the existing biomedical model was limited because it could not account for diseases or disorders that were chronic, nor could it be used for problems with no specific pathogen that caused an illness. The biomedical model also defined health exclusively in terms of the absence of a disease. However, the biopsychosocial model challenged these assumptions and proposed that a disorder was multifactorial and integrated.

Addiction can be viewed within the biopsychosocial model. Here the probability of a relapse would be determined by many factors. For instance, biological factors could be attributed to the disease model of addiction (Leone, 1989) and its genetic origins (Peele, 1988). Multiple social circumstances influenced a return to substance abuse: Relapse vulnerability was hypothesized as a result of pathological social conditions (Nida, 1988), a release from social obligations (Cox, 1990), or a way to escape the threat of achievement failure (Misra, 1980). Psychological behavioral disorder was shaped by learned, maladaptive behavior patterns that was associated with cognition, motivation and emotion (Bandura, 1977).

The biopsychosocial perspective implies that the whole person, as a system, is unique and inter-related among all of its component parts. Consequently, risk reduction involves a holistic approach requiring multivariant behavioral technological interventions, especially for an integrated outcome measurement. Psychological dependency factors are emphasized for such a program because cognitive strategies establish an awareness hierarchy of danger or harm that are learned simultaneously with the acquisition of knowledge and skills. An example of a risk reduction strategy from this model would be to teach the person to become the agent of regulating his internal mental states for perceived threats to an intention, in order to execute a skilled action for managing a relapse situation. This requires more than the execution of a performance for goal attainment. When the awareness hierarchy is ignored, order is disrupted and the system becomes dysfunctional. Consequently, the risk of relapse increases.

The Prevention Model

Prevention is society's response to maladaptive behavior. The implied message to the prevention per-spective (and probably for any other model of human intervention) is that the counselor is perceived as the agent of social control, especially by the person who is receiving services. The underlying task is to persuade the client to relinquish some freedom during intervention so he could acquire more free-dom and personal control in the long run.

Most people are rigidly set in their habits, motives and behaviors. They expect little change because there may be no intention to experience a richer life towards wellness. They resist in ways to protect their sense of freedom or personal control when they perceive it is being threatened. They react or resist change because they can not identify the motives underlying their behavior and attitudes. Furthermore, perceived failure towards compliance makes individuals feel punished, morally con-demned or socially stigmatized.

A theory of psychological reactance was generated by Brehm (1966) to account for this per-ceived loss of freedom. Further, it can be extended to the concept of risk reduction through more recent work on reactance (Brehm and Brehm, 1981; Bensley and Wu, 1991). Overcoming reactance may enhance behavioral technology and outcome measurement in risk reduction. Too much per-ceived pressure may cause a person to do the opposite of what is required or desired to minimize risk. Strong "anti" messages may be perceived as a threat to personal freedom. More effective pro-grams may require a "moderate" stance. Harm reduction models for addiction are such programs that assume a moderate stance.

Inducing clients to become more aware of their role and goal in risk reduction may also alle-viate psychological reactance. Rush and Watkins (1981) explained how role induction was asso-ciated with psychological naiveté. Usually, clients do not have much experience with professionals. Their attitudes towards these people reflect family, cultural mythology, gossip and TV/movie portrayals. Therefore, socializing clients to risk reduction via procedures that outline, demonstrate and familiarize them what to expect improves outcome. Expectations are clarified, attitudes are gradually realized and perceptions about program tasks are elicited before and after they are engaged.

As stated previously, risk reduction is a generic concept. It has modified and updated perspectives about prevention programs. They have become more personalized and they can be selectively targeted to problem areas. This becomes especially useful when a counselor works for an agency and discov-ers a specific need for such a program. People can recognize the critical role they can play to stay well. Therefore, risk reduction changes the focus from an illness model to problems viewed in the context of a wellness model. A wellness perspective teaches a client how to monitor symptoms, thoughts and intentions when faced with perceived stress. Also the wellness model can be applied to multiple pre-vention interventions.

Primary prevention aims to generally reduce the risk of new cases of disorders. Therefore, these programs are administered to everyone and not a particular population. For example, professionals attempt to teach risk prevention so a problem will not develop.

Secondary prevention is directed at people who are identified "at-risk" and they will probably develop a disorder. Here biopsychosocial risk factors are the basis that determine a risk. The aim is to reduce the potential disability of an existing condition. Usually, skill development interventions are taught to increase resiliency while support is provided to protect the person. This is the direct application of the diathesis—stress hypothesis: when an individual is biologically vulnerable for a disorder, risk is minimized by teaching him coping skills and/or modifying the environment. Consequently, the intensity and frequency of the symptoms are likely to decrease.

Tertiary prevention helps people who are already diagnosed with an illness or disorder. The aim is to reduce the risk of further impairment. Frequently risk reduction is taught in a rehab or resocializing settings for these problems. The counselor has more control over clients because they frequently attend the program. Therefore, better assessments are available to target risk reduction.

Wellness, Values Clarification and Motivation

Most of us live within a culture of illness in which wellness is defined as not being sick. However, wellness is not synonymous with health. Health is the state of active instruction and reflection pursuant to pro-health behaviors. It is concerned more with a shift in one's thinking instead of a behavioral performance. Therefore, when one operates with intention towards wellness, the experience of "doing" is consonant with thinking. Vaughn (1985) called this being authentic because one's behavior and beliefs were congruent.

Changing one's beliefs and attitudes to reduce risk implies problem skills development. Change also means taking risks to develop "skill power" not "will power" that eventually lead to life-style patterns. Concepts like self-regulation (Bandura, 1977), psychological hardiness (Kobassa, 1982) or sense of coherence (Antonovsky, 1987) emphasize a sequence of events that minimize risk: cognition governs behavior and adjustments in one's behavior can always be made when recognizing one's intentions.

Values clarification influences one's affective dispositions, which eventually effect decision making, behavior and attitudes. It gives some direction to the meaningness of life, which eventually guides behavior. Therefore, values clarification is one flexible way to provide an individual with a frame of reference to integrate, explain and conduct new experiences and relationships.

Simon et al. (1972) delineate values clarification as an internal consistency between what people say and do. They outline three steps necessary to achieve internal consistency. They are:

1. *Choosing*—The ability to choose freely between alternates and to evaluate the consequences of each alternative.

2. *Prizing*—The ability to be proud about choosing an alternative and to publicly affirm the choice.

3. *Acting*—The ability to incorporate choice into one's overt behavior and to repeat that choice.

Values clarification is a critical component of successful client education for risk reduction. It may reduce psychological reactance and attrition rates. Furthermore, it is flexible enough to help clients develop their own problem solving strategies to minimize health risks. When people can evaluate the way things are to what they want them to be, then information is activated and problems move from patterns into processes. Therefore, when the functional significance and personal meanings of a person's problems and patterns are identified, change occurs in spontaneous self-organization (Mahoney, 1983).

Spontaneous self-organization can be seen as characteristic of all systems, especially concerning the phenomenology of cognition. Maturana and Varela (1992) used the word "autopoesis" to describe this self-organization theory.

Autopoesis, briefly stated, characterizes those systems which:

- maintain their defining organization throughout a history of environmental perturbation and structural change, and

- regenerate their components in the course of their operation.

Autopoesis is endemic in all systems. Systems begin from a relative state of equlibrium so information can be assimilated. However, when information can not be assimilated anymore, the system must accommodate in order to qualitatively change its configuration. Then information can be re-assimilated into a more cohesive and qualitative whole, until the process begins again with another perturbation. This behavior of systems is non-linear and it can be demonstrated with outcome measurement. Therefore, a small intervention can produce a large output, especially when cognition is conceived in the center of the system.

The development of risk reduction programs and its behavioral technology is also non-linear and self-organizing. Furthermore, those clients who are involved in risk reduction programs change as a function of this descriptive phenomenology. Therefore, autopoesis underlies the complexity of change throughout this paper that emphasizes cognition as the center of an individual's system.

The Health Belief Model

The health belief model is a cognitive model of health behavior and compliance containing four components

1. Personal susceptibility to a negative health condition.

2. The perceived severity of the condition.

3. The value of the health related behavior.

4. Barriers to the action taken, not to be taken.

Kirscht and Joseph (1989) interpreted this model as a readiness to act when the four components are viewed holistically.

Becker (1974) originally developed the Health Belief Model. It evolved from value-expectancy theories which assume that a person's decisions are based on a cost-benefit appraisal of alternatives. For example, an individual weighs the pleasures of smoking against the risk of lung cancer. Or a person weighs the pleasures of sexual intercourse with a drug injecting abuser against the risk of AIDS. The decision to execute these behaviors depends upon the perceived seriousness of risk and the subjective probability of developing a disease or a disorder. If the negative consequences are perceived to occur in the distant future, then subtle messages of persuasion through behavioral interventions is more effective than exposing clients to threatening messages about getting sick. Further, a social systems approach to risk reduction which focuses on social pressures and negative social reactions to engaging in risk behaviors may be more effective than a threat approach in this model.

It is also important to remember that variables like ethnicity, perceived costs to treatment, socioeconomic status, age and other social-psychological variables influence the outcome of weighing the costs and benefits of a behavioral performance towards wellness and risk reduction. According to Brannon and Feist (1997) the model has been improved when one integrates aspects of other theories such as self-efficacy, intentions to behave and perceived social norms. These improvements tend to concentrate on developing a client's social cognition. These are the factors that influence the way people perceive themselves and others and form judgments about the causes of behavior.

Change and Risk Reduction

Theory of Reasoned Action and Planned Behavior

Ways to reduce risk are linked directly to health attitudes and behaviors. Fishbein et al. (1994) and Ajzen (1985) proposed a linear model of health behavior as a direct result of an intention. Behavioral intentions are made up of three parts consisting of:

1. Attitudes toward specific actions which are based on beliefs about likely outcomes of actions and beliefs about those outcomes.

2. Subjective norms regarding an action about what a person believes others think that person should do (these are called normative beliefs) and the motivation to comply with those normative references.

3. Perceived behavioral control about one's coping ability to perform a contemplated action, and also, that the action undertaken will have the intended effect (this is similar to Bandura's self-efficacy [Bandura, 1977]).

According to these theories of planned behavior and reasoned action, humans are viewed as rational with their behavior under volitional control. Any behavior can be defined by an action, a target in a context, and within a certain time frame. An intention always predicts the occurrence of a desirable behavior. An attitude also includes the affect towards performing a certain behavior.

The bottom line about these theories indicate that an intention is the best indicator that a behavior will occur. Furthermore, behavioral and normative beliefs are "cognitive structures" that influence individual attitudes and subjective norms. They eventually shape a person's intention to perform a behavior. However, shaping an intention occurs non-linearly.

When these theories are synthesized for risk reduction, behavioral and normative beliefs must be taken into account when designing behavioral change technology. Behavioral beliefs combine the outcome of a behavior with an evaluation about that outcome. For example, condom risk reduction use may raise questions and beliefs about a partner's infidelity v. caring. Normative beliefs regard others' views of a behavior to be executed and a willingness to conform to that view. Therefore, a professional counselor needs to keep in mind that different populations vary in their normative opinions, which is another level in a client's system affecting self-organization.

The literature also discusses these theories applied to such behaviors as sunscreen application (Hillhouse et al., 1996), exercise (Gatch and Kendzierski, 1990) and daily self-care habits (Madden et al., 1992).

Finnigan (1995) applied the Theory of Reasoned Action (TRA) to a drug education program as an intervention to deter or reduce heroin drug use. TRA induced and maintained behavioral change with heroin injections and also their cognitive structures underlying drug use. Fear tactics or "anti" messages even worked better when one achieved an attitude change and an intention to remain abstinent.

The Transtheoretical Model of Change

The timing of applying behavioral change technology is just as important as developing new interventions for risk reduction. It appears that people can be assessed at various levels to change. Therefore, an intervention may work better at the appropriate time. Prochaska et al. (1992) outlined a five-step model of change. It specifically addressed the problem about "when" and "what" to introduce as an intervention while clients progress through a program. The five stages are:

1. *Precontemplation:* A condition of unawareness with no intention to change.

2. *Contemplation:* An increased awareness about a problem with no commitment to take action.

3. *Preparation:* A condition of awareness to pursue a goal within a limited period of time based upon past failure to achieve that goal.

4. *Action:* A successful and active effort to change a behavior.

5. *Maintenance:* A striving to maintain a goal through effort producing successful goal attainment.

A professional counselor may be able to use this theory as an assessment for the client's cognitive skill level, strength of intention and motivation when planning educational and behavioral interventions. The stages are not linear, nor do the follow a linear path of relapsing.

To help clients progress through these stages the professional counselor must speak a language that promotes and encourages this progression. The tasks of risk reduction should be matched with the stage of change that clients are experiencing. For example, if clients are not yet resolute about their readiness to change because ambivalence is fueling denial; then it is not useful to keep them in the action stage. The precontemplation stage needs to be worked on first, perhaps by inducing clients into their role and discussing reactance.

Harm Reduction

Harm reduction minimizes problems in segments so an individual may be able to contain an affected area of a disease or disorder. People can be taught to live within the limitations of a wellness-illness continuum while simultaneously developing attitude and behavioral changes.

From the 1960's and throughout the 1990's the awareness of health problems has bombarded our society. Health risks were frequently associated with alcohol and tobacco. AIDS prevention was eventually introduced to injecting drug users (IDUs). Today there is a push for an integrated public health perspective for licit and illicit drug use and abuse.

Topics for the 21st century lead to controversies of such issues as prevalence reduction, quantity reduction of drugs, macro v. micro harm reduction, part v. total harm reduction and targeting vulnerable life style crises (adolescent, mid-life, and late adult). Furthermore, harm reduction programs posit a relationship between risk reduction, abstinence reduction and relapse. Eventually social capital will be generated for macro-harm reduction. Presently, it is also applied to ethnic communities and the cost-effectiveness is measured by program evaluation studies.

Harm reduction is specifically set within the broader context of health psychology and public health. Controversial issues arise because of peoples' political preferences and how public health dollars should be allocated. Substance-related disorders have been introduced into the harm reduction arena as an alternative treatment. It raises controversy because the harm reduction method takes the middle ground between the prohibitionistic and the legalistic approaches to substance abuse.

The prohibitionistic approach defines substance use and abuse by society. Eventually, this leads to incarcerations and politicians may capitalize on drug statistics. Therefore, a manufactured moral panic develops which marginalizes substance abusers and strains the criminal justice system. Indirectly, it sustains the black market. The legalistic approach promotes drug legality. Therefore, it assumes to wipe out the black market, reduce incarcerations and utilize health care money for improved prevention and treatment.

A novel situation arises because harm reduction assumes a neutral view about substance abuse and the substance abuser on the conceptual, practical and policy levels (Tucker, 1999). These levels are paraphrased in the following way:

- *Conceptual:* Harm reduction focuses on the problems rather than on the use of substances. It neither insists nor objects to abstinence. However, the user must take an active role in his program.

- Practical: Harm reduction decreases the immediate harmful consequences of a drug via pragmatic and low threshold programs.

- *Policy:* Harm reduction holds mid-range policy measures to match the wide spectrum of patterns of substance abuse and its related problems.

Methadone maintenance was the first harm reduction program before the term became popular. Policy issues that are struggled with and studied today are:

- Needle cleansing/exchange

- Outreach to high-risk populations

- Law enforcement cooperation

- Prescriptions for heroin and other drugs

- Tolerance zones in hygienic environments

- Tobacco programs—controlled smoking in public places, nicotine gum and patch use

Harm reduction programs are also flexible, however, they require more medical practitioners. A biopsychosocial perspective enfolds the implicate order of such programs with some ground rules. These "ground rules" come from a therapeutic community or milieu approach to substance abuse. Yet its aim is to help the individual and society contain substance abuse and related problems from spreading into epidemic proportions. Education, skills training and other cognitive-behavioral technology is continually developed to achieve successful outcomes on the micro and macro levels of addiction.

An overlooked aspect of such programs is the ethical issues. For instance, if a client comes into a program intoxicated during an assessment, it would be necessary for the counselor to ensure his safety upon leaving. He may have to stay until he is sober, a family member should be called if he can not drive, or he may need assistance getting home by train so he does not slip and fall onto the tracks. This is only one example. A counselor needs to be aware about how general precautions and policy measures should be put into such programs and managed for all parties involved—staff, referral agencies, family members and other relevant people.

Another example would be working with a referral agency that does not believe in harm reduction—only abstinence is necessary. If a client was referred to an agency in his catchment area which followed a harm reduction model, how would progress notes be written? The probation officer may need proof of abstinence while the client's polydrug abuse may never reach that level. From a harm reduction perspective the client may be working towards abstinence from heroin, but will still use marijuana daily.

Cognitive Structures Underlying Change

Helping individuals reduce harm to their health is an integrated endeavor. The models discussed suggest some adaptation to a biopsychosocial perspective that positions cognition as the center of the person-system. Therefore, behavior follows thinking. The thinking that is done is an appraisal—a way to estimate a threat, harm, or a loss when one is under stress, or in a stressful situation. If risk reduction can develop this idiosyncratic skill, then harm is minimized, outcome appears successful, and perhaps the person can generalize this skill to other risk areas in his life.

The literature says that classical appraisals are also a modifiable cognitive structure that one can be made aware of (Lazarus and Folkman, 1984). Furthermore, some underlying self-regulatory mechanism is inherent in this concept that begins the process.

Self-Regulation and Goals

Self-direction is a self-regulatory process. According to Bandura (1997) impulsivity appears to be tamed by internal regulated thought and direction for external sanctions and demands. Once self-direction is developed, risk reductions increase, intention is maintained, and pro-health behaviors are enacted.

Bandura (1977, 1986) also suggested that there was a series of steps towards self-regulation which could be learned. They are summarized as follows:

1. *Self-observation:* A form of self-monitoring.

2. *Judgment:* The skill of comparing one's own behavior to a standard.

3. *Self-response:* Acknowledgement and rewarding oneself when one's behavior meets a standard.

Self-direction and self-regulation are closely related to Bandura's concept of self-efficacy (Bandura, 1977). It centers on the development of a perception of one's competence in various life situations. Therefore, people with high self-efficacy will try harder to succeed in difficult tasks if they believe they are competent to complete these tasks. Conversely, people with low self-efficacy may not try harder in difficult tasks because they believe they are not competent in these specific areas.

The concept of self-efficacy can be applied to a variety of risk related phenomena which may center around addiction. Problems with motivation, self-esteem, interpersonal relations, sexual practices and other issues can be explained as life skills training in order to minimize a relapse and/or contraction of HIV/AIDS. People who lack self-efficacy can be taught to increase their competence in their abilities to evaluate risks to health and to succeed in pro-health performance behaviors.

Kobasa (1982) found out that those who stay well under perceived stress also have a sense of challenge, control and commitment to life. The implicit assumptions that underlie these health factors mediate situations of risk into optimistic cognitions that provide meaningfulness, direction, and excitement in life. This cognitive, mediational construct was called psychological hardiness which may be similar to self-efficacy.

Similarly Antonovsky (1987) developed a theory about what kept people healthy by observing those who have undergone extreme stress and remained in relatively good health. Despite risk factors, he concluded that these people had a number of generalized resistance resources, including social support which contributed to a sense of coherence. It was described as:

A global orientation that expresses the extent to which one has a pervasive, enduring though dynamic feeling of confidence that 1) the stimuli deriving from one's internal and external environments in the course of living are structured, predictable, and explicable; 2) the resources are available to meet the demands posed by these stimuli; and 3) these demands are challenges, worthy of investment and engagement. (Antonovsky, 1987, p.19)

The AIDS Risk Reduction Model (ARRM)

The ARRM, developed by Catania et al. (1990), was designed to explain and predict the behavior change efforts of people who may sexually transmit HIV/AIDS. It consisted of three stages that integrated the Health Belief Model, self-efficacy and one's interpersonal process. The outcomes of the stages were to:

1. *Recognize and label one's behavior as high risk.*
   Behavioral technological interventions to achieve Stage 1 are developed for the following elements of client progress.

   • People acquire knowledge of sexual activities associated with HIV.

   • People develop the belief that they are personally susceptible to contract HIV.

   • People believe that AIDS is an undesirable condition to have.

   • People learn about social norms and how to rethink.

2. *Make a commitment to reduce high-risk sexual contacts and to increase low-risk activities.*
   Behavioral technological interventions to achieve Stage 2 include:

   • Learn the costs and benefits of contracting AIDS and also engaging in low-risk activities.

   • Acquire and learn to recognize the difference between "high" and "low" self-efficacy.

   • Understand and appreciate group norms and social support that influences cost-benefit analyses and self-efficacy expectations and outcomes related to sexual practices.

3. *Take action by seeking information, obtaining remedies and enacting solutions.*
   Behavioral technological interventions to achieve Stage 3 reach the following goals.

   • Learn how to get self-help and formal help when needed.

   • Learn how to remember prior experiences with its problems and solutions.

   • Define and operationalize "self-esteem."

   • Learn the resources that can help you.

- Learn to verbally communicate to your sex partner.

- Understand and respect your sexual partner's beliefs and behaviors.

The last idea to consider when implementing a risk reduction program is the nature of systems. A system is a phenomenon that achieves totality and integration through an organizational process. Therefore, any event that occurs in the context of a total organism is considered. Normality is viewed as "unity," "consistency" and "organization." Abnormality is inferred as "fragmentation" and "disorganization." Systems develop through a sequence of events. It begins with relative equilibrium. When information can not be assimilated, accommodation throws the system into disequilibrium until a resolution is achieved and it goes back into an improved, qualitative state of differentiation and equilibrium.

Parallel processes occur with a client and a professional counselor when risk reduction begins. Both systems intersect, exchange information and energy, until a new state of equilibrium is achieved. If a counselor can keep this in mind when implementing risk reduction; then effective behavioral change technology is invented and tailored specifically for the client(s) at hand. One model, by Quirk and Wapner delineates this process that may be applied to any risk reduction problems.

The Organismic-Development Systems Perspective

Quirk and Wapner (1991) have been developing a health education model based upon autopoesis. Their organismic-developmental systems perspective describes how the person learns about himself and the skills necessary to deal with perceived problems, as a matter of fostering transactions of persons in their environments that achieve optimal functioning of the person-environment system. These transactions of the person-environment systems are teleological, such that goals are achieved by a variety of means as the system moves towards advanced differentiation and a hierarchical integrated person-environment stated that positions cognition as the critical factor to maintain optimum health. Therefore, optimum development involves the capacity to exercise freely implemented, flexible transactions required by intentions, the demands of the situation and skills acquisition.

The goal is to foster transactions of persons in environments that achieve optimal functioning of person-in-environment systems. This means that the unit of analysis is the mutually defining interaction and unity of environment and behavior. They are linked by transactions and synthesized through the functions of the person which are biological, psychological and sociocultural.

Disruption of the system occurs through perceived stress. When the system tries to reestablish a new, dynamic equilibrium in order to accomplish an intended goal, it can be facilitated or hindered by person-environment transactions.

Behavioral interventions towards risk reduction encompass all the person-environment transactions of experience and action. The modes of experience consist of knowing (cognition), feeling (affection) and valuing (valuation). Role induction may allow the client to understand that maladaptive person-environment transactions need assistance.

Risk reduction assistance fosters optimum person-environment transactions through assessment and treatment (or education). The following outlines a plan for assessment:

- Elicit specific plans about individual goals, which may be meaningful and motivating.

- Assess the modes of experience through discourse to help the person identify feelings, values and their appropriateness—and then define goals based upon these results.

- Incorporate the person's values, goals and methods into a concrete plan of action that identifies the person's barriers and resources.

Developmentally, the person-environment system achieves higher degrees of function and integration when one achieves a sense of self-mastery or competency. This competency is the achievement of self-regulation or agency discussed by Bandura, which allows the person to utilize flexible transactions. Consequently, it encourages one's ability to shift modes of experience required by goals, the demands of the situation and the actions that are available for the individual. When this new equilibrium is achieved, the person has reached a higher level of differentiation—a qualitative state of efficacy that can not go backwards—it can only change for the better, depending upon one's goals and intentions for the encounter with perceived risk.

Therefore, risk reduction education or treatment considers the following:

• The counselor and client should identify the developmental status of the person-environment system that may help the person achieve the goal of fostering optimal transactions.

• Short-term goals are subordinated to hierarchical long-term goals which enhances decision making and guides action.

• Compliance to treatment via accepting the notion of developing person-environment states may also benefit this part of the psychoeducational plan.

The overall goal promotes optimal functioning instead of teaching a client how to elicit or emit prescribed behavioral outcomes. A person may be very well able to demonstrate a positive outcome but he continues to function ineffectively through the person-environment system. Awareness or cognition is the important mediator needed to promote self-organization. "Knowing" and "doing" are two different things. However, when experience and action function as a unit, it influences hierarchical relationships between long and short-term goals and actions related to optimum functioning.

Conclusion

Human services, and its programs, are in a state of flux for 21st century delivery. There is a complexity and richness in the human experience of change, especially for risk reduction programs and the individuals associated with their planning, implementation and accountability. Many therapeutic approaches have occupied the center stage for change; but there are still gaps between science, practice and outcome. Therefore, some type of nonlinear, dynamic approach may be needed by the professional counselor in order to look at problems and see subtle dynamics, that appear to be chaotic. It may be that there is an implicit underlying order to the formation and implementation of risk reduction programming. This underlying order was brought forth in this article to stimulate a counselor's thinking and an agency's application of risk reduction programs.

References

Ajzen, I. (1985). From intentions to actions: A theory of planned action. In J. Kuhl and J. Beckman (Eds.). *Action control: From cognition to behavior.* NY: Springer.

Antonovsky, A. (1987). *Unraveling the mystery of health: How people manage stress and stay healthy.* San Francisco: Josey-Bass.

Bandura, A. (1997). *Self-efficacy: The exercise of control.* NY: Freeman.

Bandura, A. (1986). *Social foundations of thought and action: A social cognitive theory.* Englewood Cliffs, NJ: Prentice-Hall.

Bandura, A. (1977). *Social learning theory.* Englewood Cliffs, NJ: Prentice-Hall.

Becker, M.H. (1984). *The health belief model and personal health behavior.* Thorofare, NJ: Slack.

Bensley, L.S., and Wu, R. (1991). The role of psychological reactance in drinking following alcohol prevention messages. *Journal of Applied Social Psychology, 21,* 1111–1124.

Brannon, L., and Feist, J. (1997). *Health psychology: An introduction to behavior and health* (3rd ed.). Pacific Grove, CA: Brooks/Cole.

Brehm, S.S., and Brehm, J.W. (1981). *Psychological reactance: A theory of freedom and control.* NY: Academic Press.

Brehm, J.W. (1966). *A theory of psychological reactance.* NY: Academic Press.

Catania, J.A., Coates, T.J., and Kegeles, S. (1994). A test of the AIDS risk reduction model: Psychosocial correlates of condom use in the AMEN cohort survey. *Health Psychology, 13*(6), 548–555.

Cox, W.M. (1990). *Why people drink: Parameters of alcohol as a reinforcer.* NY: Garden Press.

Curran, J.P., and Monti, P.M. (Eds.). (1982). *Social skills training: A practical handbook for assessment and treatment.* NY: Guilford.

Engel, G.L. (1980). The clinical applications of the biopsychological model. *American Journal of Psychiatry, 137,* 535–544.

Finnigan, F. (1995). The cognitive structure underlying heroin-injecting behavior. *Journal of Drug Education, 25*(3), 281–287.

Fishbein, M., Middlestadt, S.E., and Hitchcock, P.J. (1994). Using information to change sexually transmitted disease-related behaviors. In R.J. DiClemente and J.L. Peterson (Eds.). *Preventing AIDS: Theories and methods of behavioral interventions* (pp. 61–78). NY: Plenum Press.

Gatch, C.L., and Kindzier-ski, D. (1990). Predicting exercise intentions: The theory of planned behavior. *Research Quarterly for Exercise and Sport, 61,* 100–102.

Hillhouse, J.J., Satir, W:W.III, and Adler, C.M. (1996). Predictions of sunbathing and sunscreen use in college undergraduates. *Journal of Behavioral Medicine, 19,* 543–562.

Jaros, G., and Baker, B. (1998). The development of healthcare technology through design and emergence. *Systems Research and Behavioral Science, 15,* 259–270.

Justice, B. (1988). *Who gets sick: How beliefs, moods and thoughts affect your health.* Los Angeles: Jeremy P. Tarcher.

Kirscht, J.P., and Joseph, S.E. (1989). The health belief model: Some implications for behavior change with reference to homosexual males. In V. Mays, G. Albee, and S. Schneider (Eds.). *Primary prevention of AIDS: Psychological approaches.* London: Sage.

Kobasa, S.C. (1982). The hardy personality: Towards a social psychology of stress and health. In G.S. Sanders and J. Suls (Eds.), *Social psychology of health and illness* (pp. 3–32). Hillsdale, NJ: Erlbaum.

Lazarus, R.S., and Folkman, S. (1984). *Stress, appraisal and coping.* NY: Springer.

Leone, B. (1989). *Chemical dependency: Opposing viewpoints.* San Diego, CA: Greenhaven.

Madden, T.J., Ellen, P.S., and Ajzen, I. (1992). A comparison of a theory of reasoned action. *Personality and Social Psychological Bulletin, 18,* 3–9.

Mahoney, M.J. (1983). Cognition, consciousness, and the process of personal change. In R.D. Craig and R.J. McMahon (Eds.), *Advances in clinical behavior therapy* (pp. 27–47). NY: Brunner/Inazel.

Maturana, H.R., and Varela, F.J. (1992). *The tree of knowledge: Biological roots of human understanding* (2nd ed.). Boston, MA: Shambala Publications.

Misra, R.K. (1980). Achievement, anxiety, and addiction. In D.J. Lettieri, M. Sayers, and H. W. Pearsons (Eds.), *Theories on drug abuse: Selected contemporary perspectives.* DHHS Publication No. ADMS4-967 (pp. 29–34). Washington, DC: U.S. Government Printing Office.

National Institute on Drug Abuse (NIDA). (1988). *Data from the drug abuse warning network: Series 1, vol. 7* (DHHS Publication No. ADM88-1584), Washington, DC: U.S. Government Printing Office.

Peele, S. (1988). *Visions of addiction: Major contemporary perspectives on addiction and alcoholism.* Lexington, MA: D.C. Health.

Prochaska, J.O., DiClemente, C.D., and Norcross, J.C. (1992). In search of how people change: Applications to addictive behaviors. *American Psychologist, 47*(1), 1102–1114.

Quirk, M., and Wapner, S. (1991). Notes on an organismic-developmental, systems perspective for health education. *Health Education Research: Theory and Practices, 6*(2), 203–210.

Rush, A.J., and Watkins, J.T. (1981). Cognitive therapy with psychologically naïve depressed outpatients. In G. Emery, S.D. Hollen and R.C. Bedrosian (Eds.), *New directions in cognitive therapy: A casebook* (pp. 5–28). NY: Guilford Press.

Sarafino, E.D. (1997). *Health psychology: Biopsychosocial interactions* (2nd ed.). NY: Wiley & Sons.

Simon, S.B., Howe, L.W., and Kirscheubaum, H. (1972). *Values clarification: A handbook of practical strategies for teachers and students.* NY: Hart Publishing Company.

Taylor, S.E. (1995). *Health psychology* (3rd ed.). NY: McGraw-Hill.

Tucker, J.A. (1999). From zero tolerance to harm reduction. *National Forum, 79*(4), 19–23.

Vaughn, F. (1985). *The inward arc.* Boston, MA: Shambala Publications.

Zubin, J., and Spring, B. (1977). Vulnerability: A new view of schizophrenia. *Journal of Abnormal Psychology, 86,* 103–126.

Advances in Medical Psychotherapy and Psychodiagnosis
2002–2003, Volume 11, pp. 35–44

An Examination of the Neuropsychological Sequelae Associated with End-Stage Pulmonary Disease Secondary to Alpha-1-Antitrypsin Deficiency

Angela L. Jefferson, M.A.
Loyola College, Baltimore, Maryland

W. David Crews, Jr., Ph.D., Donna K. Broshek, Ph.D.,
Jeffrey T. Barth, Ph.D., and Mark K. Robbins, M.D.
University of Virginia School of Medicine, Charlottesville, Virginia

Abstract

There has been a relative absence of studies examining the neuropsychological sequelae associated with end-stage pulmonary disease secondary to alpha-1-antitrypsin deficiency. In the present study, neuropsychological profiles are presented for four such patients who were evaluated as potential candidates for lung transplantation. All patients exhibited at least mild neurocognitive impairment on one measure (e.g., memory) and all three patients who completed the Minnesota Multiphasic Personality Inventory-2 displayed elevated clinical profiles that were indicative of a diversity of symptomatology ranging from somatic complaints, including lethargy and fatigue, to depression. These neuropsychological findings are discussed in light of the patients' end-stage pulmonary disease secondary to alpha-1-antitrypsin deficiency as well as their educational backgrounds and measured intellectual abilities. Implications for clinical practice and future research are also provided.

An Examination of the Neuropsychological Sequelae Associated with End-Stage Pulmonary Disease Secondary to Alpha-1-Antitrypsin Deficiency

Alpha-1-antitrypsin deficiency is an inherited metabolic error that occurs primarily in Caucasians of Western European descent (Crystal, 1990; Filipponi et al., 1994). Alpha-1-antitrypsin (AAT) has been classified as a primary protease inhibitor in human plasma (Celli, 1998; Weinberger, 1998). It is hypothesized to be responsible for neutralizing the enzyme elastase, which is capable of digesting elastin, a complex structural protein found in the alveoli walls in the lungs (Celli, 1998; Dettenmeier,

---

Address correspondence to: Jeffrey T. Barth, Ph.D., Division of Neuropsychology, Box 203, University of Virginia Health Sciences Center, Charlottesville, Virginia 22908

1992; Weinberger, 1998). If the relationship, or balance, between AAT and elastase is disturbed, damage to elastin and the alveoli walls of the lung may result (Weinberger, 1998). Alpha-1-antitrypsin deficiency is hypothesized to be responsible for an alteration in this balance leading to degradation of elastin in the lung and ultimately resulting in obstructive, pulmonary disease (Celli, 1998; Filipponi et al., 1994; Murray & Nadel, 1994; Weinberger, 1998).

Although individuals with alpha-1-antitrypsin deficiency are susceptible to the development of premature emphysema (Perlmutter & Pierce, 1989), the deficiency has not been shown to be a significant factor in the majority of patients suffering from chronic obstructive pulmonary disease (Sachs, Supinski, & Muir, 1983). In fact, alpha-1-antitrypsin deficiency reportedly only accounts for less than two percent of chronic obstructive pulmonary disease/emphysema cases (Celli, 1998; Dettenmeier, 1992).

The natural history of alpha-1-antitrypsin deficiency is highly inconsistent and evidence exists suggesting environmental or additional genetic factors may influence the development of emphysema in these patients (Zinn, 1994). Environmental factors include respiratory irritants and cigarette smoking while potential contributing genetic factors include alterations in the structure of the alveolar wall and elastolytic activity in circulating leukocytes.

There have been few studies in the scientific literature which have investigated the neuropsychological correlates of alpha-1-antitrypsin deficiency. One related study compared the intellectual functioning of 43 children with end-stage liver disease (*M* age = 10.93 years; ten of whom were positive for alpha-1-antitrypsin deficiency) to a control group consisting of patients with cystic fibrosis (*M* age = 9.31 years) and existing normative data (Stewart, Campbell, McCallon, Waller, & Andrews, 1992). Results indicated that those pediatric patients with alpha-1-antitrypsin deficiency exhibited significant deficits in Wechsler Intelligence Scale for Children-Revised (WISC-R) Verbal IQ and the acquired knowledge factor as compared to controls and normative data. It should be noted, however, that since these patients with alpha-1-antitrypsin deficiency were suffering from significant liver disease, these findings may not be generalizable to patients suffering from end-stage pulmonary disease.

Thus, appears to be a relative absence of studies in the existing literature which have specifically examined the neuropsychological sequelae associated with end-stage pulmonary disease secondary to alpha-1-antitrypsin deficiency. Therefore, the purpose of this study was to examine the neuropsychological profiles of four such patients who were being evaluated as potential lung transplant candidates.

Method

Patients

The patients in this study were four individuals with end-stage alpha-1-antitrypsin deficiency who were referred for neuropsychological evaluation as part of the lung transplant screening protocol at a large tertiary care medical center.

This sample consisted of two males and two females who ranged in age from 46 to 63 years. The education level of the sample ranged from 11 years plus General Equivalency Diploma to 20 years. Demographic data for each patient is provided in Table 1.

Patient A was diagnosed with alpha-1-antitrypsin deficiency five years prior to testing and complained of difficulty breathing upon physical exertion. Patient A's history indicated that he smoked cigarettes for 20 years prior to his diagnosis.

Patient B's diagnosis was made six years prior to testing and since that time he has experienced a series of pulmonary problems including pneumonia and a collapsed lung. Patient B's history was unremarkable for cigarette smoking.

Patient C was diagnosed with alpha-1-antitrypsin deficiency five years prior to testing with deteriorating pulmonary health for one year prior to testing. Patient C's history is unremarkable for cigarette smoking.

Table 1
Demographic Characteristics and Neuropsychological Test Data

Patient	A	B	C	D
Gender (M/F)	M	M	F	F
Age	46	63	46	50
Education	17	20	12	11 + GED
WAIS-R (Age Corrected)				
Vocabulary	13	15	—	07
Block Design	14	19	07	11
Similarities	09	09	07	08
Digit Span	—	—	04*	—
Trail Making Test				
Part A (time in seconds, errors)	21, 0	62*, 0	27, 0	30, 0
Part B (time in seconds, errors)	45, 0	76, 0	105*, 3	120, 2*
Wisconsin Card Sorting Test				
Correct	00	07	—	36
Errors	06	19	—	47
Perseveration Responses	02	00	—	00
Nonperseverative Errors	04	02	—	12
Perseverative Errors	00	17	—	35*
Categories	06	06	—	04*
WMS-R				
Logical Memory I	34	26	14*	21
Logical Memory II	29	26	12*	19
Logical Memory % Retention	85%	100%	86%	90%
Visual Reproduction I	39	41	21*	35
Visual Reproduction II	40	40	14*	17*
Visual Reproduction % Retention	100%	97%	66%	48%
Selective Reminding Test				
Recall	111*	115	—	120
Long-Term Retrieval	95*	110	—	117
Short-Term Recall	16	05	—	08
Long-Term Storage	102*	127	—	121
Consistent LTR	67*	68	—	74
Random LTR	27	41	—	38
Total Intrusions	00	00	—	00
Total Trials	12	12	—	12
Cued Recall	10/11	07/11*	—	08/11*
Delayed Recall	11/12	09/12	—	12/12
Delayed Recognition	12/12	12/12	—	12/12

Table 1 (continued)				
Patient	*A*	*B*	*C*	*D*
Rey Auditory Verbal Learning Test				
T1-T5	—	—	49	—
B	—	—	01*	—
A6	—	—	10	—

* = Impaired.

Patient D's diagnosis was made six years prior to testing and she has a history of treatment for bronchitis. She complained of difficulty breathing upon physical exertion and reported awakening at least once nightly secondary to shortness of breath. Patient D has a history of cigarette smoking but quit approximately two and one half years prior to testing.

Despite the apparent variations in the pulmonary functioning across these four patients, each patient met criteria for end-stage lung disease, which suggests comparable alpha-1-antitrypsin disease status. The physiological/medical criteria that operationally defined a patient as suffering from "end-stage" pulmonary disease and in need of a lung transplant included: a forced expiratory volume (FEV) < 25% of expected volume; a paO_2 < 60 mm Hg on room air; nonreversible and progressive disease despite medical therapies; and a 50% chance of dying within two to three years.

Procedures

To evaluate the cognitive and behavioral functioning of these patients, various neuropsychological tests were administered. All testing was conducted by an experienced neuropsychological test technician under the supervision of a licensed clinical neuropsychologist. The standardized administration and scoring procedures for each test were strictly followed. After brief rapport-building sessions and clinical interviews, the following battery was administered: portions of the Wechsler Adult Intelligence Scale-Revised (WAIS-R; Wechsler, 1981); Trail Making Test (TMT; Parts A & B; Reitan, 1979; Reitan & Wolfson, 1993); Wisconsin Card Sorting Test (WCST; Heaton, Chelune, Talley, Kay, & Curtiss, 1993); portions of the Wechsler Memory Scale-Revised (WMS-R; Wechsler, 1987); the Selective Reminding Test (Buschke & Fuld, 1974) or the Rey Auditory Verbal Learning Test (RAVLT; Rey, 1964); and the Minnesota Multiphasic Personality Inventory-2 (MMPI-2; Hathaway & McKinley, 1989).

To interpret each individual's neuropsychological test performances, scores were compared to published normative data for each test, while taking into consideration such demographic variables as gender, age, and educational level. Normative data and/or interpretations were obtained from the following sources: Graham (2000); Heaton et al., (1993); Heaton, Grant, & Matthews (1991); Spreen & Strauss (1998); and Wechsler (1981, 1987).

Results

The neurocognitive test results for each patient are provided in Table 1. On select subtests of the WAIS-R, the patients exhibited performances ranging from mentally deficient to the very superior range. Specifically, patient A exhibited age-corrected scaled scores on the Vocabulary, Block Design, and Similarities subtests which fell within the high average, superior, and average ranges respectively, while patient B's scores on these subtests fell within the superior, very superior, and average ranges respectively. Patient C exhibited age-corrected scaled scores on the Block Design, Similarities, and Digit Span subtests which fell within the low average, low average, and mentally deficient ranges respectively, while patient D's performances on the Vocabulary, Block Design, and Similarities subtests fell within the low average, average, and average ranges respectively.

Regarding neurocognitive dysfunction, patient A displayed impairment of his total recall on the Selective Reminding Test, as well as deficits in long-term retrieval, long-term storage, and consistent long-term retrieval strategies. For patient B, deficits were noted in his task completion time on the Trail Making Test, Part A, and his cued recall on the Selective Reminding Test. All other neurocognitive test results were within normal limits for both patients A and B.

Patient C exhibited impairment of her complex cognitive processing speed and flexibility on the Trail Making Test, Part B, as well as deficits in immediate and delayed (30 minutes) free recall of contextual verbal and nonverbal/figural material on the WMS-R-Logical Memory (I and II) and Visual Reproduction (I and II) subtests. A deficient performance was also noted on her recall of list B on the Rey Auditory Verbal Learning Test.

Similarly, Patient D exhibited a notable number of sequencing errors on the Trail Making Test, Part B, as well as perseverative errors on the Wisconsin Card Sorting Test. She also failed to achieve the expected number of categories on the WCST. Additional impairments were exhibited in her delayed (30 minutes) free recall of nonverbal/figural material on the WMS-R Visual Reproduction II subtest and her cued recall on the Selective Reminding Test. All other neurocognitive results were within normal limits for both patients C and D.

The results of the Minnesota Multiphasic Personality Inventory-2 for each patient are provided in Table 2. The three patients who completed this inventory generally displayed valid profiles, although patient A exhibited an elevated K scale, suggestive of some degree of defensiveness.

Both male patients displayed remarkably similar MMPI-2 clinical profiles. Specifically, clinical elevations (T-scores > 65) were noted on Scales 1 (Hypochondriasis) and 3 (Conversion Hysteria). For the one female patient (i.e., Patient D) who completed the MMPI-2, clinical elevations (T-scores > 65) were found on Scales 2 (Depression), 3 (Conversion Hysteria), 7 (Psychasthenia), and 8 (Schizophrenia), with the highest elevations on Scales 2 and 7.

Discussion

This article has presented the neuropsychological profiles of four patients suffering from end-stage pulmonary disease secondary to alpha-1-antitrypsin deficiency. A diversity of neuropsychological dysfunctions were noted in these patients ranging from impairment on tests purported to be sensitive to executive control functioning to verbal and nonverbal/figural memory deficits. Although no characteristic pattern of neurocognitive impairment was discernible across patients, all four individuals exhibited at least mild neuropsychological dysfunction on one measure. It should be noted, however, that the two males tended to exhibit fewer deficits across measures as compared to the two females which may be related to the level of pre-morbid functioning in the two male patients.

It is likely that the neurocognitive functioning of all patients in this study was negatively impacted by their progressive loss of pulmonary functioning (see Lezak, 1995). The array of deficits exhibited by these four patients with end-stage alpha-1-antitrypsin deficiency also tend to support the findings of Prigatano, Parsons, Wright, Levin, & Hawryluk (1983) who found modest impairments of abstract reasoning, memory, and speed of performance in mildly hypoxemic patients with chronic obstructive pulmonary disease.

Several other factors may have also contributed to the differential levels of impairment found among the patients in the current study. At first glance, it would appear that gender differences may have played a pivotal role in these findings. However, based on the small inter-gender differences in neuropsychological test performances which are typically found between males and females (see

Patient	A	B	C	D
Table 2				
Minnesota Multiphasic Personality Inventory-2				
L (Lie)	56	53	—	57
F (Infrequencey)	44	51	—	61
K (Correction)	66*	58	—	43
1 (Hypochondriasis)	75*	70*	—	51
2 (Depression)	52	62	—	76*
3 (Conversion Hysteria)	71*	66*	—	69*
4 (Psychopathic Deviate)	46	48	—	62
5 (Masculinity-Femininity)	34	48	—	60
6 (Paranoia)	49	39	—	59
7 (Psychasthenia)	49	49	—	76*
8 (Schizophrenia)	49	47	—	70*
9 (Hypomania)	56	43	—	51
0 (Social Introversion)	31	55	—	71

* = Impaired.

Lezak, 1995), and the fact that this study utilized normative data which considered gender when possible, it does not seem likely that gender largely accounted for the discrepancies observed between the male and female patients.

Alternatively, the differential findings of the present study were more likely related to patients' premorbid levels of functioning. Specifically, the two male patients reported significantly higher levels of formal education as compared to the females. In fact, the males had completed between five and nine additional years of formal education than the females. Furthermore, the males, versus females, also exhibited notably higher age-corrected scaled scores on select subtests of the WAIS-R that are highly correlated with Verbal and Performance intellectual functioning (Wechsler, 1981). Thus, based on the evidence that higher levels of premorbid functioning (e.g., higher levels of education and measured intelligence) may help to compensate for neuropsychological deficits resulting from injury or disease (see Lezak, 1995), the males' greater levels of formal education and measured intellectual abilities may have helped to offset, or slow the rate of detectable decline, of some of the neurocognitive impairments that may have otherwise been observed in these males (and that were seen in the females) with end-stage lung disease.

The MMPI-2 clinical profiles for patients A and B were remarkably similar as they both exhibited significant elevations (T-scores > 65) on Scales 1 (Hypochondriasis) and 3 (Conversion Hysteria). These profiles indicate that they acknowledged a diversity of somatic complaints which may have worsened during times of stress (Graham, 2000). They may have also been functioning at a reduced level of efficiency and reported feeling tired and lethargic.

Patient D exhibited significant elevations (T-scores > 65) on Scales 2 (Depression), 3 (Conversion Hysteria), 7 (Psychasthenia), and 8 (Schizophrenia), with the highest elevations on Scales 2 and 7. This profile suggested that she may have felt anxious, tense, and depressed, and that she may have had a tendency to worry excessively (Graham, 2000). This is not surprising given her respiratory difficulties. Similar to patients A and B, patient D acknowledged somatic symptoms of a generally vague nature and reported feeling tired and fatigued. Depressive symptomatology was also affirmed and she may have been somewhat pessimistic about her future, which is not unexpected given the status of her pulmonary illness. Overall, the MMPI-2 profiles of these three patients were not surprising in light of their advanced, end-stage lung disease. It should be noted that the neurocognitive deficits of these patients may have been exacerbated by their reported levels of distress as reflected by their elevated MMPI-2 profiles.

The findings presented in this paper appear to have implications for clinical practice. Previous research suggests memory is one of the cognitive components that is most strongly associated with medication compliance and medication planning accuracy (Isaac, Tamblyn, & McGill-Calgary Drug Research Team, 1993). Based on the diversity of neurocognitive and neuropsychological dysfunction found in these patients with alpha-1-antitryspin deficiency, it appears clinically important to complete comprehensive neuropsychological assessments, not only for patients with alpha-1-antitrypsin deficiency, but on all patients with end-stage disease who are potential lung transplant candidates. Since those patients who ultimately undergo lung transplantation must be able to comply with complicated treatment and/or medication regimens, comprehensive neuropsychological evaluations may be beneficial in identifying individual neurocognitive strengths and weaknesses. In turn, appropriate, remedial therapies and strategies can then be formulated for these patients to compensate for their identified difficulties and to increase their compliance with medical treatments. For instance, these patients may benefit from education regarding memory enhancement techniques. It may also be helpful to place their medication information in a verbal or visual context (depending on the patient's most efficient learning strategy) so that it is likely to be retained. Physicians may also want to provide concrete and simplified medical treatment directions to these patients to enhance their understanding.

Identification and treatment of patients who are experiencing psychological difficulties is also important to improve their levels of functioning and increase their emotional well-being and mental health. It is important to note that these patients may present issues in the context of therapy that are related to their end-stage disease and chronic medical illness, but they may also present issues related to the genetic component of their illness. Specifically, these patients may have therapeutic issues surrounding the inherited nature of their illness as well as the possibility of passing it on to their own children.

It should be noted that since alpha-1-antitrypsin deficiency is a relatively uncommon cause of chronic obstructive pulmonary disease, only a very limited number of patients diagnosed with this pulmonary disease were seen during any given year. Thus, data in this study was collected over a period of several years. This fact, along with the retrospective nature of this research, precluded the inclusion of a matched control group. Hence, comprehensive normative data from several sources were utilized to interpret the neuropsychological test performances of this group of patients with alpha-1-antitrypsin deficiency. Future, large scale, prospective studies are required which compare patients with end-stage alpha-1-antitrypsin deficiency to matched control groups across a comprehensive battery of neuropsychological tests and measures. Longitudinal research of patients with alpha-1-antitrypsin deficiency is also needed to examine potential changes in their neuropsychological functioning over time, as their health status deteriorates, as well as following successful lung transplantation.

Given the fact that alpha-1-antitrypsin deficiency is an inherited metabolic error, compromised liver function may produce a potentially toxic environment within the body and contribute to changes in cognitive and neurobehavioral status. Thus, future studies should focus on comparing patients with end-stage liver disease secondary to alpha-1-antitrypsin disease, patients with end-stage lung disease secondary to alpha-1-antitrypsin disease, and normal controls in an effort to determine the exact nature of cognitive-related declines in such patients.

References

Buschke, H., & Fuld, P. A. (1974). Evaluating storage, retention, and retrieval in disordered memory and learning. *Neurology, 11,* 1019–1025.

Celli, B. R. (1998). Clinical aspects of chronic obstructive pulmonary disease. In G. L. Baum, B. R. Celli, J. D. Crapo, & J. B. Karlinsky (Eds.), *Textbook of Pulmonary Diseases* (6th ed., Vol. 2). Philadelphia: Lippincott-Raven.

Crystal, R. G. (1990). Alpha-1-antitrypsin deficiency, emphysema, and liver disease. Genetic basis and strategies for therapy. *Journal of Clinical Investigation, 85,* 1343–1352.

Dettenmeier, P. A. (1992). *Pulmonary Nursing Care.* St. Louis: Mosby.

Filipponi, F., Soubrane, O., Labrousse, F., Devictor, D., Bernard, O., Valayer, J., & Houssin, D. (1994). Liver transplantation for end-stage liver disease associated with alpha-1-antitrypsin deficiency in children: Pretransplant natural history, timing and results of transplantation. *Journal of Hepatology, 20,* 72–78.

Graham, J. R. (2000). *MMPI-2; Assessing personality and psychopathology* (3rd ed.). New York: Oxford University Press.

Hathaway, S. R., & McKinley, J. C. (1989). *Minnesota Multiphasic Personality Inventory-2.* Minneapolis, MN: University of Minnesota Press.

Heaton, R. K., Chelune, G. J., Talley, J. L., Kay, G. G., & Curtiss, G. (1993). *Wisconsin Card Sorting Test Manual: Revised and Expanded.* Odessa, FL: Psychological Assessment Resources, Inc.

Heaton, R. K., Grant, I., & Matthews, C. G. (1991). *Comprehensive Norms for an Expanded Halstead-Reitan Battery.* Odessa, FL: Psychological Assessment Resources, Inc.

Isaac, L. M., Tamblyn, R. M., & McGill-Calgary Drug Research Team. (1993). Compliance and cognitive function: A methodological approach to measuring unintentional errors in medication compliance in the elderly. *Gerontologist, 33*(6), 772–781.

Lezak, M. D. (1995). *Neuropsychological assessment* (3rd ed.) New York: Oxford University Press.

Murray, J. F., & Nadel, J. A. (Eds.). (1994). *Textbook of respiratory medicine* (2nd ed., Vols. 1–2). Philadelphia: W. B. Saunders Company.

Perlmutter, D. H., & J. A., Pierce. (1989). The alpha-1-antitrypsin gene and emphysema. *American Journal of Physiology, 258,* L147-L162.

Prigatano, G. P., Parsons, O., Wright, E., Levin, D. C., & Hawryluk, G. (1983). Neuropsychological test performance in mildly hypoxemic COPD patients. *Journal of Consulting and Clinical Psychology, 51,* 108–116.

Reitan, R. M. (1979). *Manual of Administration of Neuropsychological Test Batteries for Adults and Children.* Tucson, AZ: Reitan Neuropsychological Laboratories.

Reitan, R. M., & Wolfson, D. (1993). *Halstead-Reitan Neuropsychological Test Battery: Theory and Clinical Interpretation* (2nd ed.) Tucson, AZ: Neuropsychology Press.

Rey, A. (1964). *L'examen clinique en psychologie.* Paris: Presses Universitaires de France.

Sachs, D., Supinski, G., & Muir, W. A. (1983). Genetic diseases of the pulmonary parenchyma. *Textbook of Pulmonary Diseases* (3rd ed.). Boston: Little, Brown, & Company.

Spreen, O., & Strauss, E. (1998). *A Compendium of Neuropsychological Tests* (2nd ed.). New York: Oxford University Press.

Stewart, S. M., Campbell, R. A., McCallon, D., Waller, D. A., & Andrews, W. S. (1992). Cognitive patterns in school-age children with end-stage liver disease. *Developmental and Behavioral Pediatrics, 13*(5), 331–338.

Wechsler, D. (1981). *WAIS-R manual.* New York: The Psychological Corporation.

Wechsler, D. (1987). *WMS-R manual: Wechsler Memory Scale Revised.* San Antonio, TX: The Psychological Corporation.

Weinberger, S. E. (Ed.). (1998). *Principles of Pulmonary Medicine* (3rd ed.). Philadelphia: W. B. Saunders Company.

Zinn, A. B. (1994). Genetic disease of the pulmonary parenchyma. In G. L. Baum & E. Wolinsky (Eds.), *Textbook of Pulmonary Diseases* (5th ed., Vol. 2). Boston: Little, Brown, & Company.

Advances in Medical Psychotherapy and Psychodiagnosis
2002–2003, Volume 11, pp. 45–58

Fibromyalgia and Psychobiological Disregulation: A Theoretical Formulation[1]

Micah R. Sadigh, Ph.D.
Good Shepherd Rehabilitation Hospital
and
Cedar Crest College

Abstract

The main objective of this paper is to provide a theoretical framework for the conceptualization of fibromyalgia as a state of psychobiological disregulation. Although for the past two decades much emphasis has been placed upon exploring fibromyalgia from a musculoskeletal stand point, an examination of the current literature suggests that this is a system wide phenomenon. Such findings suggest the need for a more expanded formulation of this disorder. The psychobiological disregulation model may be highly useful in accomplishing such a task. There is now growing evidence from diverse fields such as developmental biology, psychosomatic medicine and self psychology that offer some explanation with regard to the development of disregulatory conditions.

The psychobiological disregulation theory allows the current clinical and empirical data to be more effectively synthesized and applied to the evaluation and the treatment of disorders, such as fibromyalgia. In addition to clinical and empirical research, special emphasis needs to be placed upon detailed developmental studies that may be helpful in exploring the pathogenesis of fibromyalgia. The paper also explores therapeutic interventions based on the disregulation model.

Fibromyalgia Pain Syndrome (FMS) is currently conceptualized as a complex, painful and chronic musculoskeletal disorder whose etiology remains elusive (Crofford, 1998; Wolfe, 1995). While during the past two decades much attention has been paid to the evaluation and the treatment of this enigmatic condition, there is ample evidence that this is not a disease of the 80's or the 90's but a condition that has been documented in the annals of medicine for well over a hundred years (Simons, 1975). While musculoskeletal pain, both widespread and diffuse, is an integral, and perhaps the most obvious component of FMS, it is also accompanied by a number of other specific symptoms such as fatigue, headaches, irritable bowel syndrome, and sensitivity to climate changes (Alacorn and Bradley,1998; Semble and Wise, 1988).

Lack of quality sleep appears to be another distinguishing characteristic of FMS. More specifically, there is evidence that suggests that these patients are deficient in delta sleep. In a classic study, Moldofsky and colleagues were able to induce increased muscle stiffness and aching in normal subjects by merely depriving them of delta-sleep (Moldofsky & Sacrisbrick, 1976). It has been proposed that a deficiency in

---

Address reprint requests to Micah R. Sadigh, Ph.D., Department of Psychology, Good Shepherd Rehabilitation Hospital. Allentown, PA 18103.

1. The term "disregulation" (note the spelling) was originally coined by Schwartz (1979).

restorative sleep may be at the heart of this condition. Hence, one of the major approaches for the treatment of FMS has been to restore sleep through the use of antidepressants and anxiolytic agents (Semble & Wise, 1988). A recent meta-analytic study suggested that the use of antidepressants was associated with significant improvements in sleep quality in FMS patient (Arnold, Keck, and Welge, 2000).

Depression is often a concomitant of chronic pain. This appears to be especially true with FMS (Arnold, Keck and Welge, 2000). Several studies have documented a higher prevalence of depression in patients suffering from fibromyalgia and rheumatoid arthritis than in control groups, with fibromyalgia patients being most depressed (Goldenberg, 1989). Additionally, perfectionistic, overly driven, demanding and ambitious tendencies characterize a large number of the FMS population (Rice,1986). Yunus and colleagues (1989) suggested that stress may play an important role in the varying manifestation of symptoms in patients with fibromyalgia and noted that these patients tended to have more stress-related symptoms such as headaches, GI disorders, etc., than other patients chronic pain patients. This is consistent with other formulations that exposure to chronic stressors may significantly contribute to the emergence of symptoms seen in FMS patients by altering neurohormonal functions (Yunus, 1994).

During the past decade, many formulations regarding the pathogenesis of FMS have been offered in the literature, but the etiology of this condition remains highly disputed, especially since there is a lack of specific objective laboratory findings that support the diagnosis of this condition. There remains much to be understood about the nature of FMS. While a ten year longitudinal study has suggested that the symptoms of FMS do not necessarily disappear in time, there is also some evidence that patients can learn to cope with this condition (Kennedy & Felson, 1996).

Although much emphasis has been placed upon viewing FMS as a musculoskeletal disorder, there is a growing number of studies which have suggested that it is far more complex and seemingly system wide. In addition to the above mentioned symptoms, several studies have noted the development of ocular and vestibular disturbances, neurological, cardiovascular, and genitourinary symptoms in patients with FMS (Rosenhall, Johansson & Orndhal, 1987; Gerster & Hadj-Dijilani, 1984; Simms & Goldenberg, 1988; Pellegrino, Van Fossen, Gordon, Ryan & Waylonis, 1989; Wallace, 1990). Recent formulations have implicated the role of neuroendocrinologic and neuroimmunologic disturbances in this syndrome (Goldstein, 1998; Moldofsky, 1995). Such developments and findings cannot be ignored and thus, a more expanded, encompassing formulation of the disorder is clearly in order. With the expansion of knowledge in the fields of psychoneuroimmunology and psychneuroendocrinology (Kiecolt-Glaser and Glaser, 1991; Lloyd, 1987; Nemeroff and Loosen, 1987) it is perhaps time to synthesize some such findings in generating theoretical models that can be used to further explore FMS from a system oriented vantage point.

Precursors, Disregulation and Disease

The plethora of symptoms experienced by fibromyalgia patients suggest a systemic phenomenon at work. Again, there is evidence of disturbance in most systems in a large number of fibromyalgia patients. This may suggest that this disorder is indeed caused by a system-wide state of disarray, or more accurately, a state of psychobiological disregulation.

Currently, in the field of psychosomatic medicine much attention is being paid to the growing contributions of an exciting model of illness and disease, namely the disregulation model. Based on von Bertalanffy's general system theory, the disregulation model suggests that ultimately, all functioning systems are self-regulating (von Bertalanffy, 1968; Schwartz, 1979). However, if there is a disruption in one of the subsystems, in time, this will result in a system-wide state of disorder and disregulation. For example, with the advent of psychoneuro-immunology, there is now ample evidence that the immune "subsystem" which was once viewed as an "island" unto itself is intimately related to and is affected by other subsystems, such as the neuroendocrine subsystem and vise versa (Lloyd,1987; Klimas et al., 1992). Thus, the contributions of all subsystems are significant in the maintenance of health or the pathogenesis of many illnesses.

Recently, findings from fields including developmental biology, psychosomatic medicine and self psychology have provided further support for the disregulation model. Researchers from diverse fields are now gaining new knowledge regarding the development of self-regulatory mechanisms in human and animal infants and how early childhood experiences may enhance such mechanisms or hinder their functioning at an optimal level (Hoefer, 1975). Normally biological self-regulation is thought of as a process present at birth. However, recent findings dispute this assertion and suggest the contrary. Consider the following often quoted remarks by Weiner (1982) as he reflects on the contributions of Hoefer (1978), who advanced our understanding of the development of self-regulatory mechanisms.

> The mother, acting as the external psychobiological regulator of the infant's behavior and physiology, is crucial for the maturation and development of her infant. At some point in the life of the infant, e.g., at the time of weaning, the mother is no longer essential to the infant's complete psychobiological function. Behavior and bodily function then gradually become self-regulating. Internal autonomic mechanisms presumably take over and regulate the heart rate. But what if they did not? (p. 511).

What if the self-regulatory mechanism did not have a chance to fully develop? What if the "weaning" (psychologically and physically) took place too quickly and the child did not have the opportunity to gain the necessary momentum to fully achieve self-regulation? Theoretically speaking, such a child is likely to develop vulnerability (diathesis) to psychobiological maladjustment which may potentially result in further disorder and disease. Is it possible to conceptualize the point of premature withdrawal of the external regulatory influences, a point of disruption in the healthy development of self-regulatory functions. And if so, can proper self-regulation be re-established through exposure to externally consistent, regulatory environmental cues? We shall return to this question in our consideration of treatments of disregulation.

The internal self-regulatory mechanisms are also prone to disturbance and disorder by internal as well as external factors. Prolonged exposure to stressful stimuli, for example, may precipitate a state of disorder in psychobiological functioning (Selye, 1984). Such a state is compensated for by accessing finite coping (adaptive) resources that allow the whole system to adapt to a lack of order. Such compensation can be maintained for a period of time. If corrective actions do not occur, subsystems gradually enter disorder and the entire system ultimately manifests symptoms or signals of disorientation, disorder and disease.

McEwen and Stellar (1993) emphasized the role of heredity and early childhood developmental factors in the acceleration of physiological breakdown as a result of protracted stress. The authors expounded on the concept of allostasis in order to explain how repeated stress can promote tissue damage and organ dysfunction in conditions such as asthma, diabetes, gastrointestinal disorders, cancer and autoimmune disorders. Sterling and Eyer (1988) defined allostatsis as an operating range within which steady physiological and neurohormonal adjustments are made in order to effectively respond to various sources of demand. However, once the various systems are forced to constantly function outside this range, an increase in tissue wear and tear is likely to ensue, which predispose the body to disease (McEwen and Stellar, 1993).

Another mechanism that can increase the likelihood of the manifestation of stress-related disorders is that of ineffective regulation of affect (Taylor, 1992). It has been postulated that a lack of capacity for acknowledging and expressing emotions, such as in alexithymics, can render individuals vulnerable to both interpersonal and intrapsychic sources of stress (Sifneos, Apfel-Savitz and Frankel, 1977). Improper regulation of affect, hence, is thought to result in a build up of tension and its eventual somatic discharge in terms of the manifestation of psychosomatic disorders (Sifneos, 1973). As it will be discussed later, developmental factors, especially as related to deficits in early object relations, appear to be major contributors to disorders of psychobiological disregulation.

Fibromyalgia as a State of Disregulation

While fibromyalgia is a relatively new term attempting to describe a very complex syndrome, it has been well documented that this condition has been recognized by many other names (e.g., neurasthenia, fibrositis, psychogenic rheumatism, etc.) in the annals of medicine for well over a hundred years. However, there remains much uncertainty regarding the pathogenesis FMS. As a result of the absence of such knowledge it is improbable that effective treatments can be formulated and executed. Currently, there is one point of consensus regarding this condition, one point that research rather unanimously supports: there is no known cure for fibromyalgia (Kennedy & Felson, 1996).

This paper proposes that the reason there are no known cures for FMS is perhaps because there has been an undue emphasis placed on the symptomology of the syndrome instead of gaining a fuller perspective regarding its dynamics. First, as it was pointed out previously, there needs to be a shift from conceptualizing this condition as primarily a musculoskeletal disorder. The musculoskeletal system is a massive subsystem of the human body and tends to receive more attention, especially in terms of symptom manifestation. However, the musculoskeletal is only one of many subsystems in the body and may reveal only partial knowledge regarding the complete patho-physiological nature of the FMS. It is, therefore, only prudent to consider not only the manifestations of the musculoskeletal symptoms but also other subsystems, without attempting to overemphasize a particular sub-system at the expense of others.

By conceptualizing FMS as a system-wide phenomenon, it is quite possible that we take a giant step toward more fully appreciating the clinical data and formulating more effective methods of pursuing the central issues that concern the emergence of the symptoms. Such an approach is likely to reveal that at the heart of this condition there resides a profound level of system wide state of psychobiological disregulation. This suggests the over-regulation of some subsystems while at the same time the under-regulation of other subsystems. Under-regulated systems are likely to be compensated for by the over-regulated systems, which work overtime in order to maintain a state of balance for the moment, regardless of later costs. Prolonged disregulation leads these compensatory systems to become depleted and system-wide chaos ensues. It is the re-establishment of regulatory mechanisms which will finally result in the achievement of a state of order and a disappearance of the symptoms of disorder.

Let us now further explore how system wide disregulation might take place in the first place, while considering some of the developmental concepts that have been presented thus far. Schwartz (1979), the originator of the disregulation model, suggested that at the heart of disregulation is a state of "disattention" from self-regulatory mechanisms. The "disattention" will in turn bring about neuropsychological "disconnection," which will ultimately result in loss of systemic self-regulation (Schwartz, 1989). This process will in time bring about a state of disorder and disease. The question to be asked at this point is what causes "disattention" to regulatory mechanisms in the first place? That is, if such mechanisms are optimally operative in the first place (as it was indicated before, it is possible that such regulatory mechanisms might not have had the chance to become fully activated due to certain developmental complications such as premature weaning).

It has been postulated that the emergence of disturbing feelings that are not properly symbolized, may result in the distraction (disattention) from such affective and/or visceral experiences through the increase in muscle tone as a form of a defense mechanism (Bernstein, 1978). For example, in discussing a possible etiology for the chronic fatigue syndrome, a condition very similar to the FMS, Taerk and Gnam (1994) suggested that due to a limited capacity for symbolization, chronic fatigue patients tended to express their emotional distress in physical symptoms. They postulated that a lack of affect regulation due to disturbances in object relations was a major contributor to the emergence of symptoms in patients with chronic fatigue.

According to Winnicott (1966), the distorted symbolization, or lack of symbolization, of emotionally charged experiences of childhood is at the root of many psychosomatic disorders. In other words, in order to disconnect one's self from the experience of painful or disturbing emotions, an increase in the activity of another subsystem (e.g., the musculoskeletal or the gastrointestinal subsystems) is observed. If this persists, there is likely to be a deterioration of the functioning of one subsystem at the expense of another.

Schwartz (1989) has argued that repression is a major defense mechanism that is involved in the process of "disattention". Individuals using repression as their main form of defense tend to deny uncomfortable and distressing experiences. To achieve this, they must disavow certain feelings and experiences in order to maintain control over the distressing situation. The price for such a coping strategy is rather high, especially if this strategy is used over time. For example, Mann (1996) studied a group of patients with paroxysmal hypertension, with no detectable medical cause, and found the majority of them to consistently present with repressed emotions, especially when related to traumatic experiences. The author suggested that while repression may be used as a defense against stress, it is not without a cost to the individual's health. The unpredictable changes in the activity of the autonomic nervous system and the consequent changes in blood pressure may be such a price. Mann (1996) emphasized the role of psychotherapeutic interventions in addressing repressed emotions as a way of re-establishing homeostasis in the sympathetic-adrenal medulla axis.

In a classic study, Winnicott traced the origin of a patient's dissociative tendencies and the subsequent psychosomatic complications to a time when, as a child, the patient desperately attempted to gain her mother's attention even to a point of screaming before she abandoned all hope. By distancing (disconnecting) herself from her physical and emotional needs, the child learned to cope with the immediate situation, but such tendencies later resulted in physical and emotional dysfunction (in Winnicott, Shepherd and Davis, 1989).

In recent years, neuropsychological and neurophysiological data have further supported the above observations with regard to role of repression in the development of psychosomatic disorders. Several authors, most prominently Galin and colleagues (1977), have noted that chronic repressive tendencies can actually bring about a disruption in the communication between the two hemispheres resulting in the manifestation of affective experiences through somatic means (Fleminger, McClure & Dalton, 1980). In a more recent study, Min and Lee (1997) in their investigation of laterality in somatization further supported the formulation that the right hemisphere is significantly more involved with the experience of somatic symptoms related to emotional problems than the left hemisphere. They suggested that the possible disconnection brought on between the two hemispheres through repressive tendencies is likely to result in somatization disorder.

Another clinically significant area which has a great deal of relevance in the understanding of the symptomology of FMS has to do with sleep. As discussed earlier, lack of quality sleep appears to be a major diagnostic ingredient and a hallmark of fibromyalgia. From an intrapsychic standpoint, much happens during the nightly slumber. For one thing, the ego defense mechanisms that protect us from the experience of disturbing, internal events begin to lose their effectiveness. Hence, unresolved and painful thoughts and affect have an opportunity to manifest themselves. This process in and of itself can generate much unwanted anxiety, which is likely to result in an unconscious resistance to submit to the state of rest. This may also be viewed by the ego as a state of profound vulnerability (Fosshage, 1983). With the ego defenses largely put to rest, only a chronic state of arousal can protect the self from exposure to unwanted images tainted with affective material that may be overwhelming and possibly quite threatening. Sloan (1990) suggested that the censorship of the ego is not entirely dismantled during sleep and continues to interfere with the emergence of especially distressing affect. This formulation may explain the reason FMS patients so often complain of disturbed, non-restorative sleep.

The presence of alpha wave intrusion, which is not exclusive to FMS patients, nevertheless is not a characteristic of sleep physiology as seen in most insomniacs. This was clearly established by Molodofsky (1989) who compared fibromyalgia patients and insomniacs with regard to alpha-delta intrusion and concluded that while nearly all FMS patients showed persistent alpha activity during stages 2, 3, and 4. This tendency was not seen in the insomniacs.

Can we then propose that one function of such disruption in sleep activity is to maintain a state of hypervigilance? If this is the case, the consequences of such hypervigilance are quite obvious: impaired rest, limited recuperation and replenishment with potential disregulatory ramifications. The overly driven, perfectionistic, and even obsessive compulsive tendencies that are observed in fibromyalgia patients serve as powerful distraction and unconscious tendencies. However, these same characteristics cause disruptions of sleep cycles through arousal, and perhaps even hyperarousal to the point of exhaustion. Confronted by the experience of an inner state of emotional turmoil, the patient seeks constant stimulation and distraction even during sleep.

It is important to note that sleep brought on through exhaustion does not possess the recuperative ingredients of normal sleep. A recent study clearly demonstrated that exhausted subjects were deficient in slow wave or delta sleep, which suggests that initiating sleep through the means of merely exhausting one's self will result in impaired sleep (van Diest & Apples, 1994). This once again suggests that prolonged deficiency in restorative sleep has the obvious and deleterious consequences that have been reported in the literature.

Alexithymia as an Example of Psychobiological Disregulation

The concept and diagnosis of alexithymia (from Latin, without words for feelings), originally introduced by Sifneos, has gained much recognition especially among those interested in the pursuit of the mechanisms involved in the development of psychosomatic disorders (Sifneos, 1973). Alexithymics are described as those individuals who are unable to have awareness of their affective states. Nemiah and Sifneos (1970) suggested that a deficiency in the ability for symbolization of emotions may result in a host of psychophysiological complications and an impaired capacity for self-regulation. For the most part, these patients have to struggle to distinguish between their bodily feelings and emotions. Additionally, alexithymics tend to appear disconnected from their body parts and attend to them only when some extreme physical distress is being experienced. Even in such instances body parts are referred to as "it," that is to suggest that they are not owned (Rickles, 1986).

It is interesting to note that this process of bodily dissociation appears to be also at work with patients suffering from unremitting pain, although it may not possess the developmental attributes seen in alexithymics. Aronoff and Rutrick (1992), while referring to chronic pain patients, asserted that as physical pain persists, this process of disowning (i.e., hurting body parts becoming ego-alien) and detachment can become more intensified, and avoidant tendencies toward the self and others is likely to ensue.

In an essay describing mechanisms of symptom formation in alexithymia patients, Rickles (1986) makes the following observation—an observation which should ring at least partially true especially for those clinicians who have spent some time working with fibromyalgia patients. "In the case where personality dynamics predispose to manic defenses and obsessive-goal oriented behavior, some alexithymic patients will create lives that are fast paced and highly demanding. A state of chronic arousal obtains that, because of the deficiency in self-regulation and awareness of inner experience, may persist for years without significant relief" (pp. 218–219). Does this suggest that these patients, as a way of avoiding the inner experience and emotionally painful recollections, constantly seek excitation and overindulge themselves in external activities? Such tendencies tend to embody, most likely unconsciously, an attempt to avoid self-reflection and may be construed as a method of "disattention" and "disconnection" which will in time, based on Schwartz's formulation, bring about disregulation (Schwartz, 1989).

In further discussing alexithymics, Rickles (1986) suggested a second possible scenario which again can be applied to FMS patients, especially those suffering from accident related or posttraumatic fibromyalgia. "When life has been kinder and projective identification demands on objects have been moderately well met, the alexithymic will be psychophysiologically stable until some accident, determined either by providence or the unconscious, introduces an intrapsychic experience that cannot be rapidly eliminated. Usually this inescapable experience occurs in the form of physical pain" (p. 219). Given the inflexibility of the ego defenses in these patients, they have limited resources when it comes to coping with chronic and unyielding pain. Hence, the only mode of affective expression is through somatic means which may precipitate a state of psychophysiological disturbance (Lolas & Von Rad, 1989).

While most fibromyalgia patients may not qualify as candidates for the diagnosis of alexithymia, there are clear and distinct similarities between these disorders. Once again, this is likely to be due to the data suggesting they are both diseases of ineffective self-regulation, which are quite possibly due to issues of a developmental nature (Taylor, 1992).

Self Psychology and Self-Regulation

As it was discussed earlier, there is now growing evidence from both animal and human studies that early mother-infant relationships can profoundly affect neuroendocrinolgic and psychophysiologic, self-regulatory mechanisms (Hofer, 1984; Hofer, 1987; Schore, 1994; Taylor, Bagby and Parker, 1997; Weiner, 1982). The contributions of self psychology and the pioneering work of Kohut (1971) have advanced our understanding of how early childhood experiences can promote or thwart proper psychological and physiological functioning. A central concept in self psychology is that of the contribution of selfobjects in the development of the infant's nuclear self and its proper development. A selfobject is best described as a significant individual who is perceived as a part of the self and who performs crucial tasks such as tension and affect regulation, attunement to affective states, as well as providing soothing and self-affirming experiences. Kohut (1977) masterfully describes the importance of selfobjects in the infant's survival and development in the following paragraph:

> The child that is to survive psychologically is born into an empathic-responsive human milieu (of selfobjects) *just as he is born into an atmosphere that contains an optimal amount of oxygen* if he is to survive physically. And his nascent self "expects" . . . an empathic environment to be in tune with his psychological need-wishes with the same unquestioning certitude as the respiratory apparatus of the newborn infant may be said to "expect" oxygen to be contained in the surrounding environment. When the child's psychological balance is disturbed, the child's tensions are, under normal circumstances, empathically perceived and responded to by the selfobject. The selfobject, equipped with a mature psychological organization that realistically assesses the child's need and what is to be done about it, will include the child into its psychological organization and will remedy the child's homeostatic imbalance through actions (p. 85, emphasis was added).

Kohut (1977) goes on to emphasize the importance of voice and touch in regulating tension and providing the child with soothing experiences that are, in time, internalized (through the process of transmuting internalization) and continue to contribute to the child's natural and healthy development of a cohesive self. On the other hand, a defect in self and self-regulation may occur if the selfobject consistently fails to provide the child with empathic attunement. This defect in effective self-regulation sets the stage for the manifestation neuroendocrine and psychophysiological disorders which tend to surface, especially after exposure to a traumatic experience. At such times, system wide complications and symptoms that defy any linear (cause and effect) explanations may occur. Such distressing symptoms are often found to be refractory to conventional medical treatments and are likely to become progressively worse. Tests-after-tests fail to account for the state of physiological disarray that the patient is experiencing. Also, as symptom management fails to follow a predictable course of treatment, patients are likely to find themselves consulting with one specialist after another without lasting benefits. For example, many FMS report that prior to a minor car accident they were coping rather well, until "everything began to fall apart". Many such patients are eventually told that their "problems" are "psychological" and that they should find relief in psychological and psychiatric treatments (Taerk and Gnam, 1994). In this manner, further psychological damage occurs as a result of a lack of empathy by healthcare practitioners as the patients are likely to become more withdrawn and resistant to submitting themselves to further medical and psychological scrutiny (Berger, 1993).

The tenets of self psychology, especially as they relate to the development of disorders of regulations, provide a sound theoretical direction on two critical levels which are pertinent to the treatment process. First, this approach emphasizes the importance of empathically listening to the patient's symptoms without trying to explain them away as purely psychological (McDougall, 1989). This allows the patient to develop a therapeutic bond with the physician/therapist, which promotes improved communication. Such communication is crucial to the therapeutic task at hand. Secondly, as the therapeutic bond is strengthened, the physician/therapist begins to more effectively assume the role of a selfobject that can gradually assist the patient in re-establishing and improving his or her self-regulatory capacities.

Clinical Implications of the Disregulation Model in the Treatment of FMS

The main thesis of the disregulation model is that all living systems are self-regulatory in nature. However, if through a variety of internal or external events, self-regulatory mechanisms are compromised, a state of psychobiological chaos is likely to become manifest through the emergence of system-wide symptoms. Initially, subsystems tend to compensate and bring about a state of temporary balance. Over time, such compensatory attempts will, however, result in a depletion of available resources and breakdown, or a state of dis-ease, is likely to ensue. A weakness in the self-regulatory mechanisms may be the result of developmental insufficiencies and/or exposure to prolonged and uncontrollable stress (Taylor et al., 1997). In either case a reestablishment of self-regulatory functions should bring about greater order and amelioration of the symptoms. This suggests a reconnection to those mechanisms whose function has been interfered with through acts of disattention, such as repression. "Disowned" body parts need to be re-owned—"it" needs to become "my." Similarly, denied affect needs to be acknowledged, confronted and integrated. Through these processes of "reconnection," tremendous amounts of physical and psychological energies which were once used to maintain a disconnected state is freed. This energy is subsequently used for repair and reestablishment of homeostasis through self-regulatory means.

Creating a consistent, self-affirming, supportive and empathic environment is key in assisting FMS patients and all those who suffer from disorders of regulation. Physicians and therapists as external "regulators" can play a indispensable role in re-establishing and fortifying the patient's self-regulatory mechanism. Additionally, with the use of intensive psychotherapy, with emphasis on symbolization of affect, emotional and cognitive experiences are recognized and reintegrated (see Taerk and Gnam,

1994). Psychophysiological interventions such as autogenic training and biofeedback can be effectively used for enhancing self-regulation, and increasing self-efficacy and self-esteem (Sadigh, 1999; Sadigh, 2001; Schwartz & Schwartz, 1995; Rickles, 1981). Once the external sources of regulation (selfobjects), which constitute physicians, therapists, etc., are internalized, an improvement in system-wide symptoms is likely to be noted by the patient and those involved in his or her care.

Conclusions

Fibromyalgia pain syndrome is a complex and system-wide disorder which can best be described as a profound disorder of self-regulation. This paper attempted to integrate findings from a variety of disciplines, such as psychosomatic medicine, developmental biology, and self psychology (Kohut, 1971; Kohut & Wolf, 1978), as a way of suggesting possible mechanisms that may be at the heart of this disorder. Particular attention is paid to the contributions of the system based theory of psychobiological disregulation proposed by Schwartz (1989). The integration of this theory into neoanalytic thinking is highlighted based on the contributions of Kohut (1997) and Taylor (1992). The main premise of this paper is that FMS cannot be fully understood unless it is viewed as a system-wide phenomenon. It has been suggested that as a way of expanding our formulation of this condition, further attention needs to be paid to the importance of predisposing psychological and personality factors (Sadigh, 1998;Wofe, 1995). Hence, it is imperative to consider self-regulatory mechanisms, their development, psychobiology, function and dysfunction as a method of reconceptualizing FMS.

While much research has been conducted in the past decade with regard to the various characteristics of FMS, there also needs to be emphasis placed upon detailed case studies which focus on developmental, intrapsychic and interpersonal dimensions of this disorder and how they might affect regulatory functions. As implied in this paper, the treatment of fibromyalgia requires a multidisciplinary approach. Although this point has been emphasized in the current literature, I suggest that true interdisciplinary attempts cannot be successful unless certain philosophical and theoretical view points are shared by the team of treating professionals. The psychobiological disregulation model and contributions from self psychology can serve as such a unifying core that can guide both research and clinical practice.

References

Alarcon, G. S.,& Bradley, L. A. (1998). Advances in the treatment of fibromyalgia: Current status and future directions. *American Journal Medical Science, 315,* 397–404.

Arnold, L. M., Keck, P. E., & Welge, J. A. (2000). Antidepressant treatment of fibromyalgia: A meta-analysis and review. *Psychosomatics, 41,* 104–113.

Aronoff, G. M. (1992). *Evaluation and treatment of chronic pain.* Baltimore, Maryland: Williams & Wilkins.

Aronoff, G. M, & Rutrick, D. (1992). Psychodynamics and psychotherapy of the chronic pain syndrome. In G. F. Aronoff (Ed.), *Evaluation and treatment of chronic pain* (pp. 394–398). Baltimore, Maryland: Williams & Wilkins.

Bacall, H. A., & Newman, M. K. (1990). *Theories of object relations: Bridges to self psychology.* New York: Columbia University Press.

Berger, S. (1993). Chronic fatigue syndrome: A self psychological perspective. *Clinical Social Work Journal, 21,* 71–84.

Bernstein, A. (1978). A psychoanalytic contribution to the etiology of "back pain" and "spinal disc syndrome." *Journal of the American Academy of Psychoanalysis, 6,* 547–556.

Buckelew, S. P. (1994). Behavioral interventions with fibromyalgia. *Journal of Musculoskeletal Pain, 2,* 153–161.

Crofford, L. (1998). Neuroendocrine findings in patients with fibromyalgia. *Journal of Musculoskeletal Pain, 6,* 69–76.

Fleminger, J. J., McClure, G. M.,& Dalton, R. (1980). Lateral response to suggestion in relation to handedness and the side of psychogenic symptoms. *British Journal of Psychiatry 136,* 562–566.

Fosshage, J. (1983). The psychological function of dreams: A revised psychoanalytic perspective. *Contemporary Psychoanalytic Thought, 6,* 641–669.

Galin, D., Diamnond, R., & Braff, D. (1977). Lateralization of conversion symptoms: More frequent on the left. *American Journal of Psychiatry, 134,* 578–580.

Gerster, J. C., & Hadj-Djilani, A. (1984). Hearing and vestibular abnormalities in primary fibrositis syndrome. *Journal of Rheumatology, 11,* 678–680.

Goldenberg D. L. (1989). An overview of psychologic studies in fibromyalgia. *Journal of Rheumatology 16,* 12–14.

Goldstein, D. S. (1998). The sympathetic and the adrenomedullary hormonal systems: Differential responses to stressors. *Journal of Musculoskeletal Pain, 6,* 63–68.

Nemeroff, C. B., & Loosen, P. T. (1987). *Handbook of clinical psychoneuroendocrinology.* New York: Guilford Press.

Hoefer, M. A. (1975). Studies in how early maternal separation produces behavioral changes in rats. *Psychosomatic Medicine, 37,* 245–264.

Hoefer, M. A. (1978). Hidden regulatory processes in early social relationships. In P.P.G. Bateson, & P. H. Klopfer (Eds.), *Perspectives in ethology* (Vol. 3). New York: Plenum.

Hoefer, M. A. (1984). Relationships as regulators: A psychobiological perspective on bereavement. *Psychosomatic Medicine, 46,* 183–197.

Hoefer, M. A. (1987). Early social relationships: A psychobiologist's view. *Child Development, 58,* 633–647.

Kiecolt-Glaser, J., & Glaser, J. (1991). Stress and the immune function in humans. In R. Ader, & O. L. Felten (Eds.), *Psychoneuroimmunology* (pp. 849–867). Orlando, Florida: Academic Press.

Kennedy, M., & Felson, D. A. (1996). Prospective long term study of fibromyalgia syndrome. *Arthritis & Rheumatism, 39,* 682–685.

Klimas, N., Morgan, R., Salvato, F., Van Riel, F., Millon, C., Fletcher, M. A. (1992). Chronic fatigue syndrome and psychoneuroimmunology. In N. Scheneiderman, P. McCabe, & A. Baum (Eds.), *Perspectives in Behavioral Medicine* (pp. 121–137). Hillside, New Jersey: Lawrence Erlbaum Associates.

Kohut, H. (1971). *The analysis of the self.* New York: International Universities Press.

Kohut, H. (1977). *Restoration of the self.* New York: International Universities Press.

Kohut, H., & Wolf, E. (1978). The disorders of the self and their treatments: An outline. *International Journal of Psychoanalysis, 59,* 413–426.

Lloyd, R. (1987). *Explorations in psychoneuroimmunology.* Boston: Allyn and Bacon.

Lolas, F., & Von Rad, M. (1989). Alexithymia. In S. Cheren (Ed.), *Psychosomatic Medicine* (Vol. 1, pp. 189–237). Madison, Connecticut: International Universities Press.

McDougall, J. (1989), Theaters of the body: A Psychoanalytic approach to psychosomatic illness. New York: W. W. Norton & Co.

McEwen, B. C., & Stellar, E. (1993). Stress and the individual: Mechanisms leading to disease. *Archives of Internal Medicine, 153,* 2093–2101.

Mann, S. J. (1996). Severe paroxysmal hypertension: An automatic syndrome and its relationship to repressed emotions. *Psychosomatics, 37,* 444–450.

Min, S. K., & Lee, B. O. (1997). Lateralization in somatization. *Psychosomatic Medicine, 59,* 236–240.

Moldofsky, H., Sacrisbrick, P., & England, R., & Smythe, H. (1975). Musculoskeletal symptoms and non-REM sleep disturbance in patients with 'fibrositic' syndrome and healthy subjects. *Psychosomatic Medicine, 37,* 341–351.

Moldofsky, H., & Scarisbrick, P. (1976). Induction of neurasthenic musculoskeletal pain syndrome by selective sleep stage deprivation. *Psychosomatic Medicine, 38,* 35–44.

Moldofsky, H. (1989). Sleep and fibrositis. *Rheumatic Diseases Clinics of North America, 15,* 91–103.

Moldofsky, H. (1995). Sleep, wakefulness, neuroendocrine and immune function in fibromyalgia and chronic fatigue syndrome. *Journal of Musculoskeletal Pain, 3,* 75–79.

Nemiah, J. C., & Sifneos, P. E. (1970). Affect and fantasy in patients with psychosomatic disorders. In O. W. Hill (ed.), *Modern trends in psychosomatic medicine* (Vol. II). New York: Appleton-Century-Crofts.

Pellegrino, M. J., Van Fossen, D., Gordon C., Ryan J. M., & Waylonis, G. W. (1989) Prevalence of mitral valve prolapse in primary fibromyalgia: A pilot investigation. *Archives of Physical Medicine & Rehabilitation, 70,* 541–543.

Rice, J. R. (1986). Fibrositis syndrome. *Medical Clinics in North America, 70,* 455–468.

Rickles, W. H. (1981). Biofeedback and transitional phenomenon. *Psychiatric Annals, 11,* 23–41.

Rickles, W. H. (1986). Self psychology and somatization: An integration with alexithymia. In A. Goldberg (Ed.), *Progress in self psychology* (Vol. 2, pp. 212–226). New York: Guilford Press.

Rosenhall, U., Johansson, G., & Orndahl, G. (1987). Eye motility dysfunction in chronic primary fibromyalgia with dysesthesia. *Scandinavian Journal of Rehabilitation Medicine, 19,* 139–145.

Sadigh, M. R. (1998). Chronic pain and personality disorders: Implications for rehabilitation practice. *Journal of Rehabilitation, 64,* 4–8.

Sadigh, M. R. (1999). The treatment of recalcitrant posttraumatic nightmares with autogenic training and autogenic abreaction. *Journal of Applied Psychophysiology and Biofeedback, 24,* 203–210.

Sadigh, M. R. (2001). *Autogenic training: A mind-body approach to the treatment of fibromyalgia and chronic pain syndrome.* New York: Haworth Medical Press.

Schore, A. N. (1994). *Affect regulation and the origin of the self: The neurobiology of emotional development.* Hillsdale, NJ:Lawrence Erlbaum.

Schwartz, G. E. (1979). Disregulation and system theory: A biobehavioral framework for biofeedback and behavioral medicine. In N. Birbaumer, & H.D. Kimmel (Eds.), *Biofeedback and self-regulation* (pp. 881–891). Hillsdale, New Jersey: Earlbaum.

Schwartz, G. E. (1989). Disregulation theory and disease: Toward a general model for psychosomatic medicine. In S. Cheren (Ed), *Psychosomatic Medicine* (Vol. 1, pp. 91–117). Madison, Connecticut: International University Press.

Schwartz, N. M., & Schwartz, M. S. (1995). Definitions of biofeedback and applied psychophysiology. In M. S. Schwartz (Ed.), *Biofeedback: A practitioner's guide* (pp. 32–42). New York: Guilford Press.

Selye, H. (1984). *The stress of life.* New York: McGraw Hill.

Semble, E. L., & Wise, C. M. (1988). Fibrositis. *American Family Physician, 38,* 129–139.

Sifneos, P. E. (1973). The prevalence of "alexithymic" characteristics in psychosomatic patients. *Psychosomatic Psychotherapy, 26,* 65–70.

Sifneos, P. E., Apfel-Savitz, R,& Frankel, F. H. (1977). The phenomenon of alexithymia. *Psychotherapy and Psychosomatics, 28,* 47–57.

Simms, R. W., & Goldenbrg, D. L. (1988). Symptoms mimicking neurologic disorders in fibromyalgia syndrome. *Journal of Rheumatology, 15,* 1271–1273.

Simons, D. G. (1975). Special review, muscle pain syndrome, part I. *American Journal of Physical Medicine 54,* 289–311.

Sloan, P. (1990). *Psychoanalytic understanding of the dream.* Northvale, New Jersey: Jason Aronson.

Sterling, P., & Eyer, J. (1988). Allostasis: A new paradigm to explain arousal pathology. In J. Fisher & J. Reason (Eds.), *Handbook of life stress, cognition and health* (pp. 629–649). New York: John Wiley.

Taerk, G., & Gnam, W. (1994). A psychodynamic view of the chronic fatigue syndrome: The role of object relations in etiology and treatment. *General Hospital Psychiatry, 16,* 319–325.

Taylor, G. J. (1987). *Psychosomatic medicine and contemporary psychoanalysis.* Madison, Connecticut: International Universities Press.

Taylor, G. J. (1992). Psychoanalysis and psychosomatics: A new synthesis. *Journal of the Academy of Psychoanalysis, 20,* 251–275.

Taylor, G. J., Bagby, R. M., & Parker, J. D. A. (1997). *Disorders of affect regulation: Alexithymia in psychiatric illness.* Cambridge: Cambridge University Press.

van Diest, R., Apples, & W.P.M. (1994). Sleep characteristics of exhausted men. *Psychosomatic Medicine, 56,* 28–35.

von Bertalanffy, L. (1968). *General system theory.* New York: Braziller.

Wallace, D. J. (1990). Genitourinary manifestations of fibrositis: An association with the female urethral syndrome. *Journal of Rheumatology, 17,* 238–239.

Weiner, H. (1982). The prospect for psychosomatic medicine. *Psychosomatic Medicine 44,* 491–517.

Winnicott, D. W. (1966). Psychosomatic illness in its positive and negative aspects. *International Journal of Psychoanalysis, 47,* 510–516.

Winnicott, C., Shepherd, R., & Davis, M. (1989). *Psychonalytic explorations: D. W. Winnicott.* Cambridge, Massachusetts: Harvard University Press.

Wolfe, F. (1995). The future of fibromyalgia: Some critical issues. *Journal of Musculoskeletal, Pain, 3,* 3-15.

Yunus, M. B., Masi A.T., & Aldag, J. C. (1989). A controlled study of primary fibromyalgia syndrome: Clinical features and association with other functional syndromes. *Journal of Rheumatology, 13,* 183–186.

Yunus, M. B. (1994). Psychological aspects of fibromyalgia syndrome: A component of the dysfunctional spectrum syndrome. *Bailliere's Clinical Rheumatology, 8,* 811–837.

Advances in Medical Psychotherapy and Psychodiagnosis
2002–2003, Volume 11, pp. 59–74

A Review of Empirically Based Psychological Assessment and Intervention Procedures for Adults with Diabetes Mellitus

James E. Aikens, Ph.D. and Lynne I. Wagner, Ph.D.

Abstract

We review empirical data regarding clinical assessment and intervention for adults with diabetes mellitus, with respect to the following clinical problems: poor regimen adherence, depression, anxiety, psychophysiological effects of stress, eating disorders, and cognitive impairment. For areas in which clinically-oriented recommendations are not possible due to insufficient data, we provide tentative extrapolations based on principles derived from non-diabetes samples.

Management of diabetes mellitus, the most prevalent endocrine disorder, is heavily dependent upon patient behavior. Although data suggests that psychological distress is the fifth leading mortality predictor among persons with diabetes (Davis, Hess, & Hiss, 1988), medical settings tend to place much more emphasis on biological indices with lower predictive values. In this paper, we review basic medical aspects of diabetes, followed by consideration of research bearing on assessment and treatment of the following key clinical problem areas for adults with diabetes: depressive disorders, anxiety disorders, eating disorders, poor medical regimen adherence, stress effects on diabetes control, and cognitive impairment. We also include brief commentaries regarding the data on relevant psychotropic medication issues.

Basic Medical Overview of Diabetes

Insulin enhances cell membrane permeability to glucose, the primary fuel for routine cellular metabolism. Diabetes involves insufficient pancreatic insulin production and/or insulin ineffectiveness (Pohl, Gonder-Frederick & Cox, 1984), and if untreated results in abnormally *elevated blood glucose* (BG),or *hyperglycemia*. There are 2 major types of diabetes: insulin dependent (IDDM; also known as Type I or "juvenile onset" diabetes), and non insulin dependent (NIDDM; also termed Type II or "adult onset" diabetes). Their etiologies are both multifactorial, but differ considerably (Robbins & Kumar, 1987). In IDDM, the pancreas produces essentially no insulin, probably due to autoimmune destruction of insulin-producing cells (American Diabetes Association; ADA, 1996). NIDDM is more

---

Correspondence: James E. Aikens, Ph.D., Behavior Medicine Service, Psychiatry Department, University of Chicago, 5841 S. Maryland, MC-3077, Chicago, IL, USA, 60637-1470.

Tel: (773) 702-1526; Fax: (773) 702-6454; E-mail: jaikens@yoda.bsd.uchicago.edu.

highly associated with obesity and genetic factors, and usually involves insulin ineffectiveness (resistance) and/or insufficient insulin production (ADA, 1996; Pohl et al., 1984). In the USA, 1993 data indicate that 3.1% of the United States population has diabetes, 90–95% of whom have NIDDM. With the inclusion of probable undiagnosed NIDDM cases, actual prevalence has been estimated at up to 6% (ADA, 1996). NIDDM prevalence increases with age, and is more common in certain ethnic groups (e.g., Africans, Native Americans, Latinos). Finally, gestational diabetes, which occurs in 2–5% of pregnancies and can result in up to 50% risk for NIDDM if postpartum weight loss does not occur. Gestational diabetes is associated with increased age at pregnancy, family diabetes history, and obesity (ADA, 1996).

Diabetes can create acute hyperglycemia, which is associated with visual disturbances, mood shifts, and even life-threatening dehydration and tissue breakdown (Pohl et al., 1984). Longstanding hyperglycemia is linked with angiopathy, neuropathy, renal dysfunction, visual impairment, and hypertension. Myocardial infarction is the leading cause of death among people with diabetes. The physiologically opposite state, acute hypoglycemia (dangerously low BG), can produce irritability, anxiety episodes, disorientation, and coma.

"Metabolic control" is assessed routinely by physicians as a major indicator of illness status. However, metabolic control is complicated, multidimensional, and influenced by multiple factors. The two most commonly utilized specialized assays are glycosylated hemoglobin (HbA1 and its variants, which reflect mean blood glucose (BG) over the prior 6–12 weeks; ADA, 1996), and fasting BG (which indicates basal BG; Service, O'Brien, & Rizza, 1987). BG is often self-monitored by patients with portable reflectance assay devices, usually before meals and in response to symptoms of abnormal BG. The therapeutic BG "target" is often in the range of 60 to 180 mg/dl, but actual clinical targets vary widely between patients, depending on regimen, medical, lifestyle, and personal factors. The *diabetes treatment regimen* usually includes a calorie-limited, balanced, scheduled diet. In NIDDM, an oral hypoglycemic or insulin-sensitizing agent is often included. Multiple daily insulin injections are always necessary in IDDM and frequently in poorly controlled NIDDM as well. The contemporary "tight control" diabetes management philosophy, which specifies a narrower BG target range and frequent regimen adjustments, was recently supported by a large multisite IDDM trial (DCCT Research Group, 1993) and is thus becoming more widely utilized, and may soon be adapted for NIDDM as well. Subcutaneous insulin delivery systems ("pumps") are also increasingly being used, and pancreatic transplantation has been performed on a small group of IDDM patients (ADA, 1996).

Medical Regimen Adherence and Self Care Behavior

Because the diabetes regimen is burdensome, complex, intrusive, and lifelong, poor regimen adherence is a pervasive clinical issue. Although good adherence improves BG levels and significantly reduces long term complication rates (DCCT Research Group, 1993), noncompliance with diet recommendations and insulin administration has been reported by 58–80% of diabetes patients (Sarafino, 1994). Poor adherence is associated with depression and anxiety, maladaptive personality traits (Lustman, Frank, & McGill, 1991), and poor coping skills (Delameter, Kurtz, Bubb, White, & Santiago, 1987). In accordance with models emphasizing health beliefs and self efficacy factors, regimen behavior is predicted by patient illness attributions, perceived ability to self-manage diabetes, environmental adherence barriers, and the perceived costs versus benefits of the regimen. Social and family factors also appear to be relevant. Familial dysfunction is associated with poorer adherence in children and adolescents with IDDM (Anderson, 1990), whereas the lack of diabetes—specific family support predicts nonadherence in adults with NIDDM (Glasgow and Toobert, 1988). Another complicating factor is that diabetes patients usually do not experience the benefit of clear immediate feedback to reinforce effective diabetes self-management actions; more typically, everyday illness management behaviors performed by the patient have delayed or unclear consequences.

Regimen adherence is difficult to assess, for three reasons. First, typical clinical outpatient circumstances usually necessitate primary reliance upon self report data. Second, there is no absolute or standard criterion. Many patients simply do not receive explicit physician recommendations, especially in relation to diet and exercise. Third, regimen behavior has multiple dimensions which are only moderately intercorrelated. Medication-taking may be minimally related to dietary regulation, which may in turn be unrelated to the consistency of BG testing (Glasgow, McCaul, and Schafer, 1987). Therefore, each regimen component needs to be evaluated in isolation, with regards to frequency and consistency of medication administration, BG testing, physical activity, and relevant dimensions of eating behavior such as timing, amounts, meal composition, triggers for spontaneous eating, and consistency.

Although there are no universally accepted assessment measures of diabetes adherence, the range of research measures includes self report, self monitoring, staff and spousal observation, endocrinologic assays, and electronic records of behavior. One of the most well validated and clinically useful instruments is the Summary of Diabetes Self Care Activity (Toobert & Glasgow, 1993). This 12-item self report instrument assesses diabetes self care behavior over the preceding 7 days, covering various relevant features of diet, exercise, BG testing, and medication administration. Its brevity, ease of scoring, and reference to specific behaviors make it particularly useful in the psychology practice environment. Additional clinically useful measures are the Self-Care Inventory (LaGreca et al., 1990), the Diabetes Self-Care Scale (Hurley, 1990), and the Diabetes Health Profile (Meadows & Wise, 1992).

A variety of psychological interventions have been empirically demonstrated to improve regimen adherence. For obese diabetes patients, eating behavior and weight loss are usually primary treatment goals, with the long term goal of improved metabolic control. In general populations, effective behavioral programs typically include nutrition and exercise counseling, self-monitoring, stimulus control techniques, and contingency contracting (Sarafino, 1994; Masters, Burish, Hollon & Rimm, 1987). Hartwell, Kaplan, and Wallace (1986) describe a behavioral dietary intervention for NIDDM patients featuring the identification and alteration of environmental cues associated with eating and health care behaviors, self monitoring of medication and food intake, self-reinforcement of desired behavior changes using non-food positive reinforcers, modification of self-defeating cognitions related to the regimen, and an emphasis upon clear, discrete, verifiable, realistic goals for change. As in general obesity treatment, it is probably optimal to avoid a sole emphasis upon the target of weight loss per se, but the introduction and maintenance of healthy eating patterns. The psychological management of obesity can be a challenging and frustrating process, because progress may be slow and inconsistent. Therefore, each observable improvement should be heavily reinforced.

Cox and Gonder-Frederick (1992) reviewed NIDDM specific behavioral weight loss studies, concluding that men respond better to individual treatment whereas women respond better to couples treatment, long term medical improvement correlates with post treatment weight loss, and the most effective treatments are those which incorporate routine physical exercise and very low calorie diets. Finally, maintenance differs by regimen area, with improved medication and BG monitoring tending to maintain better than changes in diet and exercise behavior (Rubin, Peyrot, & Saudek, 1989).

Although the bulk of research focuses on adherence to BG testing, diet, and medication, other adherence domains where further research is needed include carrying emergency glucose and other supplies, and checking feet frequently for injuries.

Depression

Depression prevalence is elevated in IDDM and NIDDM, occurring at up to 6 times the rate normally observed in the general population (Lustman, Griffith, Clouse, & Cryer, 1986). However, it is not clear whether depression prevalence is higher in diabetes in comparison to chronic illnesses in general. Major depressive disorder is 5 times more likely among diabetes patients with a prior major depressive episode, and is associated with both poor illness control and increased reporting of clinical diabetes symptoms (Lustman, Griffith, Gavard, & Clouse, 1991).

There is no generally accepted current explanation for the depression-diabetes association, but several possibilities exist. First, diabetes often introduces both episodic and chronic stressors, i.e., a fluctuating course superimposed over a relatively demanding and permanent lifestyle-oriented regimen.

Second, the imperfect correlation between self care behavior and health outcome might induce a state of learned helplessness. Third, numerous metabolic and hormonal abnormalities impinge upon the brain, potentially altering emotional functioning at a neurophysiological level. Even transient BG fluctuation is associated with mood state in IDDM, e.g., angry and sad moods correlate with low BG (Gonder-Frederick, Cox, Bobbitt, &, Pennebaker, 1989). Thus, depression may possibly influence diabetes and/or be influenced by diabetes.

The potential confounding of medical status and psychological symptoms is a core assessment issue, and one which especially applies to depression in endocrine populations. It should be verified that hypothyroidism, adrenal medullary and cortical abnormalities, and other known depressogenic conditions have already been adequately assessed and if possible, medically treated. In diabetes, physical symptoms (weight loss, fatigue) and disrupted memory function could result from poorly controlled illness with persistent hyperglycemia. When such medically reversible states exist, it may be advisable to conduct assessment both before and after reasonable attempts at medical treatment.

Assessment instruments developed on general psychiatric groups have been widely utilized to quantify distress in diabetes, although content overlap between diabetes symptoms and general psychiatric symptoms has created concern over the potential for exaggerated psychopathology estimates (Bradley, 1994). The MMPI has been thus criticized as invalid for screening diabetes patients (Dunn & Turtle, 1981). The Symptom Checklist-90-Revised (Derogatis, 1977), while briefer, still contains at least 15 items rated by endocrinologists as attributable to diabetes or its treatment (Aikens, 1998). Diabetes patients with nonelevated SCL-90-R profiles score higher than community normals and similarly to psychiatric patients on most of these items, which cover content such as trembling, shakiness, faintness, bodily weakness, dizziness, numbness and tingling, sexual dysfunction, racing or pounding heart, chest pain, anergia, appetite disturbances, sleep disruption, and general concerns over somatic function. While such indicators potentially inflate psychopathology estimates, excluding them without careful consideration may decrease sensitivity and case detection rates.

The Beck Depression Inventory (BDI; Beck & Steer, 1987) also has several items which may tap potential diabetes-related problems (e.g., diminished ability to work, sleep disruption, fatigue, appetite disturbance, weight loss, health worries, and sexual problems). However, Lustman, Freedman, Carney, Hong, and Clouse (1992) found that BDI item values for depressed diabetes patients closely resemble those of depressed psychiatric patients, with little resemblance to those of nondepressed diabetes patients, supporting its application to this population. Another measure, the Well-Being Questionnaire (Bradley, 1994) has the advantage of being developed specifically for the diabetes population. Although its strengths also include good psychometric properties and the inclusion of a 16-item subscale assessing well-being, the depression subscale is limited to only 6 items. Additional useful diabetes-specific scales measuring aspects of depression and general emotional adjustment are the ATT-39 (Dunn, Smartt, Beeney, & Turtle, 1986) and the Diabetes Health Profile (Meadows & Wise, 1992).

Symptom-confound issues also apply to clinical interview techniques. The clinician must carefully weigh the possibilities that fatigue, sleep disturbance, sexual disturbance, and other somatic symptoms are attributable to diabetes, depressive disorder, or perhaps both. In this respect, Lustman, Harper, Griffith, and Clouse (1986) encourage the use of the NIMH Diagnostic Interview Schedule (Robins, Helzer, Croughan, et al., 1981). Although this interview disregards possible psychiatric symptoms attributable to medical illness, it rarely fails to detect verified psychiatric disorder in diabetes patient samples. A less psychiatrically-oriented alternative validated specifically for diabetes applications is the Meadows et al. Diabetes Interview Schedule (Meadows, Thompson, Brown, Sensky, & Wise, 1991).

Because cognitive-behavioral therapy (CBT; see Beck, Rush, Shaw, & Emery, 1979) has been consistently demonstrated to be efficacious when applied to other medically ill populations (e.g., rheumatoid arthritis, (Young, 1992) cancer (Anderson, 1992)), it is reasonable to hypothesize that CBT may benefit diabetes patients as well. The only controlled study on this issue, recently reported by Lustman, Griffith, Freedland, Kissel, and Clouse (1998), tentatively supports this possibility. A 10-week program of CBT applied in combination with diabetes education was effective for NIDDM patients with major depressive disorder. A BDI total score of less than 10 was seen in 85% of treated patients and only 27% of controls immediately after treatment, with 70% of treated patients (versus

33% of controls) still in remission six months later. Although glycosylated hemoglobin did not differ immediately post-treatment, the CBT group demonstrated significantly lower glycosylated hemoglobin levels at six month followup. These beneficial long term metabolic effects suggest that carefully-conducted CBT not only relieves major depression in NIDDM, but may also potentially improve illness control. On a precautionary note, any intervention that increases activity level or general self care may lower BG due to altered energy balance. Although such changes are medically therapeutic, diabetes medication or dietary regimen adjustments may be necessary to reduce the risk of hypoglycemia.

Various adjustments to standard CBT may be needed in tailoring the intervention for depressed diabetes patients. Frequently, illness-specific depressogenic cognitions and associated affective responses become evident during CBT with depressed diabetes patients. These can be targeted for change, but sensitivity must be used to place them within the context of the medical variability characterizing diabetes; thus therapists must be amply educated about the illness. It can also be expected that patients who are already expending significant time and energy coping with their medical problems may have difficulty progressing at the same rate as a depressed person without a chronic medical illness. Finally, psychotherapy with diabetes patients can obviously be interrupted or slowed by medical setbacks, and often patients do not consider their psychological difficulties as very major in comparison to the magnitude of their medical issues.

Antidepressant medications are potentially helpful, although currently only one controlled trial demonstrates efficacy (for nortriptyline) in diabetes (Lustman, Griffith, Clouse, et al., 1997). However, certain complications of tricyclic antidepressant agents can occasionally produce hyperglycemia due to appetite stimulation, in this respect Lustman et al (1997) found that nortriptyline actually worsened glycemic control as it helped mood. while selective serotonin reuptake inhibitors (SSRIs) possibly enhance insulin action enough to produce hypoglycemia (Goodnick, Henry, & Buki, 1995). Drugs with anticholinergic properties may also cause distressing symptom exacerbation among patients with autonomic neuropathy.

Anxiety

Generalized anxiety disorder is the most common anxiety disorder among diabetes patients, and is associated with poor metabolic control (Turkat, 1982). The lifetime prevalence rate for anxiety disorder in diabetes is as follows: 40.9% for generalized anxiety disorder, 26.3% for simple phobia, 15.8% for agoraphobia, 10.5% for social phobia, 3.5% for panic disorder, and 0.9% for obsessive-compulsive disorder (Lustman, Griffith, Crouse & Cryer, 1986). Moreover, Popkin, Callies, Lentz, et al. (1988) found that anxiety disorder prevalence is lower in IDDM than in combined diabetes populations, although still higher than in the general population.

There are several etiological hypotheses surrounding the diabetes-anxiety association. Lustman (1988) speculates that anxiety symptoms are produced by sympathetic nervous system responses to hyperglycemia. Alternatively, diabetes-related endocrine abnormalities might be exacerbated by normal physiological stress responses (Lustman, Griffith, et al., 1986). A third reasonable possibility is that the frequently burdensome psychological task of adjusting to chronic illness while also managing the daily pressures of the diabetes self-care regimen may have a nonspecific general negative impact upon coping effectiveness.

Hypoglycemia fear is a significant difficulty for some IDDM patients, and is positively associated with other psychological variables, particularly trait anxiety (Polonsky, Davis, Jacobson & Anderson, 1992). This fear often has a realistic component, as hypoglycemia is usually a highly aversive subjective experience which can exert extreme negative health consequences including unconsciousness, motor vehicle accidents, coma, and possible death. In response to hypoglycemia fear, some diabetes patients develop elaborate hypoglycemia avoidance patterns that essentially raise BG to a subjectively "safe" range via adjustment of insulin, diet and activity level. If excessive, this can cause chronic hyperglycemia and long term complications. Hypoglycemia avoidance behavior correlates with past hypoglycemia episode frequency (Irvine, Cox & Gonder-Frederick, 1992) and poor ability to discriminate between anxiety and hypoglycemic states (Polonsky et al., 1992).

Anxiety assessment in diabetes is vexed by overlap between the symptoms of altered metabolism (especially low BG) and symptoms of anxiety (Beardsley & Goldstein, 1993; Lustman, 1988). Symptom overlap may explain why anxiety in diabetes tends to be underdetected by nonpsychiatric physicians (Lustman & Harper, 1987). To increase the accuracy of anxiety detection and diagnosis in endocrine patients, Jacobson (1996) suggests that clinicians assess only emotional and behavioral symptoms such as persistent fears, worries, and obsessions or compulsions, disregarding "physiological" symptoms such as palpitations, tremor, and perspiration. Assessing psychiatric symptoms during episodes of relative metabolic control can also help differentiate metabolic from psychiatric symptoms. Additional organic rule-outs include hyperthyroidism and pheochromocytoma.

In terms of anxiety assessment instruments, the strongest validity is generally possessed by measures developed specifically for diabetes samples. The Well-Being Questionnaire mentioned above (Bradley, 1994) contains an anxiety subscale based on the well-known Zung (1974) instrument. The Fear of Hypoglycemia Scale (Cox, Irvine, Gonder-Frederick, Nowacek, & Butterfield, 1987) measures a variety of fear and avoidance behavior not covered by other existing instruments. Finally, the Diabetes Quality of Life (DQOL) Questionnaire (DCCT Research Group, 1988), is psychometrically sound and has subscales differentiating between general and diabetes-related worry.

As noted above, psychotherapeutic interventions for diabetes patients have not been systematically researched. However, a handful of treatment studies consider anxiety variables as secondary endpoints and provide some indirect information. For example, fear of hypoglycemia was found to be unimproved following blood glucose awareness training, an intervention designed to increase patients' abilities to detect the interoceptive signs of abnormal BG (Cox, Gonder-Frederick, Julian, Cryer, Lee, Richards, & Clarke, 1991). State-trait anxiety scale scores are often collected in studies of relaxation training applied to diabetes patients not specifically selected for the presence of anxiety. These studies are reviewed more thoroughly below (see following section). Not surprisingly, results generally indicate reduced state anxiety scores following relaxation training (Lane, McCaskill, Ross, Feinglos, & Surwit, 1993; Aikens, Kiolbasa, & Sobel, 1998; Jablon, Naliboff, Gilmore & Rosenthal, 1997). Some commentary is in order regarding relaxation training, which is frequently combined with other psychotherapeutic procedures when treating anxiety disorders in general populations. Relaxation training has been occasionally reported to produce concerning degrees of hypoglycemia in diabetes patients with well-controlled illness at baseline, indicating the need for close medical collaboration. Furthermore, all of the reported studies involving relaxation training for diabetes patients recruited only general (non-psychiatric) samples, i.e., patients who do not necessarily suffer from a clinically-significant anxiety disorder; generalization to those with clinically significant anxiety disorders has not yet been demonstrated.

Given this knowledge gap, Rubin and Peyrot (1992) suggest that clinicians choose interventions with demonstrated efficacy in general psychiatric and community populations or preferably, in comparable medical patient samples. Well-validated CBT interventions for specific anxiety disorders in general populations are detailed elsewhere, i.e., for panic disorder and agoraphobia (Craske & Barlow, 1993), obsessive compulsive disorder (Riggs & Foa, 1993), social phobia (Hope and Heimberg, 1993), and GAD (Brown, O'Leary, & Barlow, 1993). Since all of these interventions directly teach specific coping skills and aim to alter maintaining factors rather than distal etiologies, it seems reasonable to suspect that they might be beneficial even if ongoing metabolic abnormalities are contributory. Standard CBT for anxiety typically involves the collaborative examination of the validity of problematic cognitions, primarily through retrospective examination of relevant evidence, further discussion of the implications of beliefs, and behavioral experiments. In addition to cognitive mediation, it may also be important to target learned avoidance behavior (e.g., hypoglycemia fear) and its relationship to conditioning history. Patients may have had actual or vicarious exposure to anxiety-provoking diabetes-related morbidity and mortality via parents, siblings, or other relatives, and they frequently acquire avoidance responses that function to reduce further anxiety exposure. It is possible that such problems could be effectively reduced to modified exposure and response prevention procedures.

Pharmacological anxiety treatment in endocrine patients is relatively unexplored, and these therapies are not without risks. Lustman et al. (1995) reported that alprazolam generally improves glucose regulation, with benefits apparently independent of baseline anxiety level, regimen compliance, regimen changes, and weight alteration. Beta-blockers for physiological anxiety symptom management should be used cautiously with diabetes patients, because they might mask hypoglycemia symptoms (Jacobson, 1996). Potential problems with antidepressant agents are reviewed above (see Depression, above).

Physiological Effects of Stress

Psychological stress is distinguished from clinical anxiety disorder in several ways, but perhaps most obviously by virtue of its ubiquitous, less dramatic nature. Presumably, most clinically anxious patients are also chronically stressed, while the majority of stressed individuals are free of significant anxiety disorder. It has often been suggested that stressful events can affect diabetes; in one study, 84% of IDDM patients reported that stress affects their glucose (Cox, Taylor, Nowacek, Holley-Wilcox, and Guthrow 1984). One logical possibility, that stressful events disrupt diabetes control by interfering with regimen adherence, has not been widely supported (Cox et al., 1984; Aikens, Wallander, Bell, & Cole, 1992). A second possibility is that stress-related neurohormonal activity directly increases BG, since sympathetic nervous system activity functions to mobilize energy resources by inhibiting insulin production, blocking insulin action, and stimulating hepatic glucose release (Surwit, Schneider, & Feinglos, 1992).

Experimental stress exposure studies have yielded inconsistent BG effects in both IDDM and NIDDM, although BG effects appear stable within individuals with IDDM (see Cox & Gonder-Frederick, 1992; Surwit et al., 1992). Poor IDDM control is associated with increases in major life events stress (Grant, Kyle, Teichman, & Mendels, 1974) and minor everyday stress (Aikens, Wallander, Bell, & McNorton, 1994); similar associations with minor stress also exist in NIDDM patients (Aikens, & Mayes, 1997; Aikens, Aikens, Wallander, & Hunt, 1997). While it is not altogether clear whether stress increases BG, stress is undoubtedly produced by the abstract threat, lifestyle modifications, and frequently severe complications of diabetes.

Clinical assessment of stress as a factor in diabetes control ought to consider the likelihood that patient perceptions of their stress-BG correlation are not associated with their actual stress-BG correlation (Aikens et al., 1994). Thus, self-monitoring of daily life stress and BG levels is highly recommendable. The Daily Hassles and Uplifts Scale (Kanner, Coyne, Schaefer, & Lazarus, 1981) has been used in some diabetes research, and it has been adapted specifically for the measurement of diabetes-specific hassles (the Diabetes Hassles Scale; Gonder-Frederick, Cox, & Clark, 1986). Another useful measure is the Daily Stress Inventory (Brantley, Dietz, McKnight, Jones, & Tullery, 1988), which has been shown to covary with excreted stress hormone metabolites. While it is not always clinically feasible, a consecutive series of daily observations of both variables can be plotted with respect to time, and also subjected to single-case time series statistical analysis to yield a correlation coefficient indicating the strength and direction of stress-BG correspondence. Among adult females with IDDM who monitored hassles and glucose in this manner for 30 days, one-third showed statistically significant stress-BG associations (Aikens et al., 1994).

Behavioral stress reduction studies in diabetes have also shown mixed results. Some show improvements following biofeedback-assisted progressive muscle relaxation training, while others show no change or inconsistent responses (see prior reviews by Cox & Gonder-Frederick, 1992; Surwit et al., 1992). While it is currently unclear whether relaxation training is generally efficacious, it possibly benefits NIDDM patients who have high baseline BG (Lammers, Naliboff, & Straatmeyer, 1984) or daily stress (Bradley, Moses, Gamsu, Knight, & Ward, 1985). Contradictory findings have also been reported regarding the role of baseline anxiety symptoms in predicting treatment response (Aikens, Kiolbasa, & Sobel, 1997; Lane, McCaskill, Ross, Feinglos, & Surwit, 1993). In practice, a variety of types of relaxation training can usually be expected to produce at least some psychological benefits in most distressed medical patients who are free of clear counterindications such as uncontrolled dissociation, psychosis, or severe depression.

Eating Disorders and Obesity

The combined effects of eating disorders and endocrinology raise great concern in IDDM, given the dangerous impact of disordered eating behavior on metabolic control. In IDDM females (aged 13–45), Birk and Spencer (1989) estimated the respective prevalences of anorexia nervosa and bulimia at 1% and 10%, compared to .5% and 1% in the general population (Fairburn & Beglin, 1990; Whitaker, Johnson, Staffer, et al., 1990; American Psychiatric Association, 1994). Marcus and Wing (1990) found that 62% of eating-disordered IDDM females manipulate insulin dosing to promote weight loss, 75% are in poor metabolic control, and 48% have major IDDM complications. For 90%, the eating disorder developed after IDDM onset. Partial or complete insulin omission for weight loss purposes can produce hyperglycemia with diabetic ketoacidosis (DKA), and restricted food intake with unadjusted insulin administration can produce severe hypoglycemia. In diabetes, hypoglycemia is more likely in anorexia nervosa, whereas chronic hyperglycemia, recurrent DKA, and elevated HbA1c are more typical in bulimia nervosa (Rodin & Danemen, 1992).

Etiologically, numerous properties of IDDM may lower the threshold for eating disorder development in predisposed individuals (Rodin & Daneman, 1992). These include impaired awareness of hunger/satiety cues due to regimen-based dietary restraint or diabetes-related neuropathy, body dissatisfaction related to insulin-induced weight gain, and the availability of insulin manipulation to cause rapid weight loss. Life stress increases disordered eating in IDDM patients with poor eating inhibition (Balfour, White, Schiffrin, Dougherty & Dufresne, 1993). Additional hypothesized factors which are not yet empirically supported include food preoccupation promoted by the diabetes regimen, ongoing metabolic abnormalities, and altered family dynamics (Rodin & Daneman, 1992).

Special consideration should be given to the phenomenon of obesity in NIDDM. Although obesity is not classified as an eating disorder in the DSM-IV (APA, 1994), it is a major risk factor for NIDDM development and also for progression to chronic complications or related comorbid conditions after NIDDM diagnosis. NIDDM prevalence is tripled in people over 40% of recommended body weight (ADA, 1996), and 80% of NIDDM patients are obese (Robbins & Kumar, 1987). Yet, 20% are nonobese, and many obese people do not develop NIDDM, indicating that multiple factors (e.g., genetic predisposition, environment) probably underlie this association. Behavioral treatment of obesity and related issues are covered above (see Medical Regimen Adherence and Self Care Behavior).

Assessing eating disorders in diabetes is particularly challenging, due to content overlap between the diabetes diet and typical disordered eating patterns. The Eating Attitudes Test (Garner, Olmsted, Bohr, & Garfinkel, 1982) is widely used to detect eating disorders in general populations, but has not yet been modified for diabetes application (Rodin & Daneman, 1992). Rodin and Danemen (1992) suggest screening for the following factors: refractory metabolic control (see also Fairburn, Peveler, Davies, Mann & Mayou, 1991), binge-eating, weight preoccupation, insulin purging, laxative or diuretic abuse, and self-induced vomiting. The adoption of standard eating disorder criteria may be overly conservative, because even subclinical eating disorders can significantly alter diabetes control (Rubin & Peyrot, 1992). Finally, every existing validated comprehensive scale measuring regimen adherence (see above, Medical regimen adherence and self care behavior) also contains a subscale tapping various aspects of self-reported eating behavior, for example, the seven diet items on the Diabetes Self-Care Scale (Hurley, 1990), the Eating Restraint Failure scale from the Diabetes Health Profile; (Meadows & Wise, 1992), and the Food Regulation scale from the Self-Care Inventory (LaGreca et al., 1990). The most thoroughly-researched measure is the Summary of Self-Care Activities (Toobert & Glasgow, 1993), which has a diet subscale.

There is little research directly assessing the efficacy of eating disorders treatment in diabetes samples. However, Rodin and Daneman (1992) recommend that CBT intervention for eating-disordered IDDM patients include self-monitoring (weight, insulin, food, and BG readings), dietary planning, discussion of the relationship between disordered eating behavior and diabetes, and cognitive restructuring. Treatment should focus on the modification of extreme beliefs regarding body weight and shape, as well as of dysfunctional attitudes concerning diabetes management. Alternative coping strategies, such as relaxation techniques, programmed mild aerobic exercise, and social support may be appropriate adjuncts for patients that eat in response to distress (Balfour et al., 1993). Family members could also be taught about the numerous biological and psychological factors maintaining problem eating behavior, including an overreliance upon food as the center of family rituals, the use of food to communicate positive feelings and/or exert interpersonal control, and other problematic family communication patterns thought to support disordered eating (Jacobson, 1996; Rodin & Daneman, 1992). Regarding medical management, Rodin and Daneman (1992) warn that overly rigid regimen plans may exacerbate binge eating in predisposed diabetes patients. Hospitalization is probably indicated for severe weight loss, severe hyperglycemia, or electrolyte abnormalities.

Cognitive Impairment

Numerous endocrine abnormalities can lead to impaired cognitive functioning, and diabetes is no exception because acute and chronic BG abnormalities can disrupt cognition (Lezak, 1995; Goldman, 1993; Pohl et al., 1984). Experimentally induced hypoglycemia affects visual processing speed (Holmes, Koepke, & Thompson, 1986), visual tracking, visual-motor speed, concentration, and planning ability (Hoffman et al., 1989) independent of diabetes duration and metabolic control. In contrast, acute hyperglycemia is not clearly associated with cognitive impairment (Lezak, 1995; Richardson, 1990). Although strict regimen adherence over the 7-year DCCT intensive IDDM treatment study was unassociated with neuropsychological performance outcomes (DCCT, 1996), a good deal of evidence indicates that chronic hyperglycemia and frequent severe hypoglycemic episodes are associated with cognitive deficits (Ryan, 1994), with differential effects by diabetes type. Generally, IDDM patients are more likely to exhibit deficits in attention and psychomotor efficiency, with severe global deficits more probable if IDDM onset occurred prior to age five (Ryan, 1988). NIDDM patients are more likely to have learning and memory impairments associated with chronically poor glycemic control (Perlmuter, Hokum, Hodgson-Harrington, et al., 1984). The mechanism underlying neuropsychological deficits seems to be diffuse CNS pathology secondary to chronic metabolic abnormalities, as well as cerebrovascular disease (Lezak, 1995).

Cognitive assessment of endocrine patients should be performed by a psychologist skilled in evaluating functional impairments associated with underlying brain pathology. While standard neuropsychological batteries have been widely used in diabetes (Ryan, 1994; Lezak, 1995; Richardson, 1990), the potential effects of diabetes symptoms and complications should be carefully considered when interpreting performance. For example, numbness and pain related to peripheral neuropathy may slow motor speed, while retinopathy can obviously interfere with visual task performance. If possible, factors potentially interfering with valid assessment should be minimized prior to evaluation. The presence of cerebrovascular disease (and the possibility that a stroke may also be affecting cognition) should also be assessed prior to evaluation. Adequate eating and medication administration (i.e., per regimen) should be ensured during prolonged testing sessions, since impaired mental efficiency and other disruptions can occur with acute hypoglycemia (Hoffman et al., 1989; Richardson, 1990). For the same reasons, patient BG self-monitoring should ideally be conducted before and periodically throughout the evaluation, to establish BG range during testing.

Summary and Closing

Considering the reviewed data collectively, it is not surprising to find that the empirical status of assessment in adults with diabetes is far more solid than that of intervention. Those desiring further detail on psychological assessment in diabetes are directed to Bradley's (1994) comprehensive volume on the topic. Regarding intervention, one experiences the impression of an incomplete picture, with considerable research needed to fill in the numerous gaps. For some clinical problems, the only intervention recommendations that can be made are based upon untested extrapolations of general findings from nonmedical samples. As in other health psychology intervention research, almost all of the research focuses on the behavioral and cognitive-behavioral therapies. Although it has been reliably shown that stress management training reduces self-reported stress levels, it remains to be clearly determined whether the intervention improves metabolic functioning or not. Anxiety and eating disorders are relatively the most underresearched areas, with the most ambiguity with respect to recommended assessment and intervention procedures. The most relative progress has occurred in the area of regimen adherence, to the degree that we could only summarize a representative sample. Moreover, the existing data on CBT for depression are quite promising, but replication is needed, as well as direct comparisons to pharmacologic agents and other nonpharmacologic antidepressant therapies that are empirically-supported in general populations (e.g., problem-solving therapy, interpersonal therapy). Although there is much we do not yet know (Glasgow et al, 1999), diabetes presents diverse and interesting problems which can benefit from the judicious application of existing scientific findings.

Acknowledgements

Helpful reviews of earlier versions of this manuscript were provided by Louis Philipson, M.D., Ph.D., Peter Vanable, M.A., Lance McCracken, Ph.D., Kathleen Shay Aikens, Ph.D., Neil Pliskin, Ph.D., and Ivan Torres, Ph.D.

References

Aikens, J.E. (1998). Prevalence of somatic indicators of distress in a mixed diabetes sample: Comparison to psychiatric patients and community nonpatients. *International Journal of Psychiatry in Medicine, 28,* 265–272.

Aikens, J.E., Kiolbasa, T.K., and Sobel, R.S. (1997). Psychological predictors of glycemic change with relaxation training for non-insulin dependent diabetes mellitus (NIDDM). *Psychotherapy and Psychosomatics, 66,* 302–306.

Aikens, J.E., and Mayes, R.(1997). Elevated glycosylated albumin in NIDDM is a function of recent everyday environmental stress. *Diabetes Care 20,* 1111–1113.

Aikens J.E., Wallander J.L., Bell D.S.H., and Cole J.A. (1992). Daily stress variability, learned resourcefulness, regimen adherence, and metabolic control in Type I diabetes mellitus: Evaluation of a path model. *Journal of Consulting and Clinical Psychology, 60,* 113–118.

Aikens J.E., Wallander, J.L., Bell, D.S.H., and McNorton, A. (1994). A nomothetic-idiographic analysis of daily psychological stress and blood glucose in women with type I diabetes mellitus. *Journal of Behavioral Medicine, 17,* 535–548.

Aikens, K.S., Aikens, J.E., Wallander, J.L., and Hunt, S.L.(1997). Daily activity level buffers stress—glycemia associations in older sedentary NIDDM patients. *Journal of Behavioral Medicine, 20,* 371–388

American Diabetes Association (A.D.A.; 1996). *Vital Statistics.* Alexandria: American Diabetes Association.

American Psychiatric Association (A.P.A.; 1994). *Diagnostic and Statistical Manual of Mental Disorders: Fourth Edition.* Washington D.C.: American Psychiatric Association.

Anderson, B.L. (1992). Psychological interventions for cancer patients to enhance quality of life. *Journal of Consulting and Clinical Psychology, 60,* 552–568.

Anderson, B.J. (1990). Diabetes and adaptation in family systems. In C.S. Holmes (Ed). *Neuropsychological and Behavioral Aspects of Diabetes* (pp. 85–101). NY: Springer-Verlag.

Balfour, L., White, D.R., Schiffrin, A., Dougherty, G., and Dufresne, J. (1993). Dietary disinhibition, perceived stress, and glucose control in young, type 1 diabetic women. *Health Psychology, 12,* 33–38.

Beardsley, G., and Goldstein, M.G. (1993). Psychological factors affecting physical condition: Endocrine disease literature review. *Psychosomatics, 34,* 12–19.

Beck, A.T., Rush, A.J., Shaw, B.F., and Emery, G. (1979). *Cognitive Therapy of Depression.* NY: Guilford.

Beck A.T., and Steer RA. (1987). *Manual for the Revised Beck Depression Inventory.* San Antonio, TX: Psychological Corporation.

Birk, R. and Spencer, M.L. (1989). The prevalence of anorexia nervosa, bulimia, and induced glycosuria in IDDM females. *Diabetes Education, 15,* 336–341.

Bradley, C. (1994). *Handbook of psychology and diabetes: A guide to measurement in diabetes research and practice.* Chur, Switzerland: Harwood.

Bradley, C., Moses, J.L., Gamsu, D.S., Knight, G., and Ward, J.D. (1985). The effects of relaxation on metabolic control of type I diabetes: A matched controlled study. *Diabetes, 34,* 17A.

Brown, T.A., O'Leary, T.A., and Barlow, D.H. (1993). Generalized anxiety disorder. In Barlow, DH (Ed.), *Clinical Handbook of Psychological Disorders.* NY: Guilford, pp. 137–187.

Cox, D., Irvine, A., Gonder-Frederick, L., Nowacek, G., and Butterfield, J. (1987). Quantifying fear of hypoglycemia: A preliminary report. *Diabetes Care, 10,* 617–621.

Cox, D.J., Taylor, A.G., Nowacek, G., Holley-Wilcox, P., Pohl, S.L. (1984). The relationship between psychological stress and insulin-dependent diabetic blood glucose control: preliminary investigations. *Health Psychology, 3,* 63–75.

Cox, D.J., and Gonder-Frederick, L. (1992). Major developments in behavioral diabetes research. *Journal of Consulting and Clinical Psychology, 60,* 628–638.

Cox D.J., Gonder-Frederick, L., Julian, D., Cryer, P., Lee, J.H., Richards, F.E., Clarke, W. (1991). Intensive versus standard blood glucose awareness training (BGAT) with insulin-dependent diabetes: mechanisms and ancillary effects. *Psychosomatic Medicine, 53,* 453–62.

Craske, M.G., and Barlow, D.H. (1993). Panic disorder and agoraphobia. In D.H. Barlow, (Ed.), *Clinical Handbook of Psychological Disorders.* NY: Guilford, pp. 1–47.

DCCT Research Group (1996). Effects of intensive diabetes therapy on neuropsychological function in adults in the Diabetes Control and Complications Trial. *Annals of Internal Medicine, 124,* 379–388.

DCCT Research Group (1993). Implications of the Diabetes Control and Complications Trial. *Diabetes Care, 16,* 1517–1520.

DCCT Research Group (1988). Reliability and validity of a diabetes quality-of-life measure for the diabetes control and complications trial (DCCT). *Diabetes Care, 11,* 725–32.

Davis, W.K., Hess, G.E., and Hiss, R.G. (1988). Psychosocial correlates of survival in diabetes. *Diabetes Care, 7,* 538–545.

Delameter, A.M., Kurtz, S.M., Bubb, J., White, N.H., Santiago, J.V. (1987). Stress and coping in relation to metabolic control of adolescents with type I diabetes. *Developmental and Behavioral Pediatrics, 8,* 136–140.

Derogatis, L.R. (1977). *The SCL-90-R Administration, Scoring and Procedures Manual I.* Baltimore: Clinical Psychometric Research.

Dunn, S.M. and Turtle, J.R. (1981). The myth of the diabetic personality. *Diabetes Care, 4,* 640–646.

Dunn, S.M., Smartt, H., Beeney, L., and Turtle, J. (1986). Measurement of emotional adjustment in diabetic patients: Validity and reliability of the ATT-39. *Diabetes Care, 9,* 480–489.

Hartwell, S., Kaplan, R., and Wallace J. (1986). Comparison of behavioral interventions for control of Type II diabetes. *Behavior Therapy 17,* 447–461.

Fairburn, C.G. and Beglin, S.J. (1990). Studies of the epidemiology of bulimia nervosa. *American Journal of Psychiatry, 147,* 401–408.

Fairburn, C.G., Peveler, R.C., Davies, B., Mann, J.I., and Mayou, R.A. (1991). Eating disorders in young adults with insulin dependent diabetes mellitus: A controlled study. *British Medical Journal, 303,* 17–20.

Garner, D.M., Olmsted, M.P., Bohr, Y., and Garfinkel, P.E. (1982). The Eating Attitudes Test: Psychometric features and clinical correlates. *Psychological Medicine, 12,* 871–878.

Glasgow, R.E., Fisher, E.B., Anderson, B.J., LaGreca, A., Marrero, D., Johnson, S.B., Rubin, R.R., and Cox, D.J. (1999). Behavioral science in diabetes. *Diabetes Care, 22,* 832–843.

Glasgow, R.E., and Toobert, D. (1988). Social environment and regimen adherence among Type II diabetic patients. *Diabetes Care, 11,* 399–412.

Gonder-Frederick, L.A., Cox, D.J., Bobbitt, S.A. and Pennebaker, J.W. (1989). Mood changes associated with blood glucose fluctuations in Insulin-dependent diabetes. *Health Psychology, 8,* 45–59.

Goodnick, P.J., Henry, J.H., and Buki, V.M.V. (1995).Treatment of depression in patients with diabetes mellitus. *Journal of Clinical Psychiatry, 56,* 128–36.

Goldman, M.B. (1992). Neuropsychiatric features of endocrine disorders. In S.C. Yudofsky and R.E. Holes (Eds). *The American Psychiatric Press Textbook of Neuropsychiatry.* Washington, D.C.: American Psychiatric Association Press.

Hartwell, S., Kaplan, R., and Wallace J. (1986). Comparison of behavioral interventions for control of Type II diabetes. *Behavior Therapy 17,* 447–461.

Hoffman, R.G., Speilman, D.J., Hinnen, D.A., Conley, K.L., Guthrie, R.A., and Knapp, R.K. (1989). Changes in cortical functioning with acute hypoglycemia and hyperglycemia in Type I diabetes. *Diabetes Care, 12,* 193–197.

Holmes, C.S., Koepke, K.M., and Thompson, R.G. (1986) Simple versus complex performance at three blood glucose levels. *Psychoneuroendocrinology, 11,* 353–357.

Hope, D.A., and Heimberg, R.G. (1993). Social phobia and social anxiety. In D.H. Barlow, (Ed.), *Clinical Handbook of Psychological Disorders.* NY: Guilford, pp. 99–136.

Hurley, A.C. (1990). The health belief model: Evaluation of a diabetes scale. *Diabetes Educator, 16,* 44–48.

Irvine, A.A., Cox, D., and Gonder-Frederick, L. (1992). Fear of hypoglycemia: Relationship to physical and psychological symptoms in patients with insulin-dependent diabetes mellitus. *Health Psychology, 11,* 135–138.

Jablon, S.L., Naliboff B.D., Gilmore, S.L., Rosenthal, M.J. (1997). Effects of relaxation training on glucose tolerance and diabetic control in type II diabetes. *Applied Psychophysiology & Biofeedback, 22,* 155–69.

Jacobson, A.M. (1996). The psychological care of patients with insulin-dependent diabetes mellitus. *New England Journal of Medicine, 334,* 1249–1253.

LaGreca, A.M., Follansbee, D., and Skyler, J.S. (1990). Developmental and behavioral aspects of diabetes management in youngsters. *Children's Health Care, 19,* 132–139.

Lammers, C.A., Naliboff, B.D., and Straatmeyer, A.J. (1984). The effects of progressive muscle relaxation on stress and diabetic control. *Behavior Research and Therapy, 22,* 641–650.

Lane, J.D., McCaskill, C.C., Ross, S.L., Feinglos, M.N., and Surwit, R.S. (1993). Relaxation training for NIDDM: Predicting who may benefit. *Diabetes Care, 16,* 1087–1094.

Lezak, M.D. (1995). *Neuropsychological assessment: Third edition.* NY: Oxford University Press, Inc.

Lustman, P.J., Griffith, L.S., Gavard, J.A., and Clouse, R.E. (1991). Depression in adults with diabetes. *Diabetes Care 15,* 1631–1667.

Lustman, P.J., Frank, B.L., and McGill, J.B. (1988). Relationship of personality characteristics to glucose regulation in adults with diabetes. *Psychosomatic Medicine, 53,* 305–312.

Lustman, P.J., Griffith, L.S., Clouse, R.E., and Cryer, P.E. (1986). Psychiatric illness in diabetes mellitus: Relationship to symptoms and illness control. *The Journal of Nervous and Mental Disease, 174,* 736–742.

Lustman, P.J. (1988). Anxiety disorders in adults with diabetes mellitus. *Psychiatric Clinics of North America, 11,* 419–432.

Lustman P.J., Griffith, L.S., Freedland, K.E., Kissel, S.S., and Clouse R.E. (1998). Cognitive behavior therapy for depression in type 2 diabetes mellitus. A randomized, controlled trial. *Annals of Internal Medicine, 129,* 613–621.

Lustman, P.J., Griffith, L.S., Clouse, R.E., Freedland, K.E., Eisen, S.A., Rubin, E.H., Carney, R.M., and McGill, J.B. (1995). Effects of alprazolam on glucose regulation in diabetes. *Diabetes Care, 18,* 1133–1139.

Lustman, P.J. and Harper, G.W. (1987). Nonpsychiatric physicians' identification and treatment of depression in patients with diabetes. *Comprehensive Psychiatry, 28,* 22–27.

Masters, J.C., Burish, T.G., Hollon, S.D., Rimm, D.C. (1987). *Behavior Therapy: Techniques and Empirical Findings* (3rd ed.). San Diego, CA: Harcourt Brace Jovanovich, Publishers.

Marcus, M.D. and Wing, R.R. (1990). Eating disorders and diabetes. In CS Holmes (Ed). *Neuropsychological and Behavioral Aspects of Diabetes.* NY: Springer-Verlag.

Meadows, K.A., Thompson, C., Brown, K., Sensky, T., and Wise, P.H. (1991). The development of the Diabetes Interview Schedule (DIS) for the identification of psychosocial problems in IDDM patients. *Diabetes 40 (suppl. 1),* 539A.

Meadows, K.A., and Wise, P.H. (1992). A national profile of knowledge and psychosocial status in 2239 Type 1 diabetic patients. *Diabetic Medicine, 9 (suppl. 1),* 48A.

Perlmuter, L.C., Hokum, M.K., Hodgson-Harrington, C., Ginsberg, J., Katz, J., Singer, D.E., and Nathan, D.M. (1984). Decreased cognitive function in aging non-insulin-dependent diabetic patients. *American Journal of Medicine, 77,* 1043–1048.

Pohl, S.L., Gonder-Frederick, L., and Cox, D.J. (1984). Area review: Diabetes mellitus. *Behavioral Medicine Update, 6,* 3–7.

Popkin, M.K., Callies, A.L., Lentz, R.D. et al. (1988). Prevalence of major depression, simple phobia, and other psychiatric disorders in patients with longstanding type I diabetes mellitus. *Archives of General Psychiatry, 45,* 64–70.

Richardson, J.T. (1990). Cognitive function in diabetes mellitus. *Neuroscience & Behavioral Reviews, 14,* 385–388.

Riggs, D.S., and Foa, E.B. (1993). Obsessive compulsive disorder. In D.H. Barlow (Ed.), *Clinical Handbook of Psychological Disorders.* NY: Guilford, pp. 189–239.

Robins, L.N., Helzer, J.E., Croughan, J., and Ratcliff, K.S. (1981). National Institute of Mental Health Diagnostic Interview Schedule: Its history, characteristics, and validity. *Archives of General Psychiatry, 38,* 381–389.

Robbins, S.L., and Kumar, V. (1987). *Basic pathology* (4th ed.). Philadelphia, PA: W.B. Saunders Company.

Ryan, C.M. (1988). Neurobehavioral disturbances associated with disorders of the pancreas. In R.E. Tarter, D.H. VanThiel, and K.L. Edwards (Eds.), *Medical Neuropsychology,* New York: Plenum Press, pages 121–152.

Ryan, C.M. (1994). Measures of cognitive function. In C. Bradley (Ed). *Handbook of Psychology and Diabetes.* Chur, Switzerland: Harwood.

Robertson, P. and Rosenvinge, J.H. (1990). Insulin-dependent diabetes mellitus: A risk factor in anorexia nervosa or bulimia nervosa? An empirical study of 116 women. *Journal of Psychosomatic Research, 34,* 535–541.

Rodin, G.M. and Daneman, D. (1992). Eating disorders and IDDM: A problematic association. *Diabetes Care, 15,* 1402–1412.

Rubin, R.R., and Peyrot, M. (1992). Psychosocial problems and interventions in diabetes: A review of the literature. *Diabetes Care, 15,* 1640–1657.

Sarafino, E.P. (1994). *Health Psychology: Biopsychosocial Interactions* (2nd ed.). New York: John Wiley & Sons, Inc.

Slaby, A., Tancredi, L., and Lieb, J. (1981). *Endocrine Disorders. Clinical Psychiatric Medicine.* New York: Harper and Row.

Surwit, R.S. and Feinglos, M.N. (1983). The effects of relaxation on glucose tolerance in non-insulin-dependent diabetes. *Diabetes Care, 6,* 176–179.

Surwit, R.S., Feinglos, M.N., and Scovern, A.W. (1983). Diabetes and behavior: A paradigm for health psychology. *American Psychologist, 38,* 255–262.

Toobert, D.J., and Glasgow, R.E. (1994). Assessing diabetes self-management: The summary of diabetes self care activities questionnaire. In C. Bradley (Ed). *Handbook of Psychology and Diabetes.* Chur, Switzerland: Harwood, 351–375.

Turkat, I.D. (1982). Glycosylated hemoglobin levels in anxious and nonanxious diabetic patients. *Psychosomatics, 23,* 1056–1058.

Whitaker, A., Johnson, J., Staffer, D., Rapoport, J.L., Kalikow, K., Walsh, B.T., Davies, M., Braiman, S., and Dolinsky, A. (1990). Uncommon troubles in young people: Prevalence estimates of selected psychiatric disorders in a nonreferred adolescent populations. *Archives of General Psychiatry, 47,* 487–496.

Young, L.D. (1992). Psychological factors in rheumatoid arthritis. *Journal of Consulting and Clinical Psychology, 60,* 619–627.

Zung, W.W.K. (1974). The measurement of affects: Depression and anxiety. In P. Pichot and R. Olivier-Martin (eds). *Psychological Measurement in Psychopharmacology.* Basle: Karger.

Advances in Medical Psychotherapy and Psychodiagnosis
2002–2003, Volume 11, pp. 75–88

The Neuropsychology of Major Organ Dysfunction[1]

Robert Ruchinskas, Psy.D.
Temple University School of Medicine
Dept. of PM&R
Temple University Hospital
Philadelphia, PA 19140

Abstract

Practicing clinicians will encounter a patient with heart, lung, kidney, or liver disease more frequently than an individual with a neurologic condition. Still, when compared to neurologic diseases, our knowledge of the effects of acute and chronic major organ failure on cognition is limited. This paper will provide a brief overview of the cognitive sequelae of acute and long-term lung, heart, kidney, and liver disease. In addition, the limited research regarding secondary effects on cognition (disease synergies, medications, and depression) will be explored. While a nascent area of research, the literature suggests that medical diseases can pose significant challenges to cognitive capacity.

Introduction

As we begin the new century, neuropsychology has made great strides in recognizing and detailing the cognitive difficulties associated with numerous neurologic conditions. The prior conceptualizations of either Alzheimer's or vascular dementia have been refined to include entities such as Fronto-Temporal Dementia, Dementia with Lewy Bodies, and Semantic Dementia, among others. Diseases such as multiple sclerosis, originally regarded as producing few cognitive sequelae, have been found to entail high rates of neuropsychological abnormalities (Rao, Leo, Bernardin, & Unverzagt, 1991). Similarly, the ravages of certain autoimmune and infectious disorders on neurocognitive abilities are well documented, with burgeoning explorations of conditions such as AIDS related dementias, Lupus, and Herpes encephalitis. While alcohol-related cognitive decline is well recognized, research regarding other toxic dementias has also grown tremendously (Hartman, 1995).

Paralleling these lines of inquiries, theories have arisen regarding how neurological diseases can individually and collectively produce cognitive symptoms. Particularly, the concept of "brain reserve

---

1. Portions of this paper were presented at the 18th Annual conference of the National Academy of Neuropsychology, November 5, 1999, Washington, D.C.

I gratefully acknowledge John J. Nicholas, M.D. and the anonymous reviewers for their comments on a draft version of this article.

capacity" (Satz, 1993) has often been utilized as a framework to explain cognitive decline after neurological insult. Briefly, the theory suggests that a greater neuronal/cognitive reserve protect against the onset of cognitive decline, whereas less brain reserve capacity leaves one at risk for such symptoms. In addition, brain reserve capacity can be challenged by an aggregation of lesions or by the progression of a disease.

Unfortunately, both the volume of research and the theoretical framework concerning the neuropsychological effects of major organ dysfunction has lagged compared to more neurologically based disorders. A recent edition of *Neuropsychology Abstracts*[2] cited seventy-one abstracts on the subject of Alzheimer's Disease, one hundred seven regarding other dementias, and sixty-nine abstracts on traumatic brain injury. Regrettably, there were only four citations in this issue regarding the neuropsychology of medical conditions. Thus while less represented in the research literature, studies do exist regarding the effect of medical conditions on cognition or how "brain reserve capacity" can be impacted by non-neurological factors. This paper will 1) examine the challenge that acute and chronic disease states exert on cognition and 2) consider the relationship between major organ disease and frequently encountered "secondary effects" such as depression, medications, and concurrent medical conditions.

Acute Disease States and Cognition in General

It has long been recognized that acute organ failure can cause neurologic and systemic abnormalities.[3] Symptoms of acute organ failure include difficulty in arousal, disorientation, decreased attention and concentration, and generally disordered higher cognitive functions such as reasoning and judgment. Whether termed a "delirium" or an "encephalopathy," the presenting acute mental status change is often dramatic. Increased age is associated with a greater number of medical conditions and medications to treat the illnesses. Not surprisingly, those three factors, along with malnutrition, alcohol abuse, abnormal lab results, and poor cognitive status (decreased "cognitive reserve") have been identified as risk factors for acute mental status changes (Inouye & Charpentier, 1996; Marcantonio, et al., 1994; Trzepacz, Teague, & Lipowski, 1985). While less than one percent of community dwelling individuals surveyed met criteria for delirium, the percentages for hospital inpatients rise to between 10 and 61 percent (Folstein, Bassett, Romanoski, & Nestadt, 1991). The presence of delirium in inpatients lengthened hospital stays, increased the likelihood of medical complications and mortality, and often necessitated greater post-discharge supervision and assistance (Gustafson, et al., 1988).

Although considered in the family of "reversible dementias," there is evidence that cognition may not return to baseline once the underlying medical condition has been stabilized and the delirium has resolved. For example, Fields, MacKenzie, Charlson, and Perry (1986) screened consecutive geriatric medical admissions for one month and found a 20% incidence of delirium. Forty-seven percent of the delirious patients evidenced significant improvement on the Mini Mental State Examination (MMSE) at three-month follow-up. Only twenty-six percent, however, were judged as having returned to their baseline. There is also growing evidence regarding the lack of complete cognitive recovery in numerous specific systemic conditions. Mental status changes in thyroid disease are often included in the category of "pseudodementia," but studies have consistently cast doubt on the idea of complete improvement after treatment (e.g., Clarnette & Patterson, 1993). The question of reversibility of cognitive deficits after acute major organ failure has received some attention and will be discussed in the next section.

---

2. *Neuropsychology Abstracts* (2000). *9*(1).

3. For an excellent review, see the entire issue of *Neurologic Clinics of North America, 7*(3) from August of 1989 that is devoted to "Neurologic Manifestations of Systemic Disease."

Major Organ Systems

Acute Pulmonary Dysfunction

The resting brain consumes approximately 20% of the total available oxygen of the body. Areas of the brain particularly vulnerable to hypoxia/anoxia (terms used to describe a reduction in versus a complete lack of oxygen) are the basal ganglia and hippocampal formation. Depriving these brain regions of oxygen for more than five minutes (e.g., cardiac arrest without CPR) produces well recognized cognitive deficits including amnesia and general intellectual deterioration (Adams, Victor, & Roper, 1998). In addition, a recent report (Hopkins, et al., 1999) focussing on neuropsychological outcome one-year post acute respiratory distress syndrome (a condition that results from trauma, sepsis, and pneumonia and requires aggressive medical interventions, e.g., ventilation) found cognitive deficits in between one-third and three-quarters of their sample. Particularly affected were measures of short-term memory and concentration. The majority of patients evidenced cognitive improvement over the next year when compared to test scores obtained at hospital discharge. Still, 30% of the sample were judged as having experienced generalized intellectual decline as compared to their presumed baseline.

Research on less dramatic forms of acute hypoxia reveals that high altitude mountain climbers demonstrate acute mental status changes along with the possibility of lingering deficits in abstract reasoning and word-finding (Kida & Imai, 1993; Petiet, Townes, Brooks, & Kramer, 1988). Sleep apnea studies have also examined the relationship of nocturnal hypoxia and neuropsychological outcome, with heavy snorers exhibiting relationships between nocturnal hypoxia and measures of intelligence, verbal fluency, and verbal and non-verbal memory (Berry, Webb, Block, Bauer, & Switzer, 1986).

Chronic Pulmonary Disease

Much of our current knowledge regarding chronic hypoxia is based on the landmark works of Grant, Heaton, McSweeney, Adams, and Tims (1982) and Prigatano, Parsons, Wright, Levin, and Hawryluk (1983). Their studies suggested cognitive dysfunction in chronic obstructive pulmonary disease (COPD) patients correlated with resting arterial partial pressure of oxygen. A later study combined both populations (Grant, et. al., 1987) and found mild cognitive abnormalities in the COPD group as a whole, with the rate of neuropsychological deficit rising with the worsening of hypoxemia. Deficits in abstract reasoning, memory, and perceptual motor speed were most notable. Consistent with this research, studies have shown the beneficial effect on cognition of continuous oxygen therapy treatment aimed at increase lung efficiency (Heaton, Grant, McSweeny, Adams, & Petty, 1983). Recovery of neuropsychological function was also reported after patients engaged in a program of pulmonary rehabilitation aimed to increase both respiratory and psychosocial functioning (Emery, Leatherman, Burker, & MacIntyre; 1991).

Given the findings of cognitive deficits associated with this disease state, the question of a "dementia syndrome of COPD" has received some attention. One report (Incalzi, et al., 1993) described a pattern of impairment in verbal fluency and memory tasks, preserved visual attention, and diffuse worsening of other cognitive functions in almost half of their COPD patients. The authors believed that this unique pattern of cognitive decline was distinct from both their control group and pool of subjects with dementia. Other studies, while finding cognitive deficiencies, have failed to find a similar pattern of deficits. For example, mild global cognitive deficits in COPD sufferers which related to pressure of arterial oxygen and the degree of pulmonary impairment was described by Fix, Golden, Daughten, Kass, and Bell (1982). Stuss, Peterkin, Guzman, Guzman, and Troyer (1997) found deficiencies in verbal memory in COPD patients (along with more globally based attentional difficulties) which they ascribe to disrupted limbic systems. Another work (Ruchinskas, et al., 2000) found that end-stage lung disease patients were at risk for short-term verbal memory deficits, with almost half of the sample of lung transplant candidates showing deficits (more often severe than mild) in verbal memory. Still, the majority of the patients in the above noted studies did not evidence either a pattern or severity of cognitive decline consistent with a dementing syndrome.

In summary, both acute and chronic pulmonary system dysfunction is associated with the potential for cognitive deficiencies. While deficits are usually diffuse and global in nature, early symptoms can include subtle memory deficits that would go unnoticed on cursory examination. Finally, profound cognitive decline is only seen in a minority of individuals, perhaps secondary to the beneficial effects of treatments such as continuos oxygen therapy that appear to stabilize or improve mental status in many patients.

Acute Cardiac Disease

The cardiac and pulmonary systems work in tandem to maintain appropriate blood perfusion (and appropriate oxygenation) to the brain that is essential for maximal cognitive efficiency. As previously discussed, acute disruptions in cerebral perfusion (as in cardiac arrest without CPR), depending on the severity and length of decreased perfusion, can result in cognitive sequelae. Animal models have shown that chronic cerebrovascular insufficiency produces deficits consistent with dementia in rats (De La Torre, et al., 1992). The hippocampal formation, as in pulmonary disease, was particularly influenced by both acutely and chronically impaired cardiac functioning.

Chronic Cardiac Disease

In humans, reduced cardiac output has been related to decreased cognitive functioning. In advanced cardiac disease, LaMarche and Boll (1995) found extensive, global neuropsychological deficits in a group of heart transplant candidates. Particularly vulnerable were memory, information processing, and abstract reasoning skills. Deshields, McDonough, Mannen, and Miller (1996) found that impaired pre-transplant memory skills improved post-transplant in the majority of their patients.

The literature on less advanced forms of coronary disease is mixed. For example one report suggested that patients with chronic cerebrovascular disease who were pre-coronary artery bypass graft (CABG) surgery patients were impaired compared to controls on measures of attention/concentration and verbal memory (Townes, et al., 1989). In this study, the majority of patients evidenced no residual impairment or improved on post-surgery testing. Eleven percent of the patients, however, showed a decline on half of the neuropsychological variables at seven-month follow-up, with increased age being a significant predictor of poorer outcome. It has been contended that, if followed over a longer period of time (i.e., three years post-intervention of CABG, medication, or carotid endarterectomy), patients display stabilized cognition and normal regional cerebral blood flow (Meyer, et al., 1990). Tatemichi, Desmond, Phohovnik, and Eidelberg (1995) also demonstrated that a dementia secondary to bilateral internal carotid and unilateral vertebral artery occlusions was dramatically reversed (although perhaps not back to baseline) in one patient following successful surgery. Unfortunately, performing surgery on occluded arteries entails some risk, with approximately six percent of patients having a stroke after a procedure (Dashe, Pessin, Murphy, & Payne, 1997). One further study examined 37 patients with asymptomatic atrial fibrillation (AFIB) versus age, education, and hypertension matched controls (Farina, et al., 1997). The group with AFIB performed significantly poorer on tasks of attention, verbal memory, and long-term memory. The authors believed that such deficits arose from the effects of microembolization or diffuse hypoxic damage secondary to hypoperfusion.

Thus, cardiac disease can have a direct effect on cognitive functioning. There is no general pattern of neuropsychological difficulties in cardiac disease but rather diffuse global lowering of abilities. The risk for mental status abnormalities appears to increase with more advanced cardiac disease, although the effects of cardiac disorders in and of themselves versus secondary/conconimant conditions is difficult to disentangle (although will be reviewed later in this paper). As with pulmonary disease, treatment of the underlying condition appears to improve mental efficiency but is accompanied by risks (e.g., stroke after surgery). Post-cardiac surgery patients also have a higher incidence of delirium than other surgery patients (Trzepacz, Teague, & Lipowski; 1985). Similar to the research on delirium, there is evidence that some individuals may not return to baseline after treatment.

Acute Liver and Kidney Disease

Unlike the cardiopulmonary system, acute changes due to liver and kidney disease result in the classic picture of a delirium (i.e., disturbances in arousal, disorientation, decreased attention and concentration, impaired awareness, etc.). In addition, the initial changes due to portal-systemic encephalopathy may be mistaken as signs of a psychiatric condition. Symptoms of euphoria, depression, mental slowing, inappropriate affect, and behavioral and sleep disturbances may present alone or in combination. As the condition progresses, other classic symptoms appear such as increased disorientation, sleep pattern reversal, lethargy, asterixis (liver flap) and eventual stupor (Trzepacz, Brenner, & Van Thiel, 1989). Symptoms of renal failure include decreased arousal and attention, memory deficits, and poor perceptual-motor coordination along with mood and personality changes. As with other medical conditions, there is a question of return to baseline mental status after normalization on blood chemistries (Hart & Kreutzer, 1988).

Chronic Liver Disease

The most common form of liver disease is cirrhosis. As alcohol is the primary cause of cirrhosis, the initial neuropsychological research was confounded by both the potential direct effects of alcohol abuse/dependence and its indirect consequences on major organ systems. Over time, a body of literature has investigated non-alcoholic cirrhotic disease and consistently found cognitive functions impaired. Neuropsychological tests sensitive to attention/concentration and global cognitive status (e.g. Trails B) appear particularly useful as they correlate with measures of hepatic function and have been shown to detect pre-clinical signs of encephalopathy (Tarter, Van Thiel, & Edwards, 1988).

Interestingly, the basal ganglia have been implicated as being especially vulnerable in chronic liver disease. One study (O'Carrol et al., 1991) matched 10 non-alcoholic cirrhotic patients versus age matched controls. Besides the expected significant group differences on neuropsychological testing, an interesting pattern emerged on functional neuroimaging. Single Positron Emission Computed Tomography (SPECT) studies yielded group differences bilaterally in the basal ganglia, along with increased uptake in the right occipital regions and decreased uptake in the right anterior cingulate region. Skehan, Norris, Hegarty, Owens, and MacErlaine (1997) also reported abnormally high signal on magnetic resonance imaging (MRI) of the basal ganglia of patients with chronic liver disease. Even patients who were not yet cirrhotic were affected and these abnormalities reversed after liver transplantation. MRI spectroscopy studies have suggested that such changes were not correlated with metabolite ratios, only with blood ammonia levels (Taylor-Robinson, Oatridge, et al., 1995; Taylor-Robinson, Sargentoni, et al., 1996). Still, the basal ganglia's particular susceptibility to the effects of this disease is still not fully understood.

Chronic Renal Disease

Regarding the effects of long-term dialysis, the literature as a whole is not conclusive. Studies have shown both improvement and worsening of cognitive functioning secondary to dialysis (Fazekas, et al., 1996; Hart & Kreutzer, 1988). As with other conditions, the chronicity and severity of disease and the presence or absence of conconimant medical conditions may play a part in the lack of consensus. In addition, uremic status can quickly fluctuate in this population, which can greatly affect neuropsychological test results. In summary, while there appears to be a trend toward poorer performance in dialyzed patients, a progressive dementia is not present in most individuals.

Systemic Diseases and the Interaction With Organ Systems

Hypertension and Diabetes

While major organ disease can contribute to cognitive dysfunction, there is evidence of greater risk when comorbid diseases interact. For example, the Framingham Heart Study found the chances of developing heart failure in hypertensive compared to normotensive subjects about two-fold in men and three-fold in women (Levy, Larson, Vasan, Kannel, & Ho, 1996). Hypertension has been one of the most researched medical conditions through such large-scale longitudinal projects. Such studies have shown that positive relationships exist between blood pressure variables and cardiovascular disease. Relationships are also present between increased blood pressure and decreased cognitive abilities over time. Besides the Framingham studies, these results have also found in other longitudinal research (e.g., Guo, Fratiglioni, Winblad, & Viitanen, 1997) and cross-sectional studies (e.g., Freidl, Schmidt, Stronegger, & Reinhart, 1997). For example, the Honolulu-Asia Study also found the risk for poor cognitive functioning increased progressively as mid-life systolic blood pressure increased. When adjusted for stroke and heart disease, the relationship was weaker, but still significant (Launer, Masaki, Petrovitch, Foley, & Havlik, 1995). Hypertension approximately doubles the risk for intracerebral hemorrhage, with hypertensives under age 55, those who had stopped taking their blood pressure medication and those who also smoked cigarettes (Thrift, McNeil, Forbes, & Donnan, 1998) being more vulnerable.

The interaction of age and hypertension is also noteworthy. Young adults with hypertension generally perform worse than controls on cognitive tasks while middle-age hypertensives are similar to controls (e.g., Madden & Blumenthal, 1998; Waldstein, et al., 1996). Besides methodological limitations influencing the results, the possibility of differential effects of hypertension on the young (either a more severe type of hypertension or a distinct clinical entity from middle-age/elderly hypertension) was proposed for further study. Elderly adults also perform worse than normals, yet the old-old (>80) can perform similar or better than controls (e.g, Jensen, et al., 1997). Adequate control of blood pressure via medications may be an important factor in the results. Blood pressure control via antihypertensive medications, overall, appears to retard rather than promote cognitive decline (Elias, 1998; Starr, Whalley, & Deary, 1996; Farmer, et al., 1990; Goldstein, et al., 1990).

Also of note is a possible genetic predisposition to cognitive decline. Some evidence exists of subtle deficits on neuropsychological tests with offspring of hypertensives performing worse than offspring of normotensives (e.g., Waldstein, et al., 1994). For example, Thyrum, Blumenthal, Madden, and Siegel (1995) found poorer performance in offspring on tests of reaction time, digit span, and Trails B, while verbal and figural memory tests were equal to controls from non-hypertensive families.

Furthermore, brain morphological changes occur in some hypertensives and may explain cognitive decline. Hypertensives appear to be at higher risk for developing multifocal, hypointense lesions of the subcortical white matter than controls (Chan, Kartha, Yoon, Desmond, & Hilal, 1996). The presence of white matter lesions significantly increases the risk for dementia in elderly patients (Skoog, Palmertz, & Andresson, 1996). Functional neuroimaging (e.g., PET) has shown decreased brain blood glucose metabolism between hypertensives and normals (Jennings, et al., 1998; Salerno, et al., 1995). Over time, vascular dementia has been redefined to include white matter disease or multiple small vessel infarcts as a possible cause for cognitive dysfunction (Libon, et al., 1997; Hachinksi, 1994).

The Framingham study also suggests a greater likelihood of poor cognitive performance if hypertensives also have Type II diabetes (Elias, D'Agostino, Elias, & Wold, 1997; Wilson, 1997). A Finnish study (Kuusisto, et al., 1993) found hypertensives mildly impaired on neuropsychological tests compared to controls, although much of the impairment was in a subgroup of hypertensives with diabetes.

Hence, it appears that chronic high blood pressure often appears comorbid with heart disease and is a risk factor for cognitive decline. Adequately controlled blood pressure significantly reduces the risk of mental status inefficiency. Hypertension also increases the risk for adverse events (e.g., stroke) and appears to have a synergistic effect with some medical conditions (e.g., diabetes).

Medical Load and the Influences of Depression

Despite the studies noted above, the examination of possible synergistic effects between disease states is an area greatly in need of more research. In fact, many studies exclude patients with medical conditions or major organ disease. Nonetheless, while the body of literature is small, some conclusions can be drawn. One of the few large-scale studies found consistent but relatively small effects of diabetes, stroke, and depression on cognitive performance in the elderly (Zelinski, Crimmins, Reynolds, & Seeman, 1998). Still, demographic variables such as sex, race, education, and age were superior in predicting cognitive performance.

Another secondary effect to be considered is medication. With the presence of medical conditions also comes increasing numbers of medications to treat such illnesses, which raises the risk for delirium. Many single medications have cognitive side effects, with antihypertensive medications having received extensive research (with mixed results as to their possible effect on cognition). Unfortunately, the scope of this issue is too large to encompass in this paper, although numerous reviews are available (see Meador, 1998; Stein & Strickland, 1998). Regardless, the influence of prescription medications needs to be considered when making differential diagnoses.

A further well-researched aspect of chronic disease states is that of depression. There exists a higher incidence of depression in medical patients than in the general population. For example, twenty-eight percent of hip fracture patients were depressed (Billig, Ahmed, Kenmore, Amaral, & Shakhashiri, 1986) and thirty- to sixty-percent of stroke patients become clinically depressed. The concept of "pseudodementia" is well established (LaRue, 1992) and depression must be considered as a possible cause of cognitive inefficiency in medical patients.

Besides affecting cognitive efficiency, depression also decreases recovery from illness. Hodges, Lichtenberg, and Youngblade (1999) found that the presence of multiple medical conditions predicted increasing levels of depression and poorer activities of daily living. There is well-established evidence of poorer rehabilitation prognosis in patients with depressive spectrum disorders. In a large scale, community based, cross-sectional health survey in the Netherlands (Ormel, et al., 1998) found depression to have more contribution to poorer functioning than 14 of 18 medical conditions (exceptions are neurological condition/stroke, low back problems, and arthritis). Controlling for age, cognitive functioning, and pre-injury physical functioning, hip fracture patients who are not depressed are three times more likely to achieve independent walking and seven times more likely to return to their pre-injury level of physical abilities (Mossey, Knott, & Craik, 1990). Thus, a thorough evaluation of depression is essential when assessing the medical patient.

Conclusions

It can be concluded that acute organ failure produces observable cognitive changes. Marked dysfunction of the cardiopulmonary system creates an anoxic encephalopathy characterized by general cognitive decline, with short-term memory being particularly affected. Acute renal or hepatic failure presents as a classic delirium, again with global cognitive dysfunction but notable disturbances in arousal, attention and concentration, and higher order cognition. Given the severity of illness associated with major organ system failure, acute cognitive sequelae appear inevitable. Complete cognitive recovery, however, may not ensue after the underlying medical condition has been treated. There is a small but growing body of literature which suggests that delirium may not be the "reversible madness" that it was once thought to be, but in fact can leave lasting neuropsychological sequelae.

The effects of long-term organ disease are inclined to be more subtle and individualistic. Primary organ disorders tends to produce diffuse neuropsychological deficits that are, in general, related to the severity of the disease process. While the majority of individuals with chronic organ system failure produce minimally to mildly impaired neuropsychological profiles, there is a subset of patients who display striking cognitive deficits.

The concept of brain reserve capacity can be applied to explain both the lack of recovery after acute organ failure and the tendency for some individuals with chronic disease to show marked cognitive symptoms. Thus, patients with less neuronal reserve will be at greater risk for cognitive dysfunction after acute or chronic organ failure. This framework is also useful as consideration is also made of the direct effects of medical conditions on brain integrity (e.g., white matter lesions being associated with hypertension).

Still, in the context of medical patients, the brain reserve capacity theory needs expansion to include the effects of medical illness on cognition. Given the complex interdependency of the brain and major organ systems, a "medical reserve capacity" theory may be needed to truly start unraveling these dynamic interactions. Such a model would examine neuronal reserve and brain functioning as well as metabolic profiles, organ system health and efficiency, and genetic influences. In addition, secondary factors, such as age, number or type of medications, and depression have been associated with a lowering of cognition in medical patients. The conceptualization of both "mind and body" influences on cognition would also need to account for both the aggregate and interactive effects of greater than one disease state.

At present, however, this "meta-theory" (and the idea of brain reserve capacity) is a premise that is difficult to translate into everyday practice. A convenient algorithm does not currently exist to factor the effects of length and severity of organ dysfunction, medications, age, and education (to name just a few potential influences) on an individual's cognitive status. Thus, further work needs to be done in identifying premorbid risk factors (cognitive, demographic, and physical) that leave the individual vulnerable to acute and chronic neuropsychological deficits. In addition, greater research is needed to replicate and explain whether particular regions such as the hippocampus, basal ganglia, or right hemisphere are differentially affected by organ disease states. Investigations are needed to examine if sensitive neuropsychological measures can detect early symptoms of the disease based on brain vulnerability (e.g., memory difficulties in pulmonary conditions, concentration problems in hepatic disease).

Attempting this necessary examination of the influence of medical conditions is, however, a daunting task that yields a multitude of challenges. Unlike most of the volunteers for normative databases, many individuals encountered in clinical practice have more than one disease state. The average patient also may have less education than most volunteers, which raises challenges in comparing test results across samples and can potentially misclassify those with lower education as cognitively impaired (Marcopulos, McLain, & Giuliano, 1997). For example, applied studies utilizing urban geriatric rehabilitation settings finds patients often with ten or less years of education, four concurrent medical conditions and over four prescribed medications at admission (Ruchinskas, Singer, & Repetz, 2001; Lichtenberg, et al., 1994). Obviously, these are not the typical "normal controls" seen in research studies. Still, the question is raised regarding whether or not many of the individuals in most normative research studies are in fact representative of the general population. While evaluating the role of medical conditions in "normal aging" is inherently challenging, this is a crucial area of research that should be approached with the same scientific vigor as has been applied to neurological disorders.

Despite this limited research base, neuropsychological evaluation can potentially play a vital role in a patient's care. Given the sensitivity of neuropsychological tests, such data may be utilized as one measure of integrity of not only the brain but also of underlying organ systems. Subtle changes of mental status can be monitored over time to characterize disease progression/remission. In addition, the identification and reduction of possible iatrogenic effects will improve care, decrease length of stay, and possibly decrease morbibity.

In summary, the research to date has shown that the presence of acute organ dysfunction leads to cognitive deficits. Chronic illnesses can be associated with decreases in mental status, although variability among individuals is quite evident. Along with illness status and severity, numerous other demographic, baseline cognitive, metabolic, and affective data need to be considered when attempting to establish the relationship between medical conditions and mental status. To date, the formation of such an algorithm is more art than science whose balance should begin to turn as our body of knowledge increases.

References

Adams, K. & Victor, M. (1993). *Principles of neurology,* 5th Ed. New York: McGraw-Hill.

Berry, D., Webb, W., Block, A., Bauer, R, & Switzer, D. (1986). Nocturnal hypoxia and neuropsychological variables. *Journal of Clinical and Experimental Neuropsychology, 8*(3), 229–238.

Billig, N., Ahmed, S., Kenmore, P., Amaral, D., & Shakhashire, M. (1986). Assessment of depression and cognitive impairment after hip fracture. *Journal of the American Geriatric Society, 34,* 499–503.

Chan, S., Kartha, K., Yoon, S., Desmond, D, & Hilal, S. (1996). Multifocal hypointense cerebral lesions on gradient-echo MR are associated with chronic hypertension. *American Journal of Neuroradiology, 17*(10), 1821–7.

Clarnette, R. M. & Patterson, C. J. (1993). Hypothyroidism: Does treatment cure dementia? *Journal of Geriatric Psychiatry and Neurology, 6,* 23–27.

Dashe, J., Pessin, M., Murphy, R., & Payne, D. (1997). Carotid occlusive disease and stroke risk in coronary artery bypass graft surgery. *Neurology, 49,* 678–86.

De La Torre, J., Fortin, T., Park, G., Butler, K.,Kozlowski, P., Pappas, B., de Socarraz, H., Saunders, J., & Richard, M. (1992). Chronic cerebrovascular insufficiency induces dementia-like deficits in aged rats. *Brain Research, 582,* 186–95.

Deshields, T., McDonough, E., Mannen, R., & Miller, L. (1996). Psychological and cognitive status before and after heart transplantation. *General Hospital Psychiatry, 18,* 62s–69s.

Elias, M. (1998). Effects of chronic hypertension on cognitive functioning. *Geriatrics, 53*(Supplement 1), S49–52.

Elias, M., D'Agostino, R., Elias, P., & Wolf, P. (1995). Neuropsychological test performance, cognitive functioning, blood pressure, and age: the Framingham Heart Study. *Experimental Aging Research, 21*(4), 369–91.

Emery, C., Leatherman, N., Burker, E., & MacIntyre, N. (1991). Psychological outcomes of a pulmonary rehabilitation program. *Chest: the Cardiopulmonary Journal, 100*(3), 613–617.

Farina, E., Magni, E., Ambrosoni, F., Manfredini, R., Binda, A., Sina,C., & Mariani, C. (1997). Neuropsychological deficits in asymptomatic atrial fibrillation. *Acta Neurologica Scandinavia, 96,* 310–316.

Farmer, M., Kittner, S., Abbott, R., Wolz, M., Wolf, P., & White, L. (1990). Longitudinally measured blood pressure, antihypertensive medication use and cognitive performance: The Framingham Study. *Journal of Clinical Epidemiology, 43*(5), 475–80.

Fazekas, G., Fazekas, F., Schmidt, R., Flooh, E., Valetitsch, H., Kapeller, P., & Krejs, G. (1996). Pattern of cerebral blood flow and cognition in patients undergoing chronic haemodialysis treatment. *Nuclear Medicine Communications, 17*(7), 603–8.

Fields, S., MacKenzie, R., Charlson, M., & Perry, S. (1986). Reversibility of cognitive impairment in medical inpatients. *Archives of Internal Medicine, 146,* 1593–96.

Fix, A., Golden, C., Daughton, D, Kass, I., & Bell, C. (1982). Neuropsychological deficit among patients with chronic obstructive pulmonary disease. *International Journal of Neuroscience, 16*(2), 99–105.

Folstein, M., Bassett, S., Romanoski, A., & Nestadt, G. (1991). The epidemiology of delirium in the community: The Eastern Baltimore Mental Health Survey. *International Psychogeriatrics, 3*(2), 169–76.

Freidl, W., Schmidt, R., Stronegger, W., & Reinhart, B. (1997). The impact of sociodemographic, environmental, and behavioral factors, and cerebrovascular risk factors as potential predictors of the mattis dementia rating scale. *Journal of Gerontology: Series A, Biological Sciences & Medical Sciences 52*(2), M111–6.

Goldstein, G., Materson, B., Cushman, W., Reda, D., Freis, E., Ramirez, E., Talmers, F., White, T., Nunn, S., Chapman, R., Khatri, I., Schnaper, H., Thomas, J., Henderson, W., & Fye, C. (1990). Treatment of hypertension in the elderly: II. *Cognitive and behavioral function. Hypertension, 15,* 361–9.

Grant, I., Heaton, R., McSweeney, A., Adams, K., & Timms, R. (1982). Neuropsychological findings in hypoxemic chronic obstructive pulmonary disease. *Archives of Internal Medicine, 142,* 1470–1476.

Grant, I., Prigatano, G., Heaton, R., McSweeney, A., Wright, E., & Adams, K. (1987). Progressive neuropsychologic impairment and hypoxemia. *Archives of General Psychiatry, 44,* 999–1006.

Guo, Z., Fratiglioni, L., Winblad, B., & Viitanen, M. (1997). Blood pressure and performance on the Mini-Mental State Examination in the very old. Cross-sectional and longitudinal data from the Kungsholmen Project. *American Journal of Epidemiology, 145*(12), 1106–13.

Gustafson, Y., Berggren, D., Brannstrom, B., Bucht, G., Norberg, A., Hansson, L., & Winblad, B. (1988). Acute confusional states in elderly patients treated for femoral neck fracture. *Journal of the American Geriatrics Society, 36,* 525–530.

Hachinski, V. (1994). Vascular dementia: A radical redefinition. *Dementia, 5,* 130–132.

Hart, R. & Kreutzer, J. (1988). Renal System. In Tarter, Van Thiel, & Edwards (Eds.). *Medical Neuropsychology.* New York: Plenum Press.

Hartman, D. (1995). *Neuropsychological Toxicology: Identification and Assessment of Human Neurotoxic Syndromes.* New York: Plenum Press.

Heaton, R., Grant, I., McSweeney, A., Adams, K., & Petty, T. (1983). Psychologic effects of continuous and nocturnal oxygen therapy in hypoxemic chronic obstructive pulmonary disease. *Archives of Internal Medicine, 143*(10), 1941–1947.

Hodges, E., Lichtenberg, P., & Youngblade, L. (1999). The influences of medical burden, functional abilities and demographic characteristics on depression in older medical patients. *Advances in Medical Psychotherapy and Psychodiagnosis, 10,* 85–94.

Hopkins, R. O., Weaver, L. K., Pope, D., Orme, J. F., Bigler, E. D., & Larson-Lohr, V. (1999). Neuropsychological sequelae and impaired health status in survivors of severe acute respiratory distress syndrome. *American Journal of Respiratory and Critical Care Medicine, 160,* 50–56.

Incalzi, R., Gemma, A., Marra, C. Muzzolon, R., Capparella, O., & Carbonin, P. (1993). Chronic obstructive pulmonary disease: An original model of cognitive decline. *American Review of Respiratory Disease, 148,* 418–424.

Inouye, S. & Charpentier, P. (1996). Precipitating Factors for delirium in hospitalized elderly persons. *Journal of the American Medical Association, 275,* 852–7.

Jennings, J., Muldoon, M., Ryan, C., Mintun, M., Meltzer, C., Townsend, D., Sutton-Tyrell, K., Shapiro, A., & Manuck, S. (1998). Cerebral blood flow in hypertensive patients. *Hypertension, 31,* 1216–22.

Jensen, E., Dehlin, O., Hagberg, B., Samuelsson, G., Svensson, T., & Lidfeldt, J. (1997). Blood pressure in relation to medical, psychological and social variables in a population of 80-year-olds. Survival during 6 years. *Journal of Internal Medicine, 241*(3), 205–12.

Kida, M. & Imai, A. (1993). Cognitive performance and event-related brain potentials under simulated high altitudes. *Journal of Applied Psychology, 74*(4), 1735–1741.

Kuusisto, J., Koivisto, K., Mykkanen, L., Helkala, E., Vanhanen, M., Haninen, T., Pyorala, K, Riekkinen, P, & Laakso, M. (1993). Essential hypertension and cognitive function: The role of hyperinsulinemia. *Hypertension, 22,* 771–9.

LaMarche, J., & Boll, T. (1995). The neuropsychological evaluation of organ transplant patients: A review. *Advances in Medical Psychotherapy, 8,* 79–100.

La Rue, A. (1992). *Aging and neuropsychological assessment.* New York: Plenum Press.

Laurner, L., Masaki, K., Petrovitch, H., Foley, D., & Havlik, R. (1995). The association between midlife blood pressure levels and late-life cognitive function: The Honolulu-Asia study. *Journal of the American Medical Association, 274,* 1846–51.

Levy, D., Larson, M., Vasan, R., Kannel, W., & Ho, K. (1996). The progression from hypertension to congestive heart failure. *Journal of the American Medical Association, 275,* 1557–62.

Libon, D., Bogdanoff, B., Bonavita, J., Skalina, S., Cloud, B., Resh, R., Cass, P., & Ball, S. (1997). Dementia associated with periventricular and deep white matter alterations: A subtype of subcortical dementia. *Archives of Clinical Neuropsychology, 12*(3), 239–250.

Lichtenberg, P., Christensen, B., Metler, L., Nanna, M., Jones, G., Reyes, J., & Blumenthal, F. (1994). A preliminary investigation of the role of cognition and depression in predicting functional recovery in geriatric rehabilitation patients. *Advances in Medical Psychotherapy, 7,* 109–24.

Madden, D. & Blumenthal, J. (1998). Interaction of Hypertension and age in visual selective attention performance. *Health Psychology, 17*(1), 76–83.

Marcantonio, Goldman, L., Mangione, C., Ludwig, L., Muraca, B., Haslauer, C., Donaldson, M., Whittemore, A., Sugarbaker, D., Poss, R., Haas, S., Cook, E., Orav, J., & Lee, T., (1994). A clinical prediction rule for delirium after elective noncardiac surgery. *Journal of the American Medical Association, 271,* 134–9.

Marcopulos, B. A., McLain, C. A., & Giuliano, A. J. (1997). Cognitive impairment or inadequate norms? A study of healthy, rural older adults with limited education. *The Clinical Neuropsychologist, 11,* 111–131.

Meador, K. (1998). Cognitive effects of medications. *Neurologic Clinics of North America, 16*(1), 141–155.

Meyer, J., Lotfi, J., Martinez, B., Caroselli, J., Mortel, K., & Thornby, J. (1990). Effects of medical and surgical treatment on cerebral perfusion and cognition in patients with chronic cerebral ischemia. *Surgical Neurology, 34,* 301–8.

Mossey, J., Knott, K., & Craik, R. (1990). The effects of persistent depressive symptoms on hip fracture recovery. *Journal of Gerontology: Medical Sciences, 45,* M163–168.

O'Carrol, R., Hayes, P., Ebmeier, K., Dougall, N., Murray, C., Best, J., Bouchier, I., & Goodwin, G. (1991). Regional cerebral blood flow and cognitive function in patients with chronic liver disease. *Lancet, 337,* 1250–53.

Ormel, J., Kempen, G., Deeg, D., Brilman, E., Sonderen, E., & Relyveld, J. (1998). Functioning, well-being, and health perceptions in late middle-aged and older people: Comparing the effects of depressive symptoms and chronic medical conditions. *Journal of the American Geriatric Society, 46,* 39–48.

Petiet, C., Townes, B., Brooks, R., & Kramer, J. (1988). Neurobehavioral and psychological functioning of women exposed to high altitude in mountaineering. *Perceptual and Motor Skills, 67*(2), 443–452.

Prigatano, G., Parsons, O., Wright, E., Levin, D., & Hawryluk, G. (1983). Neuropsychological test performance in mildly hypoxemic patients with chronic obstructive pulmonary disease. *Journal of Clinical and Consulting Psychology, 51*(4), 108–116.

Rao, S., Leo, G., Bernardin, L., & Unverzagt, F. (1991). Cognitive dysfunction in multiple sclerosis. I. Frequency, patterns, and prediction. *Neurology, 41,* 685–691.

Ruchinskas, R. A., Broshek, D. K., Crews, W. D., Barth, J. T., Francis, J. P., & Robbins, M. K. (2000). A neuropsychological normative database for lung transplant candidates. *Journal of Clinical Psychology in Medical Settings, 7*(2), 107–112.

Ruchinskas, R., Singer, H. & Repetz, N. (2001). Cognitive status and ambulation in geriatric rehabilitation patients: Walking without thinking? *Archives of Physical Medicine and Rehabilitation, 81,* 1224–1233.

Salerno, J., Grady, C., Mentis, M., Gonzalez-Aviles, A., Wagner, E., Shapiro, M., & Rapoport, S. (1995). Brain metabolic function in older men with chronic essential hypertension. *Journal of Gerontology: Medical Sciences, 50A*(3), M147–54.

Satz, P. (1993). Brain reserve capacity on symptom onset after brain injury: A formulation and review of evidence for threshold theory. *Neuropsychology, 7*(3), 273–295.

Skehan, S.,Norris, S., Hegarty, J., Owens, A., & MacErlaine, D. (1997). Brain MRI changes in chronic liver disease. *European Neurology, 7*(6), 905–9.

Skoog, J., Palmertz, B., & Andresson, L. (1994). The prevalence of white-matter lesions on computed tomography of the brain in demented and non-demented 85 year-olds. *Journal of Geriatric Psychiatry and Neurology, 7,* 169–175.

Starr, J., Whalley, L., & Deary, I. (1996). The effects of antihypertensive treatment on cognitive function: Results from the HOPE study. *Journal of the American Geriatrics Society, 44,* 411–15.

Stein, R., & Strickland, T. (1998). A review of the neuropsychological effects of commonly used prescription medications. *Archives of Clinical Neuropsychology, 13*(3), 259–84.

Stuss, D.T., Peterkin, I., Guzman, D.A., Guzman, C., & Troyer, A. K. (1997). Chronic obstructive pulmonary disease: effects of hypoxia on neurological and neuropsychological measures. *Journal of Clinical and Experimental Neuropsychology, 19*(4), 515–524.

Tarter, R., Van Thiel, D., & Edwards, K. (Eds.). (1988). *Medical neuropsychology: The impact of disease on behavior.* New York: Plenum Press.

Tatemichi, T., Desmond, D., Prohovnik, I., & Eidelberg, D. (1995). Dementia associated with bilateral carotid occlusions: Neuropsychological and haemodynamic course after extracranial to intracranial bypass surgery. *Journal of Neurology, Neurosurgery, and Psychiatry, 58,* 633–6.

Taylor-Robinson, S., Oatridge, A., Hajnal, J., Burroughs, A., McIntyre, N., & deSouza, N. (1995). MR imaging of the basal ganglia in chronic liver disease. *Metabolic Brain Disease, 10*(2), 175–88.

Taylor-Robinson, S., Sargentoni, J., Oatridge, A., Bryant, D., Hajnal, J., Marcus, C., Seery, J., Hodgson, H., & deSouza, N. (1996). MR imaging and spectroscopy of the basal ganglia in chronic liver disease. *Metabolic Brain Disease, 11*(3), 249–68.

Thrift, A., McNeil, J., Forbes, A., & Donnan, G. (1998). Three important subgroups of hypertensive persons at greater risk of intracerebral hemorrhage. *Hypertension, 31,* 1223–29.

Thyrum, E., Blumenthal, J., Madden, D., & Siegel, W. (1995). Family history of hypertension influences neurobehavioral function in hypertensive patients. *Psychosomatic Medicine, 57,* 496–500.

Townes, B., Bashein, G., Hornbein, T., Coppel, D., Goldstein, D., Davis, K., Nessly, M., Bledsoe, S., Veith, R., Ivey, T., & Cohen, M. (1989). Neurobehavioral outcomes in cardiac operations. *Journal of Cardiothoracic Surgery, 98,* 774–82.

Trzepacz, P., Brenner, R., & Van Thiel. (1989). A psychiatric study of 247 liver transplantation candidates. *Psychosomatics, 30*(2), 147–153.

Trzepacz, P., Teague, G., & Lipowski, Z. (1985). Delirium and other organic mental disorders in a general hospital. *General Hospital Psychiatry, 7,* 101–6.

Waldstein, S., Jennings, J., Ryan, C., Muldoon, M., Shapiro, A., Polefrone, J., Fazzari, T., & Manuck. S. (1996). Hypertension and neuropsychological performance in men: Interactive effects of age. *Health Psychology, 15*(2), 102–9.

Wilson, P. (1997). An epidemiologic perspective of systemic hypertension, ischemic heart disease, and heart failure. A*merican Journal of Cardiology, 80*(9B), 3J–8J.22

Zilinski, E. M., Crimmins, E, Reynolds, S., & Seeman, T. (1998). Do medical conditions affect cognition in older adults? *Health Psychology, 6,* 504–512.

Advances in Medical Psychotherapy and Psychodiagnosis
2002–2003, Volume 11, pp. 89–106

Psychosocial Implications of Fecal Incontinence Following Acquired Brain Injury

Paul J. Taaffe, Ph.D. and George A. Zitnay, Ph.D.
John Jane Brain Injury Center, Charlottesville, VA

Jeffrey T. Barth, Ph.D.
University of Virginia, School of Medicine, Charlottesville, VA

Gregory O'Shanick, M.D.
Center for Neurorehabilitation Services, Midlothian, VA

Gerry Brooks, M.A.
Northeast Center for Special Care, Lake Katrine, NY

Tina Trudel, Ph.D.
Lakeview for Center Neurorehabilitation, Effingham Hills, NH

Abstract

Acquired brain injury (ABI) includes traumatic and non-traumatic insults to the brain of sufficient severity so as to cause temporary or chronic affective, behavioral, cognitive, physical, and/or social deficits. One of the most insidious yet overlooked physical sequela of ABI is incontinence. Of the limited number of studies that are available, the majority focuses on urinary incontinence (UI) while a scant few address fecal incontinence (FI). An even smaller subset delves into related psychosocial issues.

In an effort to highlight the medical/treatment and psychosocial aspects of bowel and bladder dysfunction following traumatic brain injury, the International Brain Injury Association and the Rubin Family Brain Injury Research Fund collaborated to sponsor a roundtable discussion on the topic in December of 1999. This meeting brought together a number of leading professionals representing the fields of neurology, neuropsychiatry, gastroenterology, epidemiology, physical medicine and rehabilitation, neuropsychology, physical therapy, and speech and language pathology. Case material and a review of the pertinent literature provided the backdrop for discussion.

At the outset of the meeting the decision was made to restrict the scope of work to FI in order to make the project more manageable and due to the fact that so little has been written on this subject. Further, all types of brain injury (i.e., ABI) were to be included given the relative dearth of knowledge in this broad area of study.

Two working groups (i.e., the Medical/Treatment Issues working group, and the Psychosocial Issues working group) were formed and proceeded to develop their respective portions of the questionnaire to be utilized by the primary care physician (PCP) and other healthcare providers. The information included in the Psychosocial Issues part of the questionnaire is based on expert opinion in terms of the domains of inquiry thought to be critical to a thorough evaluation of the patient (See Appendices A, B, and C). Patient and family member forms provide subjective and objective accounts of functioning. A decision tree/algorithm-type process was employed in arriving at the recommended steps to be taken by treating professionals (See Appendix D). The use of the questionnaire, in combination with the algorithms, constitutes the proposed method of psychosocial assessment with respect to FI after ABI. It is hoped that the questionnaire and algorithms will give rise to increased attention to this most humbling of conditions for a segment of our patient population that has heretofore suffered in secrecy. In addition, these instruments may be applicable to UI as well. An article detailing the findings of the Medical/Treatment Issues group is anticipated in the future.

Introduction

The term "incontinence" (or bowel and bladder dysfunction) is reminiscent of psychoanalytic theory as contained within Freud's Psychosexual Stages of Development (Hall, 1974). As Freud has postulated, during the initial stage of development—i.e., the Oral Stage—the focus of psychic energy is in the mouth, which is quite adaptive for the young child in that he is almost completely dependent upon the mother for sustenance. For physical and psychosexual reasons, elimination matters are not of primary concern at this point in life (at least not for the child). Moving on to the Anal stage (vis à vis Freud), the center of psychic energy now lies in the gastrointestinal tract and generates a feeling of tension that is relieved through defecation and urination. Holding on and letting go (i.e., control) are challenges to be mastered in the process of toilet training.

"Psychosocial" brings to mind the work of Erikson (1963) and his aptly named Psychosocial Stages of Development wherein the child interacts with his parents and through nurturance learns to trust caregivers and, hopefully, himself (i.e., the stage of Trust v. Mistrust). The Eriksonian psychosocial correlate of Freud's Anal Stage is that of Autonomy v. Shame and Doubt. Erikson suggests that the child must reconcile his willfulness with the expectations of his parents. Inevitably, there are moments in the life of the child when he is "caught with his pants down," and either knowingly or unwittingly his parents resort to shaming as a regrettable method of behavior modification. If practiced consistently, the child may come to question his abilities, resulting in his sense of self being shaken.

In the normal course of development, the child typically gains control of his bowels and bladder between the ages of two and four. The process of elimination becomes well learned and nearly automatic. Unfortunately, for the adolescent or adult who has suffered an ABI the seemingly simple steps involved in toileting prove to be complicated undertakings. In effect, there is physical and psychological "regression" that occurs whereby the afflicted individual may no longer recognize the sensations that are part and parcel of the urge to defecate or urinate. Conceivably, the sensory apparatus may be intact but the motor response system could be defective.

Whatever the exact physical cause of the incontinence, for the person who has lost his abilities as stated, the intrapsychic aspect of the regression is characterized by a sense of being out of control and a feeling of mistrust of one's body. The brain- injured individual is catapulted back to a time when his basic needs were taken care of by his parents, which was appropriate then but can be problematic now. An awareness of loss of function, status, and boundaries can create a compromised self-concept that is mired in shame and doubt. Repeated disaffirmations of competence with respect to bowel and bladder issues can lead to learned helplessness and diminished initiative. Feelings of guilt and despondency may prevail as the individual realizes what others must do for him.

Because the incontinent person cannot "produce" in expected ways he views himself as being inferior. Continence becomes a seemingly unattainable goal that he used to perform. Incontinence and all that goes along with it can shatter an individual's identity as being a capable, self-sufficient person. Whether the situation involves spouses, siblings, or parents of the brain-injured individual, role confusion occurs. "In sickness and in health" may be a well-intentioned phrase agreed to in principle at the wedding ceremony, but bowel and bladder dysfunction puts spouses' resolve to the supreme test. The afflicted person who, at first, is in denial or is reluctant to be helped may come to see himself as a burden to the caretaker.

Perhaps the intimate aspect of the marital relationship creates the greatest amount of strain. How can the mood be right for lovemaking when an "accident" may have occurred in the midst of foreplay and may repeat during intercourse. The desire for closeness in a sexual sense may dwindle to the point of both parties feeling disillusioned and isolated. If there is no improvement in the condition of the incontinent individual—and he believes that his future will be no better than his present—despair takes hold and discourages the spirit. The experiences of siblings and parents contain their own sets of interpersonal predicaments with attendant control, privacy, and "self" issues noted.

Review of the Literature

The sense of self of the incontinent individual appears to be more fragile than that of persons without bowel and bladder difficulties regardless of etiology. A review of the pertinent literature revealed a study by Thackaberry (1983) who was interested in the nursing management of the school-age child with bowel incontinence. Of primary concern was the potential for damage to self-esteem. Erikson's theory of psychosocial development was employed to coordinate nursing care intended to promote independence while enhancing the child's sense of autonomy.

Whereas Thackaberry (1983) looked at bowel incontinence with the school-age child, Hagglof, Andren, Bergstrom, Marklund, and Wendelius (1997) investigated the issue of urinary incontinence and self-esteem in children. Their results indicated that patients' self-esteem was impaired to a significant degree compared to controls prior to treatment for incontinence, and that after six months of treatment the patients' self-esteem had reached the same level as that of the controls. Further, patients who were completely continent at six months follow-up had significantly better self-esteem than patients whose incontinence persisted to some extent.

Nochi (1998) examined narrative data from 10 individuals who sustained a TBI to check on their sense of self. Three main points came out of the study including the fact that the brain injured participants struggled with who they had become, and with an accurate understanding of current abilities and limitations. In addition, their "loss of self" was quite pronounced when they were cognizant of "me" before and after injury. Third, these individuals' sense of self was sensitive to, and easily threatened by, societal labels. Another study related to the self was done by Leathem, Murphy, and Flett (1998) when they assessed TBI patients' perceptions of competency. In short, they found that respondents as a whole overrated their pre-injury competency, and that the severe TBI patients underestimated their present difficulties.

Chiverton, Wells, Brink, and Mayer (1996) determined that the incidence of depression is greater in women with urinary incontinence than in the general population. It seems that anxiety as well as depression is common in spinal cord injury (SCI) patients who named bowel dysfunction, along with impaired mobility, as a primary deficit (Glickman & Kamm, 1996). In fact, Glickman and Kamm (1996) thought that emotional troubles for this group were a function of the amount of time necessary to complete the toileting procedure and the frequency of bowel incontinence.

Grinspun (1993) advocated early intervention with brain-injured persons in terms of caring professionals providing proper empathy with regard to incontinence if self-image is to be maintained. It is likewise essential for others to be mindful of cognitive changes that prevent these patients from being aware of their own shortcomings and from taking corrective action on their own behalf. Recent work by Watts and Perlesz (1999) proposed that there now exists a clinical tool for identifying adults most likely to experience poor outcome following TBI.

In addition to the cases mentioned above involving TBI, SCI, and non-specific health problems, male ostomy patients especially reported having lower quality of life with mild to moderate depression, presumably due to a change in the perception of self (Mihalopoulos, Trunnell, Ball, & Moncur, 1994). The men had concerns about dependence on others after many years of self-reliance, and about leakage with its attendant feelings of helplessness.

There have been a number of studies on multiple sclerosis (MS) and the ramifications of this neurological disease. Jiwa (1995) proposed that alterations in self-esteem might be apportioned to MS patients engaging in negative self-talk and having fewer social contacts, for example. Another study by Seidler (1985) indicated that MS patients with incontinence felt helpless and inadequate, and that their public lives were quite restricted. Whatever the overriding physical impairment associated with incontinence, it seems that the mental condition of the disabled largely determines psychosocial outcome (Tate & Broe, 1999).

The literature to date has suggested that one's psychological state sets the stage for social functioning. This certainly appears to be the case with those who suffer from bowel and bladder dysfunction. Wyman (1987) noted that women with urinary incontinence avoided activity occurring in unfamiliar places due to worry of not knowing the locations of bathrooms. Similarly, Youngson and Alderman (1994) found that TBI individuals enrolled in a community-based rehabilitation program voiced fear of incontinence and exhibited avoidance or escape behavior. In their work with disabled older women, Simonsick, Kasper, and Phillips (1998) discovered that incontinence, along with several other factors, was associated with home confinement.

These studies demonstrate that persons with bowel and bladder dysfunction may ruminate, if they are cognitively able, about their condition to the point of developing what might be termed "incontinence-induced agoraphobia." For older individuals in particular, they may have the time and resources to actively seek out leisure pursuits but sacrifice their availability, spontaneity, and sense of adventure for the entrapments of their comfort zones. In essence, they prefer to hide than to risk being found out. Anticipatory anxiety takes hold and affected persons shield themselves from even the possibility of social mishaps and discomfort.

Over the past several years research has been undertaken to explore psychosocial accompaniments of brain injury, though incontinence is not necessarily mentioned. McLean, Dikmen, and Temkin (1993) examined patients at one and 12 months post-injury, and found that individuals, on the whole, were irritable, had trouble concentrating and remembering, and could not resume leisure activities or jobs. Consistent with earlier work (Thomsen, 1984), patients were seen to improve more so in the physical area than in the psychosocial domain.

Kreuter, Sullivan, Dahllof, and Siosteen (1998) assessed TBI and SCI patients on several variables related to psychosocial adjustment but not incontinence per se. Quality of life for the TBI group was explained by mood, physical and social functioning, severity of disability, and time since injury. For the SCI group, mood, physical and social functioning, and perceived loss of independence were noteworthy.

In a very recent paper written by Tate and Broe (1999) a vast number of predictors of psychosocial outcome were evaluated. The so-called "important variables" for study falling under the rubric of "neurophysical impairments" included gait, spasticity, weakness, and incoordination, but not incontinence. The findings suggested that the severity of injury, degree of impairments, chronicity of deficits, and level of self-esteem were most highly correlated with psychosocial adjustment. Further, certain aspects of psychosocial adjustment were separated out for investigation. Interestingly, neurophysical impairments and memory functioning were associated with successful occupational activities; chronicity, cognitive speed, and behavioral regulation predicted success in interpersonal relationships; and neurophysical impairments, behavioral regulation, and memory functioning were connected with success in independent living skills.

While Tate and Broe (1999) addressed the interpersonal relationships of TBI individuals in only a cursory fashion, clearly this factor is not to be overlooked with respect to psychosocial adjustment. In the best of situations when, premorbidly, a relationship was strong, the changes in the brain injured person would demand modifications in how the survivor, family members, and friends relate to one another. As discussed near the beginning of this paper, the impaired individual regresses physically and psychologically such that mistrust of oneself develops secondary to bowel and bladder dysfunction. This mistrust of oneself may be displaced onto concerned others who offer assistance and attempt to help with toileting. A type of hostile-dependent relationship may ensue. The brain injured person may have a sense of being out of control yet resists others' efforts to take charge of bathroom procedures. A once proud person who could manage basic as well as higher level needs may be reduced to a recalcitrant individual who tests loved ones' perseverance.

The literature is mixed with regard to the longevity of marriages. For example, Walker (1972) indicated that a high percentage (i.e., 89%) of marriages maintained subsequent to one partner suffering a TBI. On the other hand, Panting and Merry (1972) found a 40% divorce rate among severely head-injured individuals. In a more recent study, Kreuter et al. (1998) reported a 48% divorce rate for a SCI group and a 56% divorce rate for a TBI group. Presumably, the burdens endured while caring for their disabled spouses resulted in an unacceptable decline in quality of life. The authors also pointed out that brain injury did not pose a major impediment to persons establishing new relationships.

One last patient population to be discussed resides in nursing homes. Incontinence runs rampant in this setting and permits the opportunity for controlled study of the problem. Phillips, Morris, Hawes, Fries, Mor, Nennstiel, and Iannacchione (1997) looked at bowel and bladder difficulties as a part of a "physical function" factor along with "cognition" and "psychosocial status." Basically, the researchers utilized the Resident Assessment Instrument (RAI), which is a multidimensional evaluation device and problem identification system. They concluded that the implementation of the Resident Assessment Instrument (RAI) led to a slower rate of decline in seven different areas including urinary and bowel incontinence, and social engagement. It seems that with a heightened focus by the nursing staff on selected issues—and, perhaps, increased scrutiny by research nursing personnel—the patients' quality of care improved as did the patients' quality of life, in a general sense.

A final point to be made on this topic is that patients and physicians typically fail to communicate openly about incontinence. In effect, "physicians don't ask and patients don't tell" (Cohen, Robinson, Dugan, Howard, Suggs, Pearce, Carroll, McGann, & Preisser, 1999). This may be due, in part, to physicians feeling inadequate at diagnosing the underlying causes of bowel and bladder dysfunction, and prescribing effective treatment (Dovey, McNaughton, Tilyard, Gurr, Jolleys, & Wilson, 1996). Dovey et al. (1996) reported that nearly 72% of physician respondents to a questionnaire did not recall specific training in this area. This is a particularly unfortunate finding in view of the work of Reuben, Maly, Hirsch, Frank, Oakes, Siu, and Hays (1996) who wrote that approximately 82% of patients follow through with "most important" physician recommendations and 79% with "major" recommendations.

Critical Issues in FI Following ABI

From the preceding literature review it may be surmised that:

- FI is a biopsychosocial problem affecting the individual with ABI, the family, caregivers, and community at large.

- FI after ABI often results in:

  1. Reduced access to rehabilitation;

  2. Decreased rehabilitation momentum;

  3. Diminished quality of life despite rehabilitation gains;

  4. Loss of self-esteem;

  5. Anxiety;

6. Depression, possibly with hopelessness and suicidal risk;

7. Alteration of family role;

8. Loss of support system, income, and vocational opportunities;

9. Lack of control over time and life circumstances;

10. Inability to adjust to limitations regarding sexuality and intimacy;

11. Failure to attract or maintain a partner; and

12. Restricted socialization.

- While discussion and evaluation of FI is often ignored due to social stigma and because of the complexity of ABI, it may be the single most important barrier to achieving a satisfactory quality of life and cost effective outcome.

- Addressing this issue is the responsibility of all health providers including the primary care physician (PCP).

Conclusion and Recommendations

Incontinence is a common and potentially debilitating effect of ABI. Despite the tremendous psychosocial impact of incontinence secondary to ABI, there is a surprising void in the scientific literature on this topic. Of the studies that do exist, the emphasis has been on UI while FI, for the most part, has been neglected.

Spurred on by the International Brain Injury Association and the Rubin Family Research Fund, a roundtable discussion was held in Dallas, TX, December 10-12, 1999, at which time a number of leading professionals came together to address the issue of FI following ABI. The stated intent was to develop an assessment instrument for the PCP and other healthcare personnel for the purpose of increasing awareness to this problem and to help direct intervention. Further, it was determined that a decision-tree/algorithm-type process would be advanced in an effort to assist in coordinating effective, multimodal intervention.

There are two forms of the assessment questionnaire (i.e., one for the patient and one for a family member) and are composed of eight domains of inquiry including:

1. Autonomy/Personal Effectiveness;

2. Cognitive/Perceptual;

3. Economics;

4. Affective;

5. Interpersonal;

6. Intimacy;

7. Community Re-entry; and

8. Vocational.

Each of the 27 items in the questionnaire is scored from 1 to 4 with lower scores indicating a lesser level of functioning. By adding the scores together the practitioner is able to gain a more objective understanding of a patient's quality of life as it relates to FI following ABI. The algorithms, general and specific, are in place to guide medical professionals in the decision-making process as they attempt to achieve the best possible treatments for their patients.

Securing appropriate intervention for patients is incumbent upon the PCP, primarily. Other health-care professionals will be consulted as necessary. Proper intervention is predicated on the PCP communicating more openly and directly about FI. The PCP is encouraged to take on a strong advocate role for individuals with ABI who, many times, have been incorrectly stereotyped as poor treatment candidates. Caution is advised in making referrals to other disciplines given the relative inexperience that many professionals possess with respect to FI after ABI. The neuropsychiatrist or neuropsychologist in consultation with the PCP can address several of the psychosocial consequences in part or whole.

In reviewing and utilizing the materials developed by the roundtable working groups it must be kept in mind that the products of this collaboration are but the first steps of several to come. There is the hope and expectation that the expert opinion-based questionnaire and algorithms will provide the impetus for the procurement of evidence-based guidelines whereby the psychosocial implications of FI following ABI will be thrust into the forefront of general medical practice.

Fecal Incontinence Psychosocial Questionnaire— Patient Form (FIPQ-P)

NAME: DATE:

AGE:

MEDICAL PROBLEMS:

INSTRUCTIONS:

Please respond to each question below by placing a check mark under the number that best describes your situation:

1 = Most of the time (i.e., 5–7 days per week)

2 = Some of the time (i.e., 3–4 days per week)

3 = A little of the time (i.e., 1–2 days per week)

4 = None of the time

N/A = Not applicable

	1	2	3	4	N/A
1. Do you require assistance from others to go to the bathroom to move your bowels?					
2. Do you need help to carry out the steps necessary to complete a bowel movement?					
3. Have you postponed or missed any medical treatments due to fecal incontinence?					
4. Has fecal incontinence interfered with your rehabilitation?					
5. Do you have difficulty remembering your daily schedule?					
6. Do you lack the physical sensation of needing to have a bowel movement?					
7. Do your urges to have a bowel movement occur irregularly throughout the day?					

	1	2	3	4	N/A
8. Are you unsure of what to do when you feel the need to have a bowel movement?					
9. Have you spent money on any products to prevent or manage your fecal incontinence?					
10. Have you spent money on cleaning services due to fecal incontinence?					
11. Have you spent money for attendants or care personnel due to fecal incontinence?					
12. Have you experienced depression or anxiety related to fecal incontinence?*					
13. Have you felt hopeless due to fecal incontinence?*					
14. Have you experienced anger because of fecal incontinence?*					
15. Have you had suicidal thoughts due to fecal incontinence?**					
16. Are you afraid of being rejected by others due to your fecal incontinence?*					
17. Do you go to efforts to conceal your fecal incontinence from others?					
18. Do you feel others value you less due to your fecal incontinence?					
19. Do you feel your importance to your family has changed due to your fecal incontinence?					
20. Do you have trouble making or maintaining relationships due to your fecal incontinence?*					
21. Have you withdrawn emotionally from your partner or spouse due to fecal incontinence?*					
22. Have you avoided sexual activity because of fecal incontinence?*					
23. Has an episode of fecal incontinence occurred during sexual activity?					
24. Have you purposely stayed at home because of fecal incontinence?*					

	1	2	3	4	N/A
25. Has fecal incontinence limited your ability to socialize with others?					
26. Have you been reluctant to seek out education, training, or work due to fecal incontinence?					
27. Has fecal incontinence interfered with your attendance at classes, training, or work?					

*Warrants referral for further mental health assessment.

Fecal Incontinence Psychosocial Questionnaire—
Patient Form (FIPQ-P)

NAME: DATE:

AGE:

MEDICAL PROBLEMS:

INSTRUCTIONS:

Please respond to each question below by placing a check mark under the number that best describes your situation:

1 = Most of the time

2 = Some of the time

3 = A little of the time

4 = None of the time

N/A = Not applicable

	1	2	3	4	N/A
1. Does your family member require assistance from others to go to the bathroom to move his/her bowels?					
2. Does your family member need help to carry out the steps necessary to complete a bowel movement?					
3. Has your family member postponed or missed any medical treatments due to fecal incontinence?					
4. Has fecal incontinence interfered with your family member's rehabilitation?					
5. Does your family member have difficulty remembering his/her daily schedule?					
6. Does your family member lack the physical sensation of needing to have a bowel movement?					
7. Do your family member's urges to have a bowel movement occur irregularly throughout the day?					

	1	2	3	4	N/A
8. Is your family member unsure of what to do when he/she feels the need to have a bowel movement?					
9. Has your family member spent money on any products to prevent or manage his/her fecal incontinence?					
10. Has your family member spent money on cleaning services due to fecal incontinence?					
11. Has your family member spent money for attendants or care personnel due to fecal incontinence?					
12. Has your family member experienced depression or anxiety related to fecal incontinence?*					
13. Has your family member seemed hopeless due to fecal incontinence?*					
14. Has your family member seemed angry because of fecal incontinence?*					
15. Has your family member expressed or acted out on suicidal thoughts due to fecal incontinence?**					
16. Does your family member seem to fear rejection by others due to his/her fecal incontinence?*					
17. Does your family member go to efforts to conceal his/her fecal incontinence from others?					
18. Does your family member seem to feel others value him/her less due to his/her fecal incontinence?					
19. Does your family member seem to feel his/her importance to your family has changed due to his/her fecal incontinence?					
20. Does your family member have trouble making or maintaining relationships due to his/her fecal incontinence?*					
21. Has your family member withdrawn emotionally from his/her partner or spouse due to fecal incontinence? *					
22. Has your family member avoided sexual activity because of fecal incontinence?*					

	1	2	3	4	N/A
23. Has an episode of fecal incontinence occurred during sexual activity?					
24. Has your family member purposely stayed at home because of fecal incontinence? *					
25. Has fecal incontinence limited your family member's ability to socialize with others?					
26. Has your family member been reluctant to seek out education, training, or work due to fecal incontinence?					
27. Has fecal incontinence interfered with your family member's attendance at classes, training, or work?					

*Warrants referral for further mental health assessment.**

Fecal Incontinence Psychosocial Questionnaire (FIPQ):
Domains of Inquiry and Scoring Guide

The FIPQ has been developed based on expert opinion for the purpose of providing the PCP and other healthcare professionals with a screening instrument that is sensitive to critical psychosocial consequences of FI secondary to ABI. Equivalent forms are available for completion by caregivers, family members, and the patients themselves. Domains of inquiry and their corresponding questions include:

1. **Autonomy/Personal Effectiveness (#1–4);**

2. **Cognitive/Perceptual (#5–8);**

3. **Economics (#9–11);**

4. **Affective (#12–15);**

5. **Interpersonal (#16–20);**

6. **Intimacy (#21–23);**

7. **Community Re-entry (#24–25);**

8. **Vocational (#26–27).**

Scores for each item range from 1 to 4 with a 1 indicating a lesser functional level and a 4 reflecting a higher functional level with respect to fecal incontinence. Thus, in adding together the scores for all items the lower the total score, the lower the quality of life as it pertains to fecal incontinence.

The following scoring guide may be used to help classify the level of impairment of individuals with fecal incontinence:

0–54 Severe to Moderately Severe

55–80 Moderate

81–108 Mild to No Impairment

Note that a respondent may be less functional in one or more domains while he or she may function at a higher level in other areas. For this reason, qualitative assessment is recommended along with quantitative measurement so as to promote the most efficacious interventions.

Algorithm A: ABI and FI

Algorithm B: ABI and FI Psychosocial Consequences and Multimodal Interventions

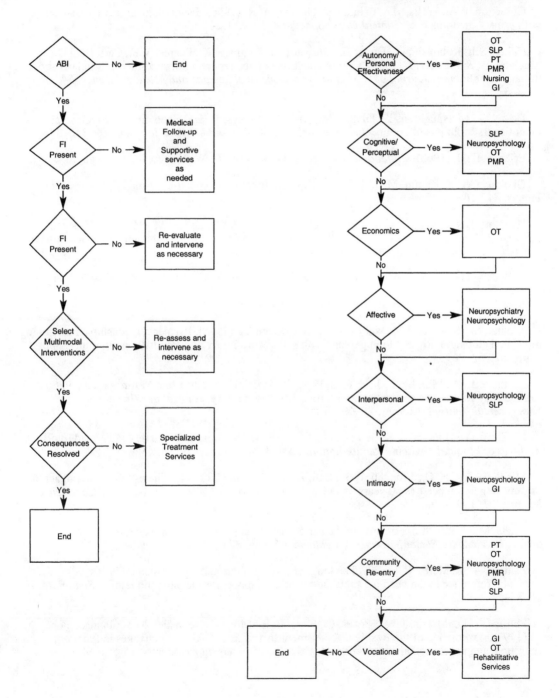

References

Chiverton, P.A., Wells, T.J., Brink, C.A., & Mayer, R. (1996). Psychological factors associated with urinary incontinence. *Clinical Nurse Specialist, 10,* 229–233.

Cohen, S.J., Robinson, D., Dugan, E., Howard, G., Suggs, P.K., Pearce, K.F., Carroll, D.D., McGann, P., & Preisser, J. (1999). Communication between older adults and their physicians about urinary incontinence. *Journal of Gerontology: A Biological Science and Medical Science, 54,* M34–37.

Dovey, S., McNaughton, T., Tilyard, M., Gurr, E., Jolleys, J., & Wilson, D. (1996). General practitioners' opinions of continence care training. *New Zealand Medical Journal, 109,* 340–343.

Erikson, E. H. (1963). *Childhood and society.* New York: W. W. Norton and Company, Inc.

Glickman, S., & Kamm, M. A. (1996). Bowel dysfunction in spinal-cord-injury patients. *The Lancet, 347,* 1651–1653.

Haggloff, B., Andren, O., Bergstrom, E., Marklund, L., &Wendelius, M. (1997). Self-esteem before and after treatment in children with nocturnal enuresis and urinary incontinence. Scandinavian *Journal of Urology and Nephrology Supplement, 183,* 79–82.

Hall, C. S. (1979). *A primer of Freudian psychology.* New York: The New American Library, Inc.

Jiwa, T.I. (1995). Multiple sclerosis and self-esteem. *Axone, 16,* 87–90.

Kreuter, M., Sullivan, M., Dahllof, A.G., & Siosteen, A. (1998). Partner relationships, functioning, mood and global quality of life in persons with spinal cord injury and traumatic brain injury. *Spinal Cord, 36,* 252–261.

Leathem, J. M., Murphy, L. J., & Flett, R. A. (1998). Self- and informant-ratings on the Patient Competency Rating Scale in patients with traumatic brain injury. *Journal of Clinical and Experimental Neuropsychology, 20,* 694–705.

McClean, A., Dikmen, S. S., & Temkin, N. R. (1993). Psychosocial recovery after head injury. *Archives of Physical Medicine Rehabilitation,* 1041–1046.

Mihalopoulos, N. G., Trunnell, E. P., Ball, K., & Moncur, C. (1994). The psychologic impact of ostomy surgery on persons 50 years of age and older. *Journal of Wound, Ostomy, and Continence in Nursing, 21,* 149–155.

Nochi, M. (1998). "Loss of self" in the narratives of people with traumatic brain injuries: a qualitative analysis. *Social Sciences in Medicine, 46,* 869–878.

Panting, A., & Merry, P. (1972). The long-term rehabilitation of severe head injuries with particular reference to the need for social and medical support for the patient's family. *Rehabilitation, 28,* 33–37.

Phillips, C. D., Morris, J. N., Hawes, C., Fries, B. E., Mor, V., Nennstiel, M., & Iannacchione, V. (1997). Association of the Resident Assessment Instrument (RAI) with changes in function, cognition, and psychosocial status. *Journal of the American Geriatric Society, 45,* 986–993.

Reuben, D. B., Maly, R. C., Hirsch, S. H., Frank, J. C., Oakes, A. M., Siu, A. L., & Hays, R. D. (1996). Physician implementation of and patient adherence to recommendations from comprehensive geriatric assessment. *American Journal of Medicine, 100,* 444–451.

Seidler, G. H. (1985). Psychosocial processing of disease exemplified by multiple sclerosis. Results of an empirical study of 27 males. *Psychosomatic Medicine and Psychoanalysis, 31,* 61–80.

Simonsick, E. M., Kasper, J. D., & Phillips, C. L. (1998). Physical disability and social interaction: factors associated with low social contact and home confinement in disabled older women (The Women's Health and Aging Study), *Journal Gerontol B Psychol Sci Soc Sci, 53,* S209–217.

Tate, R. L., & Broe, G. A. (1999). Psychosocial adjustment after traumatic brain injury: What are the important variables? *Psychological Medicine, 29,* 713–725.

Thackaberry, J. M. (1983). Nursing management of the school-age child with bowel incontinence: Utilizing Erikson's theory of psychosocial development. *Journal of School Nursing, 53,* 189–193.

Thomsen, I. V. (1984). Late outcome of severe blunt head trauma: A 10–15 year second follow-up. *Journal of Neurology, Neurosurgery, and Psychiatry, 47,* 260–268.

Walker, A. E. (1972). Long-term evaluation of the social and family adjustment of head injuries. *Scandinavian Journal of Rehabilitation Medicine, 4,* 5–8.

Watts, R., & Perlesz, A. (1999). Psychosocial outcome risk indicator: Predicting psychosocial outcome following traumatic brain injury. *Brain Injury, 13,* 113–24.

Wyman, J. F., Harkins, S. W., Choi, S. C., Taylor, J. R., & Fantl, J. A. (1987). Psychosocial impact of urinary incontinence in women. *Obstetrics and Gynecology, 70,* 378–381.

Youngson, H. A., & Alderman, N. (1994). Fear of incontinence and its effects on a community-based rehabilitation programme after severe brain injury: Successful remediation of escape behaviour using behaviour modification. *Brain Injury, 8,* 23–36.

Advances in Medical Psychotherapy and Psychodiagnosis
2002–2003, Volume 11, pp. 107–122

Specific Driving Impairments
with Aging

Daniel J. Cox, Ph.D., Donna K. Broshek, Ph.D.,
Brian Kiernan, Ph.D., and Boris P. Kovatchev, Ph.D.
Department of Psychiatric Medicine
University of Virginia Health Sciences Center

Jose Guerrier, Ph.D.
University of Miami, Miami, FL

Anthony J. Giuliano, Ph.D.
Department of Psychiatry
McLean Hospital/ Harvard University Medical School

Charles George, M.D.
London Health Sciences Centre, London, Ontario

Abstract .

The American population is growing older, and living in suburbs, necessitating continuation of driving. Automobile accidents/miles driven increase significantly with age beyond the age of 60, and are associated with greater bodily injury. This study evaluated the types of driving performance decrements that are more likely to occur with advancing age. 245 senior drivers from three different sites, 60 years of age and older, drove the interactive Atari Research Driving Simulator, completed the Mini Mental Status Exam, and the Trail Making Test, Parts A and B, as a measure of mental flexibility and capacity to shift attention. Subjects' performance was compared across five-year age increments (60–64, 65–69, 70–74, 75–79, 80+). Performance on Trails B and the Driving Simulator significantly worsened for older age groups, while Mini Mental Status Exam scores remained stable. Performance on the driving simulator and Trails B was significantly correlated. Specifically, older

This study was supported in part by the American Association for Retired Persons, NIH grant DK28-288 and a grant from the Carilion Bioengineering Institute.

Direct all correspondence to: Dr. Daniel J. Cox, Ph.D., Box 800223, University of Virginia Health Sciences Center, Charlottesville, VA 22908.

drivers were observed to demonstrate more driving risk behaviors, including swerving, steering off road and across midline, inappropriate application of brakes, missed stop signs, speed variability, slow driving, taking longer to execute left hand turns, and low speed collisions. In general, driving performance decayed most notably in the 70–79 age group. Performance in global and specific driving parameters progressively worsened for progressively older drivers, which is consistent with the types of accidents most common among senior drivers. While significantly related to more traditional brief measures of neurocognitive functioning, these relationships were weak.

Introduction

The senior population, age 65 years and older, is increasing more rapidly than any other age group. Senior citizens are expected to represent 16% of the U.S. population in the year 2020, and 17% of the population by 2030 (Bureau of the Census, 1993). Our aging society has resulted in an increasing number of senior drivers, such that 50 million drivers may be 65 years of age or older by the year 2020 (Transportation Research Board special report 218, 1988). In addition, it has been estimated that over 75% of the senior citizens will live in the suburbs in their later years, necessitating the continued use of an automobile to maintain mobility and independence (Rosenbloom, 1993).

Unfortunately, however, aging is associated with a loss of visual acuity, constriction of the visual field, decrements in problem solving and perceptual speed, response slowing due to central processing changes, decline in ability to divide and shift attention, increased reaction time, and restricted joint movement. Deficits in any of these abilities have been shown to impair driving performance (Ball & Owsley, 1991; Barrett, Mihal, Panek, Sterns & Alexander, 1977; Johnson & Keltner, 1986; Kahneman, Ben-Ishai & Lotan, 1973; Mihal & Barrett, 1976; Owsley, Ball, Sloane, Roenker & Bruni, 1991; Parasuraman & Nestor, 1991; Szylk, Seiple & Viana, 1995). Further, the older body is more fragile and less likely to survive a traumatic accident, possibly contributing to a greater crash fatality rate among the elderly (Improving safety and mobility for older people: Project proposal, 1985). In fact, motor vehicle crashes are the leading cause of death from unintentional injury for those between the ages of 65 to 74 (Waller, 1985).

While there is no observed increase in automobile crashes per driver with progressing age, there is a dramatic increase in the number of crashes per miles driven beyond the age of 60 (National Highway Traffic Safety Administration, 1988; 1989a; 1988; 1989a; 1989b). Efforts to explain this finding have included the reasonable hypothesis that older drivers may be largely aware of their cognitive-motor deficits and related driving limitations, and thus use a number of compensatory strategies, including restriction of driving in conditions of greater risk. For example, older drivers may drive only during daylight, drive on familiar roads, and only during periods of low traffic density (i.e., non-rush hours) (Solomon, 1985; Traffic safety of elderly road users, 1985). Due to these self-initiated modifications of driving behaviors, only those seniors who drive a greater number of miles are at increased risk for motor vehicle accidents.

Certain driving conditions and roadways appear to be more arduous for the older driver. Senior drivers are disproportionately involved in left-turn intersection crashes (Cooper, 1990; Garber & Srinivasan, 1991). This may be due to the increased complexity of the task, which requires more time for the older driver to select and process relevant information, engage in decision making, and execute the turn through three lanes of traffic (oncoming traffic and traffic from the right and left). Hemispatial inattention (the failure to respond to stimuli on the side of the body contralateral to a brain lesion) has also been suggested as a factor in executing left turns for patients with mild to moderate Alzheimer's dementia (Mendez, Cherrier, & Cymerman, 1997). Older drivers tend to make specific judgment errors, including failure to yield the right of way, overestimation of slower velocities, and underestimation of faster velocities (Scialfa, Guzy, Leibowitz, Garvey & Tyrrell, 1991). In addition, older drivers are often cited for violating posted traffic signs (Cooper, 1990). This may be due to a decline in visual acuity and the decreased ability to divide and alternate attention efficiently so as to keep track of the impending road conditions while reading traffic signs. Given the current data, it remains important to more thoroughly understand the components of safe driving and the senior driver.

There are at least four different ways of assessing driving skills: direct observation of on-road driving performance, actual driving records like those from the Department of Motor Vehicles (DMV), inferring driving performance from neurocognitive performance, or quantification of driving performance on a simulator. Direct observation as a research method is problematic and was not used in the current study for the following reasons: a) on-road driving demands can not be controlled, resulting in non-standard driving conditions across drivers, b) on-road driving tests can not safely expose drivers to high risk situations to see how they perform, c) on-road driving tests typically rely on the relatively subjective ratings of a driving instructor, d) on-road driving tests put the examiner at risk, and e) on-road driving tests are expensive. DMV records are problematic because they only document when accidents have occurred and been reported. In addition to under representing motor vehicle accidents (Szylk, Seiple & Viana, 1995), DMV records do not describe actual driving performance. Neurocognitive test performance has not been shown to be particularly effective in predicting either actual driving performance or future accidents, although one study found an association between performance on brief neurocognitive measures and crash risk (Sbordone & Long, 1996; Stutts, Stewart, & Martell, 1998). One study did find that a 2.5 to 3.5 hour neuropsychological battery discriminated between those elderly who were still safely driving versus those who were no longer driving due to concerns about their driving ability (Meyers, Volbrecht, & Kaster-Bundgaard, 1999). In general, however, the results from neuropsychological data are weak and/or mixed.

Due to the problems associated with these other methods of driving assessment, we used a realistic, interactive, driving simulator that has successfully differentiated high risk groups, and has demonstrated reliable test performance in previous research with other populations (Guerrier, Manivannan, Pacheco & Wilkie, 1995; Guerrier & Cox, In press). Performance on the simulator is correlated with both neuropsychological test and on-road driving performance (Guerrier & Cox, in press; Parasuraman & Nestor, 1991). Since the study design required screening a large number of subjects, a comprehensive neuropsychological test battery was not feasible due to time constraints. Instead, subjects were administered a well established screening measure of global cognitive functioning (Mini Mental Status Exam) and a measure of mental flexibility and alternating attention (Trail Making Test), which has been correlated with driving safety in past research (Guerrier & Cox, In press).

By comparing cohorts of older adult drivers, we tested the following questions: 1) Which driving skills are most sensitive to the effects of aging? 2) Does driving performance differ between aging males and females? 3) Does simulator driving performance correlate with neurocognitive performance on Trails B and MMSE?

Methods

Subjects

To maximize the generalizability of our findings, three different groups of subjects were solicited from three geographically and culturally divergent samples: 192 adults from Charlottesville, Virginia were recruited through a Senior Center; 45 adults from Miami, Florida were recruited through the Stein Gerontological Institute, and 36 adults were recruited from London, Ontario, through the London Health Sciences Center. Twenty-eight of these subjects dropped out because of simulator sickness. Older females with a history of motion sickness were more likely to experience nausea and dizziness while driving the simulator and then discontinue driving (Penberthy et al., under review). These dropout subjects did not differ from those who completed the study on any of the variables that appear in Table 1. The 245 older subjects who completed the study were all licensed drivers and generally did not differ across sites on demographic variables. Canadian drivers were slightly younger ($p = .053$) and had less formal education ($p = .047$). Overall, the sample had a mean age of 70.3 + 7 (+ standard deviation), a mean driving history of 50 + 10 years, average miles driven per year of 9,537 + 7,472, and mean Mini Mental Status Exam scores of 28.5 + 1.6 (range 20–30). The sample consisted of 122 males and 123 females. Within the age increments of 60–64, 65–69, 70–74, 76–79 and 80+, there were 53, 67, 57, 46, and 22 subjects in each age group, respectively. Data were analyzed comparing subjects across these five-year increments (See Table 1).

Procedure

To objectively assess driving in a controlled environment, the Atari Research Driving Simulator was employed. It is a realistic, interactive, fixed platform simulator that generates accurate and sensitive driving performance data. An earlier single-screen version of this simulator effectively detected: 1) the acute effects of hypoglycemia (45 mg/dl) among Type I diabetic patients (Cox, Gonder-Frederick & Clarke, 1993), which was reliable over three months (Quillian, Cox, Gonder-Frederick, Driesen & Clarke, 1994), and 2) legal intoxication (> 0.08% BAL) among college students (Cox, Quillian, Gressard, Westerman, Gonder-Frederick & Canterbury, 1995). The current three-screen version of the simulator has been used to: 1) differentiate visually compromised drivers from controls (Szylk, Seiple & Viana, 1995; Szylk, Fishman, Severing, Alexander & Viana, 1993; Szylk, Brigell & Seiple, 1993; Szylk, Alexander, Severing & Fishman, 1992; Szylk, Severing & Fishman, 1991), 2) differentiate Alzheimer's disease outpatients from age matched controls (Cox, Quillian, Thorndike, Kovatchev & Hanna, 1998), 3) differentiate middle aged from older male drivers when sober and intoxicated (Quillian, Cox, Kovatchev, & Phillips, 1999), and, 4) correlate with age-sensitive cognitive characteristics (Guerrier, Manivannan, Pacheco & Wilkie, 1995; Guerrier & Cox, in press).

The simulator has three 25″ computer screens that "wrap around" the driver, providing a 160 degree visual field, along with a programmed rear view mirror depicting rear traffic. The driving environment is realistic, incorporating a typical-sized steering wheel, gas and brake pedals, seat, and seat belt. Driving performance feedback is provided to the subject *visually* through the three screens that update at a rate of 60 times/second, *auditorially* through quadraphonic speakers delivering engine, tire and road noises, and *kinesthetically* through the steering wheel and pedal pressure.

Prior to the test drive, subjects were verbally oriented to the simulator before driving a standardized practice course to familiarize themselves with the various road conditions and operations of the simulator. The practice course was similar to the experimental courses, but there were fewer road signals and less traffic. During the practice course, room lighting was adjusted to the subject's preference to minimize glare on the monitors. After completing the standardized practice course, subjects were allowed to continue driving until they felt fully comfortable operating the simulator.

Table 1
Demographic and Descriptive Characteristics' Means ± Standard Deviations of the Subsamples

	N	Mean Age	% Males/ Females	Miles Driven/Yr	Years Licensed	Mean MMSE
60–64	53	61.4 ± 1.7	43/57%	14,160 ± 9786	41.8 ± 6.6	28.7 ± 1.9
65–69	67	66.9 ± 1.3	51/49%	9,376 ± 7022	47.7 ± 5.8	28.6 ± 1.3
70–74	57	72.1 ± 1.5	54/46%	8,377 ± 5990	52.2 ± 7.7	28.6 ± 1.1
75–79	46	77 ± 1.5	48/52%	6,644 ± 4865	56.2 ± 9.4	28.3 ± 1.8
80+	22	83.6 ± 3.1	54/46%	7,751 ± 5318	60.4 ± 13.1	28.0 ± 2.1

The driving course was designed to simulate driving demands of a typical grade 2 U.S. highway (according to standards used by the Virginia Department of Transportation). The eight-mile course took approximately 20 minutes to complete when observing the posted speed limits. The driving demands required by this course are listed in Table 2.

The simulator records data eight times a second and generates 12 driving performance variables listed in Table 3. Three of these variables reflect steering control, four variables reflect braking, and five reflect speed control. Because some subjects did not complete the course during the maximum 30 minute driving session, and because the further one drove the more likely they were to encounter a critical event, Full Stops and Collisions were calculated according to the percentage of the course completed for each subject. To incorporate time and distance across the midline into a single variable, a quadratic function was calculated incorporating these parameters into the variable, Risk Midline (see Table 3).

As a screening measure of global cognitive functioning, subjects were administered the Mini Mental Status Exam, a well established general field measure of possible cognitive decline (Folstein, Folstein, & McHugh, 1975). Scores on the MMSE range from 0 to 30, where scores of 28–30 are considered normal, 21–27 suggestive of mild dementia, 11–20 as moderate dementia and 0–10 as severe

Table 2 Driving Demands for the 8 Mile Experimental Course	
Driving Demands	*Frequency*
LEFT TURNS (driver needs to turn left at specific stop-sign intersections, negotiating on-coming and cross traffic	3
RED LIGHTS (driver needs to stop)	2
GREEN LIGHTS (driver has throughway)	4
STOP-SIGNS (driver needs to stop)	6
THROUGHWAY STOP-SIGN INTERSECTIONS (side-traffic stops)	4
SPEED LIMIT CHANGES (driver needs to change speeds)	11
SUDDEN STOPS (car in front of driver slams on brakes, object in road comes into view as driver crosses hill crest, car runs red light from left side)	3
DETOURS AT STOP-SIGN INTERSECTIONS (driver needs to obey detour arrow)	4
ENCROACHING FIXED OBJECTS (vehicle parked in driver's lane)	1

Table 3
Measured Driving Performance Variables and Explanations

Driving Variable	Driving Variable Explanation
Steering	
SD Steering	Standard deviation of steering wheel angle while on road—Swerving
Off Road	Number of times car travels off road
Risk Midline	Quadratic risk function that increases the longer and further the car crosses the midline
Braking	
Maximum Braking	Maximum foot pressue applied to the brake pedal in stop zones
Inappropriate Braking	Inappropriate braking when car is in 35 mph, 45 mph, and acceleration zones
% Missed Stops	Percentage of missed stop signs and stoplights
% Collisions	% collisions per potentially risky zone
Speed Control	
Low Speed	Average % below speed limit when car is in 35 mph and 45 mph speed zones
High Speed	Average % above speed limit when car is in 35 mph and 45 mph speed zones
SD Speed	Standard deviation of speed in 35 and 45 mph zones
Left Stop Sign Hesitation	Average time (seconds) spent stopped at left turn stop sign
Left Turning Time	Seconds required to go from a complete stop at the stop line to complete the left turn

dementia. Our sample's mean score was 28.5 (SD = 1.6). Additionally subjects were administered the Trail Making Test, Parts A and B (Reitan & Wolfson, 1993). Trails B, a measure of mental flexibility, visual scanning, and the ability to attend to two sets of stimuli simultaneously, has been previously correlated with actual driving and simulator performance (Guerrier, Manivannan, Pacheco, & Wilkie, 1995; Guerrier & Cox, in press). It has also been described as a measure of the switching of visual selective attention (Parasuraman & Nestor, 1991). Trails B involves the subject drawing a line to connect a series of randomly placed numbered and lettered circles. The subject has to alternate or shift attention between the two sequences. The time to complete the task is the primary variable, with greater time indicating a slowing of visuomotor tracking and mental flexibility.

Data Analysis

Two (Gender) X five (Age Brackets) ANOVAs were performed on the simulator, MMSE and Trails B data to determine gender and age effects. Planned contrasts compared groups to identify at the age group at which there was a significant decay in performance. Factor analysis was performed on the simulator data to develop a Total Impairment Score. Correlations between these data sets were performed to identify relationships.

Results

Effects of Age on Simulator Driving Performance

Nine of the 12 variables significantly worsened with the older age groups, involving three steering, three braking and three speed control variables. In terms of steering, older subjects swerved more (SD STEER, $F = 2.59, p < .04$), drove off the side of the road more often (OFF ROAD, $F = 8.26$, p<.001), and drove across the midline more (RISK MIDLINE, $F = 3.37, p < .01$). There was a significant Age X Gender interaction for RISK MIDLINE ($F = 2.66, p < .03$). As can be seen in Figure 1, there were several males in the 80+ age that drove extensively in the wrong lane. If these individuals are removed, the RISK MIDLINE interaction term is not significant. Figure 1 displays the significant contrasts for RISK MIDLINE, OFF-ROAD, and SD STEERING for age where these variables significantly declined at ages 70+, 75+ and 70+, respectively.

The older age groups also demonstrated greater difficulty employing the *brakes* properly: using their brakes in the open road more often (INAPPROPRIATE BRAKING, $F = 4.53, p < .002$), not stopping at stop signs (% MISSED STOPS, $F = 3.56, p < .001$), and being involved in more low speed collisions (% BUMPS, $F = 2.79, p < .03$). These problems got significantly worse at the ages of 75+, 75+ and 70+, respectively (see Figure 2). There was no difference in terms of maximum pressure on the brake pedal in deceleration zones ($F = 1.21, p = .30$), suggesting no difference in functional strength of the lower extremities across age intervals.

In terms of *speed* control, older subjects had greater variability in their speed (SD SPEED, $F = 3.47, p < .001$), drove slower relative to the posted speed limit (LOW SPEED, $F = 7.80, p < .001$), and took longer to drive through a left hand turn (LEFT TURNING TIME, $F = 5.40, p < .001$), beginning at ages 75+, 70+ and 70+, respectively. There was no difference across ages in terms of speeding (HIGH SPEED, $F = 0.72, p = .60$), nor in terms of how long subjects waited at a stop sign before accelerating (LEFT TURN HESITATION, $F = 0.72, p = .60$, see Figure 3).

In order to calculate a Total Impairment Score, we used the nine significant variables in a factor analysis (SD STEERING, OFF ROAD, RISK MIDLINE, INAPPROPRIATE BRAKING, %MISSED STOPS, % COLLISIONS, LOW SPEED, SD SPEED, LEFT TURNING TIME). These variables were converted into Z scores to ensure that the scores were comparable. Factor analysis of these variables identified five factors that explained 70% of the variance. Table 4 identifies the magnitude of variance explained by each factor.

Next, a Total Impairment Score was computed based on these five factors, with a higher Total Impairment Score indicating greater driving difficulties. As illustrated in Figure 4, there was a significant Age effect for Total Impairment Score ($F = 11.07, p < .001$), indicating worse performance for older drivers. The Total Impairment Score was significantly correlated with Trails B time to completion ($r = .29, p < .001$ and MMSE scores ($r = -.13, p = .02$).

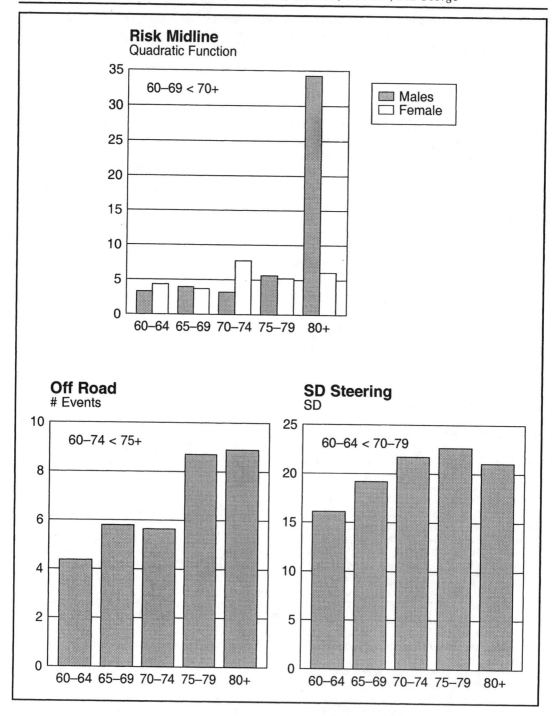

Figure 1. Significant Steering Variables

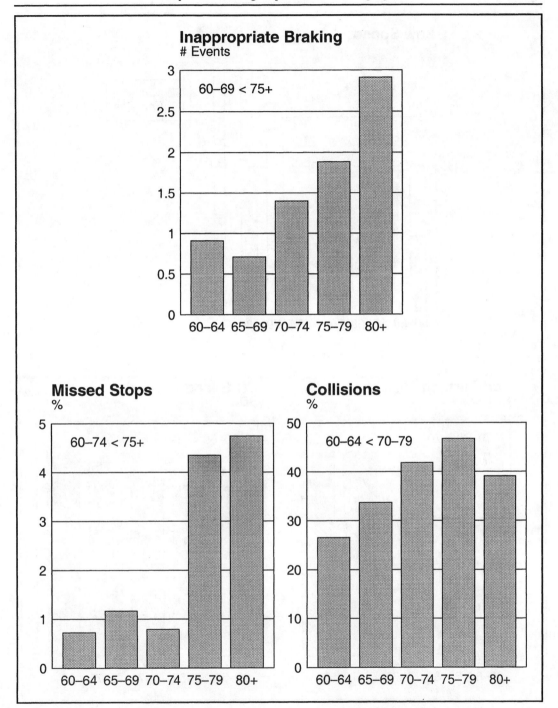

Figure 2. Significant Brake Control Variables

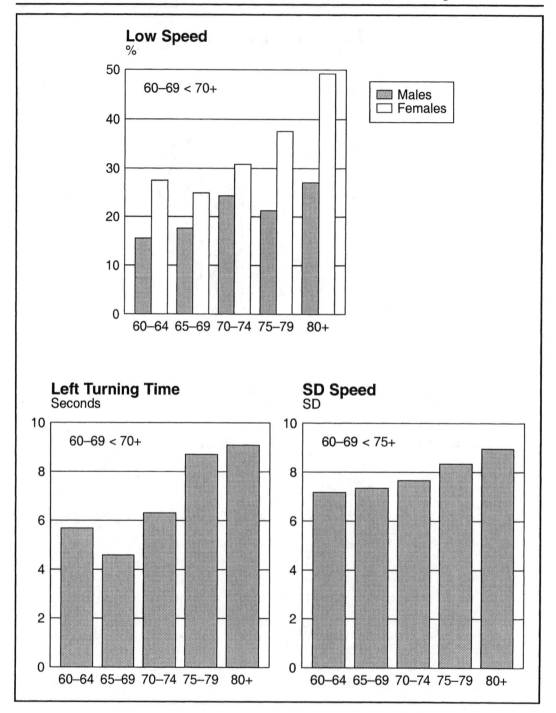

Figure 3. Significant Speed Control Variables

Gender Differences

The only significant gender difference in specific driving variables was that women drove significantly slower than males ($F = 48.85$, $p < .001$). Additionally, when compared on Total Impairment Score, females generally drove more poorly ($F = 10.99$, $p < .001$). As can be seen in Figure 4, where a larger Total Impairment Score reflects poorer driving, women had higher mean Total Impairment Scores at every age bracket. This is consistent with survey data showing older women have more accidents per miles driven (Tasca, 1997). While there was no main effect for gender on Trails B ($F = .165$, $p > .60$), there was a significant Age X Gender interaction ($F = 3.62$, $p = .007$), illustrating that women's performance on Trails B was more sensitive to age effects after age 80 (see Figure 5). While there was no interaction effect for Gender X Age for Mini Mental Status Exam, women scored slightly higher over all than their male counterparts, with respective means of 28.75 vs. 28.26 ($F = 5.87$, $p = .016$).

Neurocognitive Screening Performance

Trails B time to completion was significantly and positively correlated in the expected direction with the specific driving variables of OFF ROAD ($r = .26$, $p < .001$), % BUMPS ($r = .24$, $p < .0$), SD SPEED ($r = .11$, $p < .03$), % MISSED STOPS ($r = .31$, $p < .001$), and LEFT TURNING TIME ($r = .11$, $p < .04$). Performance on Trails B was also significantly correlated with age ($r = .24$, $p < .001$, see Figure 5). The MMSE did not significantly differ across the five age groups, with respective mean MMSE scores of 28.7, 28.6, 28.6, 28.3, 28.0.

Discussion

The current data document that driving skills are worse among progressively older subjects. There appears to be no specific area of driving which is more vulnerable to age associated decline, given that three steering, three braking and three speed control variables, as well as the Total Impairment Score, were all negatively affected. Given the general effects of aging, this is not a surprising finding. Attention to specific driving variables, however, may be warranted. There appears to be a general problem maintaining lane position, indicated by a greater degree of swerving, and driving both off road and across the midline. Preliminary data from a study employing driving diaries to heighten awareness of lane position among senior drivers suggests that this driving parameter can be improved (Kiernan, Cox, Kovatchev, Kiernan, & Giuliano, 1999). Reducing the amount of penetration into the oncoming lane of traffic could make a major impact on reducing risk of accidents.

While driving slow (LOW SPEED) may be a reasonable compensatory strategy for decreased cognitive-motor speed, it may represent a high risk behavior in certain situations, such as when crossing three lanes of traffic while making a left hand turn. This is consistent with the observation that making left hand turns is the driving event most often associated with accidents among the elderly (Cooper, 1990; Garber & Srinivasan, 1991). It has been speculated that left hand turns involve more complex information processing demands, which is what places the senior driver at relatively higher risk. The current data suggest that senior drivers are not processing this information longer (as suggested by their lack of hesitation at the stop line), but instead took longer to execute their decision. Therefore, it may be better for elderly drivers to deliberately hasten their passage through left turns, once the decision to turn has been made.

These data were generated from a driving simulator, not on-road testing. Thus the question arises: Are these data relevant to real time driving? It is reasonable to suggest that they are. Subjects from the Miami sample were also evaluated by a driving instructor sitting in the seat next to the driver traversing a standard road course. These on-road driving data were significantly correlated with driving simulator performance (Guerrier & Cox, in press). In an independent study in Charlottesville, Virginia,

Table 4
Driving Factors Accounting for 70% of Age Related Driving Variance

Factor	*Driving Variables*
Collisions	% COLLISIONS (explains 27% of the variance)
Inattention	% MISSED STOPS (explains additional 15% of the variance)
Slow Speed	LOW SPEED and LEFT TURNING TIME (explains additional 11% of the variance)
Poor Steering	SD STEERING, OFF ROAD, and RISK MIDLINE (explains additional 9% of the variance)
Erratic Speed	SD SPEED and INAPPROPRIATE BRAKING (explains additional 8% of the variance)

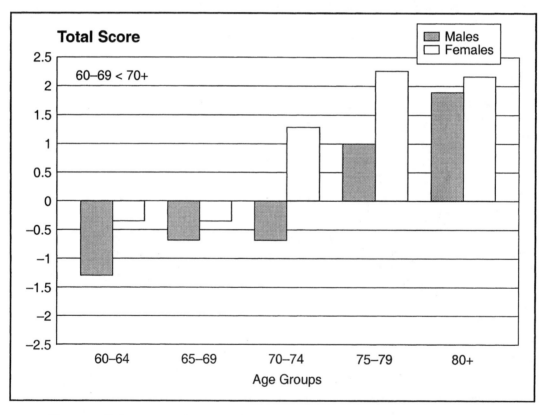

Figure 4. Driving Impairment Z Scores for Male and Female Older Drivers

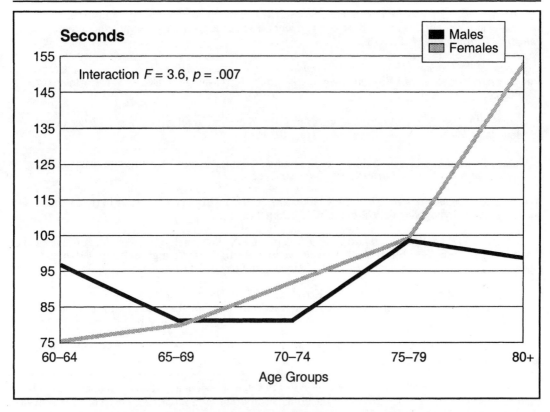

Figure 5. Mean Completion Time for Trails B

random drivers were timed as they drove through a left turn. Consistent with this simulator data, drivers estimated to be >65 years of age took approximately 30% longer to execute the left turn, compared to drivers estimated to be between 35 and 55 years of age (Cox & Cox, 1998). Consistent with on-road driving data (Tasca, 1997), we found older females drove slower than their male counterparts on the simulator. Additionally, performance on this simulator has successfully differentiated known high risk driving groups, such as intoxicated drivers, Alzheimer's disease patients and hypoglycemic subjects from age matched control groups. Finally, 18 of the best and 18 of the worst current Charlottesville subjects were surveyed 3 years after the current data was collected. The worst simulator drivers reported having over seven times more accidents (Cox, Taylor & Kovatchev, in press), suggesting that poor simulated driving performance predicts future accidents. These data would suggest that sophisticated simulation is a sound and cost-effective way of assessing driving competence, as is done with professional pilots (Hardy & David, 1997).

References

Ball, K., & Owsley, C. (1991). Identifying correlates of accident involvement for the older driver. *Human Factors, 33,* 583–595.

Barrett, G.V., Mihal, W.L., Panek, P.E., Sterns, H.L., & Alexander, R.A. (1977). Information-processing skills predictive of accident involvement for younger and older commercial drivers. *Industrial Gerontology, 4,* 173–182.

Bureau of the Census. (1993). *Current population reports: population projections of the United States by age, sex, race, and Hispanic origin, 1993 to 2050.* Washington, DC: U.S. Department of Commerce.

Cooper, P.J. (1990). Elderly drivers' views of self and driving in relation to the evidence of accident data. *Journal of Safety Research, 21*(3), 103–113.

Cox, A. & Cox, D.J. (1998). Senior's compensatory driving strategy may increase driving risk. *Journal of the American Geriatrics Society, 46,* 1063–65.

Cox, D.J., Gonder-Frederick, L.A., & Clarke, W.L. (1993). Driving decrements in type I diabetes during moderate hypoglycemia. *Diabetes, 42*(2), 239–243.

Cox, D.J., Quillian, W.C., Gressard, C.F., Westerman, P.S., Gonder-Frederick, L.A., & Canterbury, R.J. (1995). The effects of blood alcohol levels on driving variables in a high-risk population: objective and subjective measures. *Journal of Alcohol and Drug Education, 40*(3), 84–98.

Cox, D.J., Quillian WC, Thorndike FP, Kovatchev, BP, & Hanna, G. (1998). Evaluating Driving Performance of Outpatients with Alzheimer's disease. *Journal of the American Board of Family Practice. 11*(4), 264–271.

Cox, D.J., Taylor, P., & Kovatchev, B. (in press). Driving simulation performance predicts future accidents among senior drivers. *Journal of the American Geriatric Society.*

Folstein, M.F., Folstein, S.E., & McHugh, P.R. (1975). Mini-Mental State: A practical method for grading the cognitive state of patients for the clinician. *Journal of Psychiatric Research, 12,* 189–198.

Garber, N.J., & Srinivasan, R. (1991, January). Accident characteristics of elderly drivers at intersections. Paper presented at the Transportation Research Board 70th Annual Meeting, Washington, D.C.

Guerrier, J.H., & Cox, D.J. (in press). The validity of a low cost driving simulator in assessing driving performance. *Human Factors.*

Guerrier, J.H., Manivannan, P., Pacheco, A., & Wilkie, F.L. (1995). The relationship of age and cognitive characteristics of drivers to performance of driving tasks on an interactive driving simulator. *Proceedings of the Human Factors and Ergonomics Society,* 172–176.

Hardy, D. J., & Parasuraman, R. (1997). Cognition and flight performance in older pilots. *Journal of Experimental Psychology: Applied, 3*(4), 313–348.

Improving safety and mobility for older people: Project proposal. (1985). Washington, DC: Transportation Research Board.

Johnson, C., & Keltner, J. (1986). Incidence of visual field loss in 20,000 eyes and its relationship to driving performance. *Archives of Ophthalmology, 101,* 371–375.

Kahneman, D., Ben-Ishai, R., & Lotan, M. (1973). Relation of a test of attention to road accidents. *Journal of Applied Psychology, 58,* 113–115.

Kiernan, B. D., Cox, D. J., Kovatchev, B. P., Kiernan, B. S., & Giuliano, A. J. (1999). Self-monitoring improves driving performance of senior drivers. *Physical and Occupational Therapy in Geriatrics, 16*(1), 55–64.

Mendez, M. F., Cherrier, M. M., & Cymerman, J. S. (1997). Hemispatial neglect on visual search tasks in Alzheimer's disease. *Neuropsychiatry, Neuropsychology, & Behavioral Neurology, 10*(3), 203–208.

Mihal, W. L., & Barrett, G. V. (1976). Individual differences in perceptual information processing and their relation to automobile accident involvement. *Journal of Applied Psychology, 61,* 229–233.

National Highway Traffic Safety Administration. (1988). *The National Highway Traffic Safety Administration's Traffic Safety Plan for Older Persons* (Report No. DOT HS 807 316). Washington, D.C.: U.S. Department of Transportation.

National Highway Traffic Safety Administration: *Older Drivers. The Age Factor in Traffic Safety* (Report No. DOT HS 807 402). Washington, D.C.: U.S. Department of Transportation, 1989a.

National Highway Traffic Safety Administration: *Conference on Research and Development Needed to Improve Safety and Mobility of Older Drivers* (Report No. DOT HS 807 554). Washington, D.C.: U.S. Department of Transportation, 1989b.

O'Neill, D. (1992). Physicians, elderly drivers, and dementia. *Lancet, 1,* 41–43.

Owsley, C., Ball, K., Sloane, M. E., Roenker, D. L., & Bruni, J. R. (1991). Visual/cognitive correlates of vehicle accidents in older drivers. *Psychology and Aging, 6*(3), 403–415.

Parasuraman, R., & Nestor, P. G. (1991). Attention and driving skills in aging and Alzheimer's disease. *Human Factors, 33*(5), 539–557.

Penberthy, J. K., Cox, D. J., Kiernan, B. D., Kovatchev, B. P., Kiernan, B., Guerrier, J., & George, C. (under review). Driving simulator induced sickness in the older adult.

Quillian, W. C., Cox, D. J., Gonder-Frederick, L. A., Driesen, N. R., & Clarke, W. L. (1994). Reliability of driving performance during moderate hypoglycemia in adults with IDDM. *Diabetes Care, 17*(11), 1367–1368.

Quillian, W. C., Cox, D. J., Kovatchev, B. P., & Phillips, C. (1999). The effects of age and alcohol intoxication on simulated driving performance, awareness, and self-restraint. *Age and Aging, 28*(1), 59–66.

Reitan, R. M., & Wolfson, D. (1985). *The Halstead-Reitan Neuropsychological Test Battery.* Tucson, AZ: Neurospsychology Press.

Rosenbloom, S. (1993). Transportation needs of the elderly population (review). *Clinics in Geriatric Medicine, 9*(2), 297–310.

Sbordone, R.J., & Long, C.J. (1996). *Ecological validity of neuropsychological testing.* Delray Beach, FL: GR Press/St. Lucie Press.

Scialfa, C. T., Guzy, L. T., Leibowitz, H. W., Garvey, P. .M., & Tyrrell, R. A. (1991). Age differences in estimating vehicle velocity. *Psychology and Aging, 6*(1), 60–66.

Solomon, D. (1985). The older driver and highway design. In J. W. Malfetti (ed.), *Needs and problems of older drivers: Survey results and recommendations.* Falls Church, VA: AAA Foundation for Traffic Safety.

Stutts, J. C., Stewart, J. R., & Martell, C. (1998). Cognitive test performance and crash risk in an older driver population. *Accident Analysis & Prevention, 30*(3), 337–346.

Szylk, J. P., Alexander, K. R., Severing, K., & Fishman, G. A. (1992). Assessment of driving performance in patients with retinitis pigmentosa. *Archives of Ophthalmology, 110,* 1709–1713.

Szylk, J. P., Brigell, M., & Seiple, W. (1993). Effects of age and hemianoptic visual field loss on driving. *Optometry and Vision Science, 70*(12), 1031–1037.

Szylk, J. P., Fishman, G. A., Severing, K., Alexander, K. R., & Viana, M. (1993). Evaluation of driving performance in patients with juvenile macular dystrophies. *Archives of Ophthalmology, 111,* 207–2123.

Szylk, J. P., Seiple, W., & Viana, M. (1995). Relative effects of age and compromised vision of driving performance. *Human Factors, 37*(2), 430–436.

Szylk, J. P., Severing, K., & Fishman, G. A. (1991). *Peripheral visual field loss and driving performance.* Washington, DC: AAA Foundation for Traffic Safety Research Reports.

Tasca, D. (1997). *A Statistical Overview of Senior Driver Collision Involvement 1992–1994,* Ministry of Transportation of Ontario, Ontario Government Publication.

Traffic safety of elderly road users. (1985). Paris, France: Organization for Economic Cooperation and Development.

Transportation Research Board special report 218. *Transportation in an aging society: improving mobility and safety for older persons.* Vol. 1. Washington, D.C.: National Research Council, 1988: 1–12.

Waller, P. F. (1985). Preventing injury to the elderly. In H. T. Phillips and S. A. Gaylord (Eds.), *Aging and Public Health* (pp. 103–146). New York: Springer Publishing Company.

Acknowledgments

We would like to express our appreciation to Dr. Carol Manning, Dr. Robert Brashear, Ms. Paula Damgaard, and Ms. Serrita Jane of the University of Virginia's Department of Neurology. We would also like to thank Mr. Rick Moncrief, former Director of Research at Atari Corporation, Milpitas, CA and Mr. Duncan Brown, our computer programmer, for the invaluable assistance and expertise they provided with the Atari driving simulator. We would additionally like to express our appreciation to Drs. Dianne Snustad, Suzanne Holroyd and Richard Lindsay for their assistance in recommending subjects.

Advances in Medical Psychotherapy and Psychodiagnosis
2002–2003, Volume 11, pp. 123–136

Compassion Fatigue and Emotional Depletion in the Mental Health Professional

Karen L. Gold, Psy.D.
El Paso, Texas

Let us not grow weary while doing good, for in due season we shall reap if we do not lose heart.

Galations 6:9

"Do your best, then don't worry; be happy." So wrote Avatar Meher Baba, the father of Sufism, who was dubbed "The Perfect Man" by his followers. The words of this legendary healer have been read and revered by thousands. His mantra "Don't worry, Be happy" was even sung a cappella, by millions after Bobby McFerrin released a recording with the same title in 1988. Yet Baba himself spoke his last syllables on July 10, 1925. Perhaps Baba stopped speaking because he grew so very weary of talk. Or, he may have been told, as we therapists often are in our graduate training, that "The one who does the talking is the one who gets the therapy." So Baba likely became a listener and a writer, as we in the helping professions tend to do.

Some of us listen interpretatively, some reflectively, and some actively, according to our training. We listen for transference and tune into our countertransference. We analyze our clients' neurolinguistics; we hover like predatory birds, waiting to pounce on a patient's Freudian slip. We listen, and we watch, as do members of the audience in experimental theater.

Early in the 20th century, contemporaneously with Meher Baba, Lord Brain of Great Britain observed, "A clinician occupies a lonely seat in the front row of the stalls of human drama, is constantly watching, even intervening in, the tragedies, comedies and tragicomedies which form the raw material of literature." C.A. Hamman (1868–1930) obviously agreed, for he wrote, "The people in this world put on a tremendous show, and doctors have a front row seat." More than a century before, Horace Walpole told us, "The world is a comedy to those that think, a tragedy to those that feel."

Seated elsewhere in that front row are social workers, crisis responders, chaplains and other members of the clergy. Sometimes the plays we see are of the Theater of the Absurd or the Theater of Cruelty. Sometimes the plays are banal, sometimes they are gripping. Nevertheless, the consequence of our presence in the audience is that we and our clergy colleagues are particularly vulnerable to a peculiar malady which causes us exquisite pain and exhaustion. The malady is variously referred to as Compassion Fatigue, Compassionate Loneliness, Secondary Traumatic Stress, and Burnout. These terms are not interchangeable and synonymous, but they are often confused. Regardless of whatever one chooses to call it, it hurts, and its cadence drowns out "The Perfect Man's" admonition of "Do your best, then don't worry; be happy."

And so it was that I, the writer, having seen many dramas by the point at which I was more successful in my professional life than I had ever dreamed I would be, found myself feeling strangely "used up" and unhappy. Although I was rarely, if ever, alone, I was lonely. And I was tired, so very tired. Perhaps I had seen one too many dramas played out by the myriad actors I had encountered in twenty years as a therapist.

I waited for my dysphoria to pass. It didn't. I tried to leave it behind and took a vacation. It traveled along in my suitcase, round trip. I imperiously ordered it banished; it laughed. I tried to murder it; it wouldn't die. So, I decided that there was no other recourse but to get to know it, understand it and thereby find its Achilles' heel, and I did.

The words that follow have been written so that I might share my discoveries and thoughts with you, the reader. Perhaps it will provide you with an ounce of prevention so that you might forestall the malady which almost certainly awaits you as a caregiver. I speak of any of the variations of emotional depletion identified by those terms such as burnout, secondary traumatic stress disorder, compassionate stress, pathological loneliness and Compassion Fatigue. Precision requires that these terms be individually defined, although, for the reader, the variances are merely the splitting of hairs.

Burnout is a state of extreme dissatisfaction with one's work. It is characterized by excessive distancing from our clients and patients, impaired competence, low energy, increased irritability with the members of our support system, and other signs of dysfunction due to individual, social, employment, and environmental factors (Visionary Productions, 1994). Compassion Fatigue, and for that matter Secondary Traumatic Stress Disorder, are better described as "a state of tension and preoccupation with the individual or cumulative trauma of patients and clients as manifested in one or more ways: re-experiencing the traumatic events we hear our patients and clients tell us about; avoidance of or numbing ourselves to any reminders of or stimuli associated with the events they have described to us; and feeling ourselves to be in a state of persistent arousal" (Visionary Productions, 1994). Before 1950, stress was a term used in physics, and referred to the application of force great enough to distort an object or structure, such as a stanchion or a bridge (Croucher, 2000). Hans Selye brought the term to prominence as it related to the body's response to any demand made upon it. Dr. Arch Hart, in several articles written in 1984, has carefully differentiated "Stress" from "Burnout" in a variety of ways. Stress, he states in part, is characterized by overengagement, overreaction, disintegration and the loss of fuel and energy to the point that it may kill you. Burnout isn't likely to kill you, but it can make your life seem like it is not worth living. He ascribes disengagement, emotional blunting, demoralization, and grief engendered by the loss of ideals and hopes, to burnout.

The result of the malady, however identified, is that 54% of us work to restrict our emotional involvement, 60% of us suffer from depression, and 90% of us believe that our family life has suffered from the emotional demands on us due to our work (Hippocrates Magazine, 1994).

Compassion Fatigue, as the writer chooses to refer to it in the interest of simplicity and fellowship with other caregivers, is the emotional residue of the exposure to working with the suffering, particularly those suffering from the consequences of trauma. It is the inability to let go of information we acquire as a result of doing our job. It is not about supervision, licensure, insurance premiums, rent, HMO's, or hospital privileges, for these are burnout sources. It is about clients and patients.

Compassion Fatigue leads to or stems from compassionate loneliness; the kind experienced by chaplains and clergy. The loneliness is empathic more than true. It parallels the anguish, worry, bewilderment, anger, depression, fear and alienation experienced by three out of four parish ministers (Croucher). It is influenced by the desperately lonely, hurting and alienated people whom we encounter every day.

Loneliness is the price we may pay to do what we do, even if we face no personal crisis or grief in our own lives, which is highly unlikely. Perhaps it is necessary to explain further these subtle variations of the term loneliness. Many people have tried to define it. It is described as a lack of close caring relationships (emotional loneliness); the absence of an engaging social network (social loneliness); lack of a sense of meaning in one's relationships (existential loneliness); the reality of facing life experiences alone (true loneliness); and as the voluntary extreme social withdrawal usually accompanied by self-pity, listlessness, depression and inconsolable grief (pathological loneliness). Further, there is loneliness anxiety, which Clark Moustakas said distracts us from our mission and leads us to seek too much contact with others.

As the reader can imagine, over the centuries much has been written about our patients' loneliness, but very little has been said about ours. Edward Glover, in 1929, stated, "Papers on the subject matter of loneliness are as plentiful as blackberries, but only once in a while is the caregiver's loneliness subjected to scrutiny." The loneliness that goes hand in glove with Compassion Fatigue has only recently been studied. Charles Figley and his colleagues at Florida State University have identified characteristics and symptoms of Secondary Traumatic Stress and/or Compassion Fatigue. They have developed a self-test available on the Internet, as have other researchers (Visionary Productions, 1994; Museck, 1997; Bintliff, 1991). They have also developed a model to explain its etiology. Some of the hallmarks of Compassion Fatigue include memory gaps about the elements of the events described to us, feelings of estrangement from others, insomnia, irritability, exaggerated startle response, a sense of isolation, fear, preoccupation, physical fatigue, and anger towards or dislike of our colleagues. Compassion Fatigue may also manifest itself as feelings of failure or as hopelessness and disillusionment about our work.

Compassion Fatigue is not new to our field. We have many forebears who experienced it. Even our mythology addresses loneliness. Chiron, the centaur, was a physical and psychic healer who suffered from it. We can count ourselves among many eloquent hermits, monks, explorers, writers and poets who have tried to put the feelings into words. William Wordsworth wrote his famous poem, "I Wandered Lonely As A Cloud"; Henry David Thoreau, in Walden, penned the words, "The mass of men lead lives of quiet desperation. What is called resignation is confirmed desperation."

Closer to our caregiver cerebral centers, we learned how utterly lonely Sigmund Freud became when he fell from grace because of his postulated ideas, which were in fact not that much more bizarre than those of his contemporaries. Carl Jung, Harry Stack Sullivan, Wilhelm Reich, Rollo May and Otto Rank grappled with Compassion Fatigue, too. Erich Fromm said, "Loneliness is easy to catch, hard to cure, rarely fatal, but always unpleasant and sometimes wretched beyond bearing." Clark Moustakas thought loneliness was necessary for transformation, and described it as "an organic experience, which points to nothing else, is for no other purpose, and results in nothing but the realization of itself." However, for most of us who are forced to choose an organic experience to facilitate transformation, loneliness is not the one that we would select.

Paul Tournier, a Swiss colleague, believes that loneliness is the most devastating malady of our age. He says, "It is worse than homelessness. There is no departure, exile, or shelter. The lonely person is fully there, as fully as he can ever be."

A theme in our literature, as sparse as it is, suggests that the more dedicated and idealistic the clinician, the greater the depth of the loneliness, and the broader the span of it over his lifetime. Clinicians who are lonely and suffering from Compassion Fatigue are more like one another than different. There are striking developmental similarities, and there is universal vulnerability. The most prone to develop it are the deeply sensitive among us, the most caring, the most willing to work extra time and to put in more than 100%.

The Child

It is customary, but I think it is a mistake, to speak of happy childhood. Children are often anxious and acutely sensitive. Man ought to be man and master of his fate, but children are at the mercy of those around them.

Sir John Lubbock

As children, mental health practitioners typically felt lonely and different. They were deeply affected by the plight of the world's hungry, homeless, unhappy and ill. They were the most moved by natural disasters, and the most likely to ask "Why?" in the aftermath of tragedy. Many were the defenders of the "nerds," "geeks," and "dorks" who were rejected as friends by the members of the in-crowds. Dr. J. said, "As a child I didn't like being alone and as an adolescent I had an aversion to it." Dr. V. described feeling "like the kid on the outside with his nose pressed against a window wanting to be part of the group inside but not knowing how to go about it." Another practitioner said he was lost and lonely at home. One more stated, "My parents were very devouring people who never let go." He was like some others who chose loneliness. Dr. K. said that he abandoned his parents in favor of ideas, "affecting something abstract in place of something personal." Our family backgrounds were less than ideal, and this may have been the very factor which led us to our fields.

A number of us believe that we are driven by a search for compensation and a cure for personal unhappiness. Karl Menninger explained that too many of us grew up in rejecting, inadequate families. We were the family nurturers. We "developed a professional interest in lonely, eccentric, and unloved people. We were rushed into adulthood. Only selfless labor made us feel satisfied with ourselves." Many of us, throughout our young lives, developed more and worse colds and minor illnesses than our peers, and research has indeed shown long-term immunosuppressive effects of negative emotions, including excessive compassion (Rein, et al; 1995). Unfortunately, too many of us became pathological givers. We gave too much and eventually we could no longer take from others. But our motives were pure, and we simply wanted to make a difference. As George Groddeck (1866–1934) put it, "It would not be a bad thing if the elite of the medical profession would be a little less clever and would adopt a more primitive method of thinking, and reason more as children do."

The Clinician as Student

His mind must be strong indeed, if, rising above juvenile credulity, it can maintain a wise infidelity against the authority of his instructors and the bewitching delusions of their theories.

Thomas Jefferson, 1807

As high school and young college students, many of us considered medicine as a career field. One of us stated that, as an unhappy child, she looked to become a clinician because she wanted to know an interesting variety of people with whom she could engage. When we began our training, we were highly introspective, self-probing, sensitive to hurt, and unusually self-critical. For some of us, our student days marked the beginning of the lonely trek into the future, for we were taught that a competent health professional is able to submerge all needs except an abstract desire to be helpful. Some of our teachers were, however, themselves hypocrites. They had no desire to be helpful to us.

Sir William Osler, a brilliant teacher of medical students, wrote in the latter half of the 19th century that, "The successful teacher is no longer on a height, pumping knowledge at high pressure into passive receptacles . . . he is a senior student anxious to help his juniors." It seems that few, if any, teachers of mental health professionals read that section of Osler's book, *The Student Life.* On the other hand, they probably did read the more palatable writings of this scholar, who encouraged them to teach us to develop an unrealistic clinical detachment. He said, "No quality takes rank with imperturbability. It means coolness and presence of mind under all circumstances, calmness amid storm, clearness of judgment in moments of great peril. It is immobility, impassiveness, or to use an old and expressive word, Phlegm. It is the quality most appreciated by the laity although most often misunderstood by them. He who shows in his face the slightest alteration, expressive anxiety or fear has not his medullary centers under the highest control. I urge you to educate your nerve centers so that not the slightest dilator or contractor influence shall pass through the vessels of your face."

The writer is not sorry to say that some excellent clinicians must surely suffer from oppositional defiant disorder. When around trauma victims or their traumatizers, they may flinch, grimace, or become unabashedly wet-eyed, despite their training. Freud, too, in discussing the proper attitude we were to assume, admonished us to "subordinate all personal feelings in order to concentrate fully on technical operations." He said, "Emotional coldness gives the doctor desirable protection for his own emotional life and the patient the largest amount of help." No patient of the writer's has ever claimed to have been harmed by authenticity of emotion. Expressionlessness is antithetical to empathy.

Perhaps in a future article, the writer will have an opportunity to explore with the reader the training and education of interns and residents. The writer considers much of her training to have been abusive, demoralizing and hopelessly impractical. The agendas and vendettas of professors and supervisors, it seems, have been all but ignored. Teachers must be made to look beyond the student's learning problems and consider their teaching problems, as well as the emotional sources from which they spring. The teachers' and supervisors' own loneliness and their "God Complex" (which will be elaborated upon later in this paper) may cause them to feel threatened by the younger, and perhaps, considerably brighter trainee. It would have been a kindness to have heard even one professor say, as did Voltaire in 1762, "Men will always be mad and those who think they can CURE them are the maddest of all." We should have been reminded that in our future careers we would not be plying our wares, but dealing with living, suffering fellow creatures. We should have been alerted to the common problems which plague even the excellent clinicians as they march through their professional lives.

The Novitiate

Man arrives as a novice at each age of his life.

Nicholas Chamfort (1741–94)

Inexperience is what makes a young man do what an older man says is impossible.

Herbert V. Prochnow (1948)

The young practitioner charges into his future on a noble steed, determined to help and heal the suffering masses of the maladjusted and the unhappy. But the novice clinician may learn that a new practice or job position can result in an unexpected sense of isolation and estrangement. Certain factors contribute to this sense: being confined to an office, separation from colleagues, environmental deprivation, physical inactivity, and isolation imposed by confidentiality. Some novitiates grow lonely and fatigued because they see too great a contrast between themselves and their ideal, perhaps the one professor or mentor who epitomized for them all that they hoped they themselves would become. Many novitiates become unsure that they want to continue to answer the call. They even seriously contemplate leaving the profession. In reaching outside of their personal space, searching for answers, few ask for help. The best way to get help is, without doubt, from a willing senior practitioner, a mentor. Some say that the loneliness of the clinician when he or she is in a new private practice is due to a lack of guidance from a senior individual on a daily basis, and this loneliness plus lack of guidance poses serious risks. The practitioner may become intellectually stunted, hopelessly calloused or careless. Lord Byron may have had this group in mind when he wrote,

There is an order of mortals on the earth
Who do become old in their youth and die ere middle age.

The Veteran Practitioner

No wise man ever wished to be younger.

Jonathan Swift

The years between 50 and 70 are the hardest. You are always being asked to do things and you're not yet decrepit enough to turn them down.

T. S. Eliot, 1950

The most successful veteran practitioners describe a significant turning point in their work lives after 15 to 20 years in practice. It is then that they begin to work more from their own styles than that of one learned so much earlier in their student days. While the changes after the turning point are anxiety provoking, they are also satisfying and enlivening. Choosing to practice as one wants, rather than as one was taught, allows us to reap greater rewards in our profession than we have ever known. Some of the rewards are making sense out of what is confusing, having bright interesting people come to see us, discovering that we are not alone in our loneliness, and learning from our patients.

On the other hand, excessive devotion to work leads us to a loss of identity, grandiosity, secrecy, and emotional preoccupation. There are deleterious effects on our relationships with friends and family members. We become increasingly "clinical" and less real. Life is lived vicariously and we become observers rather than participants in the events and experiences of everyday living.

Clinicians, as it happens, tend to have very few friends. We explain this away as a result of the tremendous demands on our professional lives by stressors. These stressors include long hours, paperwork, therapeutic logjams, inadequate support personnel, patient non-compliance and the pressures upon us to practice our artful science defensively. Many veteran clinicians ultimately reach the conclusion that they don't need friends because they live vicariously through their patients. These are the clinicians who concern us the most. Our job is not physically arduous, but it does require sound judgment, controlled empathy, and mental stamina. These skills are eroded by Compassion Fatigue, burnout, or secondary traumatic stress disorder, just as much as they are compromised by mental illness. The isolation of solo practice increases the rate and degree of the deterioration.

At sixteen I was stupid, confused, insecure and indecisive.
At 25 I was wise, self-confident, prepossessing and assertive.
At 45, I am stupid, confused, insecure and indecisive. Who would have supposed that maturity is only a short break in adolescence?

Jules Feiffer (1974)

The Spouse

The more civilized people become the less capable they seem of lifelong happiness with one partner.

Bertrand Russell

Marriage is neither heaven nor hell. It is simply purgatory.

Abraham Lincoln

We have an unhappy track record in our marriages. Too often we treat our spouses like our patients, and they resent it. Our spouses lament that they receive less attention than do our patients. Many spouses of clinicians complain that they have often felt lonely as well as envious of the patients.

Unreasonable expectations, and assumptions by patients of our availability, lead our spouses to feelings of stress, loneliness, and even jealousy. Some of us adopt a position of superiority. There are those among us who believe that they have wonderful marriages, perfect children, cultured and profound interests, and a clear and correct grasp of current sociology. But often, this grandiosity is experienced all alone. Research conclusions tell us that, typically, the relationship between husband and wife when one or the other is a mental health practitioner lacks emotional intensity. For the most part, the emotional interaction with the spouse, while it may be positive, is only lukewarm. The practitioner speaks of his spouse with temperate placidity; he speaks of his patients with involved excitement. One clinician says our work is a safe, controlled way to be intimate. One can get close, but control it; one can be intimate, but without commitment. Another said, "I personally like the kind of deep but limited intimacy that psychotherapeutic relationships have. As a woman who in her past easily found herself merging with others once I became emotionally involved, I needed to learn about boundaries and detachments. Now I can deal with the contradiction of longing for closeness but needing separation too. I find it a valuable model for my relationships." This writer certainly worries about the health of a nonprofessional relationship fashioned on a psychotherapy model.

At highest risk are the marriages of clinicians with perfectionistic personalities, who believe wholeheartedly in the words of Martin Fisher (1879–1962): "A doctor must work eighteen hours a day and seven days a week. If you cannot console yourself to this, get out of the profession." Our obsessional traits lead us to a rigid, emotionally restricted style of interacting with our spouses, resulting in marital discord. Often, however, the spouse is blamed. One therapist admitted that her work afforded her a meaningful intimacy with a patient that she could never achieve in her personal life married to a narcissist. Too many married clinicians have substituted therapeutic relationships for personal ones, in a markedly ill-advised compromise. This, too, was never explored with us in our graduate training.

Clinicians' Children and Clinician Parents

One of the most obvious facts about grown-ups to a child is that they have forgotten what it is like to be a child.

Randall Jarrell (1914–1965)

Parents are the last people on earth who ought to have children.

Samuel Butler (1835–1902)

You can do anything with children if you only play with them.

Otto Von Bismarck (1815–1898)

Parents learn a lot from their children about coping with life.

Muriel Spark (1918–)

Clinicians' children are acutely aware of their parents' lonely, unhappy childhoods. Yet, they feel distant from the parent who often works very hard to be good at the job. Sometimes, the clinician parent is too inclined to evaluate his child as he was taught to evaluate young patients. A youngster who is not developmentally on target, who is not lawfully following Piaget's paradigm or the stages of psychosexual development outlined by Freud can become a project, or, worse still, a stigma for the parent. Other offspring complain of receiving less attention than the parent's patients. Ironically, many children of mental health caregivers go on to become clinicians themselves, seeking a means of attaining intimacy with the practitioner parents which had been lacking in their lives when they were young. Unfortunately, the children of clinicians, when they themselves become parents, replicate their own stories. They toil all day, sometimes the eighteen hours which Fisher spoke of, and look forward to a quiet meal and an evening of television entertainment. Depleted of energy, they desire neither to listen nor to speak. Those who are taken to task by their spouses or children may then escape into their solitary dens and work on the all important written reports soon due. Their worlds shrink all the more, to the point at which some reside on planets inhabited by only patients and their mental health care providers. A vast number of researchers have concluded that anywhere from 11 to 90 per cent of practitioners experience interpersonal problems not unlike those for which their patients are seeking their help.

Retirement

Doctors are mostly imposters. The older a doctor is and the more venerated he is, the more he must pretend to know everything. Of course, they grow worse with time. Always look for a doctor who is hated by the best doctors. Always seek out a bright young doctor before he comes down with nonsense.

Thornton Wilder (1897–1975)

Employment is nature's physician and is essential to human happiness.

Galen, 2nd century AD

It is true that the picture that the writer has painted of the clinician as child, student, novice, veteran, spouse, and parent is not flattering. But we are addressing the psychic damage and the scars which result from secondary traumatic stress disorder, burnout, Compassion Fatigue, and/or loneliness across the life span. This loneliness is not alleviated when the clinician reaches retirement age. Far too many of us resist retirement. What poses as professional dedication is often at heart a morbid addiction. Some of us are unwilling to leave our practices or positions even when we become infirm. Many of us talk about the value of our experience. But the question is raised as to how much experience is necessary. Can one really say that the experience of a 70 year old practitioner is better than that of someone who is only 55? For the chronically lonely clinician, patients make up for the loss of intimate contact and meaningful life experiences. The elderly clinician may no longer have his own friends; his patients' friendships and enemies are as his own. Worse yet, his sex life may be stunted, for his patients' sexual activities provided a substitute. He is highly unlikely to recognize his social deficiencies, however, or get help, for too often he sees no decline. Deterioration in sight, hearing and memory can definitely impair the elderly clinician's effectiveness, but because of the gradual shrinking of her world, she has nothing left except her work. The marriage may long be over, the relationship with the children estranged, and the friendships never nurtured. Guy and his colleagues (1987, 1989) found that no less than thirteen per cent of practitioners in mental health expect to die at their desks and do not admit that their advancing age or loneliness can be impacting negatively on their professional competence.

The God Complex

An expert is one who knows more and more about less and less.

Nicholas M. Butler (1862–1947)

In 1913, Ernest Jones wrote a paper called "The God Complex" about those of us who have a solid faith in our own importance, immortality and entitlement, unmatched by anyone else. This subgroup of us ostensibly desires aloofness, inaccessibility, and mysteriousness. As well, they display modesty and self-effacement. Clinicians marked by "The God Complex" are happiest in privacy and seclusion. They reject new knowledge, desire constant appreciation, and maintain that they protect the weak. "The God Complex" may mask loneliness, but it is not marked by Compassion Fatigue or burnout. The training of the 1930's contributed to "The God Complex." The prestige of being a "doctor" was felt to guarantee power, which led to arrogance and dictatorial attitudes. It was fed by the devoted admiration of nurses, social workers, and other "subordinates." Carl Rogers, fortunately, came forward to save most of us from ourselves. Now, the would-be Gods among us become addicted to our computer screens, exercise regimens, and private obsessions. Some of us cannot bear to "cure" our patients: we need them to need us. Those that feel this desperate need to be needed are "wounded healers" (Jung, 1951). Such clinicians have also been compared to the magnificent Wizard of Oz, who is really just an ordinary but perhaps frightened individual who hides behind a curtain. The impaired therapist who begins to question his faith in himself, and for that matter, in the God who allowed him to scale the heights to success, is too injured psychically to seek the help he needs. She may be embarrassed at her failure to practice what she had long preached to patients. The very same person who is trained to see pain and the possibilities for its reduction in others may refuse to enter into therapy herself. More than half of mental health caregivers who admit to problems such as drug use, depression, and sexual dysfunction are unwilling to seek help. They apparently will leave no alternative medicine or holistic stone unturned in trying to heal their wounds without seeing a therapist. Ironically, their self-help strategies are usually 180 degrees disparate from those they use with their own clientele. Norcross and his colleagues (1991) found that psychotherapists commonly recommend medication and helping relationships to their patients, but treat themselves via stimulus control, self-punishment and the forced imposition of will power. In other words, they struggle to change themselves from within, using the harshest interventions available to them, and which they would never use with their patients. If all else fails, and the therapist-in-distress does seek professional help, studies (Liaboe et al., 1989; Norcross et al., 1989) have indicated that the help sought will be psychoanalytical and psychodynamic, regardless of the therapist's own orientation and preferred mode of treatment provision to others. Studies also reveal that, once the therapist-patient has entered psychotherapy, he or she deems the treatment a success better than 85% of the time (Brady, et al., 1994).

Perhaps it is not such a bad thing to hurt. An Arabic proverb states, **"No man is a good physician who has never been sick."** Conversely, George Bernard Shaw observed that, **"The most tragic thing in the world is a sick doctor."** Confounding the issue further, Diderot in the mid 1700s said, **"There is less harm to be suffered in being mad among madmen than in being sane all by oneself."** In this writer's opinion, having emotional problems is not a prerequisite for being an effective therapist, but neither is it a handicap. The experience of having worked through one's problems in the present or those lingering from the past can help the therapist to mature and to reach a level of empathy never before known. Most importantly, it teaches the clinician the value of reasonable humility, and permits her to say with some conviction, "There but for the grace of God go I."

Pressure of Ethical Edicts

A clinician shall behave towards his colleagues as he would have them behave towards him.

Geneva Code of Ethics

I have noticed a tendency on the part of an occasional elder and distinguished man to think that the rules of medical ethics were meant for young fellows just starting out, but not for him.

J. Chalmers Da Costa (1863–1933)

A definite contributor to dysphoria in the practice of our craft is the invasion by third party entities who seem to hold the notion that clinical practice is superfluous entertainment. We are discouraged from treating factitious disorders, chemical dependency, eating disorders, etc. Sometimes, if truth be told, we are tempted to lie about a diagnosis so that we can get help to our patients in need, or give help longer than the period authorized. What the third party entities and others forget is that the evidence is very strong that the vast majority of patients stop treatment as soon as they can, regardless of how generous their health benefits are. We are, many of us, confused, frightened, and conflicted. How can the art and science of our profession survive in the face of Daubert, Robinson, and Kuhmo attacks, petty grievances, frivolous lawsuits, and over-zealous policing? Our licensing boards have gone way too far to the right. We fear our colleagues. We become uneasy about public playfulness, being seen unkempt, drinking, engaging in religious or political activities or getting therapy ourselves. We can be hurt by shopping at cheap stores or expensive boutiques, driving a motorcycle, enjoying unsophisticated or "adult" entertainment, or displaying anger at people who provoke us. The licensing authorities insist that we learn and adhere to tomes of ethical rules, many of which are unnecessarily restrictive at best. Why can't we simply pledge to keep the Ten Commandments and to do no harm? God asks less of us than our licensing boards. But to speak up and assert ourselves is a ticket to loneliness, ostracism and secondary stress disorder or Compassion Fatigue. The writer will remind you, the reader, that even the devil knows scripture, and being cited for ethical violations by the professions' self-appointed police can have a devastating long-term effect upon a good clinician. The prime work ethic in other Western cultures is "no dobbin' on a mate"; in the United States, of late, the ethic seems to be "It's dog eat dog." It saddens this writer to note that we as mental health professionals tend to underpathologize our colleagues and ourselves, but overdescribe others as unethical. Some practitioners throw their colleagues to the wolves quite gleefully. Ironically, the very professions that aim to assist people in accepting and coming to terms with their disabilities, feelings, shortcomings, inadequacies, mistakes, and needs often fail to tolerate or even acknowledge such human concerns within their own ranks.

Ounces of Prevention: Pounds of Cure

A good laugh and a long sleep are the best cures in the doctor's book.

Irish Proverb

Loneliness can spur us on to take a fresh look at ourselves and to grow. The professional posture of disinterested objectivity is inappropriate. We must allow relationships with patients to become more relaxed, intimate and mutual. We must put our signature style in the process of the work we do, producing for ourselves more pleasure and satisfaction. We cannot simply demand that patients struggle with their problems; we must speak of us and our problems. There are few individuals who are suited to spending all of their working hours in the practice of healing. Most clinicians benefit from diversity, which means bringing professional activities such as teaching and supervision, writing, research, consultation, administration, and other forms of clinical practice into our repertoire. Immersion in creative activity may also be vitally important. The medicine men and women among all cultures but our own understand that the shaman has to free himself from deep depression by a creative act. Involvement in such pursuits as music, poetry, dance, drawing, painting, photography, woodworking, and sculpture may help keep us sane and at peace with ourselves.

We need self-confidence and poise, combined with a great deal of humility, to withstand the emotional onslaught of our patients. We must accept that there is a significant price to be paid for being a clinician. It is the price paid for the front row seat that the healer has in the theater of the human condition. We, the other helping professionals, and the clergy who sit beside us in the front row must take steps to prevent Compassion Fatigue, secondary traumatic stress disorder, burnout, and loneliness. We must learn to use humor, for even the Bible tells us that "A merry heart doeth great good." We must give up the wish that our work will become easier. We must accept that we can only ease some of our patients' pain. We must realize that it is not unprofessional to be human, and just because Compassion Fatigue and its synonyms do not appear in the DSM IV does not mean that the disorder isn't real.

Mark Twain said, **"Be good and you will be lonesome."** Sigmund Freud defined health as the capacity to love and work. Research appears to bear out both of these sages. Healers who are the most satisfied with their work are also the most satisfied with their personal relationships. The prescription for loneliness, secondary traumatic stress, Compassion Fatigue, and burnout is human interaction and friendships.

We would do well to heed George Bernard Shaw's words: **"Make it compulsory for a doctor using a brass plate to have inscribed on it in addition to the letters indicating his qualifications, the words 'Remember that I, too, am mortal'."** Better still, perhaps we should always bear in mind "The Perfect Man's" advice: **"Do your best, then don't worry. Be happy."**

References and Bibliography

Andre', R. (1991). *Positive Solitude: A practical program for mastering loneliness and achieving self-fulfillment.* New York, New York: Harper-Collins Publisher.

Baum, R (1999). *The Truth About Tears, Parts One, Two and Three.* (Source: W. H. Frey. (1985) *Crying: The mystery of tears. Winston Press.*)

Brady, J.L., Guy, J.D. and Norcross, J.C. (1995). *Innovations in Clinical Practice,* Vol. 14. Managing your own distress: Lessons from psychotherapists healing themselves. Sarasota, Fla.: Professional Resource Press.

Brook, M. (1990). *The Practitioner.* Psychosis and Depression.

Croucher, R. (no date given). *Churchlink.* Stress and burnout in ministry.

Frazer, L. (1993). *New Physician.* Remote Possibilities.

Gorkin, M. (2000). Creative burnout. Stress Doc@aol.com

Grosch, W. & Olsen. (1994). *Innovations in Clinical Practice,* Vol 14. Therapist burnout. A self psychology and systems perspective. Sarasota, Fla.: Professional Resource Press.

Hart, A. (no date given). *Churchlink.* Stress and Burnout.

Herring, J. (1996). *Tallahassee Democrat.* While caring for others, don't forget to care for yourself.

Kerkhove, R. (1996). *Avatar Meher Baba: His Life, His Message and His Followers.* Kerhove-Peter-Milne.

Knight, B. G. (1993). *The Geontologist.* A meta-analytic review of interventions for caregiver distress: recommendations for future research.

Kottler, J. (1990). *Private Moments, Secret Selves.* Los Angeles: Jeremy P. Tarcher, Inc.

The Lancet. The doctor is unwell. (editorial), Voume 342, Number 8882, November 1993.

Lawrence, J. M. (1992). *Medical Journal of Australia.* The Impaired Doctor.

Lewis, J. M. et al (1993). *Texas Journal of Medicine.* Work satisfaction in the lives of physicians.

Maeder, T. (1989). *The Atlantic Monthly.* Wounded Healers.

Musick, J. (1997). *Family Practice Management.* How close are you to burnout? American Academy of Family Physicians.

Nuestra Pan Diario. Compassion fatigue. (editorial), June 1, 1997.

Posen, D. (1995). *The Canadian Journal of Continuing Medical Education.* Stress management for patient and physician.

Rein, G., Atkinson, M., & McCraty, M.A.(1995). *Journal of Advancement in Medicine.* The Physiological and Psychological Effects of Compassion and Anger.

Reynolds, R. & Stone, J. (eds) (1991). *On Doctoring: Stories Poems, and Essays.* New York, New York: Simon & Schuster.

Sanger, D. E. (1993). *New York Times.* The Career and the Kimono.

Stamm, B. H. (ed.) (1999). *Secondary Traumatic Stress: Self-Care Issues for Clinicians, Researchers and Educators.* Lutherville, Maryland: Sidran Press.

Sutherland, V. J. & Cooper, C. L. (1992). *British Journal of Medicine.* Job stress, satisfaction, and mental health among general practitioners before and after introduction of new contract.

Sussman, M. B. (1992). *A Curious Calling: Unconscious Motivations for Practicing Psychotherapy.* Northvale, New Jersey: Jason Aronson, Inc.

Sussman, M. B. (1995). *A Perilous Calling: The Hazards of Psychotherapy Practice.* New York: John Wiley & Sons, Inc.

The Times of India. Compassion fatigue. (editorial), December 8, 1999.

Wise, T. N. (1991). *Primary Care.* Depression and fatigue in the primary care physician.

Woodward, J. C. (1998). *The Solitude of Loneliness.* Lexington, Massachusetts: D. C. Heath and Company.

Advances in Medical Psychotherapy and Psychodiagnosis
2002–2003, Volume 11, pp. 137–154

Alzheimer's Disease and Pharmacopsychology: Implications for Psychologists

Louise Anderson-Pawlina
University of Alberta

Abstract

Alzheimer's disease (AD) is a disease that is characterized by impaired cognitive functioning suffi-cient to impede an individual's social, and occupational functioning. It is the most common cause of dementia among people who are 65 years of age and older (Czech, Tremp, & Pradier, 2000). Consequently, it behooves psychologists to have at least a basic knowledge of this disease and its treatment. This paper provides essential information on AD, its characteristics, diagnosis, treatment and management strategies. It provides guidelines for psychologists who extend services to adults, to facilitate integration of these strategies into the overall management of this disorder, as well as ethi-cal considerations.

Currently, over 250,000 seniors in Canada suffer from dementia (Canadian Medical Association, 1999). Dementia is a progressive organic mental disorder that leads to cognitive deficits not otherwise accounted for, and sufficient to impair personal social or occupational functioning. Alzheimer's demen-tia is not considered to be the result of the normal aging process, although the risk for dementia increases with age (Dringenberg, 2000). Alzheimer's disease (AD) is the most common cause of dementia among those 65 years of age and older (Czech, Tremp, & Pradier 2000). The dementia inher-ent in AD is insidious in onset, progressive, irreversible, and degenerative (Meyer, Rauch, Lechener, & Loeb, 2001). AD, is named after Alois Alzheimer, the first person to publish a paper on the topic in 1907. Although research has been ongoing since that time, more recently the focus of the research has been dedicated, not only to finding a cause and treatment, but also to preventing AD.

   The purpose of this paper is to provide an overview of the characteristics of AD, the etiology, and its assessment and treatment, from the view of a pharmacopsychologist. A computerized search of MedLine, Psychological Abstracts Information Services (PsychLit), and National Library of Medicine's search service (PubMed) was used to identify relevant literature published between 1997–2001. Key search words included: Alzheimer's, treatment, medication; behavioral; inventory; and caregiver. Limits for the search were for human, English language, review articles, studies only.

Etiology

Alzheimer's disease progresses in stages, gradually destroying neurons in various parts of the brain. Characteristics of AD include neuritic plaques (dense deposits of protein that build up outside and around neurons) and neurofibrillary tangles (i.e., insoluble twisted fibers that build up inside neurons) (Durany, Munch & Riederer, 1999). Initially, AD destroys neurons in the hippocampus (a structure deep in the mid-brain that helps encode memories) and related structures in the limbic system, caus-ing a steady decline in cognitive functioning. Areas in the cerebral cortex are also eventually compromised. As more and more areas of the brain become involved, brain regions begin to atrophy and the individual with AD becomes incontinent and totally dependent on other people for personal care (Celsis, 2000). Finally, the disease becomes so debilitating that the individual becomes bedridden and usually dies of associated complications, such as pneumonia (Gauthier, 1999).

The main diagnostic feature of AD is impaired cognitive functioning, which causes impediment to the individual's social, and occupational functioning. Cognitive impairment[1] as well as confusion resulting from delirium and depression should initially be considered when working with the confused patient, as should polypharmacy, especially with the elderly (Zapotoczky, 1998; Espino, Jules-Bradley, Johnston & Mouton, 1998). According to Celsis' (2000) review article, increasing impairment in episodic and semantic memory has been found to be a preclinical marker, with working memory showing a more gradual decline over time. A wide individual variability in the rate of progression of AD is a characteristic feature (Birks & Meizer, 2000). Alzheimer's disease usually progresses over many years (Flint & van Reekum, 1998), is very debilitating and ultimately fatal (Forsti & Kurz, 1999). On average, people who have AD typically live from 4 to 8 years after being diagnosed. However, in some cases people who have AD can live up to 20 years.

Early signs and symptoms of AD often include loss of recent memory, such as forgetting the names of familiar people and common objects, word-finding difficulties, and a decreasing ability to think clearly.[2] As the disease progresses, signs and symptoms increase and become more pronounced. Problems with verbal/oral understanding and communication, reading, writing, and thinking clearly become more frequent and observable. Agitation,[3] emotional outbursts, and disturbing behaviors, such as wandering are also common at this stage, and increase as the disease progresses. Weight loss, due to an inability to recognize food, or manipulate eating utensils can also be problematic (Delafuente & Stewart, 2001). Eventually, the person with AD loses all cognitive abilities and becomes totally dependent on other people for her/his care.

Both genetic and environmental factors have been implicated as causative factors in AD (Czech, Tremp, & Pradier, 2000). Two types of AD have been identified: 1) familial early onset (EAD), and 2) seemingly arbitrary, later onset (LAD) (where no apparent inherited pattern is observed) (Cummings & Mendez, 1997). The main distinguishing features between EAD and LAD are that in the former dementia usually develops more quickly (Meyer, Rauch, Lechener, & Loeb, 2001). Most cases of EAD are considered to be an inherited form of AD. Furthermore, EAD is observed in a much smaller percentage of the population, and usually has an earlier onset, mostly involving people 35 to 65 years of age (Prasad, Cole, Hoviand, Prasad, Nahreini, Kumar, Edwards-Prasad, & Andreatta, 1999). In addition at autopsy, in many cases of EAD, defects in genes located on chromosomes 1, 14, and 21 (Cummings & Mendez, 1997), and mutations in the genes coding for presenilin 1 (PSI) and presenilin 2 (PS2) (Czech, Tremp, & Pradier, 2000) are noted.

Although no single neurological marker for AD exists (Almkvist & Winblad, 1999), characteristics of this disease, which can only be identified post mortem, include amyloid plaques and neurofibrillary tangles (two abnormal structures in the brain) that are thought to lead to a breakdown in communication between some nerve cells in key parts of the brain causing them to stop functioning, lose connections with other nerve cells, and die (Durany, Munch & Riederer, 1999). Specifically why this occurs remains a mystery. Researchers do not yet know if amyloid plaques cause AD or are a side effect of AD (Baum, Chen, Ng, & Pang, 2000).

---

[1] See Delafuente & Stewart, 2001, for a comprehensive list of possible sources of cognitive dysfunction.

[2] Common signs and symptoms include confusion about how to do simple and familiar tasks that previously could be done without difficulty, such as simple arithmetic problems; confusion about year, month or season; disorientation; and getting lost in familiar surroundings.

[3] Unpredictable anger, and/or confusion in response to change, depression and mood changes, can be a common occurrence during the progression of AD.

The main component in neurofibrillary tangles is one form of the protein tau (Durany, Munch & Riederer, 1999), best known for its ability to bind and help stabilize microtubules (the internal framework of the cell) in the central nervous system. Also implicated in AD are various neurotransmitters, especially acetylcholine, a critical neurotransmitter commonly used by the hippocampus in the process of forming memories, and by the cerebral cortex (primary areas affect by AD) (Herrmann & Lanctot, 1997). As well, several putative factors for AD have been postulated (See Table 1).

Research involving etiological and pathophysiological factors in AD populations for which drug therapies have been tested in clinical trials include:

> aging and its impact on cell membranes, neuroplasticity, and nerve growth factor binding; exposure to toxins, for example aluminum; autoimmune and inflammatory processes; calcium channel abnormalities; increase angiotensin-converting enzyme activity impairing memory; decrease glucose utilization and abnormal mitochondrial oxidative metabolism, including free radical formation; alterations of amino acid and peptide function including decreased N-methyl-D-aspartate (NMDA) receptors and also decreased glutamate activity) and changes in gonadal hormones, thyrotrophic-releasing hormones, opioids, and arginine-vasopressin; and neurotransmitter abnormalities including acetylcholine, serotonin, and norepinephrine. (van Reekum, Black, Conn, Clarke, 1997, p. 35S)

Diagnosing AD

Currently, several methods are used by physicians and psychologists to diagnose "probable AD" when patients present with memory problems and other mental functioning difficulties. The actual diagnosis of AD can only be made post-mortem at autopsy, by examining the brain for the hallmark tangles and plaques in specific brain regions (Schmitt, Davis, Wekstein, Smith, Ashford, & Markesdery, 2000). Diagnostic tools usually include a patient history, physical examination, clinical laboratory tests, brain scans, and neurological testing, so that any medically treatable condition that might be causing the troublesome signs and symptoms, or worsening the exiting dementia, can be identified and attended to.[4] Psychological testing specific to AD which include behavioral, social and coping inventories, should be part of the psychological assessment. Since AD is a multifaceted disease, that can affect both cognitive and physical functioning, psychologists working with this population should be prepared to work in a collaborative fashion with other health professionals (e.g., nurses, social workers, occupational therapists, physiotherapists, dieticians, primary caregivers, nursing home staff), as well as physician, neurologists, neuropsychologists and psychiatrists.

---

[4]Other neurological diseases, such as Parkinson's disease can also cause dementia. Other disorders that might cause reversible dementia include, but are not limited to, severe depression, drug abuse, certain medications (e.g., analgesic, antihistamines, psychotropics (Delefuente & Stewart, 2001)), thyroid disease, severe vitamin B_{12} deficiency, cerebral thrombosis, tumors, syphilis, and other infections (Meyer, Rauch, Lechner, & Loeb, 2001); hunger, cold, dehydration, fecal impaction, and sensory misconceptions due to changes in hearing or vision (Herrmann & Lanctot, 1997).

Table 1
Putative Factors for Alzheimer's Disease and Potential Contribution

Putative Factors	Examples	Potential Contribution
Genetics	age	senescence (increasing vulnerability with age due to biological vigor and efficiency deterioration) (Delefuente & Stewart, 2001)
	gender apolipoprotein	females are overrepresented in the AD population, especially those with APOE-epsilon4 allele (Lai, Kammann, Rebeck, Anderson, Chen, & Nixon, 1999)
	Down's syndrome gene mutation	overproduction of neurotoxin Abeta (amyloid beta-peptide), due to abnormal chromosome 21 (Guo, Robinson, Mattson, 1998)
	tau	tau (a protein which plays a pivotal role in the axonal transport) implicated in neurodegeneration (Czech, Tremp, & Pradier, 2000)
Health	stroke, cardiac disease	appear to increase risk of apoptosis processes implicated in neutritic maintenance and repair (Baum, Chen, Ng, & Pang, 2000)
	menopause	decrease in estrogen substantially increases the risk of developing AD (Janicki & Dalton, 1999)
	thyroid disease	thyroid hormone system is involved in control of programmed cell death (Labudova, Cairns, Koeck, Kitzmueller, Rink, & Lubec, 1999)
	Parkinson's	has a dementia component with prominent subcortical features (Janicki & Dalton, 1999)
	prion diseases	involve deposits of abnormal proteins in the brain (Weiss & Sensi, 2000), and are characterized by a long incubation period, followed by a rapidly progressing dementia (Taber's Cyclopedic Medical Dictionary, 2001)
	diet	proper nutrition, including the role of lipids, carbohydrates, and proteins has become an important consideration (Salvioli, Ventura, & Pradelli, 1998), as has folate[1] which research indicates may be linked to brain dysfunction (Miller, 1999)

[1]As of January 1st, 1999, it became mandatory in the US to fortify all grain products with folate, based on research implicating folate deficiency in several common diseases (i.e., heart disease, stroke, nervous system disorders, including AD) (Wynn & Wynn, 1998).

Table 1 (continued)		
Putative Factors	*Examples*	*Potential Contribution*
Environment	lower education	education level and neuronal connections interrelate; linguistic skills are particularly implicated (Delefuente & Stewart, 2001)
	head injury	appears to increase risk of apoptosis processes implicated in neuritic maintenance (Baum, Chen, Ng, & Pang, 2000)
	alcohol	abuse can severely impair many neuropsychological domains (Di Sclafani, Tolou-Shams, Bloomer, Norman, & Fein, 1998)
	toxin exposure	aluminum (from drinking water), for instance, has been shown to bind with degenerating neurons regardless of the degeneration cause (Delefuente & Stewart, 2001; Janicki, Dalton, 1999)
Unspecified	lower intelligence	lower dendritic connections ((Delefuente & Stewart, 2001)
	oxidative stress	implicated in the action of diverse groups of neurotoxins; (due to free radicals that upset the delicate membrane machinery which regulates the flow of substances in and out of the cells, and/or alter the structure of certain proteins) (Prasad, Cole, Hoviand, Prasad, Nahreini, Kumar, Edwards-Prasad, & Andreatta, 1999)
	inflamation of the brain	complement proteins and many of the mediators of inflammation are produced locally by microglial brain cells (Halliday, Robinson, Shepherd, & Kril, 2000)

A patient history should be the first avenue of investigation when a psychologist is faced with a patient who presents with memory and/or mental functioning difficulties, regardless of age. This history should be obtained from the patient and corroboration of details sought from those most closely involved with the patient (e.g., spouse/partner, caregiver, treating physician, and workmates). It should detail the onset and duration of symptoms, and include objective testing of memory difficulties, evaluation of symptoms, as well as the family history of dementia. Once a thorough history and collateral information are obtained, the patient should be referred to a physician for a complete physical examination and laboratory tests, so that any treatable medical condition that might be causing the signs and symptoms, or worsening the existing dementia can be identified and attended to.

Brain scans and various neuroimaging techniques (which can be ordered by a physician, or neurologist) can also help in obtaining a differential diagnosis of dementia, as can a detailed neurological examination of the patient (which can be completed by a neuropsychologist or a neurologist). Various brain scanning procedures, including positron emission tomography (PET), single photon emission computed tomography (SPECT), and magnetic resonance imaging techniques (MRI) provide a means of detecting and characterizing the neurochemistry and the neurobiology of a disease (Phelps, 2000), as well as enabling the identification of dysfunctional changes early in the course of the disease (Nordberg, 1999). Although these techniques are expensive, they are available without cost to patients who are willing and/or able to wait for the testing to be done. An average wait period for testing is approximately 4 months for the initial referral, and approximately 2 months for subsequent referral.

A number of psychological tests and scales (see Table 3), have been, or are being developed, to help clinicians assess people with memory problems, determine stages of AD, and measure its progression. According to a review of various test batteries, conducted by Simard & van Reekum (1999), the most sensitive memory tests are the Digit Span test, the Rey Auditory Verbal Learning Test, the Buschke Selective Reminding Test and the verbal fluency tasks, with the Sandoz Clinical Assessment—Geriatric, the Gottfried-Brane-Steel scale and the Blessed Dementia Scale being the most sensitive scales. Successive assessments over time may need to be considered to either verify or confirm a possible diagnosis of AD. The techniques outlined are designed to identify difficulties commonly observed with AD, cover relevant behaviors that may occur during the course of the disease, can be administered quickly and easily, and have been found to be reliable and valid instruments.

An interesting test that has been in use since the early 1990s, and which appears to be helpful in screening for early stages of AD is the ten-point clock test. This test requires that the patient correctly write the numbers on the face of a clock and then place the hands at 10 minutes after 11 (Manos, 1999).[5]

As depression often occurs among patients with AD (Tune, 1998), it may be prudent to include in the assessment battery a depression instrument such as the Hamilton Rating Scale for Depression or the Beck Depression Inventory in the assessment battery. Concurrent medical disorders, including drugs used for their management, and alcohol or other substance use which can also cause depression, will need to be considered prior to testing. Initially, the DSM-IV may be helpful in differentiating depression from dementia. A diagnosis of major depression based on the DSM-IV requires that 5 out of 9 established criteria be met, of which 6 are observable (depressed mood, appetite, and sleep disturbances; weight loss or gain; apathy or agitation; fatigue). The three subjective criteria are feelings of worthlessness, diminished ability to think, and recurrent thoughts of death (Janicki & Dalton, 1999).

Pharmacopsychological Treatment

The primary goals in treating and managing AD are to slow, reduce, and/or reverse the associated mental and behavioral signs and symptoms, and thereby optimizing the patient's level of functioning and consequently his/her quality of life. This will also be helpful in diminishing the danger of harm from the patient, to self or others (Flint & vanReekum, 1998). Whether primary consideration should be given to pharmacological or nonpharmacological interventions will depend on the prescribing psychologist and/or physician, the patient, and/or caregiver, legal guardian, or advanced directives (e.g., as previously outlined in the patient's "living will"). However, it is likely that the patient's needs will be better served with an integrated treatment plan that addresses both cognitive and behavioral components of AD. Currently the goal of most treatments for AD include a positive response, likely to involve a slight improvement in performance or no further deterioration.

---

[5] Scoring is based on spacing of the numbers and positions of the hands (Manos, 1999).

Table 2
Instruments for Assessing Cognitive Functioning and
Behavioral Disturbances of AD

Type of Assessment	Instrument	Reference
Cognitive functioning	Mini-Mental State Examination Global Deterioration Scale	Solomon, Adam, Groccia, DeVeaux, Growdon, & Pendlebury (1999)
	Clinical Dementia Rating Scale	Schmitt, Ashford, Ernesto, Saxton, Schneider, Clark, Ferris, Mackell, Schafer, Thal, & Alzheimer's Disease Cooperative Study (1997)
	Mattis Dementia Rating Scale	Marcopulus, Gripshover, Broshek, McLain, & Brashear (1999)
	Disability Assessment for Dementia	Gelinas, Gauthier, McIntyre, & Gauthier (1999)
Sensitive memory tests	Digit Span test, Rey Auditory Verbal Learning Test, Buschke Selective Reminding Test, verbal fluency tasks	Simard & van Reekum (1999)
Sensitive memory scales	Sandoz Clinical Assessment-Geriatric, Gottfried-Brane-Steel scale, Blessed Dementia Scale	Simard & van Reekum (1999)
Behavioral disturbances cognitive functioning	Alzheimer's Disease Assessment Scale (ADAS)	Solomom, Adam, Groccia, DeVeaux, Growdon, & Pendlebury (1999)
	Revised Memory and Behavior Problem Checklist	Logsdon, Ten, Weiner, Gibbons, Raskind, Peskind, Grundman, Koss, Thomas, Thai (1999)
	Functional Assessment Staging Questionnaire (FAST)	Schafer & Thal (1997)
	Behavior Rating Scale for Dementia (C-BRSD)	Marcopulos, Gripshover, Broshek, McLain, & Brashear (1999)
	Consortium to Establish a Registry for Alzheimer's Disease (CERAD) Cohen-Mansfield Agitation Inventory (CMAI)	Logsdon, Teri, Wiener, Gibbons, Raskind, Peskind, Grundman, Koss, Thomas, Thal (1999)

Table 2 (continued)		
Type of Assessment	*Instrument*	*Reference*
Behavioral disturbances caregiver component	Behavioral Pathology in Alzheimer's Disease Rating Scale (BEHAVE-AD)	Ferris & Mackell, 1997
Cognitive impairment behavioral symptoms	Neuropsychiatric Inventory (NPI)	Hirono, Mega, Dinov, Mishkin, & Cummings (2000)
	Neuropsychiatric Inventory-carer Distress Scale (NPI-D)	Aharon-Peretz, Kliot, & Tomer (2000)
Caregiver component	Clinician's Interview-Based Impression of Change with Caregiver Input (CIBIC-plus)	Burns, Rossor, Hecker, Gauthier, Petit, Moeller, Rogers, Friedhoff, & International Donepezil Group (1999)
	Caregiver-rated Global Impression of Change	Farlow, & Cyrus, (2000)
Daily functioning	Activities of Daily Living Skills	Solomon, Adam, Groccia, DeVeaux, Growdon, & Pendlebury, (1999)
	Basic and Independent Activities of Daily Living;	Kunik, Huffrnan, Bharani, Hillman, Molinari, Orengo (2000)
Comorbid illnesses	Cumulative Illness Rating Scale	Keller, Morton, Thomas, & Potter, (1999)

A longitudinal approach to treatment for all patients with AD will be necessary given the progression and duration of the disease, and the fact that the cognitive and noncognative manifestations of the disease will evolve over time. Treatment strategies will need to be reviewed regularly by the prescribing psychologist or physician to ascertain the progression of AD, treat any other medical or mental illnesses that may occur, and monitor the effectiveness of noncognitive interventions.

If a major depressive disorder is a factor in AD, then it is likely that optimal management of signs and symptoms of major depressive disorders will initially involve a combination of antidepressants, pharmachotherapy and psychological interventions. When treating patients with AD for depression, monoamine oxidase inhibitors (MAOIs) should not be the drug of choice, in because of the strict diet constraint requirements,[6] necessary in order to prevent hypertensive crisis. Neither should tricyclic antidepressants (TCAs) be considered the drug of choice because of their adverse reactions (ADRs)

---

[6]Restrictions of amine intake (e.g. tyramine, found in cheese, yeast, wine) is essential.

(Janicki & Dalton, 1999), which include anticholinergic effects,[7] drowsiness, orthostatic hypotension, and cardiac dysrhythmias (Pagliaro & Pagliaro, 1998).

The directives for treating depression among patients who have AD are somewhat different than for treating cognitively intact patients. According to Tune's (1998) review article, prescribing psychologists or physicians should "start low, go slower, pay attention to cognitive toxicity of all medication combinations," and keep pharmacotherapy short, as "depressive symptoms do not persist as long as in cognitively intact patients" (p. 91). Selective serotonin reuptake inhibitors (SSRI's) such as fluoxetine and sertraline, that have cognitive enhancing effects, should be considered the antidepressants of choice when treating patients with AD (Tune, 1998).

In health elderly patients, the pharmacokinetics of SSRIs have been shown to be insignificantly altered. The pharmacokinetic properties of fluoxetine (Paxil®) (5 to 20 mg daily) based on multiple dosing include 94.5% protein binding, 14–28 days time to steady state, and an elimination half-life of 4 to 6 days. For sertraline (Zoloft) (25 to 100 mg/daily), also based on multiple dosing, protein binding is 98%, time to steady state is 7 days, elimination half life is 2 to 4 days, and bioavailability is increased by approximately 40% by food intake (Pagliaro & Pagliaro, 1999). The ADRs associated with the SSRI's include nausea, diarrhea, weight loss, insomnia and agitation. SSRIs are metabolized in the liver and eliminated in the urine and feces. Fluoxetine and sertraline are the only two SSRIs to form active metabolites. Concomitant illnesses to consider when prescribing SSRIs are diabetes, cardiovascular and hepatic diseases, hyponatremia, mania/hypomania, seizures, and renal impairment (especially with fluoxetine and sertraline, due to their active metabolites) (Pagliaro & Pagliaro, 1999). Treatment with medications that have been found to be helpful slowing, reducing, and/or reversing the common signs and symptoms of AD should be considered, once depressive symptoms are alleviated.

Tacrine, because of hepatoxicity and the need for frequent dosing, has been replaced for the most part by a new class of acetycholinesterase (AChE) inhibitors. Donepezil, one of several in this new class of (AChE) inhibitors is the drug of choice, because it has a longer and more selective action with manageable ADRs. Donepezil also has higher bioavailability (40–100%, compared to 3 to 8% for tacrine), a longer half life of elimination, and consequently only needs to be dosed once a day compared to tacrine's four times a day. Donepezil seems to be more effective, and for more people, is better tolerated, and seems less harmful to the liver (Nordberg & Svensson, 1998). Rivastigmine, the newest of the AChE inhibitors, is particularly relevant in regard to the elderly, because it is unlikely to interact significantly with other drugs due to its mode of action and metabolism (Birks, Iakovidou, & Tsolaki, 2000). Rivastigmine is not metabolised via liver enzymes as are other drugs in this class, but via esterases and is excreted in the urine. While drugs such as "theophylline and cimetidine have been reported to change the pharmacokinetics of tacrine and donepezil," concomitant use of various drugs with "rivastigmine does not seem to cause any drug interaction in patients with Alzheimer's disease (Perry, Pickering, Wang, Houghton, & Perry, 1998, p. 419).

Several potential treatments for AD are currently undergoing clinical trials, and are in various stages of FDA[8] approval.

---

[7]"Anticholinergic effects include blurred vision, confusion, constipation, drowsiness, dry mouth, increased heart rate (tachycardia), and urinary retention" (Pagliaro & Pagliaro, 1998, p. 168).

[8] In the US, FDA (Food and Drug Administration) approval is necessary to market any drug for use by humans.

Table 3
Medication Used to Delay and Ameliorate Cognitive Signs and Symptoms of AD[1]

Type	Examples	Action	Dosage	ADRs
Cholin-esterase inhibitor	donepezil (Aricept®) rivastigmine (Exelon®) tacrine (Cognex®)	blocks enzymes that breaks down acetylcholine	5–10 mg qd 4–6 mg qd 20–40 mg qid	nausea; vomiting; diarrhea hepatoxicity, plus above ADRs
Anti-Oxidants	vitamin E ginkgo biloba selegiline	protect neurons from oxidative damage	1000 international units (IU) bid 60 mg bid 5 mg bid	contraindications: anticoagulants confusion, hallucinations, nausea; contraindication: opiate analgesics
Anti-inflammatory drugs	nonsteroidal antiinflammatory (NSAID) aspirin, ibuprofen	prostaglandin inhibitor; counteracts inflammatory response	unknown	gastric ulcers; decreased renal function
Estrogen (females)	Estradiol	neuro-protective; promotes cell metabolism	unknown	vaginal bleeding; contraindication: breast cancer; endometrial cancer; thromboembolic disorders

[1]This table is based on combined information from the following authors: Pagliaro & Pagliaro, 1999; Delafuente & Stewart, 2001; Birk, Iakovidou, & Tsolaki, 2000; Alzheimer's Organization website, 2000.

Table 4 Potential Treatments for AD (Last Update Dec. 22, 2000)			
Type	*Example(s)*	*Action*	*FDA Status*
Cholinesterase Inhibitors	Tacrine, donepezil, besipirdine, ENA-713, eptastigmine, metrifonate, physostigmine rivastigmine	Inhibit enzyme that breaks down acetylcholine	tacrine and donepezil approved; several others in Phase III
Cholinergic Agonists	ABT-418, AFJO2B, arecoline; nicotine, RS-86, SB 202026, xanomeline	Artificially stimulate acetylcholine receptors	Several in Phase III
Calcium Channel I blockers	Nimodipine, sabeluzole	Maintain cellular calcium levels	Several in Phase III
Anti-Inflammatory Drugs	Aspirin, colchicine, hydroxycliloroquine, ibuprofen, indomethacin, prednisone	Counteract inflammatory responses	Approved for other conditions
Estrogen	Estradiol	Promotes cell metabolism and	Approved for other conditions
Anti-Oxidants	Vitamin E, vitamin C, selegiline	Protect neurons from oxidative damage	Some approved for other conditions; some in Phase III
Ampakines	CX-516	Enhance response of neuronal receptors	Clinical trials to begin soon
Neuropeplides	TRH, neuropeptide Y, somatostatin	Support memory and neuronal communication	Not yet in clinical trials
Trophic Factors	NGF, GMI, BDNF	Help neurons grow and survive	Not yet in clinical trials
Protease Inhibitors	To be developed	Inhibit production of beta-amyloid	Not yet in clinical trials

Note: From the website on AD *(http://www.alzheimers.org/potreat.html).*

Management Strategies

Nonpharmacological management of the behavioral concerns inherent in AD often a response to environmental or social factors; (Flint & van Reekum, 1998), in addition to the use of medication[9] to address the cognitive and depressive symptoms inherent in AD, is an important component for optimizing the patient's level of functioning and consequently his/her quality of life. Environmental modification and behavior management approaches have been shown to have a profound effect on the manifestation of behavioral symptoms of AD. These approaches can be instrumental in improving behaviors[10] and consequently delaying, or even preventing placement in long-term care facilities (Janicki & Dalton, 1999), by reducing both patient and caregiver stress. Behavior management interventions should initially include assessment of potential "triggers" through careful documentation of behaviors, as well as their consequences (Canadian Medical Association, 1999). This type of attention to detail will be helpful for caregivers, who should consequently be able to recognize, anticipate and minimize or avoid most situations in which problem behaviors occur.

For psychologists treating AD patients, many functional issues can result which will require attention. For instance, a driving assessment and a vocational assessment may be necessary to determine the feasibility for the patient to continue driving and/or working (Delafuente & Stewart, 2001). Certain legal issues may also need to be addressed, preferably sooner than later, to enable the AD patient to participate as much as possible in this decision making process. Some of these issues include preparing a legal will as well as a living will with advanced directives,[11] determining guardianship, and power of attorney (Delafuente & Stewart, 2001). For some patients with AD wandering becomes a problem, consequently a contingency plan may need to be formulated to avoid possible difficulties. Inappropriate sexuality can also become problematic for some patients with AD, therefore the treating psychologist should be prepared to deal with this problem as well (Janicki & Dalton, 1999). Eventually, the time may come where outside help, or a nursing home, needs to be considered. Although such a decision is never an easy one, the burden can be lessened with psychological intervention, for caregivers and family members.

Ethical Considerations

A central ethical issue in AD is the patient's loss of ability to think and make decisions. Yet research indicates that people with AD still retain an measure of insight, and consequently every effort should be made to enable them to participate in decisions regarding their own care (Adams & Page, 2000).

---

[9] Antipsychotics should only be considered as a last resort in treating the behavioral symptoms of AD, because research indicates that this population is very vulnerable to the inherent ADRs of these drugs (Janicki & Dalton, 1999). If neuroleptics are deemed necessary, olanzapine (subclassified as a serotonin, dopamine antagonist (Pagliaro & Pagliaro, 1998) an atypical antipsychotic agent with few ADRs may be the drug of choice (Janicki & Dalton, 1999). Research indicates that risperidone (Risperdal®) 1mg daily was effective and well tolerated when used to control psychosis and behavioral disturbances associated with dementia (Canadian Medical Association, 1999).

[10] Ninety percent of patients have behavioral problems, at some point during the course of AD (Canadian Medical Association, 1999). Several studies indicate that exercise-based interventions programs, such as a light exercise, mild aerobic training, or walking, are helpful in reducing behavior problems inherent in AD (Schultz, 2000).

[11] Advanced directives give individuals "the power to control the medical care or treatment they will receive, when they can no longer speak for themselves" (Delafuente & Stewart, 2001, p. 131).

The decision to allow the patient with AD to participate in decision making can be based on the following axiom: If the decision is not life threatening nor involves immediate or eminent harm to the patient or caregiver, then the patient's wishes should be honored. It will be much easier to make a case for a certain course of treatment, if the patient has participated during the initial stages.

Patients with AD should be afforded the same respect and dignity that all humans are entitled to, without exception! They should be provided with the same services, quality of care, and treatment that any other individual receives. Cost should no more be a factor for AD patients than it is for any other patient. The wishes of a patient with AD should receive the same consideration as those of any other patient, including (where legally permitted) the wish to participate in active euthanasia (subjected to euthanasia), or passive euthanasia (left to die) (Delafuente & Stewart, 2001). As well, patients with AD should never be pressured to participate in research, regardless of what the anticipated gains might be, to themselves or to society at large (Janicki & Dalton, 1999).

As well, cultural sensitivity will be necessary in multicultural societies such as Canada (Canadian Medical Association, 1999) and the United States. Consequently, psychologists will need a working knowledge of the needs of diverse ethnic groups and of how they may be affected and respond to dementing illnesses (Valle, 1998), as well as be knowledgeable about AD, its treatment, the needs of patients and caregivers, and the various supportive systems (e.g., AD associations, societies, and publications) available.

Summary

Current information for psychologists working with the adult population was presented to facilitate a basic understanding of AD. Etiological factors addressed include: characteristics and main diagnostic features of AD; symptoms, putative factors; drug therapies tested in clinical trial; and potential treatments for AD. Diagnostic methods and assessment instruments were provided, as well some information on the comorbidity of AD and depression. Treatment considerations for the AD population were addressed, as were current available medications. Given that AD has a behavioral component as well a cognitive component, management strategies were also discussed. Finally, ethical considerations were highlighted.

References

Adams, T., & Page, S. (2000). New pharmacological treatments for Alzheimer's disease: Implications for dementia care nursing. *Journal of Advanced Nursing, 31,* 1183–1188.

Aharon-Peretz, J., Kilot, D., & Tomer, R. (2000). Behavioral differences between matter lacunar dementia and Alzheimer's disease: a comparison on the neuropsychiatric inventory. *Dementia & Geriatric Cognitive Disorders, 11,* 294–298.

Almkvist O., & Winbiad, B. (1999). Early diagnosis of Alzheimer dementia based on clinical and biological factors. *European Archives of Psychiatry & Clinical Neuroscience, 249,* 3–9.

Baum, L., Chen, L., Ng, H., & Pang, C. (2000). Apolipoprotein E isoforms in Alzheimer's disease pathology and etiology. *Microscopy Research & Technique, 50,* 278–81.

Birks, J., Iakovidou, V., & Tsolaki, M. (2000). Rivastigmine for Alzheimer's disease. *Cochrane Database of Systematic Reviews, (2),* CDOO1191.

Birks, J., & Meizer, D. (2000). Donepezil for mild and moderate Alzheimer's disease. *Cochrane Database of Systematic Reviews, (2),* CDOO119O.

Burns, A., Rossor, M., Hecker, J., Gauthier, S., Petit, H., Moeller, H., Rogers, S., Friedhoff, L., & International Donepezil Group. (1999). The effects of donepezil in Alzheimer's disease—results from a multinational trial. *Dementia & Geriatric Cognitive Disorders, 10,* 237–244.

Canadian Medical Association. (1999). Management of Dementing Disorders. *Canadian Medical Association Journal, 160,* 1–15.

Castro, B., Eshleman, J., & Shearer, R. (1999). Using humor to reduce stress and improve relationships. *Seminars for nursing managers, 7,* 90–92.

Celsis, P. (2000). Age-related cognitive decline, mild cognitive impairment or preclinical Alzheimer's disease? *Annals of Medicine, 32*(1), 6–14.

Cummings, J., & Mendez, M. (1997). Alzheimer's disease: Cognitive and behavioral pharmacotherapy. *Connecticut Medicine, 61,* 543–52.

Czech, C., Tremp, G., & Pradier, L. (2000). Presenilins and Alzheimer's disease: Biological functions and pathogenic mechanisms. *Progress in Neurobiology, 60,* 363-84,

Delafuente, J., & Stewart, M. (2001). *Therapeutics in the elderly.* Cincinnati, OH: Harvey Whitney Books.

Di Sclafani, V., Clark, H., Tolou-Shams, M., Bloomer, C., Salas, G., Norman, D., & Fein, G. (1998). Premorbid brain size is a determinant of functional reserve in abstinent crack-cocaine and crack-cocaine-alcohol-dependent adults. *Journal of the International Neuropsychological Society, 4,* 559–565.

Dringenberg, H. (2000). Alzheimer's disease: More than a 'cholinergic disorder'? Evidence that cholinergic monoaminergic interactions contribute to EEG slowing and dementia. *Behavioral Brain Research, 115,* 235–249.

Durany, N., Munch, G., Michel, T., & Riederer, P. (1999). Investigations on oxidative stress and therapeutical implications in dementia. *European Archives of Psychiatry & Clinical Neuroscience, 249,* 68–73.

Espino, D., Jules-Bradley, A., Johnston, C., & Mouton, C. (1998). Diagnostic approach to the confused elderly patient. *American Family Physician, 57,* 1358–66.

Farlow, M., & Cyrus, P. (2000). Metrifonate therapy in Alzheimer's disease: A pooled analysis of four randomized, double-blind, placebo-controlled trials. *Dementia & Geriatric Cognitive Disorders, 11,* 202–11.

Ferris, S. & Mackell, J. (1997). Behavioral outcome in clinical trials for Alzheimer's disease. *Alzheimer's Disease & Associated Disorders, 11,* 10–15.

Flint, A., & van Reekum, R. (1998). The pharmacologic treatment of Alzheimer's disease: A guide for the general psychiatrist. *Canadian Journal of Psychiatry, 43,* 689–697.

Forsti, H., & Kurz, A. (1999).Clinical features of Alzheimer's disease. *European Archives of Psychiatry & Clinical Neuroscience, 249,* 288–290.

Gauthier, S. (1999). *Clinical diagnosis and management of Alzheimer's disease.* London: Martin Dunitz Ltd.

Gelinas, I., Gauthier, L., McIntyre, M., & Gauthier, S. (1999). Development of a functional measure for persons with Alzheimer's disease: The disability assessment for dementia. *American Journal of Occupational Therapy, 53,* 471–481.

Guo, Q., Robinson, N., & Mattson, M. (1998). Secreated beta-amyloid precursor protein counteracts the proapoptotic action of mutant presenilin-1 by activation of NF-kappaB and stabilization of calcium homeostasis. *Journal of Biological Chemistry, 273,* 12341–12351.

Halliday, G., Robinson, S., & Shepherd, C., & Kril, J. (2000). Alzheimer's disease and inflammation: A review of cellular and therapeutic mechanisms. *Clinical & Expeximental Pharmacology & Physiology, 27,* 1–8.

Herrmann, N., & Lanctot, K. (1997). From transmitters to treatment: The pharmacotherapy of behavioral disturbances in dementia. *Canadian Journal of Psychiatry, 42,* 51–64.

Hirono, N., Mega, M., Dinov, I., Mishkin, F., & Cummings, J. (2000). Left frontotemporal hypoperfusion in association with aggression in patients with dementia. *Archives of Neurology, 57,* 861–866.

Janicki, M., & Dalton, A. (1999). *Dementia, aging, and intellectual disabilities.* Philadelphia, PA: Brunner & Mazel.

Keller, B., Morton, J., Thomas, V., & Potter, J. (1999). The effects of visual and hearing impairments on functional status. *Journal of the American Geriatric Society, 47,* 1319–1325.

Kunik, M., Huffrnan, J., Bharani, N., Hillman, S., Molinari, V., & Orengo C. (2000). Behavioral disturbances in geropsychiatric inpatients across dementia types. *Journal of Geriatric Psychiatry & Neurology, 13,* 49–52, 2000.

Labudova, O., Cairns, N., Koeck, T., Kitzmueller, E., Rink, H., & Lubec, G. (1999). Thyroid stimulating hormone-receptor overexpression in brain of patients with Down's syndrome and Alzheimer's disease. *Life Science, 64,* 1037–1044.

Lai, F., Kammann, E., Rebeck, G., Anderson, A., Chen, Y., & Nixon, R. (1999). APOE genotype and gender effects on Alzheimer disease in 100 adults with Down syndrome. *Neurology, 53,* 331–336.

Logsdon, R., Ten, L., Weiner, M., Gibbons, L., Raskind, M.; Peskind, E.,Grundman, M., Koss, E., Thomas, R., Thai, L., & Corporate/Institutional. (1999). Assessment of agitation in Aizheimer's disease: The Agitated Behavior in Dementia Scale. *Journal of the American Geriatrics Society, 47,* 1354–1358.

Manos, P. (1999). Ten-point clock test sensitivity for Alzheimer's disease in patients with MMSE scores greater than 23. *International Journal of Geriatric Psychiatry, 14,* 454–458.

Marcopulos, B., Gripshover, D., Broshek, D., McLain, C., & Brashear, H. (1999). Neuropsychological assessment of psychiatric patients with limited education. *Clinical Neuropsychologist, 13,* 147–156.

Meyer, J., Rauch, G., Lechener, H., & Loeb, C. (2001). *Vascular dementia.* Armonk, NY: Futura.

Miller, J. (1999). Homocysteine and Alzheimer's disease. *Nutrition Reviews, 57,* 126–129.

Nordberg, A. (1999). PET studies and cholinergic therapy in Alzheimer's disease. *Revue Neurologique, 155,* S53–63.

Nordberg, A., & Svensson, A. (1998). Cholinesterase inhibitors in the treatment of Alzheimer's disease: a comparison of tolerability and pharmacology. *Drug Drug Safety, 19,* 465–480.

Pagliaro, L., Pagliaro, AM. (1998). *The pharmacological basis of psychotherapeutics.* Washington, DC: Taylor & Francis.

Pagliaro, L., & Pagliaro, AM. (1999). *Psychologist's neuropsychotropic drug reference* (PNDR). Philadelphia, PA: Bruner/Mazel.

Perry, E., Pickering, A., Wang, W., Houghton, P., & Perry, N. (1998). Medicinal plants and Alzheimer's disease: Integrating ethnobotanical and contemporary scientific evidence. *Journal of Alternative & Complementary Medicine, 4,* 419–428.

Phelps, M. (2000). PET: the merging of biology and imaging into molecular imaging. *Journal of Nuclear Medicine, 41,* 661–81.

Prasad, K., Cole, W., Hoviand, A., Prasad, K., Nahreini, P., Kumar, B., Edwards-Prasad, J., & Andreatta, C. (1999). Multiple antioxidants in the prevention and treatment of neurodegenerative disease: Analysis of biologic rationale. *Current Opinion in Neurology, 12,* 761–770.

Robertson, G., Crocker, S., Nicholson, D., & Schulz, J. (2000). Neuroprotection by the inhibition of apoptosis. *Brain Pathology, 10,* 283–292.

Salvioli, G., Ventura, F., & Pradelli, J. (1998). Impact of nutrition on cognition and affectivity in the elderly: A review. *Archives of Gerontology & Geriatrics, 6,* 458–468.

Schmitt, F., Davis, D., Wekstein, D., Smith, C., Ashford, J., & Markesdery, W. (2000). "Preclinical" AD revisited: Neuropathology of cognitively normal older adults. *Neurology, 55,* 370–376.

Schmitt, F., Ashford, W., Ernesto, C., Saxton, J., Schneider, L., Clark, C., Schafer, Thal, & Alzheimer's Disease Cooperative Study. (1997). The severe impairment battery: Concurrent validity and the assessment of longitudinal change in Alzheimer's disease. *Alzheimer's Disease & Associated Disorders, 11,* 51–56.

Schultz, R. (2000). *Handbook on dementia caregiving: Evidence-based interventions for family caregivers.* NY: Springer.

Simard, M., & van Reekum, R. (1999). Memory assessment in studies of cognition-enhancing drugs for Alzheimer's disease. *Drugs & Aging, 14,* 197–230.

Solomon, P., Adam, F., Groccia, M., DeVeaux, R., Growdon, J., & Pendlebury, W. (1999). Correlational analysis of five commonly used measures of mental status/functional abilitiesin patients with Alzheimer's disease. *Alzheimer's Disease & Associated Disorders, 13,* 147–150.

Taber's cyclopedia medical dictionary (19th ed.). (2001). Philadelphia, PA: F. A. Davis.

Tune, L.(1998). Depression and Alzheimer's disease. *Depression & Anxiety, 8,* 91–5.

Valle, R. (1998). *Caregiving across cultures.* Washington, DC: Taylor & Francis.

van Reekum, R., Black, S., Conn, D., & Clarke, D. (1997). Cognition-enhancing drugs in dementia: A guide to the near future. *Canadian Journal of Psychiatry, 42,* 35–50.

Weiss, J., & Sensi, S. (2000). Ca2+-Zn2+ permeable AMPA or kainate receptors: possible key factors in selective neurodegeneration. *Trends in Neurosciences, 23,* 365–371.

Wynn, M., & Wynn, A. (1998). Fortification of grain products with folate: should Britain follow the American example. *Nutrition & Health, 12,* 147–61.

Zapotoczky, HG. (1998). Problems of differential diagnosis between depressive pseudodementia and Alzheimer's disease. *Journal of Neural Transmission, 53,* 91–95.

Author Notes

Please send correspondence regarding this article to: Louise Anderson-Pawlina, University of Alberta, Department of Graduate Studies, Edmonton, AB, Canada.

A sincere thank-you to Ann Marie Pagliaro and Dr. L. Pagliaro for the ongoing editorial support they provided.

This paper is dedicated to my husband, Robert, who is now in the last phase of the middle stage of AD. His continued support of this paper and all my other endeavors, his resolve to enjoy every day, and his tremendous sense of humor have made each day of our lives together a privilege and a pleasure.

Advances in Medical Psychotherapy and Psychodiagnosis
2002–2003, Volume 11, pp. 155–164

Pharmacologic Treatment of Premenstrual Dysphoric Disorder

Dana von Wackerbarth
University of Alberta, Edmonton, Alberta, Canada

Abstract

The purpose of this article is to examine the pharmacological treatments of premenstrual dysphoric disorder(PMDD). Clinical literature was accessed through MEDLINE (1997–2000). Key terms used in the search included Premenstrual Syndrome and Drug Therapies. Up to 5% of women experience severe symptoms such as aggression, anger, anxiety, depression, irritability, mood swings, and tension in the luteal phase of their menstrual cycle. Antidepressants are receiving attention in treating these symptoms as well treatments such as hormone therapy, l-tryptophan, calcium and vitamin B6. Pharmacological treatments have been found, although to different degrees, to alleviate symptoms of PMDD and are discussed in this paper.

Pharmacologic Treatment of Premenstrual Dysphoric Disorder

According to Endicott's historical description, Hippocrates described the set of symptoms that occurred prior to the onset of menstruation. It was officially recognized and termed "premenstrual tension syndrome" by R.T. Frank in 1931. In the 1970s and early 1980s more research was being done in the area. In 1983, the National Institute of Mental Health made some suggestions for criteria and research methods, i.e., the requirement that there be documented at least a 30% difference in severity between the mid-follicular and late luteal phases of the menstrual cycle for changes in mood, behavior, or physical condition to be considered a premenstrual "change" or "syndrome" (Endicott, 2000). In 1987, the criteria for late luteal phase dysphoric disorder (LLPDD) were published in the *Diagnostic and Statistical Manual of Mental Disorders,* Third Edition-Revised (DSM-III-R).

In the 1990s, during the revisions and examination of a relatively large number of studies in the area, it was proposed to change the name from late luteal phase dysphoric disorder to premenstrual dysphoric disorder (PMDD). One criteria was added for the Fourth Edition of the *Diagnostic and Statistical Manual of Mental Disorders* (APA, 1994). In October 1998, an international team of experts came to the consensus that PMDD was indeed a distinct clinical entity. In November 1999, the evidence was accepted by the Food and Drug Administration Neuropharmacology Advisory Committee (Endicott, 2000).

In order to fit the DSM-IV criteria for Premenstrual Dysphoric Disorder, a woman has to have at least five of the following symptoms in most cycles for at least one year: depressed mood, feelings of hopelessness, anxiety, tension, feeling "keyed up," affective liability, lack of energy, lethargy, persistent and marked anger or irritability, decreased interest in usual activities, difficulty concentrating, changes in appetite, changes in sleep, a subjective sense of being overwhelmed; and physical symptoms such as breast tenderness, bloating or muscle pain. At least one symptom has to be a mood symptom. The symptoms must occur during the last week of the luteal phase and become absent in the week of post-menses. The symptoms must markedly interfere with work or interpersonal relationships and must not be merely an exacerbation of another disorder. These criteria must be confirmed by daily ratings for two cycles.

Prevalence

Yonkers (1999) sites the prevalence for milder premenstrual syndromes from 30% to 80%. The severe symptoms of premenstrual dysphoric disorder are at approximately 3%–5% of menstruating women (Steinberg, et al., 1999; Bhatia, et al., 1999). Steiner and Pearlstein (2000) cite research which indicates PMDD affects approximately 3–8% of women of reproductive age in the United States, United Kingdom, and France. This suggests that PMDD is not culturally bound to North America.

Etiology

There are a few suggested etiologies for Premenstrual Dysphoric Disorder. One well accepted, supported explanation is a dysregulation of serotonin. It is suggested that this is the reason the SSRI antidepressants are more effective than other categories of antidepressants. "Peripheral measures of serotonin synthesis suggest lowered serotonin function in women with PMDD" (Steinburg, et al., 1999, p. 264).

It stands to reason, because the symptoms of PMDD are so closely related to the late luteal phase of the mentrual cycle, the cyclic function of estrogen or progesterone would be causally related. Tiemstra and Patel (1998) made reference studies that found that the progesterone and estrogen levels of PMS sufferers was not different from asymptomatic control patients. The timing and the severity of symptoms were not positively correlated with fluctuations in hormone levels in symptomatic patients. More recent studies indicate that estrogen stimulates certain dopamine and serotonin receptors, the same serotonin receptors that are stimulated by the SSRI antidepressants. "PMDD is likely to involve the interaction of normal menstrual cycle hormonal fluctuations at ovulation with dysregulated neurotransmitter systems such as serotonin, norepinephrine, and gamma-aminobutyric acid (GABA)" (Pearstien & Steiner, 2000, p. 22).

The Effects of Antidepressants on Women

The effect on antidepressants (not specified) differ somewhat in men and women. One difference is in the rate of absorption. "Absorption of antidepressants may be enhanced in women because they secrete less gastric acid than men" (Bhatia, et al., 1999, p. 6). Also, the gastrointestinal transit time may be slower in women especially during high progesterone phases of the reproductive cycle which may enhance absorption. Another difference between men and women is the fact that women have a higher ratio of body fat to muscle, which gets greater with age. The larger body fat ration increases the volume of distribution for antidepressants.

The final difference is that in men, the progesterone increases microsomal and monoamine oxidase enzyme activity, whereas in women, the estrogen decreases this activity; these actions affect monoamine neurotransmitters and drug metabolism. It is important for psychologists to keep in mind is that the plasma concentrations may by higher in women so they may require a lower dose. Women may also experience drug side effects more frequently.

The Effects of Antidepressants on PMDD

Antidepressants have received attention for treating the symptoms of PMDD. "More recently, the emphasis has been on specific serotonin reuptake inhibitors (SSRIs)" (Steinberg, et al., 1999). "The current literature indicates that if simpler nonpharmacologic options are ineffective, selective serotonin selective reuptake inhibitors (SSRIs) may be used to treat patients with PMDD" (Bhatia, 1999, p. 10). The following is an examination of the current studies on the effectiveness of serotonin reuptake inhibitors, in isolation and in comparison to some tricyclic and miscellaneous antidepression categories. The antidepressants reviewed are sertaline, desipramine, fluoxetine, and bupropion.

A randomized, double-blind, parallel design treatment trial study conducted by Freeman, et al. (1999), compared the SSRI sertraline to the tricyclic antidepressant, desipramine, and a placebo. The purpose of this study was to compare the effectiveness of two classes of antidepressant drugs in the treatment of PMDD. The study was conducted at the University of Pennsylvania Medical Center. Following an intensive, 3 month screening process, 189 of the 520 subjects were chosen to participate in the study. Of these 189 subjects, 22 dropped out immediately. The remaining subjects were randomly assigned to groups and administered 50 to 150 mg of either drug or placebo.

Patients were monitored using the previously validated Penn Daily Symptom Record (DSR), Hamilton Depression Rating Scale (Ham-D), the Clinical Global Impressions-Severity Scale, the Quality of Life Scale, and Patient Global Ratings of Functioning and Improvement.

The DSR lists 17 common PMS symptoms, including the 11 symptoms of the research criteria for premenstrual dysphoric disorder (PMDD in the DSM-IV: depression, feeling hopeless or guilty, anxiety/tension, mood swings, irritability/persistent anger, decreased interest, concentration difficulties, fatigue, food cravings/increased appetite, insomnia/hypersomnia, feeling out of control/overwhelmed, poor coordination, headache, aches, swelling/bloating/weight gain, cramps and breast tenderness" (Freeman, et al., 1999, p. 4).

The DSR results showed that the sertraline group improved in all the factors, with statistical significance for the mood and pain factors. The mood factors that were significantly more improved with sertraline treatment included irritability, anxiety/tension, depression, feeling hopeless, and feeling out of control. The Patient Global Ratings of Functioning and Improvement indicated that 60% of the sertraline group rated themselves much improved or very much improved compared to 38% of the desipramine group and 29% of the placebo group. The Ham-D, CGI-Severity rating and the QOLS all reported significantly more improvement than desipramine treatment and placebo.

This study indicated that the SSRI setraline hydrochloride was much more effective in treating PMDD then either the tricyclic, desipramine hydrochloride or placebo, "Subjects receiving sertraline therapy reported significantly more improvement compared with placebo; improvement with desipramine therapy did not significantly exceed the placebo response" (Freeman, et al., 1999, p. 10).

In 1997 Yonkers et al. conducted a study to evaluate the efficacy of sertraline for treatment of premenstrual dysphoria. The study was a double-blind, randomized design. The study is significant due to the large number of subjects. Of four hundred forty-seven women evaluated for study entry, 243 completed the study. The measures used to monitor the drug's efficacy included the Daily Record of Severity of Problems (DRSP), Hamilton Rating Scale for Depression (HAM-D), Clinical Global Impression Scale (CGI), and Social Adjustment Scale (SAS).

A similar study by Pearlstein, et al. (1997) compared the efficacy of fluoxetine, a SSRI, bupropion, which falls into the miscellaneous category of antidepressants, and a placebo. This was a double blind, randomized parallel design study. Of the 44 women enrolled for the screening process, 37 women accepted for the study and 34 completed the study. The Clinical Global Impressions (CGI) Scale, Hamilton Rating Scale for Depression (HAM-D), and the Global Assessment Scale (GAS) were used to monitor the therapeutic effects of each group.

The results of this study indicated that fluoxetine was superior to both bupropion and placebo in the treatment for PMDD. Of the 10 subjects in randomized to the fluoxetine group, each women was considered a responder and requested to continue treatment. One of the four women responded to bupropion but was not satisfied with the degree of symptomatic relief and requested to change to another medication.

The Full Cycle or Half Cycle use of SSRI Antidepressants

Some evidence suggests that intermittent (premenstrual only) dosing of SSRIs might be at least as effective if not better than continuous dosing (Steiner, et al., 2000). Freeman et al. (1999) conducted a study to determine the effects of sertraline administered full cycle and half cycle (pre-menstrual). Thirty-one women, who had met the criteria for severe PMS, were randomly assigned in a double blind fashion to receive either full cycle (13 women) or half cycle dosing (18 women). The Penn Daily Symptom Report (DSR) was used to measure the effects. Of the 31 subjects, five women discontinued treatment, three for insufficient improvement (two in full cycle, one in half cycle) and one was lost to follow up. It was concluded that the side effects were similar between both groups.

The results of the study, indicated by DSR scores, were that the DSR scores were lower in the half-cycle sertraline dosing group throughout the 3 treatment months but did not statistically differ from the full-cycle dosing group in this small sample. This study indicates that half-cycle dosing of sertraline can be effective in controlling PMS symptoms. "The clinical importance of determining an optimal dose/benefit ratio for PMS patients warrants a large double-blind, placebo-controlled study of PMS patients to refute or confirm these results" (Freeman, et al., 1999, p. 7).

Adverse Drug Reactions of SSRI's

Generally, the SSRI antidepressants are well tolerated. The side effects seem mild to moderate. The most common ones seem to be headache, nausea, and decreased libido. Yonkers (1997) found the significant side effects of sertraline were nausea, diarrhea, and decreased libido. Freeman (1999) found that sertraline caused more nausea that the placebo group. In Pearlstein, et al.'s fluoxetine study, only one woman presented with each of the following complains decreased libido, rash, fatigue, insomnia and palpitations but these symptoms were categorized as mild. There was a very low rate of drop out due to adverse drug reactions: Freeman, et al. (sertraline) 23.9%; Yonkers (sertraline) 8%; Pearlstein, et al. (fluoxetine) 6.8%. In each comparative study, the SSRI was more tolerated that the other antidepressant categories and slightly more than the placebo.

Non-antidepressant Treatment of PMDD

There are several non-prescription alternatives that have been suggested for the treatment PPMD. Although not all have been proven to be effective in alleviating PMDD symptoms, they are widely used. Pearlsein et al. (2000) suggest this may be due in part to the need for increased awareness in the lay literature and by health professionals of the available treatments substantiated by research. The following is an examination of some of the well-accepted, non-antidepressant treatments of PMDD including L-tryptophan, estrogen, progesterone, ovulation suppression treatment (Danazol), calcium, and vitamin B6.

L-tryptophan

In 1999, Steinber, Annable, Young and Leyanage conducted a study comparing the effect of L-tryptophan and placebo on Premenstrual Dysphoric Disorder. The patients were recruited from the Women's Unit of St. Mary's Hospital in Montreal and screened for symptoms of PMDD using the Visual Analogue Scales (VAS). Of the 80 patients that entered the treatment, 72 completed the study (There was no statistically significant difference between treatment with respect to the incidence of premature terminations. Steinberg, et al., 1999, pp. 316.) 37 of the patients, randomly chosen, were treated with 6 g per day of L-tryptophan and 34 were given a placebo.

The rating scales used to measure the pharmacological effects were; the Visual Anaogue Scale (VAS); the Multiple Affect Adjective Checklist (MAACL); the Pleasant and Unpleasant life Events Schedule; and the Dyadic Adjustment Scale. The VAS and MAACL measured improvement in mood symptoms comprising the items of dysphoria, mood swings, tension and irritability. The Pleasant and Unpleasant Life Events Scale indicated a greater benefit of L-tryptophan for patients with higher levels of obtained pleasure at baseline.

The results of this study indicate that L-tryptophan is significantly more effective in alleviating symptoms of PMDD, specifically extreme mood swings, dysphoria, irritability, and tension than the placebo. This study indicated that L-tryptophan is well tolerated, as the side effects (i.e., dizziness) were rated as mild.

Hormone Treatments

As a result of the symptoms being related to the menstrual cycle, which is regulated by the female sex hormones, estrogen and progesterone, there was an expectation that the entire array of PMS symptoms may respond well the hormone therapy. For this reason, hormone therapy has been widely used although the results of the effectiveness have been mixed (Tiemstra & Patel, 1998).

Studies have consistently found progesterone has no benefit in lessening PMS symptoms, in fact, it has shown the opposite to be true. It is important for prescribers to be aware that progesterone may in fact aggravate preexisting PMS symptoms. "Progesterone continues to be widely used in treatment despite convincing evidence that it is not beneficial, whereas estrogen remains under-recognized as effective therapy" (Teimstra & Patel, 1998, p. 378). Estrogen, on the other hand, has been shown effective in relieving PMS symptoms although its usefulness is compromised by the need to add cyclic progesterone to the drug regiment. "Estogen alone provides adequate suppression of the cycle, but the risk of endometrial hyperplasia necessitates that progestogen is added, cyclically, which stimulates the return of many of the typical premenstrual symptoms" (O'Brien & Abukhalil, 1999, p. 19).

The estrogen and progesterone in oral contraceptives have made them an effective in reducing the physical symptoms of PMS. Evidence of their effectiveness on emotional symptoms such as irritability is less clear. There is not one type of oral contraceptive that has proven more effective than others. They should be selected on the basis of suitability of the patient, including estrogen and progesterone level combination, the side effects (which may include an increased risk of cardiovascular complications for women 30–50 years of age), and the effectiveness of reducing PMS symptoms for the individual (Tiemstra & Patel, 1998). The long-term use of oral contraceptives needs to be more adequately studied due to the risk of "menopausal" osteoporosis and cardiovascular disease.

Ovulation Suppression Therapy

Danazol is an ovulation suppression therapy used to treat troublesome premenstrual symptoms. Danazol has been reported by Pearlstein and Steiner (2000) to be effective in treating PMS symptoms at a continuous dosing of 200 mg–400 mg/day but adverse side effects make this an unappealing treatment method. Some of the adverse side effects cited were: weight gain, nausea, acne, facial hair, decreased high-density lipoproteins and depression. Although proven effective, ovulation suppression therapy should be used with great caution due to the long-term health concerns related to cardiac disease and decreased bone density that is caused by low estrogen levels.

Research has suggested that danazol is effective if given in the luteal phase only. O'Brien and Abukhalil (1999) reviewed the studies of danazol, a hormone, to treat PMS symptoms. They conducted a randomized, double blind, parallel group study using 200 mg of danazol administered in the luteal phase of the menstrual cycle. Women taking oral contraceptives had a known sensitivity to danazol or had been treated with danazol in the past three months were eliminated from the study. The results indicate that danazol, administered in the luteal phase, is not effective for the treatment of the general symptoms of premenstrual syndrome.

Calcium

There is some indication that reduced bone mineral density has been associated with both depression and PMS, and some abnormality of calcium or parathyroid hormone homeostasis may be an etiologic factor in PMS. Pearlstein and Steiner (2000) refer to studies that have indicated that calcium was more effective than placebo in reducing both emotional and physical symptoms of the PMDD diagnostic criteria except for fatigue and insomnia.

Ward and Holimon (1999) conducted a study to evaluate the use of calcium supplementation in the treatment of premenstrual syndrome. Of the 60 women selected for the study, using their own list of criteria rather than a standardized measurement tool, only 55% (33) completed the study. The most common reasons were failure to collect the study medication and noncompliance. Despite the high drop out level, of the 33 women analyzed, calcium reduced symptoms during the luteal and menstrual phases of the cycle when evaluated by a multivariate repeated-measure ANOVA. The results are encouraging considering calcium is a relatively safe, accessible and inexpensive treatment option. "Calcium supplementation of 1200–1600 mg/d, unless contraindicated, should be considered a sound treatment option in women who suffer from PMS" (Ward, et al., 1999, p. 1358). Although this study used a relatively small sample, calcium seems to be a promising treatment for PMS symptoms. It merits further research to determine the beneficial effects and any adverse long-term effects.

Vitamin B6

Pearlstein et al. (2000) suggest, because of its metabolic action, vitamin B6 as an effective treatment for PMS. They cite a recent meta-analysis of 940 women in 9 controlled studies indicate weak support for vitamin B6 (50–100 mg/day) in reducing premenstrual symptoms. Haseltine and Fauistman (2000) conducted a randomized, double blind, placebo controlled study using a Latin square design, to compare the use of 200mg/day magnesium (Mg), 50 mg Vitamin B6, 200mg/day magnesium (Mg) + 50 mg Vitamin B6, and placebo. The study was designed to investigate the possible synergy of a combined daily dietary supplement of Mg and Vitamin B6 for relief of mild premenstrual symptoms, rather than the more severe symptoms classified as PMS.

The effects were evaluated using a menstrual health questionnaire modified from Warner and Bancroft and a menstrual diary. The symptom category scores were analyzed using ANOVA, designed for use with a four-period Latin square design. "ANOVA showed no overall treatment effect in any symptom category, but extension of the analysis to investigate predefined factorial treatment contrasts of the adjusted mean scored showed a significant interaction effect Mg and Vitamin B6 supplementation for reducing anxiety-related symptoms and non-significant reduction trend in craving-related symptoms" (De Souza, 2000, pp. 136). There were no adverse side effects reported although the subjects were not specifically asked about them. This study suggests Vitamin B6 + Magnesium is a safe and effective therapy for the treatment of mild premenstrual symptoms.

Summary

It is important for physicians and prescribing psychologists to recognize PMDD as a physical and psychological disorder and to become familiar with the criteria for diagnosis and effective treatments. It is a prevalent and relatively common disorder; therefore, women seek treatment on a regular basis. The treatment of PMDD has recently been examined more closely.

The research indicates that many of the treatments that have been thought to be effective in relieving PMDD symptoms can actually aggravate them. The results of commonly used treatment are summarized in the following table:

Treatment	Efficacy	Adverse Effects	Availability	References
Sertaline	Highly Effective	Nausea, diarrhea, headache, decreased labido	Prescription	Yonkers, K., Halbreich, U., Freeman, E., Brown, C., Endicott, J., Frank, E., Parry, B., Pearlstein, T., Steiner, M., Severino, S., Stout, A., Stone, A., Harrison, W., Sondheimer, S., Polansky, M., Garcia-Espagna, B.
Fluoxetine	Highly Effective	Decreased libido, rash, fatigue, insomnia, palpitations	Prescription	Pearlstein, T., Stone, A., Lund, S., Scheft, H., Slotnick, C., Brown, W.
L-tryptophan	Moderately Effective	Dizziness	Prescription	Steinberg, S., Annable, L., Young, S., Liyanage, N.
Estrogen	Moderately Effective	Endometrial hyperplasia	Prescription	Tiemstra, J., Patel, K.
Progesterone	Ineffective	Aggravates symptoms of PMDD	Prescription	Tiemstra, J., Patel, K.

Treatment	Efficacy	Adverse Effects	Availability	References
Oral Contraceptives	Moderately Effective	Menopausal osteoporosis and cardio-vascular disease	Prescription	Tiemstra, J., Patel, K., Pearlstein, T., Steiner, M.
Danazol	Highly Effective	Cardiac disease, decreased bone density, weight gain, nausea, acne, facial hair, decreased high-density lipoproteins and depression	Prescription	Pearlstein, T., Steiner, M., O'Brien, S., Abukhalil, I.E.H.
Calcium	Moderately Effective	None Reported	Non-prescription	Pearlstein, T., Steiner, M., Ward, M., Holimon, T.
Vitamin B6	Moderately Effective	None Reported	Non-prescription	Pearlstein, T., Steiner, M., De Souza, M., Walker, A., Robinson, P., Bolland, K.

The evidence indicates a strong support for SSRIs in treating PMDD. SSRI treatment merits further study, as well as researching the levels of serotonin in PMDD sufferers, as it is suggested in the PMDD efficacy. There were limited comparisons made to both the tricyclic and miscellaneous antidepressants; need to be examined further. There was no research found on the effect of MAOIs in the treatment of PMDD, which also needs to be considered.

There are also non-prescription alternatives such as calcium and Vitamin B6 that have been proven effective in treating less severe symptoms of PMS, which may provide women with a safe alternative to antidepressants. Again, some of these alternatives need to be studied further to determine their effectiveness.

References

American Psychiatric Association. (1994). Diagnostic Statistical Manual of Mental Disorders (Fourth Edition). Washington, DC: American Psychiatric Association.

Bhatia, S.C. and Bhatia, S.K. Depression in Women: Diagnostic and Treatment Considerations. *American Academy of Family Physicians* 1999.

Endicott, J. History, Evolution, and Diagnosis of Premenstrual Dysphoric Disorder. *Journal of Clinical Psychiatry 2000;* 61(suppl 12): 5–8.

Freeman, E.W., Sondheimer, S.J., Polansky, M., Garcia-Espagna, B. Predictors of Response to Sertraline Treatment of Severe Premenstrual Syndromes. *Journal of Clinical Psychiatry 2000;* 61:8:579–584.

Freeman, E.W., Rickels, K., Arredondo, F. Kao, L., Pollack, S.E., Sondheimer, S.J. Full or Half-Cycle Treatment of Severe Premenstrual Syndrome with a Serotonergic Antidepressant. *Journal of Clinical Psychopharmacology 1999;* 19:1:3–8.

Freeman, E.W., Karl Rickels, K., Sondheimer, S.J., Polansky, M. Differential Response to Antidepressants in Women with Premenstrual Syndrome/Premenstrual Dysphoric Disorder. *Archives of General Psychiatry 1999;* 56:932–939.

Haseltine, F.P. and Faustman, D. A Sunergistic Effect of a Daily Supplement for 1 Month of 200 mg Magnesium Plus 50 mg Vitamin B6 for the Relief of Anxiety-Related Premenstrual Symptoms: A Tandomizxed, Double Blind, Crossover Study. *Journal of Women's Health & Gender-Based Medicine 2000;* 9:2:131–139.

Ling, F.W. Recognizing and Treating Premenstrual Dysphoric Disorder in Obstetric, Gynecologic, and Primary Care Practices. *Journal of Clinical Psychiatry 2000;* 6(suppl 12):9–16.

O'Brien, S. and Abukhalil, I.E.H. Tandomized controlled trial of the Management of Premenstrual Syndrome and Premenstrual Mastalgia Using Luteal Phase Only Danazol. *American Journal of Obstetrics and Gynecology 1999;* 180:1:18–23.

Pearlstein, T.B., Halbreich U., Batzar, E.D., Brown, C.S., Endicott J., Frank, E., Freeman, E.W., Harrison, W.M., Haskett, R.F., Stout, A.L., Yonkers, K.A. Psychosocial Functioning In Women With Premenstrual Dysphoric Disorder Before and After Treatment With Sertraline or Placebo. *Journal of Clinical Psychiatry 2000;* 61:2:101–109.

Pearlstein, T.B., Steiner, M. Non-Antidepressant Treatment of Premenstrual Syndrome. *Journal of Clinical Psychiatry 2000;* 6(suppl 12):22–27.

Steinberg, S., Annable, L., Young, S.N., Liyanage N. A Placebo-Controlled Clincal Trial of L-Tryptophan in Premenstrual Dysphoria. *Society of Biological Psychiatry 1999;* 45:313–320.

Steiner, M. and Pearlstein, T. Prementrual Dysphoria and the Serotonin System: Pathophysiology and Treatment. *Journal of Clinical Psychiatry 2000;* 61(suppl 12):17–21.

Tiemstra, J.D. and Patel, K. Hormonal Therapy in the Management of Prementrual Syndrome. The Journal of the American Board of Family Practice 1998; 11:378–381.

Ward, M.W. and Holimon, T.D. Calcium Treatment for Premenstrual Syndrome. *The Annals of Pharmacotherapy 1999;* 33:1356–1358.

Yonkers, K.A. Antidepressants in the Treatment of Premenstrual Dysphoric Disorder. *Journal of Clinical Psychiatry 1997;* 58(suppl 14):4–10.

Yonkers, K.A., Halbreich, U., Freeman E., Brown, C., Endicott, J., Frank, E., Parry, B., Pearlstein, T., Severino, S., Stout, A., Stone, A., Harrison, W. Symptomatic Improvement of Premenstrual Dysphoric Disorder With Sertraline Treatment. *Journal of the American Medical Association 1997;* 278:12:983–988.

Advances in Medical Psychotherapy and Psychodiagnosis
2002–2003, Volume 11, pp. 165–172

Thinking about Mind and Body for Medical Psychotherapy: Toward an Integration in Clinical Practice

Alexander Blount, Ed.D.

University of Massachusetts Memorial Health Care

Abstract

We have difficulty transcending the mind/body dichotomy because our models of medical phenomena and our terminology embody the dichotomy at every turn, even when we combine terms from both sides of the dichotomy. This discussion offers an approach to perceiving phenomena, to organizing the social roles in delivering services and to constructing the routines of clinical care that can be the beginning of an evolution toward just such a transcending of the dichotomy. This would give us access to perceiving phenomena that presently are not available because we have no ways of fitting them into our current ways of understanding.

The term "medical psychotherapy" might be considered an oxymoron, embodying as it does concepts from both sides of the mind/body split. "Medical" is often used as one half of a dichotomy of "medical" vs. "psychological," though it also has much broader uses. The term "psychotherapy" was developed to describe therapy for the "psyche" (mind) as opposed to the "soma" (body). So, while it is not completely accurate to say that "medical psychotherapy" is in the same self-contradictory category as "jumbo shrimp," the point still seems valid.

We use terms such as "medical psychotherapy," "medical family therapy," "psychosomatics," and "behavioral medicine" because we have difficulty describing work at the confluence or the overlap of our ideas of "mind" and "body." In Western cultures, most of us grow up powerfully ensnarled in the dichotomy, both conceptually and linguistically. Engel (1977) gives a concise history of the dichotomy as it relates to medicine beginning five hundred years ago. He begins with the concession by the established Church allowing the dissection of the human body. The body was seen as a mere vessel, temporarily holding the unique and eternal aspect of a person, the soul. The analytical methods of the science of Newton, Galileo and Descartes were free to examine the body as a machine without needing to include the complicating aspects of the mind which remained the province of religion. In the last hundred years, the successes of medicine and the scientific method have been so great little attention needed to be paid to complaints that an important part of what it is to be human was unaccounted for.

For those of us who try to transcend the dichotomy, there are few alternatives. We can smile sagely if a colleague says of her patient "there's nothing physically wrong with her, I'm going to refer her to a psychologist," or when the patient says, "you mean this headache is all in my mind?" knowing, as we do, that they are oversimplifying. We can say to ourselves "it's really both" or "psychological and emotional factors affect the body in very real ways and vice versa." But saying that the two sides of the dichotomy interact or inter-penetrate does nothing to relieve us of the tyranny of the dichotomy.

The Science of Mind/Body

One modern attempt at expanding the field of study, if not at transcending the dichotomy, was George Engel's "biopsychosocial model" (Engel, 1977). He put forward the model to address the dichotomy of mind and body as it was embodied in Psychiatry. The more extreme camps of the day were defining mental illnesses as "problems in living" on one hand and "biological diseases" on the other. He used the general systems theory of Ludwig von Bertalanffy (1952, 1968) to create a model of isomorphic, self-maintaining systems arranged hierarchically. Each system has it's own processes which exhibit patterns of interaction isomorphic to the systems of which it is made up and to the systems of which it is a part. Like nesting Russian dolls, the systems are arranged in a hierarchy the goes from smaller to larger: molecules, cells, organs, organisms, the person, the family, the society, and the biosphere. If a phenomenon is not explainable by breaking things into smaller units, the biopsychosocial model provides a map for the larger units in which to find the contextual factors that can help to explain it.

The biopsychosocial model does not transcend the dichotomy of mind and body as much as it arranges it differently. Instead of being different elements at the same "level" of explanation, body and mind become different levels of systems. When we move from "organism" to "person" in the hierarchy, we cross the line of the dichotomy, albeit with very little fanfare.

Even in the field that shows most promise for delivering the science that might support a move beyond this dichotomy, psychoneuroimmunology, the language of the dichotomy still structures the basic conceptualization of the work. Psychoneuroimmunology is a field that studies how psychological states and traits (mind) are associated with immunity (body) and the biological (body) and behavioral (mind) pathways for such relations. People study such interesting questions as the effects of psychological stress or joy on the immune system. They develop findings that, for example, ". . . psychological or behavioral factors may influence the incidence or progression of cancer through psychosocial influences on immune function . . ." (Kiecolt-Glaser & Glaser, 1999). This has even been extended to styles of relating and the immune system. ". . . abrasive marital interactions have important endocrinonological and immunological correlates" (Kiecolt-Glaser, Glaser, Cacioppo, & Malarky, 1998).

While the findings make intuitive sense, the statement in its structure is nonsense. It is nonsense because the term, "abrasive marital interactions," is in one *realm of description* and "the immune system" is in another. The question is analogous to the question "how does the color of the sky effect rainfall totals?" The color of the sky does not affect rainfall totals. The color of the sky, i e., our experience of meteorological phenomena, is one way of describing the weather. A measurement of rainfall totals is another. It is easier to say, "the sky is blue, it's not going to rain" than to say "when I experience the sky as blue, my observation correlates with a situation in which the air mass above me is made up of reasonably consistent temperatures throughout and is not in contact with another air mass of strikingly different temperature or levels of moisture, making it unlikely that moisture is going to be precipitated out of the air."

If we take this understanding to the study abrasive marital interactions on the immune system, we can say that we are in a similar logical situation, but one that is much more difficult to articulate. We have little or no language for the complex bodily processes that we experience as abrasive interactions. No one would expect us to say, "When I experience the cascade of neuro-chemicals that effect neuro-transmission and neural communication in certain ways, ways that in my experience I have been taught to call 'she is being abrasive,' it seems to have certain describable impact on or correlation with the long term functioning of another aspect of my chemical make up which is called my 'immune system'."

We Create the Dichotomy

The difference between mind and body is a function of the observer, not of the phenomenon being observed. "Mind" and "body" are realms of description that are different rather than different entities. By "mind" I mean the realm of meaning and intentionality. It is a realm of communication and indication. It is not dependent on energy exchange. The message that makes me filled with fury takes no more energy to deliver that the message that makes me relaxed. By "body" I mean the realm of physical structure and process, of chemical exchange, of genetics, and of physiology. Each realm of description is internally coherent or consistent and is capable of a broad range of explanations that many people find satisfactory.

If I am walking down the street and have a heart attack, there may be a description that can be offered from the world of mind, but, at first, I hope these will not be particularly interesting to the passers by. It will be the description from the world of body that I want to be interesting to observers. I want them to talk about chest compressions and resuscitation. I want physicians to talk about how the body can sustain life, about percentages of the heart muscle that are damaged, about occluded arteries and ejection fractions. Perhaps at some time in the future it might be interesting to talk about what I was worrying about when the heart attack happened or what my expectations or my family's expectations are in relation to my health. We can discuss the heart attack as an event that will impact our family relating patterns and my role in them. We can discuss how the new definition of me as a fragile person could change my understanding of myself or other people's understanding of me. Saving a life makes the world of description we call "body" interesting and takes the spotlight away from the world of description we call "mind."

From the other perspective, if we smile at each other, the smile in the world of meaning is interesting immediately, in the world of physical explanation, it is less so. I am immediately interested in what you mean by your smile and I may notice my reaction to your smile, that I feel pleasant or uncomfortable. At the same time, there is a whole world of "body" explanation that could be made. A smile can be explained as a totally biological event in that world. I could say that there are patterns of light impacting nerves in the eye translated to electrical impulses in the brain which interact with previously arranged patterns of neurons and dendrites cueing firings that control muscles in my face and at the same time cueing chemical changes that I experience as either relaxation or nervousness. We don't commonly think of the smile in the world of physical descriptions because the description that is adequate to the physical phenomena is significantly more complex than is warranted by our level of interest in those phenomena. The world of mind and meaning is much more interesting in that situation. It is observer interest that determines the description we pick, however, not the essence of the phenomena as either "mind" or "body".

Blurring the Edges

If "mind" and "body" are realms of description rather than distinct worlds of phenomena, what would a non-dichotomized world of description and experience be like? Perhaps the first step necessary is to recognize that the mind/body dichotomy is not inevitable. There are many cultures where psyche and soma are not experienced as distinct. This is shown when there are problems in the lives of people from these cultures. Authors in cross-cultural psychology assert that the less a culture is influenced by "modern" or "Western" cultures, the less differentiation there will be between physical illness and psychological disturbance (Angel and Thoits, 1987; Katon, Kleinman & Rosen, 1982; Kirmayer, 1989). Reports of "depression" in non-European countries tend to include the usual vegetative signs, but the more Western manifestations of depression such as self-deprecation, hopelessness and guilt are rarely found. (Pfeiffer, 1968).

When people from these cultures interact with people from Western cultures, they tend to gradually show their pain in ways that are more in line with Western psychiatric descriptive categories (Angel and Thoits, 1987). We observe that populations living in our culture tend to move toward a more dichotomized experience, increasingly distinguishing between emotional and bodily experience of life pain. This is seen by some Western observers to be a move in the right direction toward more mature functioning. Well-respected authors who have studied what we call "depression" in multiple cultural contexts disagree. "One caution is that this developmental paradigm is distinctly oriented to Western cultural values, in which investigators see the movement toward psychological mindedness as maturity. This view is not shared in all cultures, and its cross-cultural validity is doubtful." (Katon, Kleinman, & Rosen, 1982, page 241). One very interesting cultural take on depression is an article by Jadhav (1996) that traces the cultural vocabulary of guilt, fatigue, energy, stress and depression as expressions in the evolution and development of the institutions of British culture and the cultures in the English-speaking world.

The next step in our reasoning about depression is to question the way we use the concept. One cannot say that a person who presents with loss of libido, weight gain, sleep difficulties and pain of unexplained origin has depression but is failing to show certain symptoms. To say that a person has, in essence, the body symptoms but not the mind symptoms, is to insist on the mind and body dichotomy in the basic conceptualization and to define the person in pain as wrong in their experience of pain. Better to admit that the "Procrustean bed" of the concept doesn't fit the data. If we can find a language that transcends the dichotomy, there will be powerful payoffs in the improvement in our ability to "see" as well as to describe the complexities of human pain and disfunction.

Case Study

A 23 year old Puerto Rican woman was referred to a physician's office after her previous physician was unable to find any "cause" for her bilateral arm pain and weakness. During the first interview the patient discussed her frustration with her condition which, at the time, was impairing her self-care. When the physician asked how her husband and three children were doing, she burst into tears. She rebuked the doctor for asking about things that did not relate to her symptoms. The physician responded that he did not mean to pry and that often asking about a patient's family situation leads to information that later is helpful in treatment. She then acknowledged that she viewed herself as an incompetent wife and mother and that she had felt unworthy of anyone's love since childhood. The visit was concluded by the physician's affirming that she had suffered a great deal in her life and suggesting an extended interview at a later time.

In offering a longer interview, the physician said that it might be worthwhile to have a female staff member in his practice called the "network therapist" join at the next visit. She was a clinical social worker trained in family therapy. The patient agreed. In response to a question about what she ever did that gave her even a little relief, she said she felt some relief from her situation when writing poems. She was asked to bring some of her poems to the next visit and was asked not to change anything in her life in the meantime.

At the second visit, the patient read her poems to the physician and the "network therapist" from his staff. They tended toward themes of isolation, death and hopelessness. In the discussion of her life that reading the poems engendered, it was learned that she had been sexually abused once as a child and that she left home at 14 with her present husband who was 20 years her senior. She felt that her marriage was not working, but had no hope of being able to survive as a single person. The physician and network therapist requested that she bring her husband to the next interview.

Over the next few months, the patient and her husband spent a few sessions talking about marital issues with the network therapist and the patient participated in a support group for women who had experienced sexual abuse. Three years later the patient reported that her life was happier and more stable. Her arm pain and weakness were no longer constant, recurring only occasionally. She reported that she knew how to manage these episodes so that she had very little discomfort or deterioration of function. She never considered the alleviation of her physical symptoms to be related to her marital or group counseling experiences. (Bayona, 1998)

The primary care practice to which she came was arrayed to address its patients' pain, however that pain was presented. A physician, nurses, a "network therapist" and a service who helped patients deal with basic necessities of life were all important parts of the practice. Patients did not need to subscribe to a particular understanding of the etiology of their pain in order to hope for some relief.

The Beginnings of a Way Out

We see the dichotomy transcended in everyday parlance. In popular phrasing we use alternatives to the mind/body dichotomy, possibly because the dichotomy doesn't fit our experience even when we have no other formal system of description. Many of the phrases we use every day capture the incredibly complex way that bodily experience can be part of a complex set of human interactions. Patterns of interaction include the bodily experience of those interacting. To say "that child is a pain in the neck" compresses a great deal of popular wisdom. One aspect of taking care of a child when that is stressful for the caretaker over time can be bodily pains for the caretaker. It is part of the interaction pattern, not a by-product in another domain. This is a language that transcends the dichotomy in a particular narrow instance without being able to express a model or deliver a coherent terminology to transcend the dichotomy in any broader way.

In practice, professionals can help to move out of the bind of the dichotomy by using language that does not demand to be placed on one side or the other to be understood. These are words and phrases that are understood in both realms and do not demand clarification. Words such as "pain", "distress", "discomfort", "health", "vitality" and "stress" all can be understood by patients and professionals, usually without a demand that they be defined as indicating just body or mind.

Can We Make a New System?

How will we develop a conceptual model for working that is non-dichotomizing while still taking account of the findings of science and the experience of patients? It may be a long journey. I want to offer a possible map.

A conceptual *model of phenomena* in one domain of operation interacts with and is impacted by people's experience of the *organization of social roles* in that domain of operation. Where there is a dichotomized model of phenomena in health care, for instance, it makes sense to have very separate

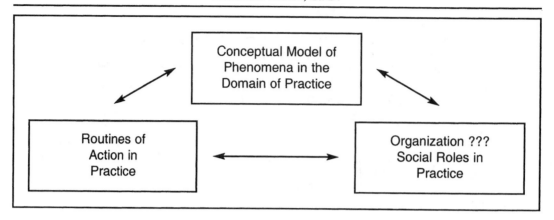

Illustration 1. Expertise in Practice

disciplines, including different training structures and funding sources for the organization of the social roles of providers. For those providers who attempt to bridge the sides (such as psychiatrists), we might expect them feel that they must choose between the sides and not feel truly at home on either. Most recently psychiatry has selected the "body" side of the dichotomy, attempting to biologically approach phenomena that presents psychosocially. With many very notable exceptions (Katon, 1995), this has made it hard for the discipline to help in primary care where the need is to be able to approach phenomena that presents biologically from a psychosocial perspective.

The *organization of social roles* impacts and is impacted by the daily routines of interaction among people practicing in the domain of operation. When physicians and psychologists first try to work together in the same practice, often neither group knows what they are supposed to do with the other (Blount, 1998; Blount and Bayona, 1994). When the routines of interaction have been structured and integrated into protocols that combine physicians and mental health providers such as in the integrated protocols developed for major depression by Katon and his colleagues (Katon, von Korff, Lin, Walker, Simon, Bush, Robinson & Russo, 1995), high participation rates by patients, high satisfaction rates for providers and patients, and high rates of improvement have been documented.

The daily *routines of interaction* also impact and are impacted by the model of phenomena guiding the practice in a particular domain of operation. We ask routine questions of our patients, directly or through research studies, that conform to our models of phenomena. Our decision trees are reflections of the basic structure of our models. If we routinely asked different questions, the different answers would begin to influence our models of phenomena, demanding in turn different questions.

This schema of models, roles and routines can be used to describe a specific domain of expertise such as health care or a much larger domain such as a culture. Because of this constantly interacting and evolving web of understandings and relationships, changes in any part of the system will ramify in changes in all parts and each part of the system will restrict the potential for change in others in evolutionary ways. It is a testimony to the need for all three dimensions to evolve together that Engel's biopsychosocial model from the seventies has had so much impact on the academic work in the field and so little impact on practice (Blount & Bayona, 1994).

It may seem that "medical psychotherapy" was dismissed at the beginning. We are now able to say how important it is along with practices like it, such as "clinical health psychology," "medical family therapy" (McDaniel, Hepworth and Doherty, 1992), "behavioral medicine" and "integrated primary care" (Blount, 1998). These practices can form the transformative routines of daily practice and the new organization of social roles that can make the "biopsychosocial model" and its successors more generally used in health care. To do this, we must make sure that our practices are not simply the usual models and practices of psychotherapy grafted onto medical settings and populations. For a clear description of what is implied by this change, see Strosahl's stimulating discussion (1998).

We need to look at the literature about how routines of practice and organization of social roles have evolved in settings where the psychotherapist becomes part of the medical team (Banta & Fox, 1972; Bloch, 1988; Blount, 1998; Coleman & Patrick, 1976; Dym & Berman, 1986; Cummings, Cummings & Johnson, 1997). We must look for ways to consult and work as team members, rather than to be specialists looking for referrals within the medical setting. We should try to share space rather than having the behavioral health space separate from the medical space. We must work hard to solve the difficulties in the routines of practice that this teamwork creates, particularly for administrative and support staff. We must structure the environment as best we can so that the routines of practice and the organization of social roles tend to be as seamlessly knit as the patients' problems and pains we address. This that requires providers who were trained on the "mind" side of the dichotomy learn the language and culture of medical service providers and work within it, even if it sometimes seems a strange culture indeed.

Finally, we must be ready to evolve in our own thinking and practice. We might, for instance, come to conceptualize the body as an organ of communication, a part of mind, and to see expressions and language and emotions as part of body and genetics. We might be able to use such ideas without have to pick between them. It is hard to imagine that such ideas would not impact basic foundational concepts such as diagnosis and psychopathology over time. If we can come to ways of thinking and describing that are a bit beyond the dichotomy that is placed on us every day, it might open up exciting new areas for practice in health care.

References

Angel, R., & Thoits. P. (1987). The impact of culture on the cognitive structure of illness. *Culture, Medicine & Psychiatry, 11*, 465–494.

Banta H. D. & Fox, R. C. (1972). Role strains of a health care team in a poverty community. *Social Science and Medicine, 6*, 698–722.

Bayona, J. (1998). Unpublished teaching case.

Bloch, D. A. (1988). The partnership of Dr. Biomedicine and Dr. Psychosocial. *Family Systems Medicine, 6*, 2–4.

Blount, A. (Ed.) (1998). *Integrated Primary Care: The Future of Medical and Mental Health Collaboration,* New York: WW Norton.

Blount, A. & Bayona, J. (1994). Toward a system of integrated primary care. *Family Systems Medicine, 12*, 171–182.

Coleman, J. V. & Patrick, D. L. (1976). Integrating mental health services into primary medical care. *Medical Care, 14*, 654–661.

Cummings, N. A., Cummings, J. L. & Johnson, J. N. (Eds.) (1997). *Behavioral Health in Primary Care.* Madison, CT: Psychosocial Press.

Dym, B. & Berman, S. (1986). The primary health care team: Family physician and family therapist in joint practice. *Family Systems Medicine, 4*, 9–21.

Engel, G. L. (1977). The need for a new medical model: A challenge for biomedicine. *Science, 196*, 129-36.

Glenn, M. L. (1987). *Collaborative health care: A family oriented approach.* New York: Praeger.

Jadhav, S. (1996). The cultural origins of western depression. *International Journal of Social Psychiatry, 42,* 269–86.

Katon, W. (1995). Collaborative care: Patient satisfaction, outcomes and medical cost-offset. *Family Systems Medicine, 13,* 351–365.

Katon, W., Kleinman, A., & Rosen, G. (1982). Depression and somatization: a review. *American Journal of Medicine, 72,* 127–135, 241–247.

Katon, W., von Korff, M., Lin, E., Walker, E., Simon, G., Bush, T., Robinson, P., Russo, J. (1995). Collaborative management to achieve treatment guidelines: Impact on depression in primary care. *Journal of the American Medical Association, 273,* 1026–1031.

Kiecolt-Glaser, J. K., & Glaser, R. (1999). Psychoneuroimmunology and cancer: fact or fiction? *European Journal of Cancer, 35,* 1603–7.

Kiecolt-Glaser, J. K., Glaser, R., Cacioppo, J. T., & Malarkey, W. B. (1998). Marital stress: immunologic, neuroendocrine, and autonomic correlates. *Annals of the New York Academy of Sciences, 840,* 656–63.

Kirmayer, L. J. (1989). Cultural variations in the response to psychiatric disorders and emotional distress. *Social Science & Medicine, 29,* 327–39.

Pfeiffer, W. (1968). The symptomatology of depression viewed transculturally. *Transcultural Psychiatry Research Review 5,* 121–123.

Strosahl, K. (1998). Integrating behavioral health and primary care services: The primary mental health care model. In A. Blount, (Ed.) *Integrated primary care: The future of medical and mental health collaboration.* New York: WW Norton.

Von Bertalanffy, L. (1968). *General systems theory.* New York: Braziller.

Von Bertalanffy, L. (1952). *Problems of life.* New York: Wiley.

Advances in Medical Psychotherapy and Psychodiagnosis
2002–2003, Volume 11, pp. 173–184

Anxiety, Depression, Hostility and General Psychopathology: An Arabian Study

Abdel-Sattar Ibrahim, Ph.D., APMPP*
Radwa M. Ibrahim, Ph.D., ABDA

Abstract

In Arabian cultures, the psycho-social characteristics of psychopathological trends including depression, anxiety, and hostility remain largely unknown. Scales measuring depression, anxiety, and hostility were administered to a voluntary sample of 989 Saudi Arabian men and 1024 Saudi women coming from different social, economical, and educational backgrounds. The principal aims of this study were to: (1) Compare Saudi men's psychopathological mean scores with mean scores of their female peers, (2) Examine the interrelations among psychopathological scores in both male and female groups, and to (3) Compare psychopathological scores among several subgroups in male and females groups. By using the Hotelling Principal Component Factor Analysis, only one unrotatable Factor, identified as general Psychopathology, was extracted in each group. Although women scored generally higher on all test scores than men, the differences were not significant. The pattern of group differences within each group separately was of more value than gender differences per se. In both groups, increased scores on depression, anxiety, hostility, and general psychopathology were reported for adolescents and younger people. Working women and house makers obtained lower mean scores. It was, also, indicated that hostility is less pathological among females. In the men group, on the other hand, police officers, secondary school students, and theology students had statistically significant higher mean scores than all other groups.

The current research results were discussed based on the theory of interaction between social roles and extent of exposure to stressful life events.

Introduction

Depression, hostility, and anxiety are among the most widespread emotional problems in most societies, and the most common psychiatric disorders for which people seek help for themselves or others in psychiatric settings, office practice, out-patients clinics and/or counseling centers (Hamilton, 1989; Kupfer & Frank, 1981). The prevalence of such problems and their relationship to psychopathology

---

*Address reprints requests to: Abdel-Sattar Ibrahim, Ph.D., The Medical Center, P. O. Box 5024, King Fahd University of Petroleum, Dhahran 31261, Saudi Arabia

has stimulated much research in Western societies. However, we are still far from knowing the incidence and demographic distribution of many such psychopathological trends in Arabian cultures. This paper aimed at estimating distribution of these characteristics in a major Arabian country, mainly Saudi Arabia.

Numerous studies have also shown that psychopathological traits are more common in females than males (e.g., Hamilton, 1989; Schwab, Brown, & Holzer, 1968; Schwab, Holzer, & Warhett, 1981; Weissman & Klerman, 1977). Hamilton (1989) has reported that depression, for example, is approximately twice as frequent in females than in males. Other studies on sex-related differences in psychopathology have shown that definite sex-related profile of psychopathology emerges (Powell, Denton, & Mattson, 1995; Schwab, Brown, & Holzer, 1968).

Obviously, research in this area is much needed to explore the interaction between sex-related and psychopathological patterns in Arabian samples. This study represented one of the attempts towards this goal.

More specifically, this research investigated depression, anxiety, hostility, and psychiatric symptom rates among groups of Saudi Arabian women, and compared women's scores in these measures with obtainable rates in men. Also, we examined the relationship among all psychopathological scores in both groups. Additionally, and in order to determine the prevalence of psychopathology in a large sample from Saudi Arabia, the present study provided psychopathology scores for Saudi women and Saudi men across several social and demographic subgroups.

Method

Subjects

The data used in this investigation were collected from 989 Saudi Arabian men and 1024 Saudi women. The men's sample ranged in age from 15.7 years to 59.1 years. In the male sample 517 were university students, 105 were employed in governmental positions, 40 secondary school teachers, 39 accountants and bank employees, and 41 policemen. The rest of the male sample came from different professional and career backgrounds. The majority of the male subjects were ethnic Saudis. Muslims accounted for over 95% of the sample.

The women group ranged in age from 15.3 years to 56.5 years. Two hundred eighty nine women were secondary school students, 203 university students drawn from different colleges and specialization including medicine, education, science and history; 133 secondary and preparatory teachers; and the rest 399 of the female sample included technicians, house-makers, and other governmental employees.

Subjects were asked to volunteer for a scientific study. They were informed in writing on the cover sheet of the research questionnaires that the study is of a research nature, and may offer no direct benefit to them. Naturally, the subjects were given the choice of withdrawing at anytime during the course of the study without any negative consequences. To ensure confidentiality, subjects were not obliged to write their names or give any other identifying information.

Measures

The Biography Questionnaire (BQ)

The BQ consists of items concerning major demographic and biographic aspects, including age, marital status, educational level, etc. Test retest reliability for the BQ was 0.89 (n = 50).

The Symptom Inventory (SI)

This inventory is designed to tap differences in general psychopathology. The SI consists of 27 items selected by Abdel-Sattar Ibrahim (Ibrahim & Alnafie, 1991) from major psychological tests of psychopathology, which were validated in Arabic Cultures, including the Minnesota Multiphasic Personality Inventory (MMPI) and the Eysenck Personality Questionnaire (EPQ) (Eysenck & Eysenck, 1975; Ibrahim, 1982). Items on this inventory represented a number of psychopathological behaviors that describe major psychiatric disorders such as sleep disturbances, social withdrawal, delusional thinking, hallucinations, and drug use.

The Depression Symptomatology Scale (DSS)

This scale consists of 18 items that have been used widely in research on depressive Symptomatology (Schwab, Holzer, & Warhett, 1981). They were based on the conceptualization of depression as a syndrome, consisting of five major dimensions. In scoring the DSS, the same technique used by Schwab and his colleagues (Schwab, Holzer, & Warhett, 1981) was implemented. Subjects rated each item on both the DSS and the SI on a scale ranging from not troubled (1) to highly troubled (3).

Ibrahim (1991) and Ibrahim and Alnafie (1991) have translated these instruments into Arabic and then made another attempt to produce a translation close to local Saudi dialects. The reliability and the validity of the above study scales were reported elsewhere (Ibrahim, 1982; 1991; Ibrahim & Alnafie, 1991; Ibrahim, 1991). Each scale was estimated for reliability by using Cronbach's alpha as a measure of internal consistency. Alpha coefficients for the SI and the DSS were 0.88 and 0.90, respectively.

The Multiple Affect Adjective Check List (MAACL)

The Multiple Affect Adjective Checklist consists of negative adjectives such as unhappy and listless, as well as positive adjectives such as strong, lucky, and free. The scale requires the subjects to respond by checking every adjective that describes "how they feel today." In scoring the MAACL, we used the scoring keys for depression (D), Anxiety (A), and hostility (H) scales (Zuckerman & Lubin, 1965).

The Cronbach's Alpha was computed as a measure of internal consistency. The mean correlation for the three subtests was found to be 0.76, well above the limit accepted for the scale reliability. In a more recent validation study (Abdel-Mawgoud & Moftah, 1995), the same group of scales were found to discriminate significantly between a total of 110 psychiatric inpatients and a comparable non patient control group.

Also, in another item analyses study (Abdel-Mawgoud and Moftah, 1995), the items have shown an overall significant decrease following an intensive eclectic psychotherapy program presented to a total of 45 hospitalized drug addicts at Al-Amal Hospital, Saudi Arabia, additionally confirming the validity of these scales as measures of psychopathology.

The *Biography Questionnaire,* the *Depressive Symptomatology Scale,* the *Symptoms Inventory,* and the *Multiple Affect Adjective CheckList* were administered to all subjects in a group-testing situation.

Results

Means, Standard Deviations, and Intercorrelations

Table 1 shows the means and standard deviations for the female/male samples for each instrument. Though not highly significant, an overall female increase on all test scores was indicated.

Table 1
Means and Standard Deviations for Males (N = 989) and Females (1024)

Variables	Males	SD	SE	Females	SD	SE
DSS	28.34	6.47	.21	29.98	6.54	.21
SI	37.93	9.02	.29	38.42	8.44	.29
MAACL (A)	6.47	3.28	.11	7.10	3.42	.11
MAACL (D)	11.95	5.37	.17	12.87	5.59	.17
MAACL (H)	7.71	3.39	.11	7.61	3.10	.09

Note. DSS = Depression Symptomatology Scale; SI = Symptom Inventory; MAACL = Multiple Affect Adjective Checklist; A = Anxiety; D = Depression; H = Hostility.

Interrelations between the questionnaires were all significant. They are displayed for both males and females in Table 2. In the male group, the highest correlation was between the *depression symptomatology scale* and the *symptom inventory scale* followed by high correlation between the *depression, hostility,* and *anxiety* scores on the *MAACL.* Also, in both groups the correlation between the *hostility* and the *depression symptomatology* scores and the *symptom inventory* scores were highly significant. However, males' correlations between *hostility* and the rest of these variables are much higher than that for the females. This may indicate that self-reported female hostility may be less pathological as compared to men.

By using the Hotelling Principal Component Factor Analysis, only one unrotatable Factor, identified as general Psychopathology, was extracted in each group. This factor accounted for 67.3%, and 63.4% for men and women, respectively. In both groups, the depression symptomatology scale and the symptom inventory scores had the highest loading on this factor. All other variables had from moderate to high loading except the hostility score in the female group, which had nonsignificant loading of 0.23. This adds more confirmation that self-reported hostility in females may be less pathological as compared to men.

Differences within the Male Subgroups

Since it has become almost customary to interpret sex-related differences in behavior as arising mainly from difference in roles, in opportunities, and social expectations, the assumption was made that it might be rewarding to analyze data according to differences in subgroups within each sex sample. Thus, 513 males were divided into seven subgroups based on over %50 of the major socio-economical, and educational backgrounds representative of the male sample. The seven groups included: government employees (n = 105), secondary school students (n = 230), secondary school teachers (n = 40), theology students (from Al-Imam Ben Saud University for Islamic Religion Studies) (n = 19), physical education (athletic) students (n = 39), police officers (n = 41), and bank employees and accountants (n = 39).

Table 3 shows the results of the one way ANOVA for the male subgroups. As can be seen from the table 3, police officers scored significantly higher than all other subgroups on almost all test variables (an overall total score of 112.67). This indicates that this subgroup, more often than other groups, endorse a great number of pathologic symptoms including *hostility, anxiety, general symptomatology,* and *depression.* Secondary school students scored the second highest subgroup, with an overall score

Table 2
Correlation Matrix for Males (N = 989) and Females (N = 1024)

Variables	DSS	SI	MAACL (A)	MAACL (D)	MAACL (H)
correlations*					
DSS	00	.74	.35	.32	.26
SI	.71	00	.36	.35	.30
MAACL (A)	.39	.37	00	.70	.59
MAACL (D)	.45	.35	.61	00	.64
MAACL (H)	.19	.20	.48	.64	00

Note. The correlation values for males are above the diagonal, and that for females are below the diagonal.
DSS = Depression Symptomatology Scale; SI = Symptom Inventory; MAACL = Multiple Affect Adjective Checklist;
A = Anxiety; D = Depression; H = Hostility.
*All correlations, $p < .05$.

of 96.08. However, secondary school students had significantly scored the highest on the *MAACL' depression scale* than all other groups. The lowest pathology scores were in favor of secondary school teachers (total of 81.78), followed by bank employees and accountants (an overall total score of 82.56).

Significant group differences were also found on the *symptom inventory* questionnaire, showing again police men and secondary school students with significantly higher psychopathological scores relative to other groups.

Differences within Women Subgroups

Six hundreds and seventy six female Ss, accounting for over % 66 of the total, sample, were also, divided into seven female subgroups based on major representative social , economical and educational backgrounds of the sample in Saudi society. The seven female subgroups selected were: secondary school students (n = 289), secondary school teachers (n = 112), liberal arts' students (n = 112), college students (n = 57), house makers (n = 41), working women (n = 44), and preparatory school teachers (n = 21).

A multivariate analysis of variance (MANOVA) indicated significant overall differences among female subgroups. ANOVAs were then computed to compare differences among female subgroups on the five test scores. The results of the ANOVAs are shown in Table 4.

Obviously, the differences among the subgroups were highly significant, with secondary school students and liberal art students scoring the highest on the *depressive Symptomatology* scores; while the working women group scored the lowest.

Significant group differences were also found on the *symptom inventory*, with secondary school students, liberal art students, and preparatory school teachers demonstrating significantly higher scores relative to the other groups, while secondary school teachers along with the working women and homemakers showed significantly lower general psychopathology scores.

Sample	Scales					
			MAACL			
	DSS	SI	A	D	H	Total
Government Employees (n = 105)						
M	26.83	34.51	5.75	10.49	7.16	16.95
SD	6.12	7.60	3.17	5.23	2.98	5.02
Secondary School Students (n = 230)						
M	28.40	39.76	6.65	12.89	8.38	19.22
SD	6.18	9.18	3.26	5.68	3.26	5.52
Secondary School Teachers (n = 40)						
M	25.20	32.68	5.65	11.35	6.90	16.36
SD	3.82	4.23	2.37	4.06	2.83	3.46
Theology Students (n = 19)						
M	28.05	37.26	6.05	13.05	8.05	18.5
D	6.34	6.33	3.02	5.76	2.56	4.8
Physical Education Students (n = 39)						
M	28.35	39.74	6.08	10.13	8.26	18.51
SD	10.95	15.59	4.23	7.65	3.93	8.47
Bank Employees and Accountants (n = 39)						
M	28.66	31.69	5.90	9.62	6.69	16.51
SD	4.84	5.41	3.80	5.07	3.76	4.58
F Ratio	10.35	12.29	2.50	2.32	5.34	
P	.000	.000	.02	.03	.000	

Table 3
F-Ratio Results of Male Subgroups—
Means, Standard Deviations and Significance Levels

Note. DSS = Depression Symptomatology Scale; SI = Symptom Inventory; MAACL = Multiple Affect Adjective Checklist; A = Anxiety; D = Depression; H = Hostility.

Sample	Scales					
Table 4 **F-Ratio Results of Female Subgroups—** **Means, Standard Deviations and Significance Levels**						
	MAACL					
	DSS	*SI*	*A*	*D*	*H*	*Total*
Secondary School Students (n = 289)						
M	31.85	42.89	7.58	13.86	8.03	20.84
SD	6.88	9.21	3.53	6.08	3.44	5.82
Secondary School Teachers (n = 112)						
M	28.56	35.53+	6.89	13.43	8.00	18.48
SD	6.35	5.88	3.01	5.10	2.74	4.62
Liberal Art Students (n = 112)						
M	31.67	39.88	7.42	13.00	7.72	19.93
D	6.74	8.72	3.48	5.28	3.07	5.46
College Students (n = 57)						
M	29.91	36.84	6.91	11.63	6.79	18.42
SD	5.92	7.35	3.48	5.26	6.86	5.77
Homemakers (n = 41)						
M	29.29	36.15	5.66	10.15	6.61	17.57
SD	6.05	6.74	3.32	5.45	2.53	4.82
Working Women (n = 44)						
M	26.17	36.03	5.18	10.52	6.25	16.83
SD	6.17	7.71	2.94	5.08	2.79	4.94
Preparatory School Teachers (n = 21)						
M	29.58	36.57	7.57	13.86	8.00	19.12
SD	5.88	6.25	2.93	3.20	2.53	4.12
F Ratio	25.18	22.10	4.23	4.20	3.22	
P	.0001	.0001	.004	.004	.004	

Note. DSS = Depression Symptomatology Scale; SI = Symptom Inventory; MAACL = Multiple Affect Adjective Checklist; A = Anxiety; D = Depression; H = Hostility.

In the case of the *Multiple Affect Adjective Checklists,* group differences were also demonstrated on the *anxiety, depression,* and *hostility* sub-scales. Clearly, secondary school students, preparatory school teachers, and the liberal art students were generally higher than other groups. The working women and house makers, on the other hand, showed significantly lower self-reported *anxiety, depression,* and *hostility* scores.

Discussion

The significant and high intercorrelations among the questionnaires add further support for the validity of these scales in tapping comparable patterns of psychopathology in both gender samples. It was anticipated, based on previous Western studies (e.g., Fleming, Offord, & Boyle, 1989; Powell, Denton, & Mattison, 1995), that psychopathology would be greater in the female subgroups than male groups in Arab cultures. This expectation was confirmed only partially, in that women scored generally higher on all test scores than men, but not to the level of significance.

As displayed in Table 4, subgroup differences within females was more significant than differences between males and females per se. It may be suggested, therefore, that the hypothesis of sex related differences in psychopathology have limited utility, at least in Saudi Arabia. Perhaps, the frequency of psychopathology in certain societies may mainly depend on other social and educational influences inside any particular society rather than on gender. Relevant here is a study of symptoms of depression in the United States and Japan carried out by Baron and Matsuyama (1988). In that study, the authors concluded that sex differences in psychopathology are not to be expected in all societies. Hence, it may be argued that certain demographic, educational, and economical factors are more responsible for psychopathology insofar as they contribute to limiting certain daily satisfactions and in restricting the capacity for successful coping with daily psychological distresses (Rosenfield, 1980). Consistent with this view is the pattern of the results in the female groups. Apparently, higher amounts of self reported *depression, anxiety,* and *hostility* were expressed by secondary school students, preparatory (junior high) school teachers, and college students. In the male group the same pattern emerged showing increased scores on all tests for secondary school students, indicating again that these groups of young people are more vulnerable to psychopathology.

Although further research is needed, one line of thinking to account for the increased scores on psychopathology variables among young groups in both sexes may be attributed to age. Most of these individuals were adolescents and young adults. It may be argued that adolescence is a period of extensive physical, social, and emotional changes. Previous research (e.g., Baron & Matsuya, 1988; Forsell, Jerom, & Strauss, 1995; Milstein, 1989; Hamburg & Takanishi, 1989) showed that adolescence is a time of particular vulnerability. In fact several longitudinal investigations of developmental differences in anxiety and depression were carried out in Saudi Arabia (Ibrahim, 1991) and other Arab cultures such as Egypt and Kuwait (e.g., Khalik, 1994). In such studies, it was reported that adolescents scored generally higher on anxiety and depression tests than all other groups; a finding that may be, in part, of cultural foundation.

Culturally speaking, older people in Arabian cultures are highly respected and are viewed as having more status and influence in social situations than younger individuals and children (Ibrahim & Ibrahim, 1999). Social anthropological studies in Arabian cultures (e.g., Al-Torki, 1986), showed that there is no limit to the realm of individual behaviors where, for example, older people such as parents must be obeyed at all times. The authority of old age extends to the selection of a major in college and to the selection and/or approval of a spouse. Although, we cannot draw from that a cause-and-effect relationship with mental health outcomes, it is certainly an interesting line of clinical investigation to study this type of age relationship cross culturally to determine its mental health implications. Based on the present results, however, preventive measures should be established within health systems in Arab cultures to confront mental and emotional health problems in these groups of young people.

That homemakers were among the lowest psychopathological groups, is inconsistent with American and Western research that usually shows that married women and homemakers are more vulnerable to stress and mental illness because of the limited opportunities available to them (Fabrega, Mezzich, Ulrich, & Benjamin, 1990; Gove, 1979a; 1979b; Gove & Tudor, 1973). Although we cannot speculate extensively about this difference, a word about the psychological implications of marriage for women in Arab conservative cultures may be in order.

In a male dominated society, which place many restrictions on male/female relationships, marriage can provide women with more chances for legitimate socialization. Married women as compared by non married females can enjoy more opportunities for making decisions relating to child support, sex, economic privileges, etc. This leaves the married in a more positive position and provides her with greater opportunities for being in control , a shield against psychopathology. Although Arab women who are married may be perceived as more restricted than working women groups, they can be proud of their dominant family role and, thus, experience less overall psychopathology.

The pattern of group differences demonstrated on the hostility scale indicated that police officers, secondary school students, and theology students were generally higher than other groups. This may indicate that psychopathological tendencies in these groups are colored by more inclination towards negative acting out in response to stress. Therefore, psychiatric and psychological services should consider providing different types of help based on group types targeted for mental health services. Obviously, research in this area is needed to explore the interaction between social groups and psychopathological patterns in Arabian samples. This research represented just one of the attempts towards this goal.

One major interpretation of group differences in psychopathology, in the current study, can be singled out based on the interaction between social roles and life's stressful events. It is assumed that some groups are more vulnerable to psychopathology because their roles expose them to more stressful life events (Bryant & Harvey, 2000; Gove, 1979b). Groups more vulnerable to the effects of stressful life events would develop a significant proportion of distress and related mental health problems (Kessler, Price, & Wortman, 1985). If this theory is accepted, it may be then concluded from this research results that, relative to other social groups in that part of the culture, adolescents, young adults including high school and junior college students, and elementary school teachers are the most vulnerable to mental health pathology. It is unfortunate, however, to indicate that the mental health care delivery system in most Arabian cultures including Saudi Arabia provides limited opportunities for mental health care of these groups. Most mental health services are centralized in large general hospitals and provide limited help in terms of prevention, mental health education, and early intervention with major emotional and mental problems if warranted. Clearly more preparedness and funding for more specialized programs in hospitals, schools, colleges, and private clinics dealing with mental health services in that part of the world is badly needed.

References

Al-Torki, S. (1986). *Women in Saudi Arabia: Ideology and behavior among the elite.* New York, N.Y.: Columbia University Press.

Abdel-Mawgoud, M., & Moftah, A. (1995). Effects of psychotherapy on psychological and behavioral disturbances among drug addicts in Saudi Arabia. *Current Psychiatry, 2,* 31–39.

Baron, N., & Matsuya, Y. (1988). Symptoms of depression and psychological distress in United States and Japanese college students. *The Journal of Social Psychology, 128,* 803–816.

Bryant, R. A., & Harvey, A. G. (2000). *Acute stress disorder.* Washington, D. C.: American Psychological Association.

Eysenck, H. J., & Eysenck, S. B. J. (1975) *Manual of the Eysenck Personality Questionnaire.* San Diego: Educational & Industrial Testing Services.

Fabrega, H., Mezzich, J., Ulrich, P., & Benjamin, L. (1990) Females and males in an intake psychiatric setting. *Psychiatry: Interpersonal and Biological Processes, 53,* 1–16.

Fleming, J. E., Offord, D. R., & Bogle, J. (1989). Epidemiology of childhood depressive disorders. Journal of American Academy of Childhood and Adolescent. *Psychiatry, 29,* 571–580.

Forsell, Y., Jerom, A. F., & Strauss, E. V. (1995). Prevalence and correlates of depression in a Population of nonagenarians. *British Journal of Psychiatry, 167,* 61–64.

Gove, W. P. (1979a). Sex, marital status, and psychiatric treatment: A research note. *Social Forces, 51,* 34–45.

Gove, W. P. (1979b). Sex differences in the epidemiology of mental disorders: Evidence and explanation. In E. S. Gomberg & V. Franks (Eds.). *Gender and disordered Behavior: Sex differences in psychopathology* (pp.73–95). New York, N.Y.: Bruner/Mazel.

Gove, W. P., & Tudor, J. F. (1973) Adult sex roles and mental illness. *American Journal of Sociology, 73,* 812–835.

Hamburg, D. A., & Takanishi, P. (1989) preparing for life: the critical transitions of adolescence. *American Psychologist, 44,* 825–827.

Hamilton, M. (1989) Frequency of symptoms in melancholia (depressive illness). *The British Journal of Psychiatry, 154,* 201–206.

Ibrahim, A-S. (1982) The factorial structure of the Eysenck Personality Questionnaire among Egyptian university students. *Journal of Psychology, 112,* 221–226.

Ibrahim, A-S., & Al-Nafie, A. (1991). Perception and concern about sociocultural change and psychopathology in Saudi Arabia. *The Journal of Social Psychology, 13,* 179–186.

Ibrahim, A-S., & Ibrahim, R. M. (1999). Cultural considerations in mental health needs and practice: An Arab experience. *Advances in Medical Psychotherapy and Psychodiagnosis, 10,* 139–150.

Ibrahim, R. M. (1991). Sociodemographic aspects of depressive symptomatology: Cross cultural comparisons. *Dissertation Abstract International, 51,* 12.

Kessler, R. C., Price, R. H. & Wortman, C. B. (1985). Social factors in psychopathology: stress, social support, and coping processes. In M. Rosenweig, & L. W. Porter (Eds.), *Annual Review of Psychology.* Palo Alto, CA: Annual Reviews Inc.

Khalik, A. M. (1994) The developmental study of anxiety. *The Annals of the Faculty of Arts, 14,* No. 90 (In Arabic).

Kupfer, D. J., & Frank, F. (1981). *Depression.* New York: Upjohn.

Millstein, S. G. (1989). Adolescent health: challenges for behavior scientists. *American Psychologist, 44,* 837–843.

Powell, J. W., Denton, R.1 & Mattison, A. (1995). Adolescent depression: Mother-adolescent dyad and locus of control. *American Journal of Orthopsychiatry, 65,* 263–273.

Rosenfield, D. (1980). Sex differences in depression: Do women always have higher rates. *Journal of Health and Social Behavior, 21,* 33–42.

Schwab, J. J., Brown, S. N., & Holzer, C. F. (1968). Depression in medical inpatients: sex and age differences. *Mental Hygiene,* 627–630.

Schwab, J. J., & Holzer, C. F., Warhett, C. W., & Schwab, R. B. (1981). Human ecology and depressive symptomatology. In J. Masserman, & S. S. Schwab (Eds.). *Social psychiatry,* Vol. III, 180–197. New York: Grune Stratton.

Weissman, M. N., & Klerman, G. L. (1977). Sex differences and the epidemiology of depression. *Archives of General Psychiatry, 34,* 98–112.

Zuckerman, N., & Lubin, B. (1965). *Multiple Affect Adjective Checklist.* San Diego: Educational and Industrial Services.

Advances in Medical Psychotherapy and Psychodiagnosis
2002–2003, Volume 11, pp. 185–200

Exploring the Mystery called AD/HD

William A. Mosier, Ed.D.,PA-C
Kettering Medical Center (Ohio)

Gabriela Z. Pickett
Kettering, Ohio

Larry F. Mosier
Chicago, Illinois

Introduction

Attention Deficit/Hyperactivity Disorder (AD/HD) is a diagnostic label that is really a hidden disability because the child with AD/HD looks normal. Since the child with AD/HD looks normal, the adults in the child's world expect him or her to act normal. The problem is that what is "normal" for a child with AD/HD is not what is generally considered acceptable behavior. The core "deficit" in AD/HD is a seemingly thick barrier between the individual with AD/HD and their understanding that there can be serious consequences, in life, for inappropriate behavior. If a child with AD/HD is asked, "Why did you do that? Didn't you know it was wrong?"; a typical response may be "Yes, I knew it was wrong, but by the time I thought about it, I had already done it." AD/HD refers to a pattern of behavior characterized by difficulty sustaining focused attention to tasks, poor impulse control, and cognitive and/or physical restlessness. Three additional frequent findings are: a pronounced preference for tactile stimulation, poor peer relationships, and a tendency toward exaggerated emotional responses to either external or internal stimuli. Even though the diagnostic label includes the word hyperactivity; it does not refer only to individuals who are physically overactive. The term hyperactivity can refer to an overactivity of thoughts, better referred to as a cognitive restlessness.[1]

The characteristics of an individual with AD/HD who does not display the symptoms of physical hyperactivity may be chronic daydreaming, being lost in one's own thoughts, appearing unmotivated, sluggish, or often staring off into space. Although the symptoms of AD/HD are present at a very early age, they are frequently not recognized until a child begins to have difficulty adjusting to a school setting. Although some AD/HD behaviors may be considered typical for early childhood, the individual with AD/HD will demonstrate these behaviors more consistently and with a greater severity than a non-AD/HD child. AD/HD is the most common cause of behavior disorders found in children and adolescents. It is probably the most common chronic neuro behavioral problem encountered in pediatric practice. It also constitutes the most frequent childhood psychiatric referral to Mental Health Professionals. About one in ten children in America fit the diagnostic criteria for AD/HD. This represents about four million school-aged children. The ratio of boys to girls diagnosed with AD/HD is 4:1. However, by adulthood. the ratio appears to be 1:1. This difference may be accounted for by factors of social conditioning and differing social expectation for boys and girls.

Although the symptoms are first noticed during childhood the residual effects can continue into adulthood, with devastating impact on both the individual with AD/HD and society.[2]

History

Even though it is often referred to as the new fad disease of the current generation, AD/HD is not a new condition. All that is new is the name. Descriptions of children displaying the symptoms of AD/HD were recorded by a German physician, Heinrich Hoffman in 1848. The first published report, in English, of children that manifest the behavioral characteristics of this syndrome appeared in 1902 in the British medical journal *Lancet*. The author, Dr. George Still, referred to these children as having "defects in character" due to their lack of emotional control, impulsivity, inattentiveness and overactivity.

In 1934, in the United States, these children began to be referred to as "organically driven." By 1940, the label "Minimal Brain Syndrome" was used. Then in 1950 that label was changed to "Minimal Brain Damage." By 1957, it was referred to as "Hyperkinetic Impulse Disorder" and in 1960 it was relabeled, "Minimal Brain Dysfunction" (M13D). Then, in 1968 with the dawn of DSM II, there was a pendulum swing away from acknowledging the syndrome as a biologically based phenomena and instead referring to it as a "Hyperkinetic Reaction of Childhood"; which implied that parenting skills was a major contributor to the manifestation. In 1982, with the publication of DSM III, the term "Attention Deficit Disorder" (ADD) was introduced. DSM III further broke-down the label into ADD with hyperactivity, ADD without hyperactivity, and (acknowledging that the syndrome can extend into adulthood) ADD—residual type. In 1987, the label for the condition ADD without hyperactivity was changed to "Undifferentiated Attention Deficit Disorder." While the diagnostic label to describe individuals with this syndrome has changed, over time, each label has been an attempt to describe the same entity, that which, since the advent of DSM-IV, 1994, is now referred to as AD/HD.[3]

AD/HD is the major cause of school failure among children today. One out of two children with AD/HD will fail at least one academic school year. One out of every two will receive a school suspension at least once. One out of ten will be expelled from school. It is estimated that half of all children with AD/HD will need special education services due to a learning disability and that seventy percent of that group will already be receiving special education for their learning disability at the time that they are finally diagnosed with AD/HD. Forty percent of all adolescents with AD/HD will become high school drop-outs. The problem of having extreme difficulty in being able to sustain focuses attention can impact heavily on academic endeavors. Without the ability to sustain focused attention, learning can be seriously impaired.

The process of learning can be facilitated when the mind is receptive to and focused on a particular area of study. When a child is unable to attend to directed learning, a child may experience school failure that eventually damages self esteem and can lead to continued failure throughout life.[4]

Etiology

AD/HD is a neuro-biological condition that is most likely genetically based. It is caused by an alteration in neurotransmitter function originating in the lower brain and limbic structures that result in frontal lobe disinhibition. The underlying neuro chemical abnormalities are probably multifaceted. The brain abnormality may be structural, chemical, or electrical. Studies have uncovered that the presence and regulation of the catecholamines dopamine (DA) and norepinephrine (NE) in the prefrontal areas of the brain are crucial to the proper functioning of the frontal lobes. An insufficiency of NE and DA can cause cerebral neurons to prematurely stop focused activity. DA is a mediator of activity level, aggressiveness, and irritability. NE mediates distractibility, level of attention, and novelty-seeking behavior. Research findings confirm an association between AD/HD and decreased DA and NE activity.[5] In individuals with AD/HD, the inhibitory function of the frontal areas may be compromised by a disregulation of DA and NE. This might result from an inadequate production of neurotransmitters, an inadequate release of neurotransmitters, or an inadequate supply of receptor sites for the neurotransmitters. It might result from a too rapid diffusion, re-uptake, or degradation of the neurotransmitters. It is also possible that the malfunction results from an abnormal pre and or post-synaptic neuronal network. Positron Emission Tomography (PET) has demonstrated a decrease in brain blood flow in areas responsible for the functions controlling activity level, novelty-seeking behavior, and focusing of attention in individuals diagnosed with AD/HD.[6]

Although substantial research provides evidence that AD/HD is genetically transmitted, there does not appear to be one common genetic origin for all cases of AD/HD. Therefore, its etiology is considered heterogeneous. Several different biochemical abnormalities may be involved, with most of them also being genetic in origin. The neurotransmitter acetylcholine, which mediates arousal level, motivation and learning, is probably also a key player. Because there are different symptom clusters representing different AD/HD subtypes, each subtype may result from a different kind of neuro-biological dysfunction.[7]

A factor that tends to confound the issue of the etiology of AD/HD is the association of alcohol abuse and/or nicotine abuse during pregnancy by some mothers of children diagnosed with AD/HD. Studies have demonstrated a higher incidence of children who display the symptoms of AD/HD among the off spring of mothers who smoked during their pregnancy.[8] Similar findings have been noted when the mother has engaged in alcohol or other drug use during pregnancy. Other studies indicate a pronounced increase in the rate of AD/HD among individuals with a family history of alcoholism.[9]

What Doesn't Cause AD/HD?

There are many myths about the causes of AD/HD. Each of the following lacks any scientific supporting evidence. AD/HD is not caused by psychogenic factors. It is not the result of poor parenting or family dysfunction. Though child abuse, divorce, and other family problems can put added stress on any one and in fact can even contribute to the symptoms of AD/HD appearing more pronounced, in themselves, they do not cause AD/HD. Although in rare instances (perhaps 2–8 percent of cases) food additives, preservatives, allergies, fluorescent lighting, lack of vitamins, food sensitivities, aspartame, or sugar can influence the behavior of some children making them appear more restless, none of them cause AD/HD.[10]

Diagnostic Criteria

The diagnostic criteria for AD/HD focuses on a triad of core symptoms: Inattention, impulsivity, and/or hyperactivity (which may be expressed as a physical and/or cognitive restlessness). The signposts for identifying AD/HD are these core symptoms being presented in a chronic and pervasive pattern that is inconsistent with adult expectations and been a problem since early childhood. The DSM-IV diagnostic criteria for AD/HD has isolated three subtypes of the disorder: AD/HD-primarily inattentive type, AD/HD primarily hyperactive/impulsive type, and AD/HD-combined type.

The nine behaviors associated with the inattentive type are:

* making careless mistakes

- having difficulty sustaining focused attention

- seeming not to pay attention when spoken to directly

- failing to complete one activity before moving on to another

- poor organizational skills/being disorganized

- reluctance to engage is tasks requiring sustained mental effort

- losing things

- easy distractibility

- forgetfulness

(Having six of the nine behaviors meets the diagnostic criteria for AD/HD-inattentive type.)

The nine behaviors associated with the hyperactive/impulsive type are grouped as follows:

Hyperactive (Restless) Criteria

- being fidgety

- unable to remain seated when expected to do so

- physical restlessness

- difficulty engaging quietly in activities without disturbing others

- acting as if driven by a motor

- excessive talking

Impulsive Criteria

- blurting out answers to questions before they are even asked

- not being able to patiently wait for a turn

- interrupting others/intruding on the activity or conversation of others

(Having six of these nine behaviors meets the diagnostic criteria for AD/HD-hyperactive/impulsive type.)

The criteria must have been observable, in the child, for at least six months to a degree that is socially mal-adaptive and inconsistent with what is considered age-appropriate behavior, present in two settings (e.g. home, school, work) and have been present prior to age seven.

The diagnosis of AD/HD is not limited to children. The wording of the DSM-IV criteria have been chosen to specifically include adult manifestations of the symptoms. To make the diagnosis in an adult, the symptoms must still have been present since early childhood.

The components of a credible assessment of AD/HD include: Medical evaluation, parent interview, teacher assessment (via behavior rating scales sent to the school and returned to the provider), child observation, achievement testing, and intellectual testing.

There are no laboratory tests currently available that will help in diagnosing AD/HD. Although there are computerized tests available to determine attention span, at the present state of the art, there is no need for EEG, elaborate brain scans, or any other high tech medical testing.[11]

Influences That Can Alter the Presentation of AD/HD

The AD/HD child's behavior can be remarkably inconsistent. Some days a child with AD/HD will wake up with the neurotransmitters firing more efficiently than on other days. Thus the child will better be able to display the behavior expected of him. This is why teachers will often complain that the AD/HD child is just lazy or not trying hard enough. There are also certain circumstances under which the symptoms seems to disappear. Some of the situations where the symptoms of AD/HD can seem to disappear are:

- during illness

- when the child is receiving constant repetitive feedback (i.e. nintendo type games)

- new or novel situations (like the doctor's office)

- a quiet environment without distractions

- a one on one situation with an adult

- intimidation (this is, however, not recommended as a way to control behavior)[12]

Differential Diagnosis

Establishing an accurate diagnosis requires gathering accurate information.

A thorough family history must be done to assess for a pattern of AD/HD criteria manifesting in other family members. The parent interview should include asking the parents to compare their child's behavior against the DSM IV criteria (the criteria, it self, can be used as a check list). Parents should be asked about the child's developmental, academic, and social history. They should also be asked to describe the specific problem behaviors they see in the child. Family functioning should be discussed as well as any previous interventions and treatment sought. Behavior rating scales can be completed by teachers as well as parents to ensure that the symptoms manifest in at least two settings. Many behavior rating scales, modeled after the DSM-IV criteria, are available.

Behavior rating scales are particularly useful because they represent a simple, quick, and economical means of gathering data that reduces rater bias and subjectivity. Because all the scales demonstrate about equal efficacy, the choice of which one to use should be based on ease of administration and scoring. Widely used are the scales by Barkley, Conners, Copeland, Sparks, and Taylor. Direct observation of the child (or interview, in the case of adolescents and adults) can uncover evidence of other psychiatric problems that will undoubtedly influence the treatment plan. It must be remembered that due to an AD/HD individuals ability to be more focused in a novel situation, direct observation in a clinical setting may not be representative of the patient's typical behavior. Psychological testing is helpful to obtain an understanding of the child's perceptual processing, visual-motor functioning, as well as intellectual and emotional states.

A physical examination and lab testing will only be useful to rule-out other medical problems. Certain medical conditions can manifest AD/HD-like symptoms. However, the individuals afflicted usually display more severe behavior problems than are found in AD/HD and often have more significant cognitive impairment. A differential diagnosis must include screening for: allergies, bipolar disorder, chronic lead poisoning, fetal alcohol syndrome, fragile X syndrome, malnutrition, medication related side-effects (i.e. anticonvulsants, antihistamines, bronchodilators,or corticosteroids), mental retardation, pervasive developmental disorders (i.e. autism), post infectious or post traumatic encephalopathy, progressive neuro degenerative disorders, schizophrenia, seizure disorders, thyroid problems, Tourette's syndrome, and untreated phenylketonuria.[13]

Comorbidity and Associated Problems

The diagnosis of AD/HD can be complicated. Although the symptoms are relatively well delineated by the DSM-IV criteria, there can be a problem in making a definitive diagnosis due to the frequency of comorbid conditions. A patients comorbidity will affect diagnosis. prognosis and treatment. For this reason, careful attention must be given to cognitive, emotional, behavioral and social assessments. Because common things happen commonly, anxiety, disruptive behavior, learning and mood disorders should be screened for routinely.

Two out of every three individuals diagnosed with AD/HD have another diagnosable Axis I psychiatric disorder. One out of every two has a comorbid oppositional-defiant disorder or conduct disorder. One out of every three will have a comorbid mood or anxiety disorder. One out of every two will have motor dis-coordination. At least one out of every three children with AD/HD has a learning disorder (LD) or communication disorder. Research indicates that when there is a comorbidity of AD/HD with LD there is a two-fold increase in the risk of academic underachievement, lowered self-esteem and delinquent behavior. Additionally, one out of every three may have Tourette's syndrome as a comorbidity.

Fifty percent of individuals with AD/HD will have one and often two comorbid conditions. Therefore, any treatment plan must include appropriate interventions to address these problems. It is rare that one medication will be sufficient to resolve all the presenting symptoms when a comorbidity is present.[14]

Positive Characteristics of AD/HD

There are positive aspects to having AD/HD. The desirable characteristics of AD/HD provide potential benefits that may out-weigh the limitations that accompany AD/HD. If a child receives the appropriate reinforcement, the following AD/HD traits can translate into valuable assets for a productive adult life:

- Persistence (As long as self-esteem stays intact, individuals with AD/HD tend to display a greater propensity to bounce back after negative feedback or failure until obstacles or objections are finally overcome.)

- Accepting and forgiving others (Individuals with AD/HD tend to be more accepting of others and usually do not hold grudges.)

- Inquisitiveness (AD/HD individuals tend to display a driving curiosity that can reinforce their ability to hyper-focus on an activity.)

- Intuitiveness (Strong emotions combined with the ability to hyper-focus can lead an AD/HD individual to have sensitive emotional responses to persons and situations.)

- High energy level (The Army recruiting campaign that states, "We do more by 9:00am than most people do by noon," may be why their is a greater percentage of individuals with AD/HD in the military than in any other single profession.)

- Imagination (Individuals with AD/HD often demonstrate a tendency toward coming up with imaginatively creative ideas.)

- Above average memory for remote events (Seemingly trivial points that may be overlooked by others, are often remembered in great detail by individuals with AD/HD.)

- Being intrigued by change and challenge (AD/HD individuals tend to be less fearful of risk-taking and less willing to give up when the going gets tough.)[15]

To treat or not to treat? That is the question!
Under identifying and untreating individuals with AD/HD increases the risk of impaired educational performance, family dysfunction, social problems, and decreased self-esteem. The potential long-term effects, not just on the person with AD/HD, but also on society, are devastating in terms of lost productivity and social adjustment. The characteristics that define AD/HD are not socially desirable traits to have. Even the diagnostic criteria specifically describe the negative aspects of being AD/HD. The positive aspects of the syndrome are usually overlooked.

The typical individual with AD/HD has been scolded since early childhood that he or she could do better if only they tried harder. This negative message heard over and over again tends to set up a cycle of self-doubt, fear of inadequacy, and sense of failure. The consequence is quite often low self-esteem. The importance of addressing self-esteem issues cannot be overemphasized. Without adequate intervention, many individuals with AD/HD are at risk for developing a life of alcohol or other substance abuse, emotional immaturity, and interpersonal difficulties.[16]

A Multi-Modal Approach to Treatment

Because AD/HD is a complex condition, a comprehensive multi-modal approach to its management is essential. When treating AD/HD medical management, behavior modification, educational intervention and psychological counseling are all important considerations. Because AD/HD is a developmental "disability" for which there is no cure, whether you are treating children or adults, successful treatment must address the behavioral, educational, medical, psychological, and social aspects of the patient's life. All patients will not manifest AD/HD in the same manner. Likewise, the treatment plan will not consist of the same intervention strategies for every patient. Some patients will be more impulsive, others more distractible and others overactive. Each requiring different but very specific behavioral interventions. The syndrome may even manifest in some individuals as under activity or lethargy. The goal of treatment must be to improve quality of life while protecting self-esteem and nurturing a sense of social competence.

To be effective a treatment plan must include:

- parenting education (to assist parents in understanding the neuro-biological basis of AD/HD)

- parenting training to help parents learn the behavior management strategies needed to assist their child developing self control)

- classroom intervention strategies (adjusting the school environment to accommodate the child's different learning style which will require educating school personnel about the nature of AD/HD)

- behavioral and cognitive therapies (to facilitate insight, coping skills, and self control)

- support groups

- assessing and treating co-morbidities

- medication management (Eighty percent of all children manifesting behavioral or learning problems caused by AD/HD will benefit from psycho stimulant medication. Of the twenty percent not benefiting from medication, most will have a co-morbidity that will respond to other pharmacotherapy.

The effectiveness of treatment will be directly related to the degree to

1. the biologic nature of the syndrome is acknowledged,

2. the support needs of the family are met,

3. school issues are addressed,

Table 1
Behavior Management Strategies for Home and School

- a positive reinforcement system must be initiated to encourage desirable behavior (Verbal reinforcements must identify the behavior that you want to encourage.)

- unacceptable behavior should be controlled with logical consequences techniques rather than with physical punishment

- avoid trying to reason with the child

- avoid giving the child more than one command at a time

- teach organizational skills

- avoid threats

- be consistent with discipline

- avoid asking the child, "Why did you do that?"

- interact with the child with eye-to-eye contact

- touch the child when you are talking to him/her (It will help the child to pay attention to what you are saying, if you precede all verbal cues with gently touching the child on the shoulder.)

Table 2
Strategies for Modifying the School Environment

- provide a quiet place for the child to study

- place child away from distractions

- place the child's desk up-front, within arms reach of the teacher

- break work assignments into a series of smaller assignments

- keep work periods short

4. co-morbidities are properly treated and

5. patient self-esteem is strengthened.

Without an effective behavior management plan to help the AD/HD child modify his or her behavior; treatment will not result in an optimal improvement in terms of a decrease in dysfunctional behavior.[16]

Psychopharmacotherapy

Medication has been used to treat AD/HD since 1937 when the disorder was referred to as"minimal brain syndrome." The use of medication is considered the single most effective treatment for AD/HD. Regardless of public opinion to the contrary, medication should not be reserved for use only after everything else tried has failed. While the use of chemical replacement therapy will benefit about 80% of children with AD/HD, it will tend to be beneficial for only about 50% of adults with AD/HD. The rationale for using medication is:

1. to enhance the effectiveness of behavior modification intervention strategies,

2. to reduce the risk of academic failure,

3. reduce the risk of the child harming self or others, and

4. to minimize damage to self-esteem caused by chronically "getting into trouble."

Responsible utilization of psychopharmacotherapy must include:

a. proper baseline assessment of target symptoms,

b. careful selection of the appropriate medication,

c. appropriate titration of medication based on clinical observation and home and school reports addressing efficacy of dose compared against side effect profile,

d. on-going monitoring and reassessment,

e. continuation of maintenance dose, and

f. eventual discontinuation.

The sympathomimetic drugs (psycho stimulants) have been used successfully to treat AD/HD for sixty years. Methylphenidate (Ritalin, Concerta, Metadate CD), the mixed amphetamine salt (Adderall), and d-amphetamine (dexedrine) are the main stay of the pharmacological treatment of AD/HD. Seventy percent of patients will respond to the first trial. Of the 30 percent who are non-responders to the initial trial, 70 percent of them will respond to the second sympathomimetic tried. Contrary to public opinion, the safety and efficacy of these psycho stimulants for the treatment of AD/HD has been substantiated in more than a hundred clinical studies reported over the last 55 years in professional journals. There are over 1.5 million patients currently taking psycho stimulants for the treatment of AD/HD.

Prescriptions written for psycho stimulants to treat AD/HD have tripled since 1990. The reason for this phenomenon is that more children and adults are being presented to medical clinics for evaluation and more clinicians are doing a better job of diagnosing the disorder and prescribing the proper medication.[17]

How Do the Psycho Stimulants Help?

The psycho stimulants effect on DA and NE transmission is what is useful for a patient with AD/HD. Just as reading glasses allow a person to better focus on what one is attempting to read, the psycho stimulants help the child or adult with AD/HD to sustain focused attention to tasks. Though the basic mechanism of action of the psycho stimulants is indirect, the result is an increase in the intrasyaptic availability of DA and NE.

This action results from blocking their reuptake by binding to the sites for DA and NE transport. Research on the effectiveness of the psycho stimulants have consistently demonstrated that with medication subjects are better able to display:

a. deceased motor restlessness,

b. improved ability to modulate motor activity,

c. decreased distractibility,

d. increased concentration,

e. decreased impulsiveness,

f. increased time on task,

g. increased self-control,

h. improved self-regulation,

i. enhanced motivation,

j. increased compliance to directives,

k. increased effort on tasks,

l. decreased physical and verbal hostility,

m. a decrease in negative behavior,

n. increased academic productivity,

o. increased accuracy of actual work performed,

p. improved handwriting and

q. improved overall academic performance.[18]

Dosing of Psycho Stimulants

In prescribing of medication for AD/HD, three important questions are: 1. How much medication is needed per dose in order for the individual to be symptom free? 2. How frequently should the medication be dosed? and 3. What periods of the day should the individual be on medication?

We must remember that if a child is diagnosed with AD/HD we are acknowledging that the behaviors displayed are neurologically based. Therefore, the need for medication must be assessed for each hour of the day and not just for use during school hours. AD/HD is not a school disability but rather a life disability. Placing a child on medication only during school hours will usually result in improved school performance; however, there will be a risk of continued behavior problems and poor social adjustment during the non-school hours if the medication is not used then as well.[19]

Contrary to popular belief, body weight has very little to do with the actual amount of medication necessary to achieve an effective response. The effect of the psycho stimulant is not directly related to the mg/kg dose. The amount of medication to be administered is more realistically determined by clinical response. Therefore, the dose must be adjusted based on how the patient is performing. There are many commercially available medication effectiveness reports (MER) that should be given to parents and teacher to complete so that the clinician has a marker for a response to a given dose. (The MER by Barkley, Conners, Copeland, and Taylor are widely used.) In the case of methylphenidate, due to its very short half life, the doses must be timed to ensure the maintenance of a brain concentration that exceeds the therapeutic threshold in order to sustain the desired effect. For example, only 5 mgs dosed at 8 am, noon, and 4 pm may be effective to facilitate decreased distractibility and sustain focused attention in one child. Yet, in another child of the same age and weight, 20 mgs doses might be necessary in order to achieve the same favorable response. The effects of methylphenidate usually appear within 20–30 minutes. The effect lasts about four hours. There is only a marginal cumulative effect. This lack of cumulative effect is, in part, why the medication is so safe for children. It also is why it is unnecessary to wean a child off the medication.

A pearl to remember when dosing methylphenidate is what I call the "Rule Of Fours." (Dose the medication at roughly four hour intervals with no dose administered after 4 pm.) The dosing at roughly four hour intervals is expected to maintain the desired effect of the medication above the therapeutic threshold throughout the day. Not dosing after 4 pm tends to minimize a potential risk of insomnia if dosing occurs too close to bedtime. The most important pearl to remember is, "DOSE LOW AND GO SLOW." A typical starting dose is 5 mg/day. Titration will depend on the child's initial reaction. Sustained release methylphenidate is available in 18 mg, 20 mg, 36 mg, and 54 mg strength and is quite variable in the duration of effect. In some patients it will only last 4 hours while in others it my last 6–8 hours. The psycho stimulants should be administered seven days a week, without drug holidays.

The old idea of providing the child a vacation from the medication was based on the false assumption that the medication would stunt growth without periodic breaks in administration. The major reason for not stopping the medication when the child is out of school is because when the medication is not in place the child 's behavior pattern of distractibility, impulsiveness and restlessness is reinforcing itself. Therefore, maintaining the medication at the therapeutic level all year round is actually best for using it as a tool for teaching self control.

The drug Adderall contains about 75% of the dextro (d) isomer amphetamine which appears to be more specific for inhibiting DA re-uptake and about 25% of the levo (l) isomer amphetamine which appears to be more specific for inhibiting NE re-uptake. This psycho stimulant has a half-life of 8 to 12 hours. It is generally well tolerated with a similar side effect profile as the other psycho stimulants. It is indicated for use in children three years of age and older. The starting dose of Adderall is 2.5 mg qAM for children three to five years and 5 mg once or twice daily in children six years and older.

This drug does not appear to have any significant advantage or disadvantage over methylphenidate in actual application.

In reference to d-amphetamine a general rule of thumb for its administration is to start with a morning dose of 2.5 mg. It is also available in spansules(which is a sustained release composition). The spansule form may avoid the need for a noon dosing. As with methylphenidate, its on-set of action is about 30 minutes. It also tends to work best following the rule of fours.

Pemoline (Cylert) is considered to be a second line choice for the treatment of AD/HD due to the risk of hepatic dysfunction. Its greatest convenience has been its once a day dosing and since it is a non-amphetamine composition, its minimal prescribing restrictions due to being a schedule IV substance. Initial starting dose is usually 37.5 mg qAM. It can be titrated weekly by 18.75 mg until the desired clinical response is achieved. Maximum daily dose is 112.5 mg. It is absolutely necessary to obtain baseline and periodic monitoring of hepatic function.[20]

Desired Outcome

Individuals with AD/HD often suffer from a lack of behavioral skills that are necessary for adequate academic and social adjustment. The medication, alone, does not teach the appropriate behaviors for coping with life's choices. However, medication in combination with the proper behavior modification training can facilitate establishing a routine for socially competent behavior. The role of the medication is to help the child gain self-control not to control the child. The medication helps the individual to be more responsive to social cues and educational opportunities. It is vital to the ultimate success of the treatment plan for the child to be held accountable for his or her behavior.

When this is accomplished the medication can be expected to facilitate behavior improvement that is sustained over time, even once the individual is off the medication. The goal is for the brain to receive sufficient reinforced for the preferred pattern of behavior. This provides the individual with a memory for what it feels like to be in control of their impulses; thus gaining more facility at maintaining self control.[21]

Monitoring Medication

Monitoring the effectiveness of the medication using standardized reports from the parents and the school is vital to obtaining a successful outcome from chemical replacement therapy. Weekly reports should be used to indicate the effects of the medication in facilitating better self control in the child. Medication effectiveness reports (MER) also help the provider to monitor for side effects and track changes in behavior that occur over time. Assessing the need for dosage adjustment should be done by comparing the child's behavior, with medication in place, against the DSM-IV criteria for

AD/HD. The goal is to be symptom free. To accomplish the treatment goal of self control over impulsiveness, distractibility and cognitive and/or behavioral restlessness, the medication may be necessary as an integral part of treatment for at least a three to five year period.[22]

Contraindications

The psycho stimulants are remarkably safe agents. Glaucoma and high blood pressure are the only real contraindications to using the psycho stimulants. Seizure disorder is not a contraindication to the use of psycho stimulants but careful monitoring for seizure activity with periodic EEGs should be an integral part of medical management. Psycho stimulants may trigger tics to appear more pronounced in patients with Tourette's Syndrome (TS). However, it is important to understand that the psycho stimulants do not cause tic disorders. Previously undetected tics may simply be brought to the surface.

Very often, TS will present as a learning disability or misdiagnosed as AD/HD long before the tic manifestations of the condition appear. If facial tics are observed after a child is started on one of the psycho stimulants it should be interpreted as a sign that the patient has TS. Lowering the dose of the psycho stimulant may diminish the tic. However, if a tic seem to worsen, clodidine can be added or the psycho stimulant can be discontinued.[23]

Managing Side Effects

There are very few serious side effects with the psycho stimulants. Serious side effects from the psycho stimulants are less common than serious side effects from acetaminophen (Tylenol). Just as Tylenol is a relatively safe medication for children, the psycho stimulants are very safe for use with children as young as age three.

The common side effects that often are of great concern to parents are decreased appetite, abdominal discomfort, Insomnia, and afternoon rebound. The side effect profile is often dose related. At lower doses the side effects are often negligible. A decrease in appetite will be observed in about 60% of individuals started on the psycho stimulants. However, the side effect does not lead to any serious health risk and will wear off over time. The concern over a possible inhibition of growth hormone (GH) is misguided. Since GH is released at night when a child is off the medication, research has confirmed that there is no risk of stunting growth from the use of the psycho stimulants. Administering the medication with meals (usually breakfast and lunch) will often resolve the problem of abdominal cramping. Symptoms of sleep disturbance can usually be resolved by giving a smaller afternoon dose of the psycho stimulant. When this is not sufficient, this is often an indication that a previously undetected comorbidity of depression is present. Once the depression is treated the insomnia will resolve. The problem of afternoon rebound is often resolved by adding an after school dose.[24]

Noncompliance Issues

Anywhere from 40 to 60 percent of patients that start treatment will discontinue treatment prematurely. The social stigma against using medication is one of the principal reasons. Other reasons for premature discontinuance are: resistance of the child and the family, shopping for other treatment modalities.[25]

Other Medications Used in Place of or With the Psycho Stimulants

The psycho stimulants will not address the target symptoms of most co-morbid states. Therefore, individuals manifesting the DSM-IV criteria for anxiety disorder, unipolar or bipolar depression, disruptive behavior disorders or any psychotic features must be considered candidates for additional pharmacotherapy.

Central alpha agonists such as clonidine (Catapres), guanfacine (Tenex), or guanabenz (Wytensin) are useful in conjunction with a psycho stimulant if an AD/HD child is displaying aggressive outbursts or if tics are present. However, these drugs are not appropriate for uncomplicated cases of AD/HD. The antidepressants may occasionally be useful as mono-therapy in mild cases of AD/HD, but are more often indicated if the patient has a comorbidity of a mood disorder. Bupropion (Wellbutrin), venlafaxine (Effexor), or the tricyclics, desipramine (Norpramin) or imipramine (Tofranil) may adequately address the symptoms of mild AD/HD. However, most often they need to be combined with a psycho stimulant. This will almost always indicate that the child has a comorbidity of depression. Other antidepressants that have been found to be both safe and efficacious, when there is a comorbidity of depression or obsessive-compulsive disorder are: the 5-HT reuptake inhibitors (SSRIs) such as: fluoxamine (Luvox), fluoxetine (Prozac), paroxetine (Paxil), and sertraline (Zoloft).

The neuroleptics such as risperidone (Risperdal) and quetiapine (Seroquel) are only occasionally useful. This class of drugs can be especially useful with a retarded child, if that child is also very aggressive. Often this type of child will not respond well to Methylphehidate HCI.[26]

Conclusion

AD/HD is a chronic syndrome that may produce adjustment problems even into adulthood. Individuals with AD/HD and their families need a support system and available resources to help them in coping with the potentially lifelong complications resulting from the syndrome. A multi modal approach to treatment must include planning for ensuring a clearly structured environment at both home and school that has well defined behavioral expectations reinforced with an appropriate behavior modification plan.

Proper classroom placement is absolutely vital to the success of the treatment plan. Additional tutoring, and assistance with developing adequate organizational skills may also be necessary. The best results will grow out of a team approach to management that includes the home, school, and health care providers working together in the best interest of the child. Mental Health Providers have a responsibility to educate clients and their families about AD/HD and attack the myths surrounding its causes and treatment. Although medication is a first line treatment for AD/HD, it must be clearly understood that medication alone is not an adequate intervention. Without a plan that includes behavior modification strategies, medication effectiveness will be limited. By the same token, psychotherapy without medication and behavior modification is of very limited value for the child with AD/HD. Despite marketing ploys attempted intervention by making changes in the child's diet or by adding nutritional supplement, such as pycnogenol, sea weed, or vitamins will not have any appreciable effect on decreasing the negative behaviors associated with AD/HD. Although there are claims that Acupuncture and Chiropractic can treat AD/HD, neither has shown any efficacy in controlled studies.[27]

Of all the treatments that are ineffective for treating AD/HD, physical punishment is the most destructive. Physical punishment should be avoided. Children with AD/HD will tend to demonstrate defiance and aggressive behavior towards others in response to being disciplined with physical punishment. Though spanking may produce temporary compliance, the flood of emotions that the child experiences in response to a spanking will tend to have a seriously negative impact on both the child's self-esteem and sense of what constitutes socially acceptable behavior. Recognizing that the typical forms of discipline will tend not to work on a child with AD/HD is a crucial first step. Parents must be provided with alternatives to spanking or spoiling.

Organizations such as Children and Adults with Attention Deficit Disorders (CHADD) (800) 233-4050 and the National Attention Deficit Disorder Association (ADDA) (800) 487-2282 can be contacted to provide persons with AD/HD and their families educational resources and emotional support.[27]

References

1. Barkley R. A. *Attention Deficit Hyperactivity Disorder: A Handbook for Diagnosis and Treatment.* New York: Guilford Press; 1990.

2. Quinn PO. *Attention Deficit Disorder: Diagnosis and Treatment from Infancy to Adulthood.* New York: Brunner/Mazel, Inc.; 1997.

3. Taylor JF. *Helping your Hyperactive/Attention Deficit Child.* 2nd edition. Rocklin, CA: Prima Publishing; 1994.

4. Barkley RA, et al. Frontal lobe functions in attention deficit disorder with and without hyperactivity: A review and research report. *Journal of Abnormal Child Psychology.* 1992; 20:163–188.

5. Pliszka S, McCracken J, Maas J. Catecholamines in attention-deficit hyperactivity disorder: Current perspectives. *Journal of the American Academy of Child and Adolescent Psychiatry.* 1996; 35:264–272.

6. Voeller KS. What can neurological models of attention, intention and arousal tell us about AD/HD? *Journal of Neuro psychiatry* 1991; 3(2), 209–216.

7. Reiff M, Banez G, Culbert T. Children who have attentional disorders: Diagnosis and evaluation. *Pediatrics in Review.* 1993; 14:455–465.

8. Wender PH. *Attention-Deficit Hyperactivity Disorder in Adults.* New York: Oxford University Press; 1995.

9. Matson J. (Editor). *Handbook of Hyperactivity in Children.* Boston: Allyn and Bacon; 1993.

10. American Psychiatric Association. *Diagnostic and Statishcal Manual of Mental Disorders.* 4th ed. (DSM-IV). Washington, D.C.: American Psychiatric Association; 1994.

11. Hallowell EM, Ratey JJ. *Driven to Distraction.* New York: Pantheon Books; 1993.

12. Rostrain A. Attention deficit disorders in children and adolescents. *Pediatric Clinics of North America.* 1991; 38:607–635.

13. Biederman J, et al. Comorbidity of attention deficit hyperactivity disorder with conduct, depressive, anxiety, and other disorders. *Am J Psychiatry* 1991; 148:564–577.

14. Copps SC. *The Attending Physician: Attention Deficit Disorder (A Guide for Pediatricians and Family Physicians)*. Atlanta: SPI Press; 1992.

15. Ingersoll BD, Goldstein S. *Attention deficit disorder and learning disabilities: Realities, myths and controversial treatments*. New York: Doubleday; 1993.

16. Braswell L, Bloomquist M. *Cognitive-Behavioral Therapy with AD/HD Children: Child, Family and School Interventions*. New York: Guilford Press; 1991.

17. Goldstein S, Goldstein M. *Managing Attention Disorders in Children: A Guide for Practitioners*. New York: John Wiley & Sons, Inc.; 1990.

18. Greenhill L, Osman B. (Eds) *Ritalin: Theory and Patient Management*. New York: Mary Ann Liebert Inc. Publishers; 1991.

19. Copeland ED. *Medications for Attention Disorders and Related Medical Problems*. Atlanta: SPI Press; 1991.

20. Swanson J, et al. Effect of Stimulant Medication on Children with Attention Deficit Disorder: A Review of Reviews. *Exceptional Children*. 1993; 60(2):154–162.

21. Silver LB. *Attention-Deficit Hyperactivity Disorder: A Clinical Guide to Diagnosis and Treatment*. Washington, D.C.: American Psychiatric Press, Inc; 1992.

22. Weiss G. (Guest Ed) *Child and Adolescent Psychiatric Clinics of North America: Attention-Deficit Hyperactivity Disorder*. 1992; 1(2).

23. Coming DE. *Tourette Syndrome and Human Behavior*. Duarte, Calif.: Hope Press; 1990.

24. Brown F, Voigt R, Elksnin N. AD/HD: A neurodevelopmental perspective. *Contemporary Pediatrics*. 1996; 13:25–44.

25. Nadeau KG. (Ed) *A Comprehensive Guide to Attention Deficit Disorder In Adults: Research, Diagnosis, and Treatment*. New York: Brunner/Mazel Publishers; 1995.

26. Hunt RD, et al. An open trial of guanfacine in the treatment of attention deficit hyperactivity disorder. *Journal of the American Academy of Child and Adolescent Psychiatry*. 1995; 34:50–54.

27. Mosier WA. Attention Deficit/Hyperactivity Disorder: Separating Fact from Fallacy. *Advance for Physician Assistants*. 1997; 5(2):14–21.

28. Garber SW, et al. B*eyond Ritalin: Facts About Medication and other Strategies for Helping Children, Adolescents, and Adults with Attention Deficit Disorders*. New York: Villard Books; 1996.

Advances in Medical Psychotherapy and Psychodiagnosis
2002–2003, Volume 11, pp. 201–210

Does Writing Really Heal?

David Lingiah, Ph.D.
Glasgow, Scotland

Writing As Therapy

Writing is a therapeutic activity. The writer of a letter, or poem, or book goes through a process of therapy, of self-healing. In this process, a variety of emotions are experienced and expressed in words; the intensity of thought is conveyed in words, expressions and phrases that mean something to the writer. This act, this creative activity is healing to the whole being of the writer. Whether his/her writing is private, to treasure for oneself or meant to be read by others, does not matter. What matters is that the writer is able to live or relive through some of the experiences that may be posing as a problem or block to one's further development. Once the writing activity has occurred the writer very often feels much better. If the writing contribution is meant for the general public, in many cases the readers too may find healing. Whatever the reason, writing is proving to be a valuable vehicle of liberation and self-realization. For many people it has provided a route into self-expression, to finding a voice and speaking out, and a way into the making of art. Schneider and Killick (1998) aptly observed : "We believe that personal writing has been much undervalued both as a potent form of self-expression and as a contribution to art."

"When I write about my life I lay claim to it and give it value. My life is then not just something that has happened to me but belongs to me. Writing helps me to stand in my own shoes. Creating finished pieces of work out of my personal world is also important, as if by giving the writing shape I also create an inner sense of completion and order" (Elke Dutton, quoted in Schneider & Killick, 1998). Hunt & Sampson (1998) in *The Self on the Page* also referred to another writer, Virginia Woolf, whose writings had helped to heal wounds. She wrote about her obsession with her mother, saying: "It is perfectly true that she obsessed me, inspite of the fact that she died when I was thirteen, until I was forty-four. I wrote the book *(To the Lighthouse)* very quickly; and when it was written, I ceased to be obsessed by my mother. I no longer hear her voice; I don't see her . . . I did for myself what psychoanalysts do for their patients. I expressed some very long felt and deeply felt emotion. And, in expressing it I explained it and then laid it to rest." It must be pointed out that many writers do not specifically set out on a therapeutic quest; whatever healing benefit they may derive from their writing comes by default in many cases rather than by design.

Writing is commonly used as a form of healing and for self-expression at moments of intense emotions. A woman who finds herself deeply in love for the first time might find that poetry is the only vehicle through which she can express her feelings. A recently divorced man may try to make sense of his situation by retracing his autobiography. Indeed, so many life-events, both happy and sad, find their most accurate expression through writing—bereavement, divorce, child-birth, adolescence, estrangement, marriage—the list is endless (Thomas, 1995: p. 34).

Writing in Counselling

According to Murphy and Mitchell (1998: 24): "Good writers are able to communicate emotions in their works. Books can make us laugh, bring us to tears, or draw out anger and indignation." In the counselling context these researchers noted that "At the end of the therapeutic encounter clients have a story of their success that is rife with their participation in their own healing. We believe that this will prove empowering for clients and will serve to help maintain changes after therapy is terminated" (p. 29).

The very process of writing externalizes the client's problems. As they write or type, the written representation of their issues appear before them on the paper or computer screen. It is believed that this process can enhance the externalisation of the problems, and therefore promote therapeutic change. As we write, we are typically reading what we are writing. This in turn has the potential to impact on ourselves and to impact on what we write next. For this reason some counsellors encourage their clients to write out their concerns; these are then discussed with the clients in sessions in explaining ways of enabling the clients to make desirable changes in their lives. When no one talks about his critical, angry, or hurt feelings, there is no chance to clear up the communication. Eventually, the unexpressed negative feelings can corrode what live positive feelings there are. The first step is to bring it out of the dark closet of your private thoughts and into the open air.

Vance (1998) used letter writing with clients who were afraid to express their feelings to important people in their lives. Their inability to express feelings left these clients in conflict, desperate to move on in their lives. "The goal of letter therapy is to communicate from the heart in a way that opens up new possibilities for intimacy and growth." The act of writing is not just a form of communication but also a means of making sense of experience and arrive at a deeper understanding of the self. The combination of the creativity of the process with the achievement of something tangible increase feelings of self-confidence and self-value. Writing about his personal story of recovery from the trauma of his mother's suicide Lukas (1987) concluded in these words: "I do not feel stuck anymore. I do not grieve as I used to; I am no longer crippled by my mother's suicide. Part of my ability to respond has been created by the research and the writing of this book. If it has helped no one else, it has helped me."

Therapeutic Writing Research

Creative writing has been recognized as a form of complementary therapy to talking and reflecting (Bolton, 1998). "With creative writing you do more than voice your difficulties, you transcend the pain by changing the problems into something worthwhile," observed Clare Douglas, the director of the Charity Survivor's Poetry. With reference to poetry writing she says poetry's therapeutic effects can work for anyone: "It is a concise expression of extreme emotion or experience. In a few carefully chosen words, a poem can communicate something very powerful" (Bee, 2000: p. 15). Dr. Bolton is presently conducting research in poetry therapy at the University of Sheffield's Institute of Primary Care and General Practice. She has used this form of therapy with healthcare practitioners and patients, and finds it helps them to put their troubles and fears into perspectives.

The Times (May 9/2000) reported major research is under way into poetry therapy for mental illness in an article titled: "Can poetry replace pills?" by Peta Bee. She writes: "It could be that the process of writing verse helped to cure their (patients) depression and lift their spirits far better than modern medication. Now psychologists and therapists are musing over the healing power of poetry in aiding recovery from a host of mental illnesses ranging from stress to eating disorders" (p. 15). Dr. Robin Phillipp, a consultant occupational physician at the Bristol Royal Infirmary, has long used creative writing to help sufferers of mental illness. *The Lancet* (1996) published his study confirming the benefits of his poetry therapy research.

His study revealed that two thirds of the subjects found reading poems helpful because they could identify with the rhythm. The same number said it was the best form of catharsis because it helped them articulate their disordered thoughts. Eight percent (8%) of those questioned reported that, under the supervision of their GP, they had been weaned off anti-depressants and tranquilizers, purely because poetry had been so effective in helping them cope with their emotions. Dr. Phillipp says there is physiological explanation for the soothing effects of poetry. The effects are linked to the interplay of the left and right hemispheres of the brain. The visualization of images and response to rhythm that occur when reading a poem may stimulate the limbic system, which is responsible for emotions. Now he is carrying out a large scale clinical trial as part of a World Health Organization project on mental health involving "poetry intervention" in the form of weekly poetry reading, writing or listening to poetry. There is great hopes for those involved in any form of reading or writing.

Poetry Emotion

Chris McAulay (2000) reported in *The Glaswegian* of a writing group called Survivors Poetry Scotland. The link between mental illness and creativity is well known. He noted that many of the most brilliant minds in history have suffered from psychological flaws of one form or another. The group is funded by the Greater Glasgow Health Board, Glasgow City Council along with the Scottish Arts Council with the aims of providing an artistic outlet for people suffering from mental health problems and for people who have come through major traumas and other upheavals in their lives such as alcoholism, drug addiction, child abuse or disability. The organisation exists mainly to meet the needs of the users who all have one thing in common: "they have come through a harrowing personal experience and survived." Jack Withers, one of the regular visitors to the writing group and one of its founders, have already published three books of his writings. Another user of this group, a disabled person, said: "This group helps me a lot in improving my confidence through writing." A sixty-year old woman, Mrs Malik, a biscuit factory worker, who lost her husband recently, attended the group to "pick myself up, and writing can be very therapeutic. I like the idea of somehow leaving your mark, and hoping that some people will appreciate the messages you're trying to get across."

Yesterday, I Cried

In her book, *Yesterday, I cried,* Iyanla Vanzant (2000) takes stock and reflects on the hardships and huge obstacles she has had to overcome. The pain of the past does not have to become the reality of the present. She is an example of how yesterday's tears become the seeds of today's hope and renewed strength. She expressed her lost and pain in a wonderful poem forming the basis of her book told through the life of Rhonda.

She wrote:

> *"I cried a soulful cry yesterday, and it is so good.*
> *It felt so very, very bad.*
> *In the midst of my crying, I felt my freedom coming,*
> *Because*
> *Yesterday I cried with an agenda."*

Reprinted with the permission of Simon & Schuster from *Yesterday, I Cried* by Iyanla Vanzant. Copyright © 1998 Inner Visions Worldwide Network, Inc.

Finally, she had worked through her tears, her problems and set herself on the road to self-recovery. She was ready to celebrate "the lessons that had brought you to a deeper realization of yourself, of the child within you" (p. 28). She noted: "Giving birth to this book has been one of the most challenging experiences I have faced in quite a while. It was yet another opportunity for me to review my life. It was a blessing in disguise that forced me to search my soul, revisit old wounds, assess where I am, and make some decisions about where I want to go." That was made possible after she had cried "with an agenda." Crying over spilt milk is a waste of time; but doing so with a plan provides a map to move forward with one's life. Vanzant realized this point when she remarked that:

> *"My journey is not over yet by a long shot. I still have some deep wounds that require intensive care. There are places in my heart that are still closed. Writing this book helped me to realize that." She had used her negative life experiences to educate herself and liberate others. Diane Abbott, MP commented on this work thus: "She offers salvation to all women (and men) who are on the road to self-discovery."*

Tears of Rage

Following the abduction and murder of his young son, John Walsh (1998) described his experiences of loss and rage in a devastating story with an enormous amount of integrity and passion. He described how the police had botched the case and how he never really got justice for his son, Adam. A man who thought he was invincible, when faced with his tragic loss, broke down. Although he and his family will never get over this ghastly tragedy, John decided to turn this horrid tragedy into saving the lives of countless children. John went on to create laws to hunt down criminals in order to protect children today in America. John Walsh's act of writing this book helped him to come through his immense tragedy, a story which has caused a lot of people to shed tears about this family's struggle, perseverance and triumph. He became a crusader for justice. He was featured recently on Montel Williams' Show, with a shocked audience in tears.

Personal Griefwork and Writing

I suffered the bereavement of my wife over four years ago. She was killed in a horrible road accident. The grief was overwhelming; the trauma was deep. To embark on my healing process I took to writing as a form of personal therapy. That process led me on to a research study which culminated in a higher degree dissertation in Counselling Studies very appropriately. It was a tremendously painful experience. That writing engagement was like a wrestling match with myself; words and emotions becoming meaningful, like the potter working his mud clay into a creative work of art. The emotions that were kept "silent" had to be expressed. They found expressions through my writing therapy which provided an outlet for my healing.

In *Solitude* Storr (1989: p. 129) had in fact suggested that the creative act of writing "is one of the ways of overcoming the state of helplessness. It is a coping mechanism, a way of exercising control as well as a way of expressing emotions". Again, C. S. Lewis (1966: p. 50) following the death of his wife from cancer, wrote *A Grief Observed* as something he had to do as "partly a defence against total collapse, a safety valve." Indeed, as Dr Radhakrishnan (1965) remarked the intensity of experience combined with the magic of words reveals "a man's dialogue with himself." Such dialogues have produced great literature and healing at the same time.

Grief Poetry on Mother's Day

An opportunity presented itself for my son to express his silent grief. It was Mother's Day; the children attending the Glasgow Sathya Sai Spiritual Centre Human Values classes were preparing to celebrate Easwaramma's Day. Jason was asked to write a poem to be read at the celebration in 1997. His grief found expression in his poem as he accepted that saintly lady as his mother "who has gone forever so soon without saying a loving word." Only a few lines of this poem which was printed in both Mauritian Abroad (1999, vol. 2, Issue 4, p. 27) and Sai Reflections (1997, May Issue, p. 17), is reproduced here to show the deep feelings and thoughts, that inner dialogues, which produced that composition:

I will be twelve soon
My mum has gone forever,
So soon.
Without saying a loving word
Nor a see-you-soon, bye-bye
In case I cry.

The Client Speaks

This personal dialogue as a form of healing through writing is especially effective in bereavement care. Bereavement counsellors are very aware of the healing process through writing; they often use this technique to assist their clients to come to terms with their loss. This is well demonstrated by Mrs. JS's letter in *Cruse Chronicle,* the Newsletter for bereaved people (Dec/Jan,1999/2000):

"I was 43 years old with a teenage son when my husband died last year. I started writing in what I called my Thoughts Book. It became my relief and comfort and in it I wrote endlessly, words and statements which now appear rather frightening! I also wrote poems, which obviously helped express my anger, hurt, pain and confusion. My Thoughts Book became a lifeline in a world that seemed to have been utterly destroyed. I continue to write in it but reading it again and looking at the dates I can see that I write less often now.

"Sometimes, as when it was the first anniversary of my husband's death, I go back to writing page after page of words, words, words! I write about my anger, my rage, my feeling of falling into empty blackness with no way out, my wish to be left alone. I write whatever is in my head. I hope that by expressing my thoughts and feelings, my life will be more bearable. I don't know whether a Thoughts Books would help others but I believe it has helped me."

Researching the Oppressed

In *Writing for Self-Discovery*, Schneider and Killick (1998) quoted Elke Dutton as saying: "The simple act of letter writing can help us confront our problems and ultimately change our lives. This therapeutic approach to problems has helped many people to transform themselves." At the same time, very often such people make a remarkable contribution to their society. For example, a chance reading of the Titmus Report from the Brunel University library shelf stirred Sam Lingayah emotionally and spurred him into action. "It was a heart-breaking experience," he wrote. That experience led him "to find the truth for myself whether the destitute, the disabled and the poor were exposed to dehumanised and cruel treatment." His search for truth led to a PhD awarded by Middlesex University published as *Social Welfare in Mauritius*. He wrote about this episode and his struggle for higher education in *From Child Labourer to PhD*. He writes from his personal experiences of pain and lowly background; this helps him to come to terms with his inner self, and simultaneously, makes an impact on many others in similar situation. Very inspiring indeed.

Strength in Death

Sam Lingayah at age 26 in 1956 left Mauritius for India. He wrote two letters to his loving father. Two years later he received very upsetting news of his father's sudden death, aged 52. As the eldest son of the family, the news devastated Sam who was deeply hurt and shocked. It was like an arrow which has transfixed my heart unexpectedly and unprepared." Yet in the only letter written to his mother he asked himself many questions and prayed in supplications to Lord Rama thus:

"How I am to lead my steps safely in the dark desert of life when my blazing torch has blown out? How am I to rest my head in a house whose principal pillar has crumbled to pieces? How am I to find happiness when the source where I drank the water of inspiration and fortitude, hope and indeed life has run out?"

These soul-searching questions are the dialogues he engaged himself in to reach an acceptance of the inevitable facts of life. Such inner quest leads to spring wells of healing. Thinking of the heavy responsibility on his shoulders for his brothers and sisters he exclaimed in agony:

"The sudden demise of our great papa is a tremendous blow to us. Now whose protection are we to seek in time of danger? Now whose comfort are we to seek in time of distress? Now whose affectionate pat are we to seek in time of prosperity? Now whose feet are we to worship?"

I like to share with you his very encouraging words to his mother—words of immense healing capacity for himself; uplifting words to himself too. Regrettably he did not have the means to attend the funeral and be together with the rest of his kith and kin. However, the act of thinking and soul-questioning which poured out words of strength and energy provided the means for his own healing and recovery; they also offered hope and inspiration to his mother and the rest of the family as seen from the words that follow:

"Our papa is no more. No more can we set eyes upon his extraordinary person. No more can we hear his sweet voice. But for that are we to keep on shedding tears, beating our breast, and tearing our hair? Ma, as lamentation brings nothing but ruination, it is pernicious to give way to it. Therefore, let us pluck up courage and start life afresh with renewed patience and resolution. Let by-gone be by-gone. Let us now with united force and determination hold high the flag of duties and responsibilities that our immortal father has handed over to us.

"Papa has departed from us for ever. But we are very grateful to the Infinite that you are here and we will daily ask Him to let you live for many more years amidst us, who now need your guidance and protection, affection and comfort. Ma, be content for it is only when you are in a contented state that we may work harder and lead a happier life" (pp. 15–16).

The reading of this letter is enough to bring tears to one's eyes. It also immediately calls to mind that great Indian epic film, *Mother India.* I don't intend to discuss this film here. But many readers who have seen it will appreciate Sam's situations. Sam's letter to his mother also reminds one of Abraham Lincoln's historic letter of condolence to Mrs. Bixby who lost five sons on the field of battle. I am sure every time she read that letter she derived much comfort in the fact that her great loss was for a noble cause.

Lincoln & Cowper's Healing Words

Lincoln (printed in Ghosh,1960) wrote :

"I feel how weak and fruitless must be any words of mine which should attempt to beguile you from the grief of a loss so overwhelming. But I cannot refrain from tendering to you the consolation that may be found in the thanks of the Republic that they died to save. I pray that the Heavenly Father may assuage the anguish of your bereavement and leave you only the cherished memory of the loved and lost, and the solemn pride that must be yours to have laid so costly a sacrifice upon the altar of freedom."

Often one offers words of comfort to another in such a way that both derive much help in the process: the writer and the reader; the giver and the receiver of the words. A sharing of a painful experience has a beneficial effect. Cowper's letter to Joseph Hill on the death of his mother is an instance. Cowper (printed in Ghosh,1960) wrote:

"Your mother lived to see you rise, at least to see you comfortably established in the world: mine, dying when I was six years old, did not live to see me sink in it. You may remember with pleasure, while you live, a blessing vouchsafed to you so long; and while I live, must regret a comfort of which I was deprived so early. I can truly say that not a week passes in which I do not think of her. Such was the impression her tenderness made upon me, though the opportunity she had for showing it was so short."

A Labourer's Writings

I referred earlier to Sam Lingayah's condolence letter to his mother. But there is more to learn from his writings. His many painful experiences and memories are written in the form of letters, Notes and Stories addressed to various people. He saw life as a poor child labourer, as a young soldier, as a penniless student in India. He touched upon many different subjects in a little less well- known work entitled *A Labourer's Writings* published in the 1960s. Doctor heals thyself. He had no professional counselling to support him in his traumatic life experiences. He devised his own therapy by turning thoughts and emotions into words that heal. He was prepared to share his thoughts to his readers "in the field of writing, an art which I am so poor in but so deeply in love with" although he described himself as "an ordinary peasant, with an awkward civilization, and an almost an illiterate." There was a sensitive discernment in the course of his self-exploration. As Dr. Krishna Gokak (1975) observed: "A transparent sincerity permeates this piece of writing. The writer takes his readers into confidence regarding all the changes in his thoughts and moods. We come to know every bend of the road he has taken and the direction of each step. This is what makes it a genuine document of human sensitivity and of the psychology of profound inner changes." His dialogues with himself created his therapeutic space and marvellous work of art in the bargain.

All these examples and instances are given simply to show the power of words in healing the self or others. The act of putting these thoughts and feelings down have a miraculous tendency to generate a healing effect. These examples may give the impression that all forms of writing therapy to explore emotions especially in the context of grief counselling bring healing. This is not the case.

Latest research findings by Dr.Margaret Stroebe at the University of Utretch and others including Dr. Emmanuelle Zech of the University of Louvain appear to contradict current knowledge thus far. In a paper prepared by Stroebe, Zech and Schut titled "The Role of Social Sharing in Adjustment to Loss" presented at the meeting of the European Association of Experimental Social Psychology, in Austria, 1999, they concluded thus: *"we seemed to have failed to find any evidence that disclosure to others helped bereaved individuals to adjust to their loss"* (italics mine). The notion that social sharing is a panacea for all traumatic events should therefore be viewed in a new light.

Stroebe and Schut in a special chapter: "Meaning Making in the dual process model of coping with Bereavement" to a book entitled "A Meaning Reconstruction and the Experience of Loss" edited by R.A. Neimeyer (in press) reviewed the works of a number of researchers including those of Pannenbaker in this area; they failed to identify beneficial effects of this type of confrontation. The dual process model of coping with bereavement is also published in *Death Studies* (1999). Similarly, Dr. E. Zech (2000) has carried out an extensive literature search in her doctoral thesis at the Catholic University of Louvain where the effects of communication of emotional experiences have been studied. She asked: "Does talking or writing about emotions really make people feel good?"

Counsellors involved in griefwork using writing as a tool should exercise some restraint and care in the light of these current research findings.

Acknowledgements

I wish to thank Drs Margaret Stroebe and Emmanuelle Zech for providing the materials based on their latest research mentioned in this article.

References

Bee, P. (2000) "Can Poetry replace pills?" *The Times,* May 9, p. 15.

Bolton, G. (1998) *The Therapeutic Potential of Creative Writing.* London: Jessica Kingsley Publishers.

Cowper, W. (printed in Ghosh, R.P. 1960: p. 45).

Cruse Chronicle, the Newsletter for bereaved people (Dec/Jan, 1999/2000): Surrey: Cruse Bereavement Care.

Douglas, C. (2000) in Peta Bee, *The Times,* op. cit.

Ghosh, R. P. (1960) *Good English.* Calcutta: Modern Book Agency Ltd.

Gokak,V. K. (1975) *"Foreword": Holy Man and the Psychiatrist* by Dr. S. H. Sandweiss. SSSBook Trust: India.

Hunt, C. and Sampson, F. (eds), (1998) *The Self on the Page.* London: Jessica Kingsley Publishers.

Lewis, C. S. (1966) *A Grief Observed.* London: Faber and Faber.

Lincoln, A. (printed in Ghosh, R. P, 1960: p. 46).

Lingayah, S. (1996) *Social Welfare in Mauritius.* Sanskris Publishing.
   (1996) *From Child Labourer to PhD.* Sanskris Publishing.
   (1961) *A Labourer's Writings.* Mauritius.

Lukas, C. and Seiden, H. (1987) *Silent Grief: Living in the Wake of Suicide.* NY: Science, p. 208.

Mauritian Abroad (1999: vol. 2. Issue 4, p. 27). Kent: Sanskris Publishing Ltd.

Murphy, L. J. and Mitchell, D. L. (1998) *British Journal of Guidance and Counselling,* Vol. 26, No. 1. pp. 21–32.

Phillipp, R. (2000) in Peta Bee, *The Times,* op. cit.

Radhakrishnan, S. (1965). Speeches and Writings: "The Magic of Words." India: Ministry of Information. p. 216.

Sai Reflections (1997 May Issue, p. 17). Sathya Sai Organisation, UK.

Schineider, M. and Killick, J. (1998). *Writing for Self-Discovery.* Shaftsbury: Elements Books.

Storr, A. (1989) *Solitude.* London: Flamingo.

Stroebe, M., Zech and Schut, H. (1999) "The Role of Social Sharing in Adjustment to Loss" paper presented at the meeting of the European Association of Experimental Social Psychology, Austria. (Personal communication).

Stroebe, M. and Schut, E. (2000). "Meaning Making in the dual process model of coping with Bereavement" in *Meaning Reconstruction and the Experience of Loss* (Ed) R.A. Neimeyer (in press). (Personal Communication).

Stroebe, M. and Schut, H. (1999). *Journal of Death Studies,* 1999, (23) pp. 197–224.

Thomas, S. (1995). *Creative Writing.* Nottingham: Department of Adult Education University of Nottingham.

Vance, T. (1998). *Letters Home: How Writing Can Change your Life.* New York: Pantheon Books.

Vanzant, I. (2000). *Yesterday, I Cried.* London: Pocket Books.

Walsh, J. (1998). *Tears of Rage.* USA: Pocket Books.

Zech, E. (2000). The effects of communication of emotional experiences. Unpublished PhD Thesis, Catholic University of Louvain, Belgium. (Personal communication).

Further Reading & Contacts

The Healing Word by Fiona Sampson. The Poetry Society. 020-7420-9880) www.poetrysoc.com Survivors' Poetry, Diorama Arts Centre, 32 Osnaburgh Street, London NW1 3ND (020-7916-5317) survivor@survivorspoetry.org.uk.

Advances in Medical Psychotherapy and Psychodiagnosis
2002–2003, Volume 11, pp. 211–218

Book Review Section

Rhoda Olkin, Ph.D.
What Psychotherapists Should Know About Disability
New York: Guilford Press, 1999, 368 pages, $42.00 ($22.00 pbk). ISBN: 1-57230-643-2
Reviewed by: Wayne D'Agaro, PsyD

Dr. Olkin has written a lucid and comprehensive book that will pull clinicians beyond their limiting assumptions about disability and provide ample practical recommendations to guide sensitive and effective clinical treatment of people with disabilities. Olkin communicates her ideas and experiences in a highly accessible, frank, and conceptually coherent style. As a result of her own experience with disability (her husband has multiple sclerosis and she contracted polio as an infant in the 1950s) and as a professor at the California School of Professional Psychology in Alameda, California with considerable hands-on experience working with people with disabilities, Olkin is able to sensitize the reader to the big and small ways that the disability experience influences an individual's identity development, relationships, school and work, and family life. It would be hard not to be influenced by Olkin's work in ways that matter as a psychotherapist: one's capacity for empathy, informed listening, clear, systems-sensitive thinking, and practical intervention will be enhanced by a careful reading of this book.

Olkin begins with a personal invitation to plumb the range of human experiences and terminology that characterizes the disability community. She offers as her hope that the reader "will come to see disability in a whole new way." Olkin regards people with disability not as heroic, though she acknowledges that some may well be, but rather as other human beings going about the routines and challenges of everyday life. In contrast to the medical and moral models of disability, Olkin's work contributes to the growing recognition of the social origins of disability in a disabling environment and interpersonal matrix. The ABs (or able-bodied) reader will be gradually transformed by Olkin's words, ideas, and candor. To appreciate at a deep level that the physical challenges may be constant, and that interpersonal relationships and social interchange are profoundly affected by disability is useful in itself. Like Olkin, who herself tried for most of her early adult life to "pass" as "normal," we are compelled by the consciousness-raising experience she provides to "come out" and confront our stereotypes, negative attitudes, and private myths and fallacious assumptions about people with disabilities. The process is worthwhile, as any sensitive reader will more fully understand disability in the context of a specific person and be more able to address disability issues effectively in treatment.

What Psychotherapists Should Know About Disability is deliberately not organized around separate chapters that explicate the seemingly unique features and challenges of specific disabling conditions. Instead, Olkin asserts that while there are certainly idiosyncrasies of each disabling condition, the tremendous overlap in the experiences of persons with disabilities requires an appreciation of the commonalities (which she names the "disability experience"). Olkin deftly organizes the commonalities of the disability experience into a penetrating conceptual model in Chapter 2. Importantly, Olkin fully embraces a family systems orientation, and develops a minority model of disability. Olkin explicates the similarities and differences in experiences between disability and other minority or out-groups. She identifies malignant social factors as prejudice, discrimination, and stigma as core similarities and essential features of minority experience. She further develops the idea of "multiple minority status," suggesting that other factors such as gender and/or ethnicity have synergistic effects and multiple sources of discrimination. Olkin's minority model reliably places the person with disability in a social context and resists all temptations to more simply consider disability as an entity in isolation. For example, she identifies education as a critical moderator of disability effects, particularly in the domains of work and economic resources, as well as providing opportunities for socializing and purpose in life. The implications clearly follow, namely, that any clinical role must contribute to marshalling support for continued

Thomas Grisso, Ph.D. & Paul S. Applebaum, MD
Assessing Competence to Consent to Treatment
New York: Oxford University Press, 1998, 211 pages ($33.00) ISBN: 0-19-501372-6
Reviewed by: Andrew Nathan, PsyD, Manchester Counseling Services, Bedford, NH

The clinical problems and pitfalls inherent to evaluating patients' decision-making capacities represent considerable challenges to most clinicians. The practical task of distinguishing competent from incompetent patients can be bewildering and overwhelming. Grisso and Applebaum's *Assessing Competence to Consent to Treatment* is an authoritative and practical clinical guide for such knotty tasks. The authors have deftly managed to integrate clinical, legal, and scientific scholarship into a concise yet highly informative handbook that is amply illustrated by focused clinical vignettes. Their truly impressive accomplishment was recently recognized by the American Psychiatric Association and American Academy of Psychology and the Law's co-sponsored annual Manfred S. Guttmacher Award (2000) for outstanding contributions to the literature of forensic psychiatry.

Assessing Competence to Consent to Treatment is the rich product of a long-term and comprehensive research study of patients' capacities to make treatment decisions conducted by the authors at the University of Massachusetts Medical School. Its relevant empirical foundations are apparent throughout the text. As importantly, the authors' clarity of exposition and capacity to identify essential elements of complex issues is superb. Not a word is wasted with each of the eight chapters limited to 20 pages or less. Both their style and organization are clearly born out of sustained scholarship and thoughtful teaching. The book is thus highly readable, and, as good teachers do, the reader is moved through the concepts, issues, and practice recommendations supportively while deepening understanding and sophistication.

Grisso and Applebaum begin their handbook by locating the pivotal concept of competence within the doctrine of informed consent. By the second page, the reader is drawn into thinking deeply about the centrality of competence to decision-making by using an interesting neurosurgery case. The historical evolution of consent to medical treatment is then surveyed by parsimoniously weaving together case law, the influence of Enlightenment philosophers, and medical practices within a sociohistorical context. The chapter concludes with an exposition of the critical elements of informed consent: reasonable disclosure of relevant information, voluntariness, and competence. Grisso and Applebaum emphasize that informed consent is not necessarily an "event," but is really best regarded as a process that both favors and empowers patient autonomy, and evolves over time in a treatment relationship. The ultimate goal of informed consent is meaningful participation by patients in decisions about their care.

The second chapter outlines and clarifies concepts and presumptions underlying competence to consent to treatment in the form of five maxims. Legal competence is: (1) related to, but not the same as, impaired mental states; (2) refers to functional deficits; (3) depends on functional demands; (4) depends on consequences; and (5) can change. The authors then make use of these five maxims in their development of a working definition of incompetence which informs the remainder of their book and practice recommendations and is consistent with both the ethical and legal notions of competence.

Incompetence constitutes a status of the individual that is defined by functional deficits (due to mental illness, mental retardation, or other mental conditions) judged to be sufficiently great that the person currently cannot meet the demands of a specific decision-making situation, weighed in light of its potential consequences (p. 27).

The chapter concludes with a cogent analysis of the implications for assessment objectives and the kinds of information that should be obtained and considered in evaluating the competence of patients to consent to treatment. These include the patient's clinical condition, the patient's functioning in tasks involving decision-making abilities, and the specific demands of the patient's treatment situation.

The third chapter identifies and defines the types of decision-making abilities that are particularly relevant to the competence assessment. These include the ability to: (1) express a choice; (2) understand information relevant to treatment decision-making; (3) appreciate the significance of that information for one's own situation, especially concerning one's illness and the probable consequences of one's treatment options; and (4) reason with relevant information so as to engage in logical process of weighing treatment options. While the authors' research studies have suggested that patients' understanding and reasoning with treatment information are substantially correlated, they sometimes dissociate in individual patients, and both only weakly predict appreciation. Chapters 4 to 6 go on to elaborate and recommend when and how these relevant decision-making abilities should be assessed.

The four circumstances that are regarded as "red flags" indicating the need for an evaluation of patients' decision-making capacities include abrupt changes in patients' mental states, patients' refusal of recommended treatment, patients' consent to especially invasive or risky treatment, and the presence of one or more risk factors to impaired decision-making (such as age). Chapter 5 covers issues relevant to competence evaluation in general, and Chapter 6 provides a detailed examination of one approach to structured assessment of patients' decision-making using an instrument derived from the authors' research: The MacArthur Competence Assessment Tool for Treatment (MacCAT-T). The appendix provides the manual for the MacCAT-T, including instructions for its administration, a form to guide clinicians in organizing the interview and recording patients' responses, and a guide for rating responses.

Chapter 7 explains in very practical terms how to use the data collected in an assessment to reach conclusions or judgments about patients' abilities to make meaningful treatment decisions given the circumstances with which he or she is faced. Throughout, Grisso and Applebaum emphasize the value of regarding any judgment as a balance scale with "autonomy" on one end and "protection" on the other, with "ties" favoring autonomy—deprivation of autonomy should be substantiated by the absolute necessity of protection.

The chapter concludes with recommendations about how best to document the competence judgment.

In the last chapter (8), Grisso and Applebaum review what happens when patients lose the capacity to make decisions, and the process of substitute decision-making for incompetent patients. This chapter begins with a review of how patients can proactively control medical treatment decisions through the use of advance directives and standards for making decisions that rely on patients' preferences to guide the choice of treatment.

Grisso and Applebaum have produced a masterful work that is superbly written and organized, conceptually precise and empirically sound, and eminently useful. There are few books that have the power to influence and improve individual practice in such a comprehensive way. This is one of them.

Mark E. Maruish (Ed.)
The Use of Psychological Testing for Treatment Planning and Outcomes Assessment
New York: Lawrence Erlbaum Associates, 1999, 1520 pages, ISBN: 0-8058-2761-7 ($105.00)

Handbook of Psychological Assessment in Primary Care Settings
New York: Lawrence Erlbaum Associates, 2000, 856 pages, ISBN: 0-8058-2999-7 ($75.00)
Reviewed by: Anthony J. Giuliano, Ph.D., McLean Hospital, Belmont, MA

Amidst these uncertain and sometimes gloomy times when managed care has largely altered the traditional practice of psychological assessment, Mark Maruish has edited two comprehensive and highly useful volumes that will guide clinicians in the thoughtful application of psychological testing to behavioral healthcare service delivery. These edited volumes represent remarkable achievements, as it is no small task to bring together numerous recognized experts into one-volume reviews of the psychological assessment literature. *Use's* 47 chapters authored by 88 contributors is organized into four sections which include General Considerations, Child and Adolescent Assessment Instrumentation, Adult Assessment Instrumentation, and Future Directions. The *Handbook* is similarly organized and includes 26 chapters written by 49 authors divided into four sections that include General Considerations, Assessment Instruments, Primary and Behavioral Health Care Integration Projects, and Future Directions.

Though both books are quite lengthy, Maruish and his contributors are successful on many levels. Most importantly, they succeed in demonstrating that psychological assessment, if used wisely, can contribute significantly if not uniquely to improvements in individual treatment and outcomes management, and in facilitating the essential mission of primary care. Maruish and his contributors work hard to articulate opportunity, value, and need in their reviews, and provide a managed-care sensitive context for the use of psychological assessment instruments and consultation. At their core, both texts also function as a compendium of psychological assessment measures that have utility in general clinical and/or primary care settings. Both are also prefaced by a set of chapters that address principles and practices of testing and are followed by a final section that focuses on future directions in the use of psychological assessment in treatment planning and outcome assessment or primary care.

The purpose of this second edition of *Use's,* like the first edition before it, is well-captured by Mariush in his preface: ". . . for those skilled in its use, psychological testing's ability to help quickly identify psychological problems, plan and monitor treatment, and document treatment effectiveness presents many potentially rewarding opportunities during a time when health care organizations must (a) provide problem-focused, time-limited treatment; (b) demonstrate the effectiveness of treatment to payers and patients; and (c) implement quality improvement initiatives" (p. xiii). Clearly these tasks will never be simple ones, however, this book helps to make these tasks more clear and more likely to be successful. Thus, the book's organization contributes to understanding some of the key issues and practice guidelines to be considered in the use of psychological testing for treatment planning and outcome assessment in today's behavioral health care environment. The second and third sections focus on issues related to the use of specific psychological tests and scales for these same purposes.

Mariush's introductory chapter provides an overview of the status of the contemporary health care deliver system and the ways in which testing might contribute to making that system more clinically and cost-effective. Two chapters are devoted to issues related to treatment planning. The chapter by Larry Beutler and his colleagues is a particularly good example of integrating research and practice to develop a thoughtful framework for using psychological tests for treatment planning. For example, Beutler and his associates discuss how testing may be used as predictor of differential treatment responses and outcomes. The subsequent four chapters focus on issues related to outcome assessment. The first by Michael and John Lambert provides an historical summary of outcome assessment, its current status, and its measures and methods. Particularly interesting is its discussion of the distinction between clinically and statistically significant differences in outcome assessment, as well as some outcomes-related issues that need additional study (e.g., cost-effectiveness and provider profiling). The next chapter develops a set of specific guidelines that can be valuable to clinicians in their selection of psychological measures for assessing treatment outcomes and, by extension, for treatment planning purposes. The last two chapters of the first section provide an accessible and practical discussion of statistical procedures and research design issues related to the measurement of treatment progress and outcomes with psychological tests. While these "introductory" chapters may be considered by some as "too technical" or "too research focused," their value in many ways outpaces what most may regard as the "meat" of the volume, those chapters in the second and third section that deal with specific psychological instruments. In short, these introductory eight chapters represent the value-added part of the book, and will provide clinicians with the kind of knowledge that provides a foundation for developing or sustaining an effective treatment evaluation process or program in any clinical setting.

The second and third sections address the use of a wide range of specific psychological instruments for treatment planning and outcome assessment purposes in a pediatric and adult/geriatric population. While there is some unevenness in the quality of the chapters, each chapter is generally organized around three important areas: describing what the instrument does and how it was developed; how it should be used for treatment planning and monitoring; and how it should be used to assess treatment outcomes. Each chapter is also written by the test's developer or a well-recognized expert on that particular test. Excluded from the text are neuropsychological and other cognitive measures. The child and adolescent instruments reviewed include: Children's Depression Inventory, Multidimensional Anxiety Scale for Children (MASC), Revised Children's Manifest Anxiety Scale, Minnesota Multiphasic Personality Inventory-Adolescent version (MMPIA), Millon Adolescent Clinical and Personality Inventories, Personality Inventory for Children and for Youth, Child Behavior Checklist and Related Instruments, Conners Rating Scales-Revised, Youth Outcome Questionnaire, Devereux Scales of Mental Disorders, Behavior Assessment System for Children (BASC), Personal Experience Inventory, and the relatively new Child and Adolescent Functional Assessment Scale (CAFAS). This section concludes with a review of a new and unique tool designed to assess the outcome of psychosocial treatment and care in children called the Child Health Questionnaire (CHQ).

The adult assessment instruments include the majority of well-known tests and scales such as the SCL-90-R, BPRS, PRIME-MD, BDI/BHI, Beck Anxiety Inventory, Hamilton Depression Inventory, STAVSTAXI, MMPI-2, MCMI-III, PAI, Rorschach Inkblot Method, Katz Adjustment Scales, and the SF-36 Health Scale, as well as many that are probably in less widely known or used. The latter include the Behavior and Symptom Identification Scale (BASIS-32), The Outcome Questionnaire, Butcher Treatment Planning Inventory, Marital Satisfaction Inventory, Adult Personality Inventory, Quality of Life Inventory, the UCSF Client Satisfaction Scales, and the Consumer Satisfaction Survey.

The final section of the book presents a discussion of the future of psychological assessment. Most interesting is the chapter by Kevin Moreland and his colleagues who describe anticipated advances in the field of testing as well as future legislative and medical care mandates that may affect the manner in which psychological testing is likely to be used in the next decade.

The purpose of the *Handbook* has a more limited focus, namely, to guide the reader to a systems-level and practical understanding of how to integrate behavioral healthcare services into primary medical practices, such as improving how to identify and monitor mental health and substance abuse problems. The first section provides a general overview of issues related to integrating psychological testing into both adult and pediatric primary care settings. The chapter by Derogatis and Lynn offers a particularly insightful framework for screening and monitoring psychiatric disorders in primary care populations, and pulls together a range of epidemiological research relevant to this important task.

The chapters in the second section provide detailed reviews of many well-known general instruments and recently developed disease-specific instruments likely to be useful in an integrated delivery system. For example, the PRIME-MD, COMPASS-PC, Quick PsychoDiagnostics (QPD) Panel, SCL-90 R and BSI, Symptom Assessment (SA)-45, Daily and Weekly Stress inventories, SF-36 Health Survey, and the Self-Administered Alcoholism Screening Test (SAAST) are all given detailed coverage in their own chapters. Given the prevalence of depression in primary care populations, several chapters are devoted to the detection and monitoring of depression: Beck Depression Inventory (BDI), Center for Epidemiologic Studies Depression Scale (CES-D), Hamilton Depression Inventory, and the Geriatric Depression Scale (GDS). This section also includes two relatively unique chapters. One is by Murray and Safran that reviews a new tool for measuring, monitoring, and improving primary care called the Primary Care Assessment Survey. The second addresses a too-often overlooked variable in primary care service delivery, namely, the quality of the doctor-patient relationship: the Difficult Doctor Patient Relationship Questionnaire by Hahn.

The third section is devoted to providing three in-depth case studies of primary care organizations in which psychological assessment has been implemented. Robinson and Strosahl take up the task of improving patient care by identifying and treating depression in a primary and behavioral health care integration project. Beck and Nimmer describe the Kaiser Permanente Integrated Care Project and a third chapter, co-authored by the editor, describes the INOVA primary behavioral health care pilot project. Each is rich in the kind of insight that comes from the experience of working over time to integrate behavioral healthcare services into primary medical practices, and addresses both the benefits and costs of this evolving trend. The final section is made up of a single chapter devoted to examining how technology will likely affect and facilitate the use of psychological assessment instruments in primary care settings in the future.

Overall, both volumes represent truly useful, even indispensable, resources for psychologists, students, physicians (including psychiatrists and primary care providers), and researchers who are interested in increasing their knowledge of opportunities for and applications of psychological assessment instruments in behavioral health care settings. The *Handbook* additionally functions as a resource for thinking through how to capitalize on the movement to integrate primary care and behavioral healthcare through the use of psychological testing. Both can also serve as guides on how to survive and thrive in the era of managed behavioral healthcare and for designing and implementing outcomes assessment systems within managed behavioral healthcare organizations. Such practical real-world resources are unique, and deserve the serious consideration of every thoughtful clinician, particularly those in care management and supervisory positions, that work in managed behavioral healthcare settings.

Melvin Delgado (Ed.)

Alcohol Use/Abuse Among Latinos: Issues and Examples of Culturally Competent Services
New York: Haworth Press, 1998. 208pp.
Reviewed by: Joseph R. Pereira, LICSW, North Shore Medical Center, Salem, MA

The effectiveness of substance abuse treatment depends on a number of different considerations. The ability of an individual to initiate and remain in treatment for an adequate period of time is crucial to the success of any treatment. A significant factor that contributes to a person starting and staying in treatment is the degree to which the services being provided address the specific concerns of the individual. Therefore, any substance abuse treatment approach must take into consideration a person's age, gender, and ethnic and cultural background as a means of attracting and retaining the person in treatment. Given the importance of providing services that are relevant to the individual, the need for clinicians to be culturally competent is essential.

Dr. Melvin Delgado, a professor at the Graduate School of Social Work at Boston University, edited this volume which is co-published in the Alcoholism Treatment Quarterly, Volume 16, Numbers 1–2, 1998. Delgado has written extensively on a number of different subjects including how to improve the cultural competence of alcohol and other drug abuse treatment professionals. In *Alcohol Use/Abuse Among Latinos,* Dr. Delgado raises the standard of multicultural therapy with Latino clients and their families.

In his introduction, Delgado states that, "The topic of this volume is on how the field of alcohol, tobacco, and other drug abuse (ATOD) has attempted to operationalize culturally competent services for Latinos in the United States." The chapters in the book together provide a multidimensional approach that leads to a rich sociocultural analysis that reflects much of the heterogeneity and complexity of Latinos' cultures. Though cultural stereotypes leak out from time to time among the authors, Delgado and his contributors are successful in helping therapists improve their sensitivity to sociocultural issues in developing and providing treatment services. In addition, the book provides ample clinical examples that help to ground the reader.

This book is divided into four sections. The first section, "Setting the Context," addresses why cultural competence with Latinos is critical to the field. The second section, "A View from the Field," is probably the most interesting and offers a picture of how cultural competence has been formally and informally developed across Latino subgroups. The third section, "Group Specific," focuses on research and case studies of various Latino sub-groups. The fourth section, "Summary of Key Practice, Research, and Policy Implications" represents Delgados view of essential practice emphases, policy implications, and future directions for the field.

While the title of the volume indicates a focus on alcohol use and abuse, one of its strengths is that a number of different authors focus on other drug use among Latinos. For example, De La Rosa's chapter, "Prevalence and consequences of alcohol, cigarette, and drug use among Hispanics," summarizes useful statistical information from government sources such as the Substance Abuse and Mental Health Services Administration. He provides epidemiological data on alcohol use as well as nicotine, marijuana, cocaine, and heroin use and compares Latino substance use rates with African-American and European-Americans.

Another significant strength of the volume is the uniqueness of some of the areas covered. Delgado provides a case study that illustrates and explores the role of Latina beauty parlors and their potential use as sources of outreach, including links to Latinas in the community who may not otherwise come to the attention of traditional substance abuse treatment providers. Mora focuses on the treatment of alcohol dependency among Latinas within the frameworks of feminist, cultural, and community perspectives. The chapter by Reyes discusses the particular needs and concerns of substance abusing Latina Lesbians. In the area of policy and administration, the chapter by Cervantes and Pena offers useful guidelines for maximizing cultural competence in the evaluation of Latino programs. In the final section, Rodriguez-Andrew explores issues and reviews examples of culturally-sensitive services for the treatment of alcohol use and abuse disorders among Latinos.

Despite a few limitations in advancing cultural stereotypes and limited integration of perspectives, the many strengths of *Alcohol Use/Abuse Among Latinos* make it a useful resource for a wide range of readers, particularly social workers. Clinicians who work with Latinos will find helpful guidance in understanding the sociocultural dynamics of many Latino individuals, families, and communities. It will certainly aid clinicians in developing and considering sociocultural hypotheses regarding Latinos who abuse substances. On some occasions, clinicians will be exposed to novel ideas in addressing cultural and gender matters and around which to organize intervention efforts. Its strong clinical and policy foundations contribute to raising the standard for the growing multicultural counseling and therapy field.

G. Alan Marlatt (Ed.)

Harm Reduction: Pragmatic Strategies for Managing High-Risk Behaviors
New York: Guilford Press, 1998. 390ppp. ISBN: 1-57230-397-2
Reviewed by: Christopher Dunstan, Ph.D., The Providence Center, Providence, RI

In *Harm Reduction,* G. Alan Marlatt provides the most articulate and lucid discussion of the theoretical framework and principles of harm reduction in the available literature. *Harm Reduction* represents essential reading for all clinicians whose clients' lives have been touched by substance use and its associated consequences. In contrast to traditional interventions and social-legal policies toward substance use, Marlatt proposes that harm reduction (or harm minimization) represents an alternative approach that costs less on many levels (i.e., less stigmatization and marginalization of drug users, less costly and complicated criminal justice interventions).

Marlatt begins his edited volume with three introductory chapters that review the history of harm reduction and the principles underlying the approach. His first and second chapters introduce the historical roots of harm-reduction approaches in the context of his visit to the Netherlands in 1990. Most interesting is Marlatt's sensitivity to the sociocultural contexts in which modern harm-reduction approaches have emerged, particularly in the Netherlands, Canada, and the United Kingdom. Marlatt then provides a brief but insightful analysis of the essential differences between Dutch public policy and current US policy. The reader comes away appreciating that the interesting differences in social contexts, welfare and healthcare systems, and ideologies may make imitation difficult.

The five basic principles of harm-reduction approaches are then articulated in Marlatt's third introductory chapter and provide another useful contrast to current US policies and treatment assumptions. Harm reduction: (l) is a public health alternative to the moral/criminal and disease models of drug use and addiction, (2) recognizes abstinence as an ideal outcome, but accepts harm reducing alternatives; (3) has emerged as a "bottom-up" approach based on the advocacy of drug users, rather than a "top-down" policy promoted by drug policy makers; (4) promotes low-threshold access to services as an alternative to traditional, high-threshold approaches (i.e., harm reduction approaches send clinicians into the field to share park benches with addicts, while traditional approaches require drug users to make meetings at certain times in sanctioned centers); and (S) is based on the tenets of compassionate humanism and pragmatism versus moralistic idealism.

With these principles as a guide, Marlatt provides four chapters that outline a variety of specific harm-reduction focused programs aimed at alcohol and nicotine, illegal substances, and HIV and AIDS prevention. In so doing, the specific concerns of a wide range of potential clinical groups are considered such as college students, gay males, and substance dependent individuals of all ages. Two subsequent chapters consider the special needs and concerns of African-Americans and Native Americans, and address issues associated with bringing harm reduction approaches into these two ethnic communities and without flinching from the hard lessons of past failures. Particularly poignant is how"zero tolerance" and "abstinence-only" policies have likely strengthened the inaccessibility of outreach and treatment efforts. The chapter focusing on Native Americans calls for the serious and sustained integration of substance use approaches with the cultural practices of the community.

In Marlatt's concluding chapter, harm reduction is reviewed in relation to current public policy, and he provides a cogent counterpoint to the variety of misconceptions about harm-reduction approaches. For example, though often distorted in this fashion, Marlatt emphasizes that harm reduction approaches are not about legalizing drugs, nor tolerating widespread and unbridled use of drugs. This is brought together well in a summary of the arguments for and against syringe exchanges that highlights the significant philosophical differences between harm reduction and current public policies. Is it possible to help those who are still using? The conflict of the models is worth exploring and understanding.

In the end, it will be up to the reader to decide where and with whom harm reduction strategies may be worth pursuing. Whatever the point of view of the reader, the book will provide a well-written and thoughtful overview and analysis of harm reduction approaches and ideas for implementation that will improve conceptual clarity and facilitate thinking through these thorny social issues.

The International Directory of Medical Psychotherapists and Psychodiagnosticians 2002–2003

ALABAMA

Adams, Martha S.
Ball, James C.
Ballew, Michael S.
Blanton, Donald W.
Covin, Theron M.
Crook, Jr., Donald H.
Crowder, James E.
Crowe, Jr., L. Kenneth
Dubin, Edward R.
Estis, Willis C.
Floyd, H. Hugh
Hale, Halina W.
Hayward, Eric
Herrick, Charlotte A.
Hill, L. Donald
Hoke, Daniel M.
Hovater, John G.
James, Doyle
Jolley, Windell L.
Kogelschatz, Joan L.
Kramer, Luther E.
Kringel, William F.
Kutzman, Gerald R.
Michel, Thomas J.
Oatsvall, Robert D.
Petrella, Rocco G.
Preston, Frankie L.

Rhodes, Ray Lamar
Robbins, Douglas E.
Schell, David W.
Smith, James A.
Snow, Diana D.
Suess, James F.
Thomas, David B.
Wells, Annie M.
Williamson, W. Windell

ALASKA

Kappes, Bruno M.
Kleinke, Chris L.
Mueller, Royce K.
Severson, Larry J.

ARIZONA

Baldwin, Carol M.
Behrens, Vergie Lee
Brundage, Janice K.
Cohn, Linda D.
Cohn, Michael J.
Crockett, Norma D.
Daniel, Stephen P.

DeJesus, Nelson H.
Dereli, Atila H.
Elias, Dennis C.
Gurgevich, Steven
Howard, Timothy J.
Jenkins, Charles G.
Love, Lois M.
Malone, Gloria M.
McDonald, Craydon D.
Nayeri, Babak M.
Nicholls, Christopher J.
Nicholson, Elaine R.
Patascher, Steven
Prato, Anthony C.
Rousseau, Andre M.
Ryan, Anne
Sasmor, James C.
Schlamowitz, Kevan E.
Schwager, Herbert A.
Seidner, Meryl L.
Shutt, Darold L.
Smith, Richard K.
Tarte, Claire J.
West, Julia S.
White, Cynthia A.
Wiseman, Judith A.

ARKANSAS

Back, Bettye R.
Dunn, Paul Andrew
Fair, Catherine F.
Gantner, Rose K.
Goodsell, Rodney
Harrendorf, Cagle
Johnson, Judy W.
Porter, Becky L.
Souheaver, Gary T.
Tursi, Patricia P.

CALIFORNIA

Abeliuk, Mary Ellyn G.
Ackerland, Valerie L.
Agras, W. Stewart
Aldavoud, Fazlollah
Allen, Francis D.
Andrew, Russell S.
Auh, Chule H.
Baccaro, Maria M.
Bachelor, Barry G.
Bailey, Michael J.
Baras, Hugh L.
Bauer, Bernard D.
Baumbach, H. Dale
Baxley, Bruce C.
Bennington, Kent F.
Bercun, Corey S.
Blum, Richard H.
Blumenfeld, Arnold I.
Blustein, Ronald S.
Boer, Arend P.
Boroskin, Alan
Boudreau, June A.
Bower, Rosemary A.
Boxley, Russell L.
Brace, Susan M.
Budwin, Howard M.
Burger, Donald G.
Burnell, Diana P.
Busey, Joseph S.
Caracena, Philip F.
Carptenter, Jr., Austin A.
Carr, Les
Christian, Kathleen A.
Clapp, John A.
Clark, Craig G.
Cockrell, Marjorie L.
Cole, James R.
Coleman, Joseph H.
Comeau, Allan J.
Congdon, Clyde S.
Cordrey, Diane L.

Coull, Charles E.
Coven, Berdeen E.
Covington, Stephanie S.
Cram, Jeffrey R.
Crary, William G.
Crenshaw Sr., Booker T
Crews, Richard L.
Damluji, Namir F.
Davis, Bobbie Karon
Davis, David P.
Deardorff, William W.
Deitch, David A.
DeJarnette, James E.
Deskin, Gerald
Distler, Luther S.
Dorn, Robert M.
Drake, D. Philip
Duncan, Edward M.
Dwarshuis, Louis K.
Edwards, Horace F.
Elkin, Ann J.
Ellsworth, Richard G.
Evans, Robert W.
Fabrizio, Jr., Carl
Feinberg, Richard A.
Field, Eleanor S.
Finkelstein, David E.
Finneberg Herndon, Elaine
Fisher, Robert L.
Floyd, Karl A.
Freeman, Barbara L.
Friedman, William J.
Galbreath, Robert
Gallway, Robert A.
Gardner, David C.
Gardner, Grace Joely
Gayten, Warren
Gerson, Allan R.
Geshuri, Yosef
Gilbert, Gary S.
Glidden-Gunter, Ralph
Goldstein, Ross E.
Gorman, Ira Ronald
Gray, John H.

Greeley, James E.
Green, Sharon
Green, Stanford
Grewal, Baljinder S.
Gross, Bruce H.
Guttman, Kenneth
Haddock, Dean M.
Hardey, Thomas R.
Harris, Joan A.
Hart, Irvin H.
Hayes, Gary A.
Helm, David P.
Hersh, Neil A.
Hoey, Henry P.
Hoffman, Mark L.
Horner, David A.
Iger, Linda M.
Izzi, Roger A.
Jackson, Barbara L.
Jacobson, Patricia L.
James, Edward V.
James, Paula
Jones, David R.
Jospe, Michael L.
Kaiser, William W
Kal, Edmund F.
Kalm, Ellen
Kappler, Kevin
Kashoff, Shirley L.
Katz, Stan J.
Kerr, J. Michael
Kilbourne, Kenneth B.
Klein, Richard S.
Kopley, Margot B.
Kovan, Robert A.
Kovelman, Joyce A.
Kracklauer, Karl
Kramer, Jonathan M.
Kremsdorf, Ross B.
Kushner, Malcolm
Ledig, Claire
Lee, Daniel D.
Lehrer, Marc

Lemon, Marilynn A.
Lepkowsky, Charles M.
Leventhal, Fayne M.
Levy, Donald J.
Lewis, Arthur L.
Liebert, Douglas S.
Lindsay, Jon M.
Londot, Kenneth L.
Lowman, Melody Matthews
Lundgren, Kathe D.
Maibaum, Matthew
Manning, Bradley A.
Marks, R. Cindy
Mars, David S.
Marshak, Mel D.
Matano, Robert A.
Matusiak, Robert M.
Maurer, Robert J.
Maynard, Marianne
McCullough, Janell
Mehl, Carter D.
Mendlowitz, Debra Ruth
Miller, L.D.
Miller, Michael R.
Miller, Sarah M.
Moore, Lawrence E.
Morford, Sherral K.
Munday, Claude S.
Mycena, Myra
Napoleon, Anthony B.
Natelson, Bernard F.
Nathan, Howard W.
Neudeck-Decker, Marilyn
Noel, William M.
Nogales, Ana Ledwin
Norris, Frederic W.
Olinger, Leonard B.
Palmer, Beverly B.
Parker, Kenneth A.
Pasino, James A.
Pazdernik, Joseph M.
Perry, William
Pham, To Quang

Piciucco, Luigi
Pickering, William C.
Piro, Philip S.
Pirojnikoff, Leo A.
Podboy, John W.
Popell, Catherine
Pratt, George J.
Premselaar, Mark A.
Prosise, John B.
Proud, Ernest
Puk, Gerald
Reinhart, Gail E.
Richardson, Robert L.
Riggs, David
Roberts, Ronald H.
Robinson, Dennis J.
Rofsky, Marvin
Romero-Romero, Hector Raul
Rose, Leslie T.
Rubanowitz, Daniel E.
Rubin, Howard S.
Rubin, Seth I.
Russell, Laura
Sarnoff, Sandra K.M.
Schroeder, Gerald L.
Schwarz, Doris A.
Scott, James D.
Seldin, Nathan E.
Shapiro, Jerrold L.
Shein, Jeffrey D.
Shiba, Debra L.
Shields, Andrea L.
Shoemaker, James E.
Short, Barbara L.
Sieck, Michael H.
Simon, Gerold R.
Skenderian, Daniel
Sluzki, Carlos E.
Smith, Curtis E.
Solomon, Robert S.
Somerville, Addison W.
Spindell, William A.
Springer, Gerda M.

Steinberg, Richard D.
Straatmeyer, Alvin J.
Strahle, Gary K.
Tepperman, Jerome H.
Thomas, Arlo
Tobias, Manuel D.
Tobin, Thomas J.
Tondow, Murray
Torres, David L.
Townsend, Richard E.
Turner, Ray A.
Ullman-Duarte, Wendy L.
Vahedian, Ahmad
Varni, Margaret B.
Veurink, Reginald L.
Vogt, Gregory M.
Waddell, Linda H.
Walter, David H.
Wanlass, Richard L.
Weinberg-Smith, Carol A.
Weiner, Richard S.
Weinstein, Karen A.
Weiss, Daniel S.
Wells, Robert D.
White, Kathryn P.
Whitley, Miles M.
Wilson, David L.
Xenos, Jr., Steve A.
Yee, Raymond
Yellen, Andrew G.
Yellen, Heidi Lauren Duboe
Young, William B.
Zappert, Laraine T.
Zweig, Richard L.

COLORADO

Barnett, Larry L.
Bassoff, Evelyn S.
Berger, Natalie S.

Bermudez, John M.
Dirks, Jerald F.
Downing, Elaine M.
Duskis, Ronald Alan
Faneli-Gledhill, Diane
Haburchak, Lawrence M
Hummel, William F.
Kannegieter, Ruthan B.
Kaplan, Glenn M.
Landau, Judith
Levine, Peter A.
O'Reilly, Brenda K.
Pender, Jr., Alexander W.
Peniston, Eugene
Perri, Ben
Powers, Harvey B.
Rifkin, John R.
Ross, James M.
Rothschild, Bertram H.
Schrader, Eleanor M.
Schwartz, Ted W.
Stark, Arlynne
Storaasli, Ragnar D.
Timmons, Frank R.
Vega, Jose G.
Vogenthaler, Donald R.
Walker, Stephen E.
Werner (Fromkin), Kristine R.
Wood, G. Vernon
Young, J. Christopher

CONNECTICUT

Bachrach, Andrea E.
Bonesi, Suzanne H.
Cashman-Janowski, Regina
Cline, John C.
DeCarli, Robert P.
Derry, Suzanne M.
Desiderato, Otello
Dreyfus, Joan King

Ellovich, E. Michael
Fitzgerald, John F.
Friedman, Estelle R.
Gagnon, John H.
Grant, Ronald A.
Isenberg, David P.
Janowski, Stanley J.
Karashik, Steven E.
Kreisman, Rhoda L.
Lerner, Hank S.
Levin, Roger B.
Margolies, Robert
Marone, Joseph G.
Millian, Lenore Z.
Molnar-Cronin, Marie L.
Nunno, Frances A.
Opsahl, Charles A.
Owens-Lane, Janice
Pawlowski, Walter J.
Pioli, John J.
Rayne, J. Thomas
Reid, Thomas A.
Reneson, Jr., Joseph E.
Sass, Kimberlee J.
Server, Janice L.
Sherman, William M.
Silverman, Stephen E.
Snyder, Peter J.
Spodick, Pearl B.
Stern, Michael L.
Stolzenberg, Jonathan B.
Sullivan, James M.
Sylvester, Phillip T.
Tolor, Alexander
Walker, Preston J.

DELAWARE

Brams, Marvin R.
Brubaker, Herbert L.
Elwood, Lawrence K.

Iqbal, S. Mohammed
Jacobs, Sharon B.

DISTRICT OF COLUMBIA

Borriello, John F.
Brooks, Renana E.
Hunt, (Sister) Anne M.
Jacobstein, Diane M.
Jones, Molly Modrall

FLORIDA

Acken, Lucille G.
Andrasik, Frank
Arucas, Julian A.
Barnett, Mark H.
Bedinger, George M.
Bekoff, Oscar
Berdell, Starr
Berger, Karan
Billion, Larry
Bingham, John E.
Bone, J. Michael
Bradman, Leo H.
Brigham, Deirdre D.
Broman, Harvey J.
Brown, Hugh
Brugnoli, Robert J.
Buffone, Gary W.
Cabada-Rovirosa, Heriberto
Carlin, Barbara K.
Carnes, John W.
Chesire, Margaret M. Brennan
Chiappy-Ortiz, Daisy
Clements, Paul R.
Cohrssen-Hollister, Geraldine C.
Conley, Harold I.
Cosma, Guillermo W.

Crown, Barry M.
Dee, William M.
Deluca, Joseph N.
Denholm, Diana B.
Dieffenbach, Thair Reed
DiGregorio, Joan M.
Dingfelder, Steven P.
Donovan, Dennis J.
Dorfman, William I.
Edenfield, William H.
Epstein, Joel J.
Erlichman, Eliot D.
Erlichman, S. Roy
Fellows, Cheryl W.
Fernandez, Rebeca
Ferriolo, Michael F.
Finamore, Dora
Fischer, Roy J.
Fleisher, Lynda K.
Forman, Bruce D.
Fortson, Francine A.
Fuentes, Dainery M.
Furr, Sheila Cohen
Gerow, Nancy S.
Gibson, Douglas P.
Gibson, Gina G.
Gilmore, David
Goldstein, Perry C.
Gonzalez, Julie
Gonzalez, Michael
Greenfield, Nancy Lee
Griffin, Adrienne M.
Haber, Audrey R.
Hall, Richard C.W.
Harrison, Noble W.
Hartman, Wayne L.
Hennig, Jr., Elbert Glenn
Herman, Steven H.
Hernandez, Oren
Herrera, Lourdes L.
Herrera-Pino, Jorge
Herrero, Luis A.

Hirsch, Jeffrey M.
Hodan, Gerald J.
Horowitz, Judith E.
Jackson, Melanie J.
Jacobson, Leonard I.
Johnson, Frances A.
Josephson, Gilda S.
Kaikobad, James J.
Kasper, Mary Elizabeth
Katell, Alan D.
Katz, Andrew
Katz, William D.
Kaushik, Pankaj K.
Killian, Grant A.
Kimmel, Joel I.
Krimsky, Eileen
LaMarche, Judith A.
Leder, Marcia B.
Levick, Myra F.
Liang, Jeffrey S.
Lightfoot, Lynn E.
Lopez, Celestino
Lowe, Ronald E.
Mahon, Christopher B.
Mansfield, Tobi E.
Mara, Barbara A.
Mason, Renee F.
McGovern, James M.
McIntyre, Deborah
Merin, Sidney J.
Merritt, Sr., Henry N.
Meyers, James
Meyers, Judith E.
Miller, Howard B.
Montealegre, Elias
Moore, Robert H.
Moorehead, Melodie K.
Moreland, John R.
Morgan, Mary K.
Napier, Robert E.
Nelson-Wernick, Eleanor
Newcomb, Joyce E. Strom

Newton, V. Miller
O'Higgins, Timothy
Ogilvie, Victor N.
Paskow, Joan B.
Patterson, Roger
Peake, Thomas H.
Perez-Noy, Antonio
Perkins, Hiram T.
Permesly, Roxanne G.
Quintero-Lumberas,
Francisco
Rexroat, Regina V.
Rievman, Steven Paul
Rivas-Vazquez, Ana A.
Rothard, Anita B.
Rousseau, Roger
Rubin, Joy
Saland, Deborah
Sands, Joel B.
Sapp, Jr., James W.
Schapiro, Sarita R.
Schneider, Barry A.
Shapiro-Ross, Sheri
Shotz, Frederick A.
Shotz, Linda F.
Shumaker, Robert G.
Simon, Franck D.
Spellman, Michael B.
Stewart, Donald A.
Stiles, Linda Rose
Svenson, Christine S.
Tarnowski, Kenneth J.
Toister, Richard P.
Traub, Gary
Valdes, Orlando J.
Volland, Michelle M.
Wasserman, Lori
Weaver, Richard G.
Wells-Crowley, Judith K.
Wernick, Robert L.
Winograd, Sessile S.
Yates, Philip R.

GEORGIA

Adams, David B.
Adams, Jr., John C.
Binder, Jeffrey L.
Brinnon, Dana C.
Brooks-Bolton, Lynda L.
Brown, E. Sue
Budd, Barbara E.
Burns, Thomas C.
Capone, Antonio
Christie, Hugh A.
Cook, Roy R.
Cox-Pursley, Carol S.
Darsey, William D.
Doverspike, William F.
Dudley, Gary E.
Durden, Gerald
Flick, Arthur B.
Frey, Ph.D., B.H.
Gustin, Ann W.
Hamby, Charles S.
Lewis, Kathleen S.
Lioi, Geriann C.
McAleer, Charles A.
McGarry, Michael S.
McRae, Jr., Harold W.
Mehrvarz, Iraj
Nease, Virginia L.
O'Hara, Christiane C.
Patterson, David L.
Pedigo, Thomas K.
Peterson, Helen S.
Rice, Janet S.
Schwartz, David M
Smith, Gary W.
Smith, M. Sharon
Smith, Robert D.
Stallworth, Felicia NMI
Stankovic, Srdjan R.
Stone, Herbert K.

Tilford, Van W.
Triolo, Santo James
Uomoto, Jay M.
Weinstein, Marc Glenn
Wolfe, John C.
Ziegler, J. Stephen

HAWAII

Annon, Jack S.
Claspell, Emily L.
Folen, Raymond A.
Ginandes, Sheila L.
Gitter, Olaf K.
Glass, Thomas A.
Hernandez, Julie S.
Kappenberg, Richard P.
Kellar, Michael A.
Merrill, Thomas Selfridge
Mora, Ralph
Newton, Barbara J.
Onorato, Vincent A.
Ramos, Franklin
Rogers, Joseph P.
Shaw, Virginia R.
Sword, Richard M.
Torigoe, Rodney Y.
Tsushima, William T.
Wade, Terence C.
Wood, Carol J.

IDAHO

Chittick, Eldon V.
Deatherage, Edward
O'Reilly, Brin
Rice, Charles M.
Stempf, Craig R.

ILLINOIS

Alexander, Marvin E.
Allert, Adrienne
Alsup, Sr., Patricia J.
Andrise, Patricia J.
Ballesteros, Helen M.
Brown, Peter R.
Charley, Michael J.
Chiappetta, Michael F.
Cunat, Ronald F.
Curns, Eileen B.
Dallas, Dan G.
Erickson, James H.
Errek, Henry K.
Forbes, Gordon B.
Goebel, James B.
Goldstein, Mark L.
Graham, Alan R.
Grant, Richard L.
Green, Theophilus E.
Harley, J. Preston
Hennessy, Darlene L.
Hogsett, Stanley G.
Hunter, Richard H.
Jann, Earl B.
Jennings, Michael C.
Jones, John W.
Khan, Mazhar A.
Kornel, Esther
Kornhaber, Bruce D.
Kroll, Larry J.
Lee, William W.
Levitt, John L.
Lipman, Jonathan J.
Liss, Madeline
Lucas, Jeff
Manka, Matthew J.
Mathews, Jr., Dewey L.
Nordstrom, Rodney R.

Ostrov, Eric
Otero-Zeno, Tulio M.
Parker, Jeffrey S.
Patterson, Wanda Sue
Poprick, Mary Ann
Saeed, S. Atezaz
Saunders, Antoinette M.
Schulze, Peggy H.
Sponsler, Ruth E.
Staples, Barrion J.
Stone, Mark H.
Stout, Chris E.
Suran, Bernard G.
Tracy, Jean K.
Weiss, Marc F.
Widen, Helen A.
Williams, Jay T.
Wolf, Harvey M.
Wolfe, Anne R.
Zebrowski, Mark M.

INDIANA

Dicken, Richard J.
Dimitroff, Michael L.
Dooley, James P.
Eglen, Jan A.
Frauman, David C.
Gleckman, Ari
Grana, Richard K.
Haley, Shirley C.
Harrison, John Stephen
Hasan, Leela
Hasan, Syed Al
Ipes, Jr., Thomas P.
Jasinski, Edward J.
Kristevski, Alexander C.
Manders, Karl
Moser, Adolph J.

Ott, John A.
Pancner, Ronald J.
Pinto, Rodger P.
Pueschel, Kathleen M.
Schilson, Elizabeth A.
Sims, Debbie D.
Sims, Tom E.
Smith, Nancy M.
Thompson, Stephen D.
Tucker, John W.
Vecera, Vincent P.

IOWA

Dawdy, Steven C.
Hartzell, John P.
Lonning, Philip E.
Moran, Marcene R.
Richards, Mary A.
Rosberg, Gary R.
Salter, Karen K.
Seager, Kathleen M.

KANSAS

Carpenter, Chrystee
Deutch, Neal B.
Guthrie, Diana W.
Hill, David O.
Moeller, Theodore A.
Naramore, Stan
Read, Marsha R.
Riordan, Hugh Desaix
Smith, James E.
Sward, Jon M.
Trotter, Jr., H. Darby
Zaremski, Barbara

KENTUCKY

Bach, M. Taylor
Borders, Jr., John K. (Jack)
Ferzacca, William
Frager, Stanley R.
Hill, Brien F.
Hoersting, Steven R.
Irvin, William R.
Mahoney, David J.
Meegan, William J.
Patel, P.D.
Riback, Nira B.
Shirazi, Camellia
Sprague, Dennis B.
Valentine, Mary H.
Washam, Jr., Charles W.
Whittington, Greg K.

LOUISIANA

Allanach, Robert C.
Appleton, Patricia N.
Boutte, Margaret A.
Dolan, John D.
Goldstein, Jack
Hollingsworth, David K.
Istre, Clifton O.
Jacques, III, Charles G.
La Barbera, Robert R.
Menard, Terry J.
Moan, Charles E.
Smelley, Sherry V.
Texidor, Margaret S.
York, J. Steven

MAINE

Cialfi, Jr., Alfred F.

Niles, David P.
Parker, Larry D.

MARYLAND

Albert, Suzanne P.
Berman, Merrill I.
Bronheim, Suzanne M.
Bush, Robert J.
Bussey, Phillip
Citrenbaum, Charles M.
Clapperton, Jr., Gilbert
Clymer, Roy E.
Craig, Michael J.
Culbertson, Stuart A.
Dale, Jr., Grady
Davis, Estelle L.
Denniston-Brooks, Eileen P.
Donner, Lawrence
Fowler, John C.
Fox, Rhea L.
Fuhrmaneck, Joseph J.S.
Geraty, Edward M.
Glantz, Meyer D.
Hawkins, Patricia D.
Hertzman, Rebecca Z.
Hewick, Walter E.
Hiland, David N.
Holmes, Elizabeth K.
Hopson, Natalie W.
Hutchins, Argin M.
Jeffreys, John S.
Jennings, Pamela K.
Johnson, Greg William
Karlsberg, Robert C.
Kayton, Robert
Khayat, A. Victor
Kirwan, William T.
Koeppl, Peter M.
Krell, Daniel M.
Lamott, James Robert

Lasson, Morris S.
Leeb, Jack
Lemaire, Theo E.
Lewis, James E.
Long, William R.
Lubell, Elyse C.
Magrab, Phyllis R.
McCarthy, Marie C.
McDonough, John P.
Mestanas, Gregory S.
Morris, Harry J.
Morrison, Reed A.
Nacev, Vladimir
Napora, Joseph P.
Noonberg, Aaron R.
Pickett, Eugenia
Plotkin, Alan L.
Podd, Marvin H.
Raznick, David J.
Reichert-Boggs, Carol J.
Rubin, Jerome
Rubin, Richard R.
Sachs, Kenneth S.
Samorajczyk, John F.
Savage, Jr., Rudolph P.
Schultze, Edward W.
Seelig, Donald P.
Shaw, Kathleen May
Solomon, Frema S.
Stern, Samuel N.
Suit, James L.
Sumner, Morris E.
Sweeney, Gladys A.
Sweetbaum, Harvey
Thurmond, Denise R.
Wilbur, Iris B.
Williams, Jon E.
Williams, William W.
Wolman, Elaine M.
Woods, Joyce V.
Young, Philip John

MASSACHUSETTS

Amira, Stephen A.
Amit, Uri
Arone, Vincent J.
Audette, Gerald N.
Cautela, Joseph R.
Chirban, John T.
Climo, Lawrence H.
DiMeo, Lorna E.
Dimitri, Robert H.
Dube, Rodney P.
Edmands, Margaret S.
Eskedal, Glen A.
Fein, Sherman E.
Franklin, Seena S.
Ghannam, Huda
Gracey, Harry L.
Greenfield, Paul E.
Grossbart, Ted A.
Hough, Sigmund
Kames, Linda D.
Kirley, Marion R.
Larsen, Larry L.
Lee, Bom Sang
Lisowski, Kathleen A.
Maloof, Bruce A.
Marion, Tovah S.
McGlynn, Martin J.
McVeigh, Jane T.
Meyer, Jr., James
Mintz, Norbett L.
Mortarelli, Paul L.
Neumann, John L.
Nigrosh, Barry J.
Nisenbaum, Steven
O'Brien, Jr., John R.
Post, David L.
Ratner, Joseph S.
Reardon, Joyce A.
Reilly, Charles J.
Riley, John M.
Rothfarb, Herbert I.

Rudin, Stephen G.
Shapse, Steven N.
Siegert, Barbara M.
Smith, Barbara A.
Solomon, Francine
Sprague, Rick
Stiegel, Jon M.
Strasnick, Brian J.
Stubenhaus, Eric C.
Vernick, Sheila K.
Weissberger, Ruth M.
Wellington, Jean
Zoldbrod, Aline

MICHIGAN

Abbasi, Tariq A.
Adams, Robert H.
Alessi, Galen J.
Alt, Nan
Arellano-Lopez, Juan J.
Baker, Brenda J.
Barton, Annette E.
Braciszeski, Terry L.
Brandt, Frans MJ
Briskin, Gerald J.
Bull Ehinger, Mary Ann
Chandler, Lynn J.
Cloud, Jack L.
DeBoer, Ronald P.
DeBruyne, John R.
DeVries, Edward J.
Disend, Meredith M.
Drasnin, David R.
Duiven, John P.
Eggertsen, Claude
Ehnis, Richard W.
Gallagher, John T.
Grothaus, Kay L.
Hand, John S.
Hendrickson, Christine

Hinderer, Steven R.
Hinds, William C.
Jerome, John A.
Kron, Audrey C.
Laufer, Charles D.
Leer, Wilbur B.
Lichtenberg, Peter A.
Lorandos, Demosthenes A.
MacRae, David R.
Marshall-Reed, Diane
Matthews, Scott R.
McPhail, John D.
Mehboob, Mohammad Iqal
Montgomery, Gertrude E.
Moore, Howard E.
Moore, Robert C.
Moriarty, James JP
Nicholson, William N.
Petras, John W.
Price, Daniel C.
Riessinger, Camala A.
Rowe, Robert J.
Schulz, Karen A.
Sczomak, John M.
Sherman, Kenneth J.
Shinedling, Martin M.
Silverstein, Avery M.
Smolarski, Ronald T.
Sooho, Alan M.
Stehouwer, R. Scott
Stern, Charles R.
Thimotheose, K.G.
Vander Goot, Mary E.
Wannen, Herbert R.
Zarr, Michael L.

MINNESOTA

Alberta, Richard G.
Ascano, Ricardo P.
Axen, Dianne M.

Hoffman, Richard G.
Huber, James W.
Karol, Robert L.
Kent, Phillip L.
Lesar, David J.
Martin, Jodi A.
Numan, Ina M.
Ollendick, Duane G.
Schubert, Charles M.
Speare, Jonathan
VanReken, Mary K.
Yellin, Absalom M.
Ziesemer, Gerald E.

MISSISSIPPI

Branton, Camille B.
Donohoe, Timothy L.
Ferguson, Debbie J.
Graham, Kenneth E.
Henrion, Rosemary P.
Hodges, Joan M.
O'Brien, Mary A.
Osborn, William P.
Quinn, Kathleen
Robbins, Eugenia Cleary
Smith, Stanley G.
Stamm, Patricia A.

MISSOURI

Anderson, Frances J.
Blinder, Max
Carney, Robert M
Courtois, Stephen V.
Culbertson, Nola B.
Dolenz, John J.
Duckro, Paul N.
Forgey, Donna M.
Geller, Robert A.

Gilner, Frank H.
Glotzbach, Louise M.
Halligan, Fredrica R.
Hewitt, Jack L.
Humphrey, Joseph A.
Jones, Fowler C.
Kabat, Syrtiller M.
Klingensmith, Philip C.
Kweskin, Edward F.
Margolis, Ronald B.
McCaskill, Eddie
Metzl, Marilyn N.
Miller, Melvin P.
Miriani, Dorothy N.
Piech, Mary L
Reedy, Ron
Ro-Trock, Larry G.
Saunders, Caryln L.
Schmidt, Bruce A.
Shealy, C. Norman
Skibinski, Gregory J.
Snow Sheridan, Deborah
Wenner, Frances C.
Wetzel, Richard D.
Witt, Frederick W.

MONTANA

Bach, Paul J.
Cheatle, Martin D.
English, James V
Jarvis, Lawrence G.
Johnson, Mark H.
Johnson, Rennae I.
Krajacich, Thomas
LeLieuvre, Robert B.
Segerstrom, David C.
Shea, Robert A.
Shubat, Edward E.
Stivers, Peter L.
Velin, Robert A.
Wemple, James R.

NEBRASKA

Beischel, Mark L.
Bizzell, Daniel L.
Denton, Jerry L.
Essien, Essien A.
Evans, Marleen E.
Folcik, John C.
Hairston, James R.
McIlvain, Helen E.
Parker, C. Tommie
Sime, Andrea J.

NEVADA

Altamura, Wendy O.
Bondy, Dorothy R.
Butler, Samuel F.
Carter-Hargrove, James A.
Colosimo, Charles P.
DiOrio, Robert J.
Ekstrom, Maurice
Etcoff, Lewis M.
Glovinsky, Marvin A.
Graudins, Lothar E.
Green, George H.
Hopper, David L.
Kotkov, Leigh W.
Mellor, Dennis L.
Mortillaro, Louis
Noyes, Patty
Reed, Renee
Retfalvy, M.V. Rhianon
Rogina, Julius M.
Sharp, Harlan D.
Stock, Dennis T.
Wallace, Richard L.

NEW HAMPSHIRE

Bass, Stephen M.
Berke, Richard
Claiborn, James M.
Conte, Frank D.
Ellsworth, June A.
Finn, Paul E.
Flynn, William B.
Guare, F. Richard
Kalfas, Nicholas S.
Katz, Lynda
Krueger-Andes, David A.
Mill, Michael W.
Pollak, Jerrold M.
Scalese, Vincent N.
Warshaw, Steve
Williams, Robert B.

NEW JERSEY

Abrams, Michael
Accaria, Philip L.
Achor, Marian B.
Adams, Benjamin H.
Adelman, Howard
Benanti, Sal C.
Bennett, Barbara L.
Blanding, Z. Benjamin
Blatt, Irwin B.
Boksay, Istvan J.E.
Brennan, Jewel
Brogan, George D.
Bruner, Gladys
Centofanti, Carmen C.
Charuk, John M.
Colis, Michael J.
Cordier, David M.
Costanzo, Wandz
Daniel, Alan L.

DiTomasso, Robert A.
Dooley, Christopher
Epstein, Yakov M.
Evan, R. Isaac
Evers, Sean R.
Fabrikant, Craig S.
Falkowski, Glenn L.
Figurelli, Jennifer C.
Fraser, Ronald B.
Fried, Stephani R
Friedman, Joseph
Ganz, Joseph
Gebhard, Thomasina
Geller, Marc D.
Goldstein, Gary Neil
Gordon, Jonathan D.
Gough, Thomas J.
Greenfield, Daniel P.
Greenfield, Terry L.
Hanbury, Jr., Raymond F.
Hartman, Bernard
Hartnett, Kathleen Sullivan
Haydon, Martin H.
Healy, Patricia A.
Howard, Harvey
Humphreys, Edward J.
Joensen, John P.
Kilroy, James J.
Lanez, Carmencita T.
Lazarus, Arnold A.
Loffredo, Ronald D.
Mangel, Howard R.
Manginelli, Michael
Massoth, Neil A.
McGugan, Anthony W.
McLeod, Iris H.
Medina, Caroline B.
Millner, Elaine S.
Moeller, Tamerra P.
Mollod, Ruth W.
Moore-Russell, Martha E.
Moser, Rosemarie S.

Nusbaum, Geoffrey D.
Oliver, Elise P.
Parisi, Irene E.
Pasahow, Robert J.
Pellegrino, Argentino C.
Perfetti, Lawrence J.
Pollak, Catherine A.
Robak, Rostyslaw W.
Ruderman, Jerome
Salierno, Carmine A.
Saraduke, Paul
Scannella, Anthony M.
Scheiner, Lillian C.
Schucker, Burton C.
Schul, Leon
Seccafico, John C.
Seeland, A. (Arthur) David
Shrensel, Sharon R.
Silverman, Hirsch Lazaar
Silvestri, James J.
Singer, Marie
Slepian, Howard J.
Solomon, Victor M.
Spitalny, James M.
Steinberg, Jakob
Sugarman, Daniel A.
Watral, David M.
White, Mark
Wiernaz, Michael J.

NEW MEXICO

Agoos, Lawrence D.
Andorfer, Joseph C.
Collins, John L.
Heisey, Marion J.
Reif, Laurie L.
Rose, Anne

NEW YORK

Arinoldo, Carlo G.
Baker, II, John W.
Barile, Frank A.
Basu, Born
Behar, Joe
Ben-Yishau, Yehuda
Berger, Harris
Bindler, Paul R.
Birnbaum, Steven R.
Blackstein, Neal Martin
Blair, Carole L.
Bordan, Terry
Botkin, Evelyn B.
Burhenne, Diane P.
Buxbaum, Joan
Capson, Stephen A.
Carll, Elizabeth K.
Cavanagh, Patrick J.
Chesler, Norman
Cilente, Jerald
Cohen, Roberta G.
Confusione, Michael J.
Cormack, Peter H.
Deluty, Marvin Z.
DeMatteo, Patricia D.
Dewart, Dorothy B.
Diner, Martin K.
Doonan, Marijanet
Dumas, Juan
Duplak, Christina
Dustman, Alan V.
Dwivedi, Suresh C.
Ehrlich, Roy E.
Ellis (Honorary), Albert
Engelhardt, Jo Ann Z.
Eron, Tijen B.
Fancher, Edwin C.
Feldman, Robert N.
Feldman, Roger L.
Filewich, Robert J.
Friedin, Bruce D.

Friedman, Irving
Fullard, David A.
Gilchrist, Rhonn D.
Glick, Bruce J.
Gold, Judy R.
Greenberg, Roger P.
Greenfield, Lynn A.
Griffin, Raymond A.
Gunser, Paul
Hadjolian, Serge Edward
Halpern, Seymour
Hamling, Richard A.
Hawkins, Michael R.
Hershman, Allen L.
Hoffman, Helen R.
Honor, Stephen
Hott, Jacqueline Rose
Isacoff, Mark
Isele, Frank W.
Jelsma, Beth M.
Judge, Joseph B.
Jungels, Georgiana H.
Jurmann, Judith A.
Kaminsky, Irene
Kapotes, Charles N.
Katzenberg, Arlene Chmil
Klopstech, Angela
Kolin, Elizabeth Ann
Kuttner, Michael J.
Langer, Karen G.
Lewittes, Don J.
Linden, Eric R.
Liteanu, Ronald R.
Lobacz, Frank M.
Loeb, Nancy
Lombardo, John P.
Lupu, Marian F.
Marsanico, Linda
Matseoane, Carol T.
McAleer, Margaret P.
Merker, Robert A.
Mihovich, Eva G.
Miller, Laurence R.

Miller, Leo Richard
Milo, Gennaro D.
Molinaro, Mario A.
Moran, Ambrose William
Mordock, Jr., John B.
Mulvi, Thomas J.
Munschauer, Carol A.
Nadler, Leslie G.
Norris, S. Louise
Oesterreicher, Lea
Pillai, A.K. Balakrishna
Pollack, Matthew B.
Ratmeyer, Harlan E.
Reich, Ilana
Ross, Barbara P.
Rubin, Gretel B.
Salkind, Theda M.
Samuels, Bennett S.
Scaturo, Douglas J.
Schachner, Chana
Scherer, Marcia J.
Schienberg, Paul
Schuster, Richard J.
Schweiger, Avraham
Shimkunas, Algimantas M.
Siefring, John
Sisley, Emily L.
Snow, Barry R.
Sokolow, Lloyd B.
Soracco, Audrey
Sorrel, William E.
Sperduto, William A.
Stern, Leon
Sternberg, Simone F.
Szarvas, Robert F.
Terenzi, Rickard E.
Terzaghi, Mari
Weafer, Jr., John J.
Weinhold, Paul M.
Weinstein, Pearl A.
Wilner, R. Stephanie
Zorn, William A.

NORTH CAROLINA

Acevedo, Jose C.
Anderson, Robert J.
Ballard, James H.
Bass, Mary Catherine
Berg, Richard A.
Burkett, Rose R.
Campbell, Herbert L.
Carr, Lewis C.
Carroll, Elizabeth K.
Chalnick, Marla K.
Chapman, Tom A.
Clougherty, Christopher H.
Collins, William L.
Ellis, Michael S.
Engelstatter, Gerolf H.
Flint, Linda A.
Greenfield, Gary R.
Guyer II, Charles G.
Hunter, Linda L.
Kennedy, Hilda B.
Kinney, Barry H.
Krasner, Paul R.
Lanier, Sr., Joe H.
Liberman, David B.
Love, Jr., Maston
Luedtke, Kurt A.
Marshall, William R.
Mitchell, Joseph J.
Morgan, James T.
Nelson, Arnold E.
Reback, Donald K
Sawyer, Glenda C.
Smith, Vivian Christine
Strag, Gerald A.
Sultan, Faye E.
Sutton, William A.
Warren, III, John F.
Weichert, Patrick D.
Whitehead-Metz, Lynn Dee
Winston, Jr., Robert W.
Wood, D. Clifton

NORTH DAKOTA

Duke, Bill J.

OHIO

Alfano, Anthony M.
Angelotta, John W.
Arnold, Kevin D.
Aronson, David E.
Ashenberg, Zev S.
Austin, Sean Harlan
Beckmann, Esther S.
Black, Joseph E.
Carino, Fernando Jaico
Daniels, Robert W.
Dember, Cynthia F.
Dickison, Harry W.
Eppley, Susan R.
Ferri, Frederick P.
Flexman, Jerry E.
Gary, John J.
Genardi, Dick A.
Goodman, Hubert T.
Grant, Richard A.
Heretick, Donna M.
Hodges, Douglas D.
Hood-Lawson, Janice
Hurles, M. Jay
Hustak, Thomas L.
Kayloe, Judith C.
Keck, Gregory C.
Kirkhart, Robert O.
Kline, Bruce E.
Knight, III, John L.
Kuna, Daniel J.
Lavin, Louise M.
Lee, Jung
Lepidi-Carino, Madeline J.
Mack, Kathleen A.
McCafferty, Patrick A.

McDonald, Michael
Meiring, Thomas E.
Miller, Richard K.
Monsour, Noel
Morgillo, Mary D.
Moss, Sharon E.
Mulick, James A.
Murray, Donna
North, George E.
Pernotto, Maryann L.
Rak, Carl F.
Rodebaugh, Helen D.
Ryder, Mary L.
Schultz, Janet R.
Schwartz, Janet M.
Segraves, Kathleen
Sidharta, Nathanael O.
Smucker, Nancy Jo
Spencer, Donald L.
Stoer-Scaggs, Linda
Swimmer, Glenn I.
Taylor, Jr., Purcell
Torppa, Alan J.
Travis, Fiona H.
Tritt, Donald G.
Umana, Roseann F.
Weitman, Carl Usher
Williams, Sheila Y.
Wood, Kathleen S.
Zupnick, Stanley M.

OKLAHOMA

Beasley, Jr., Stewart R.
Brady, Douglas O.
Carella, Stephen D.
Darks, Helen J.
Flores, Andrea L.
Lukens, Jr., Horace C.
Nye, Ronald R.
Pikler, Elaine G.

Sanders, Gilbert O.
Stapp, B. Michael
Swink, Richard H.
Walker, Anita

OREGON

Agen, Jack R.
Anderson, Dorothy J.
Bates-Smith, Karen S.
Berger, Karan
Blose, Patricia W.
Bufford, Rodger K.
Garfunkel, Joel
Garwood, John Ernest
Gordon, Jerome S.
Hart, Larry S.
Hawkins, Nancy E.
Hennings, Bill
Henry, Robert F.
Hersen, Michel
Johnson, James (Jim) C.
Johnson, Jim
Lahman, Frank G.
Lazere, Richard
LeBray, Peter R.
Lechnyr, Ronald J.
Lee Selinger, Rosemary C.
Louks, John L.
Morrell, Eric M.
Reiman, John Warren
Reinhart, David F.
Reiter, Gregg F.
Rethinger, Paul J.
Saslow, Julia A.
Selinger, Rosemary C. Lee
Smith, James R.
Starker, Steven
Swanson, Keith A.
Waksman, Steven A.
Warner, Peter D.

PENNSYLVANIA

Addis, John W.
Asken, Michael J.
Auritt, Joycellen Young
Bader, Alan P.
Badillo, Frank
Baird, James W.
Bogovich, Kristina
Bowman, Helen L.
Bricklin, Barry
Bright, Priscilla D.
Brotman, Lloyd E.
Campanella, Sandra A.
Charney, Natalie J.
Cobbett, Allen A.
Coburn, P. Christopher
Conner, Louise C.
D'Agaro, Wayne R.
Dickey, Esther W.
DiMalta, Vincent F.
DonGiovanni, Vito John
Dubrow-Eichel, Steve K.
Edwards, Barbara L.
Fiorenzo, Craig J.
Frank, Marion R.
George, Theresa
Gerstein, Alvin L.
Ginsberg, Barry G.
Ginsberg, Jerry
Gitlin, Sidney
Golin, Sanford
Gribetz, Michael D.
Gudowski, Richard M.
Haaz, Edward
Hake, Donald J.
Heiser, Raymond D.
Heisey, Gloria N.
Hoch, Carolyn C.
Huha, James G.
Ivins, Richard G.
Jennings, Donald E.
Johnson, Jerry A.
Karlin, Robert M.

Karpf, Ronald J.
Kayes, Barry L.
Kennedy, Charles J.
Knapp, Nancy H.
Kraybill, Donald E.
Lande, Stephen D.
Lee, William G.
Levit, Herbert I.
Liberi, William P.
Lizzi, Frank
Lucey, George R.
Lyness-Richard, D'Arcy
Maguire, Brent L.
Malatesta, Victor J.
Markiewicz, Marc F.
McConnell, Harry W.
McCusker, Peter J.
Miller, David J.
Miller, Richard J.
Mintzer, Lawrence G.
Nachtwey, Peter H.
O'Connell, David F.
O'Shell, Wallace D.
Pappas, George P.
Pastushak, Roman J.
Pauza, Joseph A.
Pellow, Rita B.
Perovich, George M.
Perry, Joseph P.
Pokea, Sondra T.
Poloni, Louis D.
Ramm, Douglas R.
Ramsden, Elsa L.
Ramsey, David A.
Rarig, Kathleen G.
Redd, Cathy A.
Reed, Lorraine C.
Rosenberg, Steven M.
Rosencrantz, Elliot
Ruby, J. Richard
Sadigh, Micah R.
Schneider, Stanley E.
Schorr-Ribera, Hilda K.
Scott, Kitty Lee

Sherman, Geoffrey K.
Smith, Larry D.
Smith, Marie E.
Smith, Molly A.
Sowa, Martin S.
Stauffer, Don A.
Stettner, Donald H.
Strauss, Judith B.
Strick, Sadie E.
Surmacz, Gerald E.
Sutton, Lawrence R.
Sylvester, Kevin E.
Thomas, David A.
Thompson, Diane L.
Truckenmiller, James L.
Turoczi, John C.
Tyrrell, Thomas J.
Wagner, Mark S.
Walker, Jasen M.
Walker, Larry D.
Weinberger, David M.
Weiss, Esther V.
West-Moore, Kimberly
Williams, James E.
Woodruff, Guy C.
Zivan, Morton

PUERTO RICO

Cruz-Lopez, Miguel A.
DeJesus, Miguel A.
Egozcue, Angel R.
Santos, William L.
Torruella, Juan E.

RHODE ISLAND

D'Aloia, Donna M.
Dorry, William A.
Esposito, Ronald A.

SOUTH CAROLINA

Barnard, Barbara N.
Bradley, Jr., John K.
Crews, Freda V.
Doskocil, Karl V.
Frier, Ronald C.
Harley, Jr., A.B.
Heffler, Joel B.
Hightower, Marjorie M.
Hoffman, Robert J.
Hollander, Sheila K.
Holmes, George R.
Kaplan, Candia P.
McCarthy, Robert E.
Platt, Randolph E.
Rainwater, III, Avie J.
Rekers, George A.
Strader, George
Switzer, III, Paul K.
Waller, Edward D.
Zaepfel, Glenn P.

SOUTH DAKOTA

Hauck, William C.
Phares, Robert E.
Terry, Thomas G.

TENNESSEE

Anchor, Felicia
Anchor, Kenneth N.
Azimi, Amin
Battle, Allen O.
Bernard, Maxine L.
Bernard, Sam D.
Blackerby, William F.
Bottari, Michael A.

Boyd, Jr., William R.
Buchanan, H. Ray
Busch, Carole A.
Carrico, Kenneth L.
Downs, John M.
Eichler, Jr., Renald C.
Engum, Eric S.
Favara, David M.
Friedlob, James W.
Frye, Evelyn M.
Griffin, Nathaniel
Guinsburg, Philip F.
Haney, David P.
Hannaford, Charles P.
Hazelton, Joseph Edward
Hester, Larry R.
Horwitz, Alex
Hughes, Robert B.
Jacobson, Howard A.
Jones, Glenna M.
Lancaster, John W.
Loranger, Jon W.
Luscomb, Richard L.
Lynch, Timothy D.
McGee, William E.
Morris, Sharon T.
Murray, III, Lindley
Nottingham, IV, Edgar J.
Oliveira, O.H.
Pendergrass, Thomas M.
Pitt, Rosalyn R.
Potts, Ray
Saunders, Mollie
Spence, Felicitas IB
Vernon, Minta F.
Walker, Lois B.
Walter, Charles L.
Way, John G.
West, G. Norman
Willson, Ellen M.
Yium, Mildred M.

TEXAS

Abney, Lucille A.
Arnold, Bill
Austin, Sue A.
Bailey, A. Kathleen
Bannister, Geraldine Love
Borda, Robert P.
Branaman, Timothy F.
Bridges, Charles F.
Brockman, Leslie R. "Dick"
Brody, Marjorie E.
Brunson, Bradford I.
Cadwalder, Maurice H.
Campbell, Michael E.
Casey, Robert P.
Chavez, Sylvia P.
Contreras, Jose A.
Cookerly, J. Richard
Cooksey, Vance S.
Cuencas-Zamora, Ramon
Daner, Francine
Darsa, Stephanie D.
DeArana, Olga Ruiz C.
DeLeon, Lauro R.
Dempsey, George L.
Dixon-Floyd, Izola
Drum, Candyce D.
Duncan, III, Marion W.
Dunn, Charleta J.
Durbin, Jr., Harvey
Erikson, Melvin Lee
Ferguson, Nancy L.
Fraser, Jaine E.
Fryer, John H.
Garza-Trevino, Enrique S.
Genaro, Lorayne E.
Gold, Karen L.
Gonzalez, George A.
Grant, Robert W.
Gregory, Mary K.

Gruen, Shirley N.
Haire, Carol D.
Haley, Michael
Hall, James R.
Hall, Karyn D.
Harrell, T. Walter
Harris, Betty H.
Haven, Lillian C.
Heikens, George A.
Hodges, Randolph K.
Houston, Marilyn
Hyden, Jr., James Monty
Ingram, Jr., C. Robert
Jacobs, John A.
Johnson, David L.
Jolley, Aubrey H.
Jones, Richard G.
Jones, Ronald W.
Justice, D. (David) Blair
Justice, Rita N.
Kershaw, Carol J.
Kowis, Lucinda K.
Kramer, Jr., George H.
Lawrence, Carl W.
Lennhoff, Michael
Lerman, Marty H.
Levy, Harriette J.
Lilliker, Shelley L.
Longano, Bernie
Loomstein, Harvey A.
Maldonado, Gilbert
Mangos, Rae Carol
Marrero, Magaly V,
Martin, Jack G.
McCoy, Walter J.
McCraw, Ronald K.
McGee, P. Daniel
McGill, Jerry C.
McIntosh, Edith Marie
McKinney, Mark E.
Mendez, Susana E.
Micklin, Harvey G.

Miller, Duane C.
Miller, Kenneth L.
Milliken, Katherine
Morciglio-Benkert, Myrta M.
Morrow, Henry W.
Moses, Rick P.
Murrah, Jeffrey D.
Nicolau, Juan
Noblitt, James Randall
Norton, John H.
Nunley, Elma P.
Nutt, Johnnie W.
O'Brien, Eugene P.
O'Brien, Shawna L.
Orman, Teresa E.
Orner, Marc M.
Overman, Tommy M.
Pagonas, P. Keith
Pascaretta, Anthony L.
Paulson-Lee, Frankiemae
Peek, Leon A.
Peniston, Eugene
Peppers, Walter R.
Permenter, Sue A.
Phelan, P. Caren
Pichitino, John P.
Poston, III, Walker S.
Powell, Sharon L.
Raphaeli, Avi
Rose, Lucien D.
Ruiz, Edmundo J.
Sahley, Billie J.
Scholwinski, Edward J.
Shane, David S.
Shaughnessy, Dennis M.
Shaw, Mary Ann
Shinder, James N.
Sicard, R. Augustin
Siegel, Jeffrey C.
Stansell, Vance D.
Steinman, David R.

Stockton, Curtis O.
Thrift, Robert D.
Tracktir, Jack
Tucker, Ann
Tumlin, Shari L.
Uzzell, Barbara P.
Vazquez, Steven R.
Vickrey, Noreen
Wall, Robert H.
Watson, William E.
Weinberger, Robert N.
Weyandt, Linda
Wigodsky, Ann
Wilcox, Allison H.
Wilhelm, Sonja G.
Williams, Marlot W.
Willingham, Welborn K.
Wilson, James O'Brien
Wolf, Christina M.
Womack, Michael A.
Yaacoubi, Ghanem I.
Yentis, Richard D.

UTAH

Goldstein, Samuel J.
Smith Benjamin, Lorna

VERMONT

Benay, Elliott M.
Bethell, Charles F.
Gauthier, David A.
Henault, Jr., Armand J.
Kotkov, Benjamin
Langelier, Regis
Miller, Joel R.
Trombley, Henry Ira

VIRGINIA

Al-Falaij, A. Rahman
Anderson, Gregory L.
Archer, Robert P.
Auerbach, Anita L.
Ball, John D.
Barth, Jeffrey T.
Beckman-Brindley, Sharon J.
Bellino, Thomas T.
Berg, Phyllis A.
Brennan, Philip I.
Brown, William D.
Carpenter, Johnice G.
Dane, Joseph R.
Decker, William A.
Elion, Victor H.
Emanuelson, Margaret S.
Engel, Wayne E.
Federici, Ronald S.
Fielding, Michael F.
Fletcher, Constance N.
Fletcher, Samuel J.
Fletcher-Janzen, David
Forssmann-Falck, Renate
Gerstle, Robert M.
Gillikin, Lynn S.
Gluhareff, Robert S.
Green, Meredith W.
Hatt, Clifford V.
Hauenstein, Emily J.
Heddings, Faith D.
Hoffmann, Fred J.
Kirby, Deborah M.
Lyon, Seaborn L.
Manganiello, James A.
Mendelsohn, Mark B.
Michaelson, Geoffrey K.
Mosier, William A.
Mountz, Jr., Thomas C.
Mullins, Jr., Frank A.
Neis, Gertrude M.
Nidiffer, Jr., Frank D.

Peck, III, Edward A.
Rostafinski, Michael J.
Seda, Jr., Gilbert
Spiro, Marilyn L.
Strosnider, J. Steve
Stutts, Michael L.
Sutton, Nancy Z.
Thoben, Karen A.
Wenzel, Charlotte K.
West-Moore, Kimberly
Zitnay, George A.

WASHINGTON

Beavers, Daniel J.
Carlson, Gary E.
Chen, Jeanette J.
Cooper, Cecilia R.
DeHerrera, Larry (Lorenzo) J.
Erickson, Richard C.
Fordyce, Honorary, Wilbert E.
Foss, Hazel M.
Gluck, Michael
Goodwin, Glenn T.
Harris, Lance A.
Hawkins-Mitchell, Vali
Hellman, John R.
Hymen, Steven P.
Jensen, Craig C.
Kelly, Dennis A.
Kosins, David J.
Langer, Stephen M.
Lloyd, John T.
Malakoff, Cheryl A.
Marlowe, Wendy B.
Mazer, Irene R.
McCarty, Eileen R.
McIvor, Daniel L.
Meagher, Christopher R.
Meier, Monty L.
Ovens, Wallace

Pautler, Thomas G.
Peterson, Norman F.
Phillips, Sr., Hosea A.
Piper, Jr., August T.
Rarick, William J.
Reisenauer, Timothy M.
Shultz, Kenneth A.
Slater, Charles B.
Stokes, DeVon
Thorpe, Sylvia A.
Uomoto, Jay M.
Uomoto, Katy P.
Uslan, Donald W.
Vanderway, Robert C.
Vizzard, J. Stephen
Wall, Thomas W.
Wanwig, John D.
Weathers, Lawrence R.
Weathers, Mary B.
Williams, Dennis J.
Zucchero, Carol

WEST VIRGINIA

Capage, James E.
Cerra, Victor
Gomez, Margaret J.
Goots, Samuel
Harlow, Jeffrey L.
Kurland, Nadine J.
Lawhon, Delbert A.
Leavitt, Priscilla F.
Lee, Fred T.
Rittenhouse, Ronni
Rush, Barbara L.
Sella, Gabriel E.
Webb, Donna O.
Webb, III, Deleno H.
Webb, William B.

WISCONSIN

Ackerman, Marc J.
Anderson, Michael F.
Buda, Edward
Caulfield, Timothy G.
Cohn, Lucile M.
Daut, Randall L.
DeSantis, John-Francis
Gibson, Keith D.
Gillespie, Robert A.
Glass, Paul Kenneth
Green, Cornelia A.
Groh, Thomas R.
Heinz, Harlan R.
Heinz, Sharon A.
Hoffman, Deborah A.
Holzer, Jr., John M.
Jansky, John L.
Kane, Andrew W.
Kane, III, Lawrence A.
Kaufman, Harvey L.
Krings, Judith B.
Lindner, Elizabeth A.
Listiak, Richard L.
Mancuso, Joseph E.
Muntz, Eleni S.
Pipp, Sr. Mercita
Polder, Gordon J.
Polder, Sarah K.
Rice, David G.
Scheets, Raymond W.
Schlagheck, James F.
Schneider, Steven V.
Silva, Milton N.
Stolldorf, Dean E.
Van Rixel, Sheila C.
Venardos, Marlene G.
Wagner, Melvyn M.

WYOMING

Smith, James E.

Country

AUSTRALIA

Costello, Brian R.
Endrey, Anthony J.

CANADA

Andres, J. Edward
Arora, Sunder Singh
Baron, Dov
Bhatt, Vasantrai D.
Borsellino, Charles C.
Chong, Dennis K.
Deneuve, Mitra D.
DePaul, Elizabeth M.
Dvali, Irene P.
Enright, Robert Charles
Epelbaum, Mikhail
Gamsa, Ann
Gormandy, Winston D.
Guzman, Rogelio (Roger)
Hassam, Abdul S.
Hill, Knolly D.
Hill, Mariana G.
Joshi, Dilip A.
Kaur, Rupinder
Machanic, Mindy
McNab, Brian R.
McSherry, James
Mensah, Joseph A.
Neehall, Joan
O'Brien, Elizabeth P.
Pagliaro, Louis A.
Pare, Michael F.
Poon, Vincent H.K.
Pulvermacher, Gerald D.
Rajabian, Nancy
Richardson, Donald W.

Robertson, Grace A.
Ruznisky, Sonja A.
Shepel, Larry Francis
Shiffman, David P.
Sirman, Mehmet Rauf
Sousa-Poza, Joachim F.
St-Onge, Robert G.
Stewart, Daniel L.
Thauberger, Patrick C.
Theriault, Serge A.
Thomas, Roger E.
Utendale, Kent A.
Vickram, Cameron I.
Voyageur, Evelyn May
Wilson, Michael S.
Wong, David
Yung, Christoph Y.
Zabinsky, Laverne H.

COLUMBIA

Fergusson, Alberto

ENGLAND

Berke, Joseph H.
Nelson, William C.
Young, Raymond

FRANCE

Seid, Kathy J.

GERMANY

Brickwedde, Rebecca L.
Garcia, Ivan O.

GUAM

Kallingal, George K.

HONG KONG

Cheng, Louis Y.

ISRAEL

Lahad, Shmuel D.
Wanderer, Zev W.
Weisenberg, Matisyohu

MEXICO

Lauderdale, John J.
Snyder, Robert L.

MICRONESIA

Zimmern-Reed, Annette W.

PAKISTAN

Rana, Shabbir A.

SAUDI ARABIA

Ibrahim, Abdel-Sattar
Ibrahim, El Sheikh

SOUTH AFRICA

Hoosen, Ismail G.
Schlebusch, Lourens

SWITZERLAND

Punnett, Audrey F.

SYRIA

Hajjar, Mohamad Hamdi

TAIWAN ROC

Chan, Chin-Hong

UNITED KINGDOM

Kaiser, Faward
Lingiah, David Bassana
Mathews, Subash C.
Rana, Tanvir A.

WEST INDIES

Daniel, Walton H.

DISABILITY ANALYSIS IN PRACTICE: FUNDAMENTAL FRAMEWORK FOR AN INTERDISCIPLINARY SCIENCE
Co-Edited by Kenneth N. Anchor, Ph.D., ABPP
and Thomas C. Felicetti, Ph.D., ABDA

Topics Include:
* Life Care Planning: The Interdisciplinary Team Approach
* Disability and Classroom Inclusion
* Attitudes Toward People with Disabilities
* Urologic Problems Relating to Disabilities
* The Role of the Respiratory Care Practitioner in Disability Analysis
* Transdisciplinary Evaluation of Chronic Pain: The Health Psychology Perspective
* Evaluation of Soft Tissue Injury
* Uses and Misuses of Psychopharmacology: What Every Disability Analyst Should Know
* Functional Capacities Assessment
* Orthotics and Prosthetics: A Team Approach to Functional Independence
* Extremity Joint Mobilization: Concepts of Assessment and Treatment
* Osteopathic Medicine and the Role of Manipulation in the Treatment of Chronic Pain
* The Disabling Impulse to Set Fires
* Seeking Legitimacy: The Pilgrimage of Those Claiming to Have Multiple Chemical Sensitivity
* Communication Disorders: A Profession in Evolution
* Clinical Evaluation: From Validation to Practice
* On the Complexities of Shopping: The Story of Interdisciplinary Team Rehabilitation
* Interdisciplinary Team Process: A Model Used in a Residential Facility for Traumatically Brain Injured Adults
* The Neuropsychological Sequelae and Assessment of Head Trauma
* Cognitive Rehabilitation for Traumatic Brain Injury
* The Further Education and Credentialing of the Disability Analyst

Contributors:
Kenneth N. Anchor, PhD, Dan Bagwell, RN, Jeffrey T. Barth, PhD, Matthew W. Bowen, PhD, Donna K. Broshek, PhD, Tracey Brown, PT, Elaine L. Bukowski, PhD, Chetwyn C.H. Chan, PhD, Howard H. Covitz, PhD, Robert Diamond, PhD, Allan O. Diefendorf, PhD, Tom Felicetti, PhD, Linda Ference, MA, H. Hugh Floyd, PhD, Karen L. Gold, PsyD, T. Walter Harrell, PhD, Larry J. Kopelman, PhT, Renee Kusner, BA, Tatia M.C. Lee, PhD, Ralph G. Leverett, PhD, Jonathan J. Lipman, PhD, Josephine Maimone, PT, Robert Male, PhD, Tom Malinowski, BA, Phyllis Marks, MEd, Gregory W. Nevens, EdD, Louise Pate, MS, Don Rhodes, MA, Bethany Rouland, PT, Heidi J. Rubin, MS, Loreen Scott, BA, Randy Scott, BA, Robert A. Seegmiller, PhD, Gabriel Sella, MD, Donald F. Stanton, DO, Carol A. Straiton, BS, William B. Turner, BS, Paul T. Webber, CO, J. Michael Wieting, DO, Alex C. Willingham, MD, Marie Wilson, RN

THE DISABILITY ANALYSIS HANDBOOK:
TOOLS FOR INDEPENDENT PRACTICE
Edited by Kenneth N. Anchor, Ph.D., ABPP

Topics Include:
* The Disability Revolution: Emerging Career Track for the 21st Century
* The Education of a Disability Analyst
* Pain and Disability
* A Legal Perspective on the Social Security Disability Programs
* Catastrophic Injury: A Model of Disability Analysis, Treatment Planning, and Case Management
* Diabetes as a Disability
* Chronic Renal Failure: Analysis of Disability and Rehabilitation
* Alcohol and Other Substance Abuse Among the Disabled
* Psychosocial Issues in Burn Injury Rehabilitation
* Aging and Disability
* Nursing Perspectives on Disability and Rehabilitation
* Environmental Neurobehavioral Toxicology
* Nonverbal Learning Disorder
* Evaluating Economic Losses in Personal Injuries
* Back Injury Disability Management
* The National Directory of Disability Analysts

Contributors:
Kenneth N. Anchor, PhD, Rose Bianchi, DNSc, RN, CS, Ronald T. Brown, MD, William H. Burke, PhD, Phyllis M. Connolly, PhD, RN, Kim N. Dietrich, PhD, William F. Doverspike, PhD, Mark A. Doyne, MD, Lewis M. Etcoff, PhD, David A. Ettinger, JD, Thomas Felicetti, PhD, Melissa Freizinger, MA, Peter B. Griffin, PhD, Diana W. Guthrie, PhD, Lee Ann Hoff, PhD, RN, Robert N Jamison, PhD, Karen M. Kampfer, MA, Stanley Lee, MD, Joseph Magaddino, PhD, Ann Marie Pagliaro, PhD, Louis A. Pagliaro, PhD, Victoria K. Palmer-Erbs, PhD, RN, CS, Roger L. Patterson, PhD, Mary R. Saunders, BA, Howard G. Shertzer, PhD, Kenneth J. Tarnowski, PhD, David L. Weatherford, PhD.

ORDER FORM

Please mark the number of copies for each book selected in the spaces preceding the book titles.

_____ Disability Analysis in Practice: Fundamental Framework for an Interdisciplinary Science: $50.00

_____ The Disability Analysis Handbook: Tools for Independent Practice: $60.00

_____ The International Directory of Disability Analysts: $40.00

_____ The Catastrophic Injury Handbook: $75.00

_____ All of the above: $160.00

Payment by: (check one)
Check ☐   Visa ☐   Mastercard ☐

Credit Card Number: _____ Exp. Date: _____

Name as it appears on card: _____

Total cost of order: $ _____ (payments in U.S. dollars includes s/h)

Ship book(s) to:

Name: _____

Address: _____

City/State/Zip: _____

Send or fax this form to ABDA Book Orders, Park Plaza Medical Building, 345 24th Avenue North, Suite 200, Nashville, TN 37203-1520. Fax # (615) 327-9235.

AMERICAN BOARD OF DISABILITY ANALYSTS

* * * <u>Time Limited Grandfathering</u> * * *

Health and allied health care professionals are invited to apply, Board certification is available at two levels depending upon experience: **Disability Analyst and Fellow** (minimum 4 years) or **Senior Disability Analyst and Diplomate** (9 years or more). Those selected will be listed to <u>The National Directory of Disability Analysis</u>, receive ABDA publications and reduced fees for all training events in the U.S. and elsewhere. For a detailed application packet write, fax or call: Alexander Horwitz, M.D., Executive Office, ABDA, Park Plaza Medical Building, 345 24th Avenue North, Suite 200, Nashville, TN 37203-1520, FAX: (615) 327-9235, Tel: (615) 327-2984, E-mail: Americanbd@aol.com